INTERNATIONAL
ECONOMICS
IN AN
INTEGRATED WORLD

INTERNATIONAL ECONOMICS IN AN INTEGRATED WORLD

Arthur B. Laffer
University of Southern California

Marc A. Miles
Rutgers—The State University of New Jersey

Scott, Foresman and Company

Glenview, Illinois

Dallas, Tex.   Oakland, N.J.   Palo Alto, Cal.   Tucker, Ga.   London, England

Library of Congress Cataloging in Publication Data

LAFFER, ARTHUR B.
   International economics in an integrated world.

   Includes index.

      1. International economic relations—Mathematical
   models.   I. Miles, Marc A., 1948–   II. Title.
   HF1411.L334   337'.0724   81-6297
   ISBN   0-8302-4028-4   AACR2

Printed in the United States of America

ISBN: 0-673-16020-3

10   9   8   7   6   5   4   3   2   1

Acquisitions Editor: Jim Boyd
Supervising Production Editor: Pam Price
Compositor: Computer Typesetting Services, Inc.
Cover and Text Designer: Kenny Beck
Art: etc. Graphics

To William G. Laffer
To the memory of Hans Krieks—
Two men who helped us view the world
Through a different light.

CONTENTS

PREFACE

Collaboration on this book began some seven years ago. At that time, Arthur Laffer was on the faculty and Marc Miles was a graduate student at the University of Chicago. A view of the global economy, something quite different from the received wisdom, was taking form at Chicago. This view was evolving and being extended by a number of people at the University of Chicago, including the authors of this book. The economic events of the time literally inundated the environment with stimulus and data. These events, in conjunction with the seeds of thought found in the new "global monetarist" view of the world economy, accelerated the advancement of the model. A sharp schism developed between the more traditional perspective on trade and payments theory and the global monetarist view.

To the vast majority in the economics profession, the move toward demonetarization of gold and floating exchange rates that centered on the Camp David pronouncements of August 1971 was clearly in the right direction. Dollar depreciation was thought not only to improve the U.S. competitive position, but also to improve the country's trade balance, increase domestic employment, and have minor inflationary consequences. Laffer, however, went on record arguing that each percent the currency depreciates would result in an additional percent of U.S. inflation. Depreciation would thereby neither improve the country's competitive position nor result in increased employment at home. Thus, from the global monetarist perspective, devaluation caused inflation without any corresponding benefits. At the time, this view was rejected by the entire political system and all but a handful of economists. The potential for simultaneous inflation and economic contraction was simply not part of traditional thought. It remained beyond the focus of most economic discussions for a few years until the inflation–recession of 1974 suddenly caught everyone's undivided attention and created a serious paradox for the conventional theories. Since 1974 the global monetarist view has become a serious challenger to the traditional view.

From the vantage of the traditional view, the political steps taken in the late 1960s and early 1970s are quite understandable. From the perspective of global monetarism these steps make almost no sense whatsoever. Furthermore, it was likely that such steps would continue, since it was evident that the conventional approach was receiving exclusive attention in international economics courses. Yet, the growing dissatisfaction with the conventional approach that was emanating from the University of Chicago was contributing to the development of a reasoned, alternative theory to explain the international movements of money, goods, and capital. These explanations became embodied in the Monetary Approach to the Balance of Payments, or "global monetarism."

The Monetary Approach, as it developed at Chicago, had its roots in two papers, Robert Mundell's "Growth and the Balance of Payments," and Arthur Laffer's "An Anti-Traditional Theory of the Balance of Payments Under Fixed Exchange Rates." These articles were drafted in the mid-1960s at Chicago and Stanford. Mundell's article was subsequently published in his book *International Economics*, while Laffer's contribution was never published.

These two articles served as the foundation upon which many of the ideas and articles of Chicago students and faculty, as well as others interested in the Monetary Approach, were developed in the late 1960s and the 1970s. They also served as the source of many of the ideas which received much attention in Harry Johnson's famous series of articles on the Monetary Approach.

These two original articles contained two basic themes. First, the analysis of economies should be conducted within general equilibrium rather than partial equilibrium models. The market for goods is integrally linked to the market for money and bonds through Walras' Law. Attempts to analyze any one market in isolation often led to inappropriate conclusions. Second, the proper framework for analyzing international movements within markets was a global economy of highly integrated country economies. Countries were treated as one of many economies closely intertwined, not as economically distinct units which could be analyzed in isolation.

Seven years ago there was no source to which the interested person could turn in order to get a basic understanding of this alternative approach. The ideas were dispersed in articles in a wide variety of books and journals. Some of the ideas remained unpublished. Other ideas had yet to be fully developed. At the time, we undertook to fill this void by creating a source which would pull together these ideas and present them in a usable form.

We also felt that any treatment of international economics should include basic "pure" or "real" trade theory as well as payments theory. The two branches of international economics are often treated as separate, distinct subjects. However, both parts are needed for a complete theory of how the international economy works. Furthermore, within a truly general equilibrium model, the two parts must be internally consistent. It is only logical to presume that relationships which hold in pure trade theory will hold in payments theory as well. This book, therefore, encompasses both subjects, and an effort is made to show how they are related.

The inclusion of both subjects also permits us to emphasize some confusions between pure trade and payments theory created by earlier approaches. For example, some approaches seem to imply that the trade balance and balance of payments are synonymous. Often, the terms of trade (the relative price of goods) and the exchange rate (the relative price of monies) are used interchangeably. A change in one of these variables is assumed to cause a similar change in the corresponding other variable. However, the overall treatment contained in this book permits a sharp distinction to be drawn between these variables, and shows how they in fact may move in different directions. The explanation stands as a warning that potential policy errors may result from failing to realize the distinction.

This book is not a traditional eclectic textbook. It does not simply present a collection of ideas on international trade arising over the last two hundred years. Rather, this book takes an approach that departs from conventional wisdom by investigating new alternatives contained in the Monetary Approach. Much of the analysis builds upon our own work and the works of others concerning the implications of integrated markets. The validity of the assumption that world markets are integrated is an empirical issue. The integrated markets perspective, however, is a useful starting point and is far more constructive as a basis for systematic thought than the traditional alternative of essentially segmented markets. The integrated markets approach provides new and different insights into the functioning of the world and country economies, which are not provided by more conventional approaches. The result is a treatment of international economics that is both intuitive and internally consistent. This approach provides a perspective into the world economic environment, and helps to anticipate the effects of private or government actions on world markets. We would like the reader, whether a student, business executive, professor, or government official, not merely to learn about international theory, but rather to carry away a sense of what underlies the economic phenomena observed in the world, so that he can use it to his own advantage in dealing with the future.

To this end, we have sought to summarize and integrate theoretical and empirical ideas which existed not only seven years ago, but which have been developed since. The major ideas include the development of a basic Monetary Approach model of the balance of payments and its policy implications; development of a corresponding absorption model of the trade balance; the internationalization of domestic money or "currency substitution;" and the important limits these ideas place on discretionary monetary policy, even under perfectly floating rates. The incorporation of some concepts of "supply side" economics into international trade, inflation as an international rather than domestic phenomenon, the impact of the Eurodollar market on domestic monetary policy, and a reexamination of the conventional wisdoms concerning such policies as capital controls, devaluation, and floating exchange rates are also dealt with in detail.

The pure trade theory is contained in the first eight chapters. Chapter 1 presents an overview of trade and the Ricardian one-factor model. Chapters 2 and 3 expand the basic model of the supply side to the traditional $2 \times 2 \times 2$ case. Chapter 4 brings in demand and the gains from trade. Chapter 5 shows the effects of introducing tariffs and quotas, and compares the two policies. Chapter 6 examines whether trade barriers are the optimal commercial policy tool for problems involving traded goods, and what some alternative policies might be. This chapter also includes a discussion of the optimum tariff and the infant industry argument. Chapter 7 deals with the effects of transfers, growth, changes in the terms of trade, and factor mobility on trade among countries. Chapter 8 departs from traditional pure theory analysis by showing how "supply side" economics can be incorporated into trade theory. First, a basic "wedge" model of a closed economy is described. Then the "supply side" model is extended to the two-country case to show the effects of demand and supply shocks on a country's trade balance.

Analysis of the international payments system encompasses the remaining thirteen chapters. Chapters 9 through 11 set the stage by describing the relationship between the pure theory barter model and the complete payments model, comparing adjustment mechanisms in open and closed economies, describing the balance of payments accounts and related concepts, and providing empirical evidence that the world, in fact, behaves as an integrated market. Chapters 12 and 13 describe the behavior of the money market in an integrated world. A basic Monetary Approach model is developed. The emergence of world-wide inflation in the 1970s is discussed, along with the role of Eurodollars and the breakdown of the Bretton Woods System in creating these inflationary pressures. Chapter 14 contains a model of the trade balance which is consistent with both the Monetary Approach model of Chapter 12 and the "supply side" model of Chapter 8. The models in Chapters 12 and 14 are taken from Laffer's article "The Anti-Traditional Theory."

Chapter 15 completes the basic model by describing a model of the capital market in an integrated world. It also discusses why, once the interaction of the money, goods, and capital markets is considered, capital controls are not likely to achieve their objective. Chapter 16 presents an alternative model, the more traditional Keynesian model of internal-external balance. This chapter provides an opportunity for emphasizing some of the basic differences between the traditional and the integrated market approaches. Chapter 17 reexamines both theoretically and empirically the effects of devaluation. Chapter 18 examines the role of a reserve currency country on a fixed exchange rate system and the implications of its unique position. Chapter 19 is devoted to the phenomenon of currency substitution or diversification of money portfolios and why it changes basic monetary theory. Chapter 20 takes a new look at the arguments for floating rates and indicates why returning to fixed rates may be the most efficient way of ending world inflation. Finally, Chapter 21 looks at recent developments in the international economy. Did the Carter Administration's attempt to "talk down" the dollar have the desired effects? What forces influence the value of the dollar exchange rate in an integrated world? What happened when the Carter Administration finally tried to stop the dollar's slide? Is the European Monetary System likely to have an important effect on the global economy?

The book is aimed at the advanced undergraduate and MBA levels, though graduate students probably will also find the book useful as a basic description of the Monetary Approach. The emphasis is on developing a framework for understanding the world, so the book should be useful for businessmen and government officials. The book is ideally suited for a two-quarter sequence in pure trade theory and balance of payments theory. The book has also been successfully employed in a one semester combined course, using Chapters 1-6, 9-17, and 20. Those who want a two-semester sequence will want to choose a book of readings to supplement the pure trade theory section.

Books, of course, are not written in a vacuum. The process of writing a book such as this involves constant interaction with the thoughts of other people. With many people it is difficult to delineate where your thoughts end and where their thoughts begin. So in lieu of such an impossible task, we would like to thank those who have been particularly helpful in formulating the ideas in this book. The list is headed by Robert Mundell, whose work serves as the source and catalyst for many of the basic ideas. Special thanks are also extended to Victor Canto for his many hours of help in avoiding errors, changing presentations, developing the *mutatis mutandis* demand and supply curves, and developing the wedge model of the open economy. Others who contributed in one way or another in developing the ideas include Douglas Joines, Bluford Putnam, R. David Ranson, James C. Turney, Robert Webb, and Sykes Wilford.

The presentation of the book benefitted, in addition, from those who served as reviewers: Robert Oliver (California Institute of Technology), Thomas Grennes (North Carolina State University), Franklin Walker (SUNY-Albany), Thomas Layman (Arizona State University), Henry Goldstein (University of Oregon), and James E. Anderson (Boston College). We would also like to thank many students at the University of Chicago, Rutgers University, and the University of Southern California whose comments helped improve the presentation. In addition, we would be remiss if we did not thank those to whom we entrusted the typing of the manuscript at the seemingly endless stages of revision: Mary Carmen, Beverly Davidson, Gerri Dructor, Gladys Durkin, Betty Hafner, Virginia Normann, and Edie Trimble. Finally, while we know that these people have all doubtlessly helped us avoid major errors, errors always remain. We accept responsibility for any you may find.

ARTHUR B. LAFFER
University of Southern California
Los Angeles, California

MARC A. MILES
Rutgers—The State University of New Jersey
New Brunswick, New Jersey

INTERNATIONAL
ECONOMICS
IN AN
INTEGRATED WORLD

SECTION ONE

THE PURE THEORY OF TRADE

CHAPTER 1

Introduction

The subjects covered in the first section of this book are contained under the general heading of the *real* or *pure* theory of international trade. This real or pure theory deals exclusively with transactions in goods and services. Money does not enter into the analysis. Within the framework of the pure theory, goods and services are exchanged for other goods and services. As a consequence, all incomes and prices are denominated in terms of one or more of the goods produced. This type of analysis may be unfamiliar at first and may even appear to have little relevance to the "real world." Yet, given time and exposure to the basic elements of the moneyless framework, it will become clear that this analytic framework does provide convenient and revealing insights for analyzing both the pattern and level of trade. Many of these insights are not initially intuitive. However, as the analysis progresses, they will become almost obvious.

In the second section of the book the basic framework is expanded to include markets for money and bonds as well as goods. However, the basic concepts developed for goods alone in the first part of the book will still remain valid. Thus, by the end of the book, a complete model of international transactions that integrates the markets for goods, money, and bonds will have been constructed. This overall comprehensive framework, however, is constructed one step at a time. The construction begins in this chapter with a highly simplified overview of the basic determinants of trade in goods. The chapter concludes with a simple Ricardian model of trade.

AN OVERVIEW OF TRADE

International trade theory (real theory) is simply an application of the principles of much of the microeconomic theory you already know. Trade theory deals with such familiar concepts as supply, demand, and relative prices. To provide 'an overview of the theory of trade and how familiar concepts fit into the analysis, we begin with the analysis of a market for a single traded good, for instance, corn.

Analysis of the market for a single good comes directly from microeconomics. As in most microeconomic analyses, the discussion is in *partial equilibrium* terms. As the name partial equilibrium implies, such a model analyzes only *part* of what can happen. This form of analysis assumes that "other things" do not change, when in fact they may. Usually the other things that are assumed not to change include the demand for and supply of (and thus prices of) other goods. While partial equilibrium analysis may at times be appropriate for a single market in isolation, it is clearly not suited for analyzing the trade of a country as a whole. Virtually all of the discussion of the determinants of trade in the main part of this book is, therefore, in *general equilibrium* terms. General equilibrium analysis allows all variables to change simultaneously. However, in spite of the shortcomings, the simplicity of the partial equilibrium analysis does provide a convenient framework from which to start. This chapter therefore begins the analysis of international trade in the partial equilibrium framework.

The determinants of trade in the market for a single good like corn are, not surprisingly, the supply of and the demand for corn. More specifically, the determinants of trade are domestic supply and domestic demand. If more corn is produced domestically at the prevailing price than is domestically demanded, surplus corn will be available for export. Conversely, if more corn is demanded in the country than is supplied at the prevailing price, the excess of demand over supply will have to be satisfied by imports from abroad. So, to determine the direction of trade in corn, three things must be known: (a) the quantities of corn supplied at different prices, (b) the quantities of corn demanded at different prices, and (c) the prevailing world price of corn. Therefore, in order to analyze a country's net trade in goods, the determinants of the domestic supply of each good and the domestic demand for each good must first be analyzed individually. We shall proceed first to the determinants of supply.

Perfect competition among producers is an underlying supply assumption. Perfect competition, as you will recall, usually implies the following production characteristics:

a. Each industry is comprised of enough firms to assure that no firm by itself is able to affect any market price. This characteristic of the competitive market is often referred to as *atomistic competition.*

b. Capacity within each industry is sufficiently flexible to allow the industry to expand or contract production either through free entry and exit of firms or through the capability of existing competing firms to vary their scale of production.

c. Each product produced by the various firms within an industry is sufficiently homogenous to avoid product differentiation.

d. There is no collusion among the firms.

Perfect competition together with a given level of technology and factor prices suffice to define what it would cost each individual producer to produce an additional unit of output at various levels of output. Such a curve is shown in Figure 1–1(a). This curve corresponds to the supply curve or marginal cost curve of a specific producer. It is a partial equilibrium curve in the sense that each farmer's supply curve is based on the premise that other farmers do not alter their output, and thus do not alter good or factor prices.

Just as any one producer has such a supply curve, so does each and every producer have a supply curve. At a given point in time, all supply curves can be added horizontally to obtain a total supply curve for that market. In the simplified economy of Figure 1–1, there are two producers of corn with supply curves S_1S_1 and S_2S_2. When these individual supply curves are added horizontally, the market supply curve S_MS_M is obtained. For example, at a price of $2/bushel, Farmer 1 is willing to supply ten thousand bushels while Farmer 2 is willing to supply twenty thousand bushels. Thus, at $2/bushel, the total supply of corn in the economy will be thirty thousand bushels.

Figure 1–1 is intended only as an illustration. Furthermore, Figure 1–1 is constructed with the caveat "at any point in time." At that given moment in time, the two farmers are willing to supply corn at the rate of thirty thousand bushels per unit of production time at a prevailing price of $2/bushel. However, an implication of perfect competition is that firms may be entering and leaving the industry. A market supply curve that exists at one point in time may be quite different than the same market's supply curve after several firms have had time to enter or leave. For

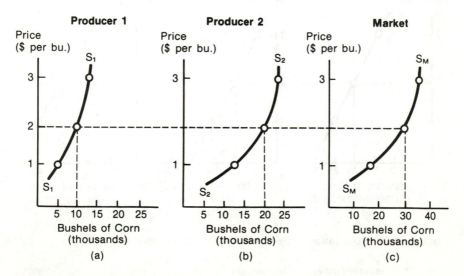

Figure 1–1   The Derivation of the Market Supply Curve for Corn

this reason, the market supply curve at a given point in time is usually referred to as a *short-run* supply curve.*

The market demand curve can be derived in a similar fashion. Again, it is assumed that an individual economic agent in the market, (this time the demander), is unable to affect the market price. Products purchased in the market are assumed to be homogeneous, and collusion by demanders does not exist. Furthermore, since the level of demand varies with the amount of income in the market place, the level of income of the individual is taken as constant.

Given these assumptions, it is now possible to describe each individual consumer's quantity of corn demanded at various prices. This curve corresponds to D_1D_1 and D_2D_2 in Figure 1–2. Just as with the supply curves, these individual demand curves are added horizontally to obtain the total quantity of corn demanded per unit time at different prices. Total market demand is represented by the demand curve D_MD_M. Again, the total number of market participants (demanders) is assumed given at the point in time depicted by the demand curve.

At this point, we should discuss the precise nature of the price which is measured along the vertical axes of Figures 1–1 and 1–2. The usual custom is to think of such prices as the price of corn in terms of currency or money—let's say, dollars. But, in fact, the price that is actually being measured is the relative price of corn, that is, the price in terms of other goods. The traditional use of dollar prices reflects the partial equilibrium nature of the analysis. When the demand and supply curves for corn are drawn in terms of money prices, it is assumed that the demand and sup-

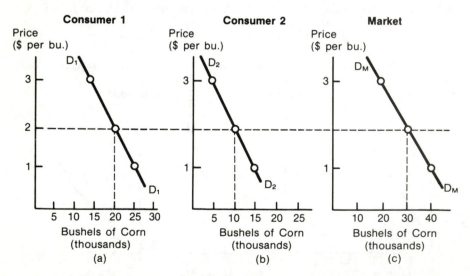

Figure 1–2   The Derivation of the Market Demand Curve for Corn

*Over time, the supply curve may be more nearly horizontal, a point that may be important in distinguishing between trade adjustment in the short and long run.

ply (and thereby the price) of every other good is constant. Given the assumption that other prices remain constant, the behavior of the relative price of corn is identical to the behavior of the dollar price of corn alone. It is important to grasp this point fully, because later, when the analysis moves to a more general equilibrium model, the distinction between dollar prices and relative prices must again be made. Invariably, our pure trade analysis will be explicitly in terms of relative prices.

With the market supply and demand curves defined as above, market equilibrium can now be determined. One possible equilibrium occurs where the market demand curve intersects the market supply curve, or as shown in Figure 1–3(a), at $2/bushel. At the price of $2/bushel of corn, the domestic supply of corn is precisely equal to the domestic demand for corn. But, if domestic supply equals domestic demand, there is no excess supply to be exported abroad, nor excess demand that must be satisfied by imports from abroad. In other words, $2/bushel represents the *autarky* price of corn, that is, the domestic price of corn that prevails when no corn is being exported or imported.

Of course, $2/bushel is not the only possible price of corn. It happens to be, however, the only price at which corn is neither exported nor imported. At any price of corn higher than $2, corn is in domestic excess supply and must be exported. At any lower price, corn is in domestic excess demand and must be imported from abroad. Figure 1–3(a) then provides a great deal more information than merely the price of corn at which domestic supply equals domestic demand. Figure 1–3(a) also indicates the prices of corn at which the country is a net exporter or importer, and in what quantities. At prices above $2/bushel, as supply increases and demand falls from the autarky level, the country is a net exporter of corn. The reverse occurs at any price below $2/bushel.

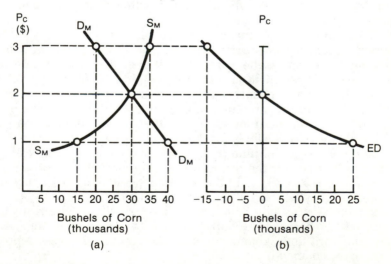

Figure 1–3   The Derivation of an Excess Demand Curve for Corn from Market Demand and Supply Curves

The net trade position of the country in corn at different prices can be illustrated even more clearly by using an excess supply or demand curve. The excess demand curve in Figure 1-3(b) is traced by taking the horizontal distance between the demand and supply curves at each price and plotting this quantity against price. Thus, at $2/bushel where domestic demand for corn just equals domestic supply, the intersection of the demand and supply curves means that excess demand is zero. The excess demand curve intersects the vertical axis in Figure 1-3(b) at $2. At any price above $2, the domestic supply curve is to the right of the domestic demand curve, implying an excess supply (a negative excess demand) of corn in the country. For example, in Figure 1-3(a), at $3/bushel, the domestic supply curve is to the right of the domestic demand curve by fifteen thousand bushels. This distance is reflected in Figure 1-3(b) by a negative excess demand of fifteen thousand bushels at $3/bushel. At any price below $2/bushel, the domestic demand curve is to the right of the domestic supply curve, representing positive excess demand. Thus, in Figure 1-3(b) at $1/bushel, there is an excess demand for corn of 25,000 bushels.

Precisely which trading opportunity the country chooses depends upon the equivalent conditions in the rest of the world now. There are two general frameworks within which the determination can be carried out. If the country under consideration is a "small" country, then the country itself is a price taker just like a purely competitive firm. Total demand and supply in the small country is so negligible in comparison to total demand and supply in the world, that the country cannot influence the price of corn on the world market. With a given excess demand curve for corn, determination of the country's trade is easy. All that is required in this case is to find the prevailing price for corn on world markets. The excess demand curve shows the net trade position of the small country at that price.

If the country is "large" the analysis is slightly more complicated. The country is no longer a pure price taker and the excess supply or demand of the country influences the world price of corn. The equilibrium world price of corn is determined at that price where total excess demand in one part of the world equals the total excess supply in the rest of the world. In terms of the present example, the equilibrium price occurs where the excess demand (or supply) in the "large" country at a given price equals the excess supply (or demand) in the rest of the world. Determination of this equilibrium price can be shown by superimposing the excess supply curve for the rest of the world onto Figure 1-3(b). This is done in Figure 1-4 as ES_{ROW}. In the example, world equilibrium occurs at $1.25/bushel. At $1.25/bushel the excess demand in the country (twenty thousand bushels) exactly equals the excess supply in the rest of the world. At $1.25/bushel total world demand for corn equals total world supply, and corn flows among countries from areas of excess supply to areas of excess demand.

In sum, if a country can be considered purely as a price taker, it can be analyzed by itself, using the prevailing world market prices as a

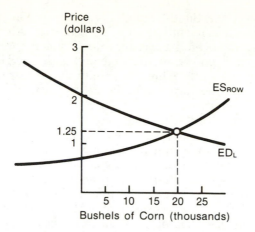

Figure 1–4   Determination of Trade in Corn for a "Large" Country

datum. However, if the country influences the world price, it cannot be analyzed in isolation. Rather, demand and supply of the country have to be analyzed in conjunction with demand and supply in all other countries.

The preceding analysis may be useful for analyzing the market for one particular good, such as corn. However, changes in the net export or import of corn should not be taken as an indication of changes in the net export or import of all goods. The reason is simply that changes in the net demand for corn may, in turn, produce changes in the net demand for other goods. Such interaction of the net demands of various goods cannot be analyzed in the partial equilibrium model just presented. In that model the demand and supplies of other goods are assumed constant. But it is quite probable that, say, exporting more of one good leads to importing more of another good. After all, the motivation of people to produce and sell goods is to buy other goods. An increase in exports or sales to foreigners provides more income to purchase goods from foreigners. As often as not, an increase in exports is associated with a similar increase in imports of other goods. Consequently, to analyze the behavior of a country's total trade, the interaction between exports and imports must be considered in a general equilibrium model of trade.

THE RICARDIAN ONE-FACTOR MODEL

The analysis of fully general models of trade begins with a model containing only one factor of production, labor. This model of international trade was developed by the nineteenth-century British economist David Ricardo. Following closely on the trade theory of Adam Smith, another British economist, the Ricardian model stresses the gains from trade when different countries have different technological capabilities in producing goods. Whereas Smith argued that countries will export goods that they produce more efficiently than other countries, Ricardo's modification emphasizes that even if a country is less efficient than all other countries in producing all goods, it will still export those goods that it produces *relatively* more efficiently. Thus, the Smith model is referred to as the theory of *absolute advantage*, while the Ricardian theory is the theory of *comparative advantage*.

The assumption of differing technologies as the source of trade patterns differs from the assumptions used to develop trade patterns in following chapters. Commencing in Chapter 2 a second model of trade among countries is developed, which considers more than one factor of production and relies on differences in endowments of productive factors such as land, labor, and capital. Hence, after this first chapter, countries are assumed to have equivalent technological capabilities. The framework of this first chapter, however, stresses different technological capabilities and ignores different factor endowments. Interest in the Ricardian framework stems both from the fact that it was the precursor of modern international trade theory and also from the fact that many of its implications have remained unblemished to this date.

By assuming the presence of only one factor of production, attention is focused in the Ricardian model on the country's endowment of labor and how that labor is transformed into one product or another. A one-factor model is obviously less complicated than a two-factor model. On the other hand, the two-factor model introduced in subsequent chapters has richer implications. However, these additional implications are acquired at the cost of greater complexity. With a two-factor model, the focus is on the initial endowments of both factors and also on the proportions in which these two factors are combined in production of each good. But while we are concerned here with only one factor of production, the model still contains two goods. All trade models require at least two products in order for an exchange to occur.

The underlying assumptions of this one-factor model are summarized by the following factors:

a. There are two countries;

b. Each country produces the same two goods;

c. Each country has a given amount of labor, which is the only variable factor of production;

d. Although there are constant costs of production for each good within a country, over the relevant ranges of possible production, the costs differ between the two countries.

Only one factor of production and constant costs of production implies that in both countries the output of either good is directly proportional to the amount of labor used in its production. And since each country has a limited amount of labor, the production of both goods is strictly limited.

The relationship between quantity of labor available, the quantity of output, and the incentives for trade can be described in a numerical example. Suppose that the world consists of two countries, the U.S. and Italy, which can produce two goods, shoes and corn. While both goods can be produced in each country, since technology differs between countries, a unit of labor is not equally efficient in the two countries. For example, (as shown in Table 1–1), a unit of labor in the U.S. can produce either four pairs of shoes or three bushels of corn. A unit of labor in Italy, however, can produce only two pairs of shoes or one bushel of corn.

In terms of Adam Smith's theory, the U.S. has an absolute advantage in producing both goods. One unit of labor can produce more of both goods in the U.S. than in Italy. Alternatively, production of either good requires fewer labor hours in the U.S. This absolute advantage would appear to give the U.S. the edge in exporting both goods. However, if the U.S. exported both goods to Italy, what would Italy trade in return? Obviously, in a two-country, two-good world, one country exports one good and the second country exports the other. It is also obvious that the concept of absolute advantage does not provide us with sufficient information to determine the pattern of trade.

The concept of comparative advantage, on the other hand, does permit the determination of trade patterns in this example. While the U.S. may have absolute advantage in both goods, it can have comparative advantage in only one good. As will now be illustrated, the U.S. has a comparative advantage in corn production, and Italy has a comparative advantage in shoe production.

Consider the cost in terms of foregone shoes of shifting a worker from shoe production to corn production in the two countries. In the U.S., such a shift of labor produces three more bushels of corn, but four fewer pairs of shoes. In other words, for each additional bushel of corn that is produced in the U.S., four-thirds fewer pairs of shoes are produced. Hence, the price of a bushel of corn in the U.S. in terms of shoes ($P_{C/S}^{U.S.}$) is four-thirds.

If a worker is shifted from shoe to corn production in Italy, one additional bushel of corn is produced at the expense of two pairs of shoes. Hence, in Italy the price of corn in terms of shoes ($P_{C/S}^{Italy}$) is two. By increasing corn production in the U.S. instead of Italy, fewer pairs of shoes are sacrificed.

Similarly, the price of shoes in terms of corn in the U.S. ($P_{S/C}^{U.S.}$) and Italy ($P_{S/C}^{Italy}$) can be determined. This price shows how much corn production is decreased when an additional pair of shoes is produced. From Table 1–2 it is clear that this price is simply the inverse of the price of corn.

Table 1–1   Production of One Unit of Labor

	Shoes (Pairs)	Corn (Bushels)
U.S.	4	3
Italy	2	1

Table 1–2   The Relative Prices of Goods in the Two Countries

	Price of Corn in Terms of Shoes $P_{C/S}$	Price of Shoes in Terms of Corn $P_{S/C}$
U.S.	4/3	3/4
Italy	2	1/2

Notice in Table 1–2 that although it is relatively cheaper to produce corn in the U.S., shoe production is relatively cheaper in terms of corn in Italy. The U.S. therefore has a comparative advantage in corn while Italy has a comparative advantage in shoes. With trade, the U.S. is expected to specialize in producing and exporting corn, while Italy should specialize in producing and exporting shoes.

This information about production of the two goods permits us to derive graphically the maximum production in the two countries and to show the gains from trade. Suppose that both the U.S. and Italy have one hundred units of labor. If all U.S. labor were put into shoe production, four hundred pairs of shoes could be produced. Alternatively, with all labor employed in corn production, three hundred bushels of corn would be produced. These two possibilities are graphed in Figure 1–5(a). However, these two points on the graph represent only two of many possible output combinations. All additional possible production combinations are summarized by the production possibilities curve connecting these two points.

This production possibilities curve is a straight line (see Appendix A to this chapter) since constant cost of production is assumed in both indus-

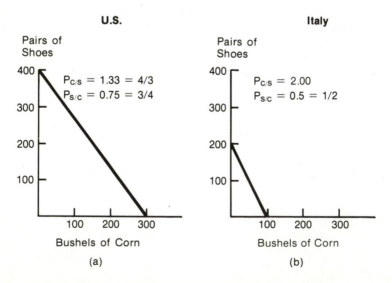

Figure 1–5   The Production Possibilities Curves of the U.S. and Italy

tries. Each additional unit of labor produces the same amount of shoes or corn. The slope of this line therefore represents the rate at which corn production can be transformed into shoe production by switching one laborer from the cornfields to the shoe factory. In other words, it represents the ratio of the marginal product of labor in the two industries. For example, in the U.S. case, shifting a worker from producing corn to shoes increases shoe production by four pairs but it reduces corn production by three bushels. Alternatively, for every additional bushel of corn that is produced in the U.S., four-thirds pairs less of shoes are produced. Hence, four thirds is the marginal cost of a bushel of corn, expressed in terms of shoes. This marginal cost is also known as the *marginal rate of transformation* (MRT) of shoe production into corn production.

The slope of the line also represents the relative price at which these two goods would have to trade in the U.S. in autarky. In autarky, both goods are produced at home because neither is supplied through foreign trade. If both goods are produced, then, from the example it is known that the goods can be substituted in production at the rate of four pairs of shoes for every three bushels of corn. Since this is the relative rate at which the two goods are supplied, consumers trying to get the most they can with their limited incomes or budget constraints consume each good until the relative values of the goods are four pairs of shoes to three bushels of corn. The relative value of goods in consumption is known as the *marginal rate of substitution* between shoes and corn (MRS). In equilibrium then, the marginal rate of transformation in production (MRT) has to equal the marginal rate of substitution in consumption (MRS). From above, MRT = 4/3, so the autarkic equilibrium price of corn in terms of shoes must also be 4/3 ($P_{C/S}^{U.S.}$ = 1.33). One and a third pairs of shoes have to be surrendered in order to obtain one bushel of corn. (A proof that the marginal rates of transformation and consumption are equal in autarky is presented in Appendix B of this chapter.)

Similarly, a hypothetical production possibilities curve for Italy is presented in Figure 1–5(b). If all labor in Italy were employed in the shoe industry, two hundred pairs of shoes could be produced. If, instead, all one hundred units of labor were employed producing corn, one hundred bushels of corn would be produced. Notice that the rates at which shoes can be transformed into corn, and thus the autarkic prices, are not the same in the two countries. In the U.S., the price of corn in terms of shoes is 1.33. But in Italy, for every bushel of corn sacrificed, two more pairs of shoes are produced. Thus, in autarkic equilibrium, two pairs of shoes have to be foregone to purchase a bushel of corn. In other words $P_{C/S}^{Italy}$ = 2.0.

The difference in production techniques immediately provides the *raison d'être* for trade between the two countries. Each country finds that it can produce one good relatively less expensively than the other country, since in autarky the relative price of goods differs between the two countries. It is then to the benefit of each country to purchase the good that it has relatively more difficulty producing. To use the present example, only 1.33 pairs of shoes must be sacrificed to produce one bushel of corn in the U.S., versus 2.0 pairs in Italy. Thus, U.S. producers can produce corn for only one and a third pairs of shoes, while Italian consumers would be willing to pay up to two pairs for the corn. Clearly, there is room for both sides to gain.

Similarly, shoes are relatively less expensive to produce in Italy than they are in the U.S. In the U.S., each pair of shoes requires the sacrifice of .75 bushels of corn, while in Italy one pair of shoes requires the sacrifice of only .50 bushels of corn. Again there is room for U.S. consumers and Italian producers to gain.

If the autarky prices in the U.S. and Italy did not differ, there would be no room for either country to gain. There would be no natural incentive to trade. Two basic propositions about trade have therefore been illustrated:

1. If relative prices in two countries do not differ in autarky, there is no incentive to trade.

2. Given different relative prices in autarky, when trade commences, goods tend to flow from the country that produces the goods relatively less expensively to the other country. The country that produces a particular good relatively cheaper is said to have a *comparative advantage* in that good. In the numerical example above, the U.S. has a comparative advantage in corn while Italy has a comparative advantage in shoes. Notice that the concept of comparative advantage refers to relative and not absolute prices. With two goods and two countries, each country has a comparative advantage in one good. Neither country can have a comparative advantage in both goods, though in trade equilibrium one country may produce both goods.

When free trade exists between two countries, the relative price of goods can no longer differ between the countries as they did in autarky. If the relative prices continued to differ, there would be an incentive for arbitrage. That is, people would buy in the relatively cheaper country and sell in the more expensive. This arbitrage in and of itself would produce a self-correcting force which would make relative prices rise in the cheaper country and fall in the more expensive. For example, when trade opens, if the $P_{S/C}^{U.S.}$ remains at .75 and the $P_{S/C}^{Italy}$ at .50, then someone could make a profit by buying shoes in Italy and selling them in the U.S. In turn, he could then make additional profits by buying corn in the U.S. and selling the corn for shoes in Italy. But reducing the supply of shoes in Italy should raise their relative price there. Similarly, selling shoes in the U.S. should lower their relative price there, and so on. The relative prices in the two countries converge. The incentive to arbitrage, and thus the movement in relative prices, disappears only when relative prices in the two countries become equal.

While the relative prices in the two countries must be equal following the opening of trade, what precisely will the equilibrium price be? The answer is that with this type of trade model the final price is not known without more information. Final equilibrium prices are determined by the interplay of the forces of both supply and demand. But the Ricardian model only provides information about the supply or production sides in the two countries. There is no information about comparative demands. The precise equilibrium relative price cannot be determined.

There exists, however, information about the final price in spite of the inability to determine the exact equilibrium price. The supply side information does provide information about the range within which the equilibrium price must fall. For example, it is known that the final value of $P_{S/C}$ cannot fall below .50. If this price fell below .50, Italian shoe producers would not sell abroad. Both Americans and Italians would try to import shoes with no one selling them. Remember that Italian shoe producers can always get .50 bushels of corn for shoes at home, so .50 is the minimum price they demand to supply shoes to the world market. Similarly, the equilibrium price would not rise above .75 because consumers in the U.S. could always get shoes from domestic producers for .75 bushels of corn. So the final relative price of the two goods would be .50 $\leq$ $P_{S/C}$ $\leq$ .75 (or equivalently 1.33 $\leq$ $P_{C/S}$ $\leq$ 2.0). The precise price could be determined by supplying sufficient information about demand conditions.

This final relative price of the two goods is called the *terms of trade*, that is, literally, the terms on which one good trades for another on world markets. It is especially important in Section II of this book to distinguish the concept of the terms of trade from the concept of the exchange rate, which is the relative price of currencies.

If the two countries are about equally sized, that is, neither is a "small" country, then the final equilibrium price lies between the two autarky prices. Notice that since the equilibrium price does not equal either country's autarky price, each country specializes completely in the production of the good in which it has a comparative advantage. For example, Italy has a comparative advantage in shoes. If $P_{S/C}^{U.S.} = .50$, Italy would trade, but would probably produce both goods. In this case, Italy would export some shoes and import some corn, while the U.S. would produce only corn. If $P_{S/C}^{Italy} > .50$, the Italian shoe producers could get more for their shoes abroad than it would cost to make them, while Italian corn producers could get less now in terms of shoes for their corn than the cost of production. Italian shoe manufacturing would expand and Italian corn farmers would go out of business. Italy would specialize in producing shoes. In the U.S., just the reverse would happen, with shoe manufacturers going out of business and specialization occurring in corn. Since both countries would be better off than if they did not trade, calls for protection to prevent Italian corn farmers or U.S. shoe manufacturers from going out of business would not be in the interest of either country. After all, there would be no initial incentive to trade unless people felt it would make them better off.

An indication of these gains from trade is presented in Figure 1–6. Assume that in autarky the U.S. produces 80 pairs of shoes and 240 bushels of corn (point A). Italy, on the other hand, produces 100 pairs of shoes

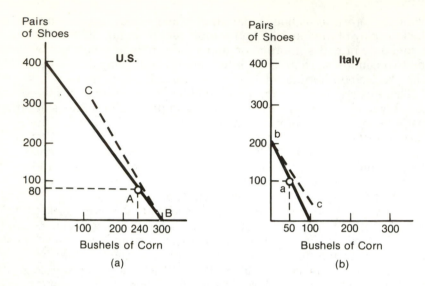

Figure 1–6   The Gains from Trade in the Ricardian Model

and 50 bushels of corn (point a). Total world production is 180 pairs of shoes and 290 bushels of corn. However, if with trade both countries specialize in the good in which they have a comparative advantage, production moves to points B and b. The U.S. produces 300 bushels of corn and Italy produces 200 pairs of shoes. The total world production of both goods rises. The world as a whole is clearly better off.

In addition, if the free trade terms of trade lie between the autarky terms of trade of the two countries, both countries can be shown to gain from trade. For example, if the free trade price of corn in terms of shoes were 5/3, the consumption opportunities for the U.S. would be described by the dotted line BC. Notice that since BC lies to the right of the initial production possibilities curve, the U.S. can consume more of both goods than under autarky. Similarly, the free trade consumption opportunities for Italy are described by the dotted line bc. Italy's total consumption also rises under free trade. A more detailed description of these gains from trade is provided in Chapter 4.

The simple Ricardian model therefore illustrates many of the basic results which will be shown to hold in the more complete trade models:

a. Trade equalizes the relative price of goods among trading partners.

b. The equilibrium relative price lies between the autarkic prices.

c. Comparative advantage is determined by factors such as differing technology.

d. Countries are shown to export the good in which they have a comparative advantage.

e. Both countries gain from the existence of trade.

These same results are now derived for the more complete and interesting models of trade.

SUMMARY

The *real* or *pure* theory of trade considers only the *barter* model, where one set of goods and services are exchanged for another set. The pattern of trade between countries of the barter model depends on the quantities of the various goods supplied and demanded at each relative price, and the prevailing equilibrium world relative price of the goods. The equilibrium world relative price is the one at which the excess supply of goods in one part of the world equals the excess demand for goods in the rest of the world. Given this equilibrium price, goods then flow from areas of excess supply to areas of excess demand.

The *Ricardian model* of trade assumes that only one factor of production, labor, is used in each country, and analyzes the pattern of trade by considering only the supply side. It differs from Adam Smith's theory of trade by stressing *relative* or *comparative advantage* rather than *absolute advantage*. If production techniques differ between countries, then *autarkic* relative prices differ and comparative advantage exists. Arbitrage assures that free trade equalizes relative goods prices in both countries, and goods flow from the country with comparative advantage to the other country. The fianl equilibrium price of goods is called the *terms of trade*, and must lie between the autarkic prices in the two countries. The precise equilibrium price cannot be determined, however, since the model considers only the supply side, and not demand. Free trade then increases the welfare of the two countries by increasing the quantity of goods produced and consumed.

REFERENCES

RICARDO, DAVID. *Principles of Political Economy and Taxation*, London, 1817. (Reprinted New York: Dutton, Everyman's Library, 1969). Especially Chapter 7.

SMITH, ADAM, *The Wealth of Nations*, 1776. (Reprinted New York: The Modern Library, 1937).

APPENDIX 1
SOME BASIC PROPOSITIONS OF THE
RICARDIAN MODEL

In Chapter 1, two assertions are made about the slope of the production possibilities curve in the Ricardian model. First, it is asserted that the slope is a constant and equals the ratio of the marginal products of labor in the two industries, which in turn equals the marginal rate of transformation MRT. Second, it is asserted that the slope equals the autarkic equilibrium relative price of the two goods. These two assertions are now derived with the help of a simple algebraic model.

A. The Ricardian Production Possibilities Curve Is a Straight Line Whose Slope Is the Ratio of the Marginal Products of Labor in the Two Industries

Assume that within a country two goods are produced, shoes and corn. Production of both goods involves constant returns to scale. In other words, the production of shoes or corn will be proportional to the amount of the one factor of production labor that is employed in producing the good. In algebraic terms, the production functions for the two goods may be represented as

$$C = \alpha L_C \qquad\qquad (1A-1)$$

$$S = \beta L_S \qquad\qquad (1A-2)$$

where

C = the quantity of corn produced

S = the quantity of shoes produced

L_S, L_C = the quantity of labor in the shoe and corn industries respectively

α = the additional bushels of corn produced by one additional worker in the corn industry

β = the additional pairs of shoes produced by one additional worker in the shoe industry

The only limit on the total quantity of production is the total quantity of labor L in the country. It is assumed that at any moment all labor is fully employed between the two industries so that

$$L = L_C + L_S. \qquad\qquad (1A-3)$$

Given these three assumptions, the basic characteristics of the Ricardian production possibilities curve can be shown. Rearranging equation (1A-3) yields a description of the amount of labor in the corn industry in terms of total labor and labor in the shoe industry

$$L_C = L - L_S. \qquad\qquad (1A-3')$$

Substituting (1A-3') into the production function for corn yields

$$C = \alpha(L - L_S) \qquad\qquad (1A-1')$$

which in turn can be solved for labor in the shoe industry

$$L_S = \frac{\alpha L - C}{\alpha}. \qquad\qquad (1A-4)$$

Substituting (1A–4) into the production function for shoes yields

$$S = \beta L - \left(\frac{\beta}{\alpha}\right)C. \qquad (1A\text{--}5)$$

Equation (1A–5) describes the Ricardian production function. It shows that with a given amount of labor the quantity of shoes produced is negatively related in the proportion β/α to the quantity of corn produced. Equation (1A–5) is therefore a linear or straight-line relationship with slope β/α. The Ricardian production possibilities curve is therefore a straight line.

It can now be easily shown that the slope of the line is the ratio of the marginal products of labor in the two industries. The coefficient β is described as the additional pairs of shoes produced by an additional worker in the shoe industry. Hence, β is simply the marginal product of labor in shoe production. Similarly, the coefficient α is the marginal product of labor in corn production. Thus, the slope of the Ricardian production possibilities curve is the ratio of the marginal product of labor in shoe production to the marginal product of labor in corn production.

The production possibilities curve for the U.S. in Figure 1–6 can provide numerical verification of these results. If it is assumed that there are four hundred workers in the U.S., the production functions for corn and shoes will be

$$C = \frac{3}{4} \cdot L_C$$

$$S = 1 \cdot L_S.$$

The four hundred units of labor are capable of producing the three hundred bushels of corn or four hundred pairs of shoes shown on the horizontal and vertical intercepts respectively. In this numerical example, then, $\alpha = \frac{3}{4}$ and $\beta = 1$. From equation (1A–5) the relationship between corn and shoe production is

$$S = 400 - \frac{4}{3}C.$$

The production possibilities curve is a straight line with a slope of 4/3, just as assumed in the chapter. Furthermore, this constant marginal rate of transformation is equal to the ratio of the marginal products of labor.*

---

*This numerical derivation of the U.S. curve in Figure 1–6 assumes that there are four hundred units of labor in order to avoid the use of constant terms. If the U.S. had only 100 workers, as assumed in the numerical example in Chapter 1, then the production functions for corn and shoes would become

$$C = 225 + \frac{3}{4} \cdot L_C$$

$$S = 300 + 1 \cdot L_S.$$

The undesirable aspect of constant terms is that they imply positive output even with zero workers.

B. The Slope of the Production Possibilities Curve Equals the Autarkic Equilibrium Relative Price of the Two Goods

Since the Ricardian model is only a model of the supply side, the autarkic equilibrium price must be derived from supply side considerations. It will be assumed that the primary force for determining the equilibrium price is profit maximization by producers. Profit in either industry is defined as the revenues from production minus the (labor) costs of production. However, since there is no numeraire such as money in this barter model, the value of labor and production in both industries must be denominated in a common good. Shoes are chosen as the numeraire. Profits in the corn industry (denominated in shoes) are therefore

$$\pi_{C/S} = P_{C/S} \cdot C - P_{C/S} \cdot W_C \cdot L_C \qquad (1A\text{--}6)$$

where

$\pi_{C/S}$ = profits in the corn industry in terms of shoes

$P_{C/S}$ = price of corn in terms of shoes

W_C = wages paid in the corn industry in terms of corn.

Similarly, profits in the shoe industry are

$$\pi_S = P_{S/S} \cdot S - W_S \cdot L_S \qquad (1A\text{--}7)$$

where

π_S = profits in the shoe industry in terms of shoes

$P_{S/S}$ = the price of shoes in terms of shoes

W_S = wages in the shoe industry in terms of shoes.

The price of shoes in terms of shoes of course equals one, and therefore can be ignored.

If (1A–6) and (1A–7) represent the profits of individual firms in the industries, each firm being a price taker in the goods and labor markets, then the only way individual firms can maximize profits is to vary the quantity of labor hired. The profit functions can be rewritten

$$\pi_{C/S} = P_{C/S}(\alpha L_C) - P_{C/S} W_C L_C \qquad (1A\text{--}6')$$

and

$$\pi_S = (\beta L_S) - W_S L_S, \qquad (1A\text{--}7')$$

and the first order conditions for profit maximization are

$$\frac{\partial \pi_{C/S}}{\partial L_C} = P_{C/S} \cdot \alpha - P_{C/S} \cdot W_C \qquad (1A\text{--}8)$$

and

$$\frac{\partial \pi_S}{\partial L_S} = \beta - W_S. \qquad (1A\text{--}9)$$

Together (1A–8) and (1A–9) imply

$$\frac{P_{C/S} \cdot \alpha}{\beta} = \frac{P_{C/S} \cdot W_C}{W_S}.$$ (1A–10)

Since labor is assumed mobile, labor will move between industries until the real wage is equalized, i.e. $P_{C/S} \cdot W_C = W_S$. Labor mobility therefore implies that the right hand term in (1A–10) equals one. Equation (1A–10) can therefore be rearranged to

$$P_{C/S} = \frac{\beta}{\alpha}.$$ (1A–10′)

In other words, when producers are in profit-maximizing equilibrium, the autarkic relative price of corn in terms of shoes must equal the slope of the production possibilities curve or marginal rate of transformation.

CHAPTER 2

The Supply Side in a Nontrading Country

The model of trade is now expanded from the single-factor Ricardian model to consider two factors of production—capital and labor. In order to determine the pattern of trade among countries, we must first know the quantities of goods at various prices that countries are willing and able to relinquish in the exchange process. The determination of trade, like any other economic question, has two sides—supply and demand. The supply side represents a country's possible combinations of production at various prices. The demand side represents the possible combinations of goods which satisfy a country's total demand at various prices. Which goods are in excess supply and which are in excess demand can be determined by comparing equilibrium supply combinations to equilibrium demand combinations at a given relative price. Excess supplies of goods can be exported, and excess demands can be satisfied by importing the desired goods. Trade patterns emerge.

Before analyzing trade patterns, however, it is obviously necessary first to describe the underlying determinants of supply and demand of goods. This chapter explores the basis of goods supply within a nontrading country producing two goods with two factors of production. The following chapter, Chapter 3, explains how trade in goods or factors affects the supply of goods and the returns to factors within a country. Finally, Chapter 4 incorporates the demand side of the goods markets and describes the gains from trade.

THE PRODUCTION POSSIBILITIES CURVE, PRODUCTION FUNCTIONS, AND FACTORS OF PRODUCTION

The supply side of a country can be summarized by the production possibilities curve (PPC) (which is shown in Figure 2–10). This curve describes the maximum possible combinations of two goods A and B which can be produced in a particular country under the conditions of efficient production and full employment. To derive the PPC, one must first know how much of the two factors of production, capital (K) and labor (L), are available and how the limited quantities of factors must be combined to produce the two goods A and B. The relationship between quantities of factors of production and quantities of goods produced is described in the production function. Therefore an understanding of some of the properties of the underlying production function is essential to understand what quantities of goods A and B are available for the economy's consumption.

A production function simply describes the maximum output obtainable from limited quantities of factor inputs. The production function therefore assumes that the factors of production such as labor, capital, and land are being used in the most efficient combination possible to produce the final product. For each product this maximum relationship can be represented by the expression:

$$Q_i = \text{function}_i(K_i, L_i) = f(K_i, L_i) \qquad (2\text{--}1)$$

where Q_i is the maximum amount of product i that can be produced, and K_i and L_i are the quantities of factor inputs of capital and labor.

The production function implicitly assumes a specific level of technical knowledge. As the level of technical knowledge changes, so should the relationship between quantities of inputs and maximum outputs. The greater the technology, the more "efficiently" the inputs can be used, and the more output that is possible from a given quantity of inputs. So, Q_i above represents the maximum output of good i that can be obtained from given amounts of inputs *under the state of currently available technical knowledge.*

In the analysis of this book, only two homogeneous factors of production, capital, K and labor, L, are considered. Of course, the production function could potentially be described in terms of many factors of production, but there is no loss of generality from restricting the analysis to two factors. In most cases the same basic economic principles described hold regardless of the number of inputs. The use of only two factors simply makes the analysis more manageable and amenable to graphs. To many people these two factors of production are visualized most easily as machines and workers. However, in some particular applications a more general approach may be useful by interpreting K and L according to the context at hand.*

If both capital and labor were freely available, given any production functions for the two outputs, an unlimited amount of A and B could be produced. But both capital and labor are scarce resources, and the econ-

---

*For example, an alternative dichotomy might be skilled versus unskilled labor. Other factor inputs relevant to particular applications could include land, technology, natural resources, and entrepreneurial talent. More generally, any productive resource whose characteristics are distinctly different from the characteristics of other resources can be thought of as a separate input. Note also that factor inputs may be the outputs of a separate production function, for example physical or human capital.

omy is assumed to have a specific endowment of each. The amount of physical capital available at any moment in time is denoted as K, so the economy operates under the constraint that the amount of capital employed in the two industries must sum to K, that is, $K_A + K_B = K$. Similarly, the labor force L is allocated across the two industries so that $L_A + L_B = L$.

It is the assumption of scarce factors of production that, in turn, results in the scarcity of outputs A and B. A positive value or price is placed on additional units of goods A and B because not enough of either can be produced to satiate completely the demand for them. More of each good is always preferred to less. The inputs in turn must also have a positive value because additional units of inputs are required in order to produce additional units of output. The prices paid these factors of production are called "factor rewards." Factor rewards determine the allocation of the scarce inputs among producers.

The factor reward of capital represents the price of hiring physical capital for some prespecified unit of time, in other words its "rental rate," r. The price of hiring labor, again for a prespecified unit of time, is called its "wage rate," w. One possibility is to denominate these factor rewards in terms of a money numeraire such as dollars. However, as is obvious by now, the discussion in this section of the book is in terms of a barter economy, that is, one without money. Another numeraire must therefore be chosen. Any final product i or, for that matter, input, in the economy could be used. In general a final product will be used as numeraire in this book. Factor rewards are therefore written as r_i or w_i, where the subscript i refers to the good in which the factor is assumed paid.

For example, the wage rate in an automobile factory could be described as the number of cars each worker could buy with his wages. The wage rate would be represented by w_A, where A denotes that wages are denominated in terms of automobiles, perhaps two cars per year per worker. Likewise, the profits, rents, etc. accruing to the firm's physical capital could be described by r_A. Thus a large stamping machine could be said to earn five cars per year. In a two product world, the returns to factors could just as easily be described in terms of the "other" good. If wheat is the other product, one might alternatively state that the factory worker earns 2,000 bushels of wheat per year and the stamping machine 5,000 bushels per year.*

As factors of production enter the production function, two properties are assumed to hold:

---

*From experience we tend to think of wages and rents as some dollar amount. However, the use of money here as a numeraire is unnecessary and, without additional insights, tends to confuse the analysis. If necessary, money could be introduced as a commodity in its own right, and the same theorems would hold. This context is reserved for issues relating to the balance of payments in the second part of the book. Otherwise, it is both risky and unnecessary to think in terms of money prices, money wages, or monetary variables. Many of the most common errors of analysis result from this quite intuitive, but misleading, practice.

a. Each factor of production by itself is assumed to obey the law of diminishing returns. In other words, if the quantity of one factor is held constant, then, as additional units of the other factor are added, total output continues to increase, but eventually by smaller and smaller amounts per additional unit.

b. Increasing all factors of production proportionally produces equiproportional increases in output. This property is called constant returns to scale. Thus, doubling both the quantity of labor and capital used to produce a single product results in a doubling in the amount of the good produced.

This second property of the production function is also referred to as "homogeneity of degree one" since if all factors of production are increased by the proportion λ, then output increases by the proportion λ raised to the power one, that is,

$$\lambda^1 Q_i = f(\lambda K_i, \lambda L_i) \qquad (2\text{-}1')$$

Evidence from both engineering and econometric studies suggests that these characteristics do not grossly misrepresent the real world.

An important implication of constant returns to scale, known as Euler's theorem, relates to the disposition of total output between the two factors of production. Under conditions of perfect competition each factor is paid its marginal product. Combining constant returns to scale with perfect competition assures that the total compensation of labor and the total returns of capital always sum precisely to total output. This result is true within each industry as well as over all industries. The implied relationships in the two factor, two good case are:

$$w_i L_i + r_i K_i = Q_i \text{ for either industry A or B} \qquad (2\text{-}2)$$

and

$$w_A(L_A + L_B) + r_A(K_A + K_B) = Q_A + P_{B/A}Q_B \qquad (2\text{-}3)$$

for the two good economy as a whole, where

L_i, K_i = quantity of labor or capital used in industry i (either A or B)

w_i, r_i = factor rewards in terms of good i (either A or B)

$P_{B/A}$ = price of good B in terms of numeraire good A

A derivation of Euler's theorem as it is used here appears in the appendix to this chapter.

FACTOR PROPORTIONS AND FACTOR RETURNS WITHIN A GIVEN INDUSTRY

This section examines the way in which changing factor proportions within a given industry affects output, and the way in which producers determine the proper factor proportions. As is shown, changing factor proportions is one way of affecting factor rewards. The other way is through changing output prices, which will be described in the next chapter in the section on the Stolper-Samuelson theorem.

With constant returns to scale in this analysis, the production function can be expressed on a per worker basis. This adjustment is possible because, as its name implies, constant returns to scale mean that scale variables affect inputs and outputs identically. Doubling inputs means doubling output. In terms of equation (2–1′) above, doubling means that the scale factor by which all variables are multiplied is two. In theory, any number can be used as a scale variable. The particular scale variable chosen in this section is the inverse of the number of units of labor, that is, 1/L. This chosen scale variable permits the analysis to proceed on a per worker basis.

Dropping subscripts from (2–1′) the production function becomes:

$$\frac{1}{L} \cdot Q = f\left(\frac{1}{L} \cdot K, \frac{1}{L} \cdot L\right) \qquad (2\text{–}4)$$

or

$$\frac{Q}{L} = f\left(\frac{K}{L}\right). \qquad (2\text{–}5)$$

In this form the production function shows that the amount of output per worker depends solely on the amount of capital per worker, that is, the number of machines employed per worker. This relationship between outputs and inputs can alternatively be expressed

$$Q = L \cdot f\left(\frac{K}{L}\right). \qquad (2\text{–}5')$$

This form emphasizes that given the capital-labor ratio in the industry, total output is proportional to the quantity of labor employed. From this relationship it is clear that the amount of output produced still depends upon the total quantity of labor input and the total quantity of capital input.

The production function relating output per worker to capital per worker in a given industry i is shown diagrammatically in Figure 2–1. In the diagram each point along the production function OP relates the maximum amount of output per worker that can be obtained from a corresponding amount of capital at the worker's disposal. Over the entire production function, as the quantity of capital at a worker's disposal increases, the maximum potential output of the worker also increases. But the convexity (diminishing slope) of the production function means that the additional maximum output added by each additional unit of capital becomes smaller and smaller. These smaller additions to output correspond to the law of diminishing returns for each factor as described in assumption A on page 25.

At any one point along the production function in Figure 2–1, the slope represents the change in output per worker divided by the change in the

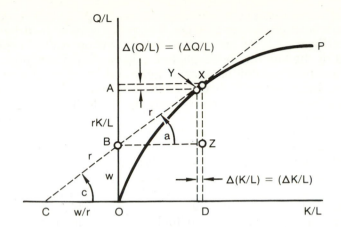

Figure 2–1   The Production Function

amount of capital per worker. This ratio is the change in output associated with a one unit change in the amount of capital, that is, the marginal product of capital.

To show that the slope of the production function is literally the marginal product of capital, we need only compare the change between two points (X and Y) arbitrarily close along the curve. The horizontal distance between the two points is $\Delta(K/L) = \Delta K/L$ (since the numeraire L can be considered constant), and the vertical distance is $\Delta(Q/L) = \Delta Q/L$. The slope (the vertical change divided by the horizontal change) is therefore $\Delta Q/\Delta K$ or the marginal product of capital. In terms of Figure 2–1, if the industry operates at point X, the horizontal distance between the two vertical dotted lines represents the increment in capital per worker $\Delta K/L$ as output increases to point X. The vertical distance between the two horizontal dotted lines represents the increment in output per worker $\Delta Q/L$ as point X is reached. The slope of the production function at point X is therefore equivalent to $\Delta Q/\Delta K$ or the marginal product of capital. This value diminishes as point X moves farther to the right. Thus, along the production function, the marginal product of capital can be seen to diminish with an increase in the ratio of capital to labor, as the law of diminishing returns implies.

Furthermore, under perfect competition, this slope of the production function at point X is exactly equal to the rental rate of capital, r. It is evident from Figure 2–1 that the slope at point X is also equal to the hypotenuse (BX) of triangle BZX. These two additional pieces of information in turn permit the identification of how total production is divided between capital and labor. If the rental rate is multiplied by the factor proportion K/L, the returns to capital per worker rK/L are obtained. The distance AB in Figure 2–1 therefore represents capital's share of the total output per period per worker employed, and the distance OB is labor's share of total output. A proof of this assertion follows.

The question is to determine what proportion of the total output per worker Q/L (measured by the distance OA in Figure 2–1) is received by capital, and what proportion by labor. The proof is aided by drawing the line BZ in Figure 2–1. As just shown, the returns per unit of capital are measured by the line BX, the tangent of angle a. At point X, the number of units of capital per unit of labor is measured by BZ = OD. From geometry, we know that multiplying the tangent of an angle by the adjacent side yields the value of the side opposite the angle. Thus, the returns to capital per worker rK/L equal the distance XZ which also equals AB. Since total output per worker is OA and capital's share is AB, by the Euler theorem relationship described in equation (2–2), the remaining output OB goes to labor and represents labor's share.

A few more observations are now possible. Since the number of workers per worker must, by definition, equal one, the distance OB (wL/L) must also equal the wage rate w. Also, COB and BZX are similar triangles, implying that the tangent to angle c is again the rental rate r. This result in turn implies that the distance CO represents the wage-rental ratio, w/r.

An important relationship can now be demonstrated—the relationship between the two key variables, the capital-labor ratio K/L and the wage-rental ratio w/r. Consider an increase in the capital-labor ratio that moves the point X up and to the right along the production curve. The slope CX declines as the capital-labor rises, and the distance CO increases. As the capital-labor rises, the marginal product of capital declines, marginal product of labor increases, and the ratio of wages to the return to capital rises. In other words, the wage-rental ratio is an increasing function of the captial-labor ratio over the entire range of the production function.

The positive relationship between the wage-rental ratio and the capital-labor ratio can also be shown in terms of the isoquants for good A in Figures 2–2 and 2–3. An isoquant simply describes the various combinations of capital and labor which can produce a given amount of a particu-

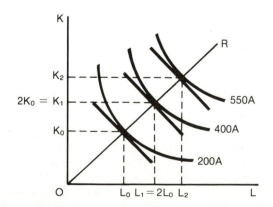

Figure 2–2 Isoquants of Good A

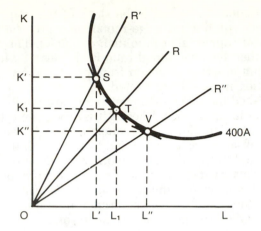

Figure 2–3   The Relationship between Wage-Rental Ratios and Capital-Labor Ratios along the Isoquant

lar good. Since isoquants are derived directly from the production functions, they should reflect similar properties. For example, one property of the homogeneous production functions used in this text is that as both capital and labor are increased in the same proportion, output also increases by that proportion. Thus, in Figure 2–2, as the initial quantities of capital and labor (K_0 and L_0) employed in producing good A are doubled to $K_1 = (2K_0)$ and $L_1 = (2L_0)$, the quantity of good A produced also doubles from 200 to 400 units. If the quantity of both capital and labor were increased by an additional 37.5% (to K_2 and L_2), output would increase to 550 units of good A.

Another property of the production function is that a given wage-rental ratio should be associated with a given capital-labor ratio, regardless of the level of output. This property is also illustrated in Figure 2–2. The capital-labor ratio is reflected in the ray OR from the origin. Along that ray the capital-labor ratio is constant. The wage-rental ratio is reflected in the slope of the isoquant at a given point. As drawn, the slope of the isoquant equals the ratio of the marginal products of labor and capital. In profit maximizing equilibrium this ratio must also equal the wage-rental ratio. Notice in Figure 2–2 that along ray OR the slopes of the isoquants are equal. Hence, the constant capital-labor ratios are associated with constant wage-rental ratios.

As the wage-rental ratios change, however, the capital-labor ratios also change. The precise relationship between the two ratios is shown in Figure 2–3, which analyzes only the isoquant for 400 units of good A. Point T represents the initial situation where K_1 units of capital and L_1 units of labor are used to produce 400 units of good A. However, other combinations of capital and labor are possible. For instance, if more capital (K') and less labor (L') were employed, production would occur at point S on the isoquant. At point S the slope of the isoquant is steeper, implying a higher equilibrium wage-rental ratio. Alternatively, point V represents a lower capital-labor ratio than at point T. The lower slope at point V means that the wage-rental ratio is also less. So for movements along the isoquant in either direction from point T, the wage-rental and capital-labor ratios are positively related.

Having described the relationship between the capital-labor ratio and wage-rental ratio in terms of geometry, it is worthwhile to express the same point on a more intuitive and economic level. When the K/L ratio rises, each unit of labor has more capital to work with than before, and each unit of capital has less labor to work with. Each unit of labor becomes more productive and each unit of capital less productive, implying that the marginal product (and thus the wages) of labor rises and the marginal product of capital falls. The wage-rental ratio must rise.

Alternatively, when the price of one factor of production rises vis-à-vis the other factor, cost-conscious producers will, under normal conditions, tend to use less of the now higher-priced factor relative to the now lower-priced factor. Thus, if the wage rate rises relative to the rental rate, profit-seeking entrepreneurs hire less labor and more capital, or in other ways raise the amount of capital per worker. Similarly, if the rental rate on capital rises relative to the wage rate, businessmen and women attempt to conserve on their capital requirements. The K/L ratio is reduced and the increase in the number of workers per unit of capital raises the marginal product of capital in order to finance the increased capital rental rate.

Thus, irrespective of how the change occurs, there should be a positive relationship between the wage-rental ratio and the capital-labor ratio. The cheaper capital is relative to labor, the more capital per worker firms employ and vice versa. Such a positive relationship is summarized by the positively sloped curve in Figure 2–4.

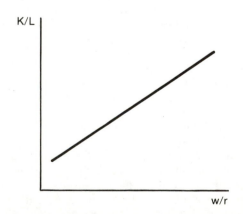

Figure 2–4   The Relationship between the Capital-Labor and Wage-Rental Ratios

FACTOR PROPORTIONS ACROSS INDUSTRIES

The previous section concludes that within a specific industry there is a positive relationship between the capital-labor ratio and the wage-rental ratio. This section discusses the relationship of factor proportions across industries. Specifically, a second industry with a different production function is introduced, and it is then determined how the limited supplies of labor and capital in the economy are allocated between the two industries.*

Assume that the economy being analyzed produces two goods. Many economic texts describe the two goods as guns and butter or food and clothing, but we will use the general description of good A and good B. The production functions of the two goods can therefore be represented by f_A and f_B. Both production functions have the same general characteristics as those described previously. Each production function has labor and capital as the only two inputs and displays constant returns to scale. Increasing the relative amount of one input in each production function results in diminishing marginal product for that factor. There are, however, differences in the two production functions. Specifically the production process in one industry always uses capital more intensively than the production process in the other industry. This assumption about the intensity with which factors are used means that at any given wage-rental ratio, the capital-labor ratios differ in the two industries.

As described in the previous section, given the properties of the production function, the precise positive relationship between the capital-labor and wage-rental ratios within each industry can be derived. Because the production functions in both industries A and B have the previously defined general characteristics, there must be a positive relationship between the two ratios in both industries. Thus a graph relating K/L to w/r would have a postive slope for each industry. But because the precise way in which inputs are transformed into outputs differs in the two industries, the graphs for the two industries do not coincide. The relationship between K/L and w/r for two possible industries is shown in Figure 2-5.

In Figure 2-5 the capital-labor ratio rises with the wage-rental ratio for both industries. In fact, since the lines are arbitrarily represented as parallel, the change in K/L for a given change in w/r is exactly the same in both industries. However, for any given level of w/r, the level of K/L differs between the two industries. Specifically, industry A in Figure 2-5 uses capital more efficiently than industry B. The greater efficiency means that at a given amount of capital per worker, capital has a higher

---

*The supply relationships of this and the next section are demonstrated through the use of the Lerner-Pearce diagram and algebraic expressions. However, in the appendix these same relationships are demonstrated with an alternative, diagrammatic approach called the Edgeworth Box.

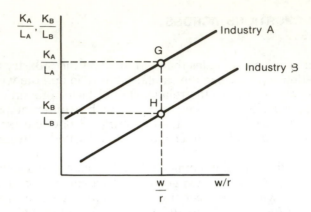

Figure 2-5 Relative Factor Proportions in Industries A and B

marginal product in industry A than in industry B. Thus, industry A employs relatively more capital per worker. Good A can therefore be referred to as the (relatively) "capital-intensive" product and good B the (relatively) "labor-intensive" product.

The implications of differing production functions in the two industries can be summarized in an isoquant graph. Figure 2-3 described the combinations of capital and labor which produce 400 units of good A. However, a second good, good B, is now produced. A second isoquant, representing the output of 300 units of good B, is therefore added to the graph in Figure 2-6.

Since the production functions for good A and good B differ, the isoquants for the two goods differ. More precisely, if the two industries face the same wage-rental ratio, (as represented by the line WW in Figure 2-6) the capital-labor ratios in the two industries differ. Thus the ray from the origin OR_A, which represents the equilibrium capital-labor ratio in industry A, has a steeper slope than the ray OR_B. Industry A employs K_A units of capital and L_A units of labor. Industry B, on the other hand, employs fewer units of capital and more units of labor. So at the common equilibrium wage-rental ratio facing the two industries, industry A is employing more units of capital per unit of labor than is industry B. Good A is the (relatively) capital-intensive good.

The economy as a whole has a limited quantity of capital K and of labor L. Now that the relative uses of K and L in the two industries have been described, how the limited quantities of factors are allocated between the industries can be determined. Only one further piece of information is needed in order to determine the distribution. The piece of information is that under competitive conditions and costless factor mobility, the wage-rental ratio must be the same in both industries. In fact not only the ratio but the absolute factor rewards in terms of either good must be the same.

The logic of this assumption is quite straightforward. Owners of both labor services and capital seek out the highest wage rates and rental rates

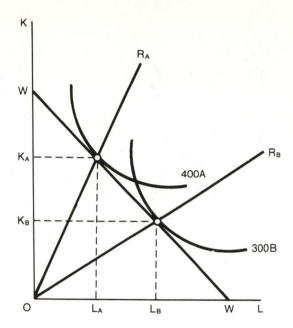

Figure 2–6   Isoquants for Good A and Good B

available to them. In contrast, firms try to pay as little as possible for both labor services and capital. Attaining a solution for these conflicting goals requires that both the relative and absolute factor rewards be the same in both industries. If the equalities did not exist across industries, competitive pressures would force the economy back to that equilibrium. Factors would immediately seek to move from the low-paying industry to the high-paying industry. Similarly, producers in the high-paying industry, recognizing an opportunity to cut costs, would try to reduce the factor rewards of their industry. These competitive forces disappear only when the equality of factor rewards is reestablished across the industries.

The distribution of factors between the two industries can easily be determined graphically with the isoquant diagram. Suppose, for example, that the economy is producing 400 units of A and 300 units of B, as shown in Figure 2–7. Suppose further that the prevailing wage-rental ratio is reflected in the line WW. Production occurs at points A_0 and B_0, where the isoquants are tangent to the same wage-rental ratio. How many factors of production are needed to produce these quantities of the two goods? Production in industry A requires L_A units of labor and K_A units of capital. Production in industry B uses L_B units of labor and K_B units of capital. As shown in Figure 2–7, the quantities of labor employed in the two industries, $OL_A + OL_B$, just sum to OL_E. This quantity is the total labor required. Similarly, the distances OK_A and OK_B, the quantities of capital required in the two industries, just sum to OK_E. The total factor requirements are summarized by the point E in Figure 2–7.

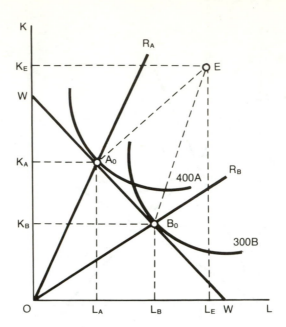

Figure 2–7   Distribution of Factor Employment through Vector Addition

If factors were freely available to the economy, the technique just employed could be used to determine total employment or point E. But the choice which the economy faces is quite different. The economy's factor endowment or point E is usually given. The economy must then decide, given the technology embodied in the isoquants and the prevailing wage-rental ratio, how to allocate the limited factors between the industries. For the economy to maximize its production, all factors must be employed. Full employment of factors in turn implies that the quantities of capital and labor used in industry A plus the quantities used in industry B just add up to the quantities represented by point E. In other words, a graphic method is needed to add the factors used in the two industries to see if they just equal the given overall endowment of factors.

The graphic technique for adding the factor employments in the two industries to just equal the overall endowment constraint is called vector addition. The technique involves basically adding the rays OR_A and OR_B so that they just equal point E. The procedure (as illustrated in Figure 2–7) is as follows: First, use the prevailing wage-rental rate to determine the equilibrium capital-labor rays in the two industries. The rays pass through the point on the isoquants tangent to the wage-rental ratio. These rays are OR_A and OR_B in Figure 2–7. While these rays are obtained from isoquants representing specific levels of output, remember that with homogeneous production functions, isoquants of any other output level are also tangent to the wage-rental ratio along these rays. Second, constrained to using factors in these proportions, total factor employment must equal point E. This condition is fulfilled by drawing one line parallel to OR_B between the ray OR_A and point E (the dotted line A_0E) and a second line parallel to OR_A between point E and the ray OR_B (the dotted line B_0E). The result is a parallelogram OA_0EB_0 which determines both factor distribution and output.

At the prevailing wage-rental ratio, therefore, factors employed in industry A are represented by the point A_0 and factors employed in industry B by point B_0. This is the only distribution of factors between the two industries which is consistent with both the prevailing capital-labor ratios in the two industries and the overall factor endowment. Output of good A in this example in turn is determined by the isoquant passing through point A_0, or 400 units of A. Output of B is determined by the isoquant passing through point B_0 (300 units of B). This graph, which shows how the given factor endowment of the economy is allocated between two industries with differing production functions to determine equilibrium levels of output, is called the *Lerner-Pearce diagram*.

The distribution of factors and level of outputs can alternatively be determined algebraically. Given that the wage-rental ratio must be the same across industries, the combinations of possible capital-labor ratios can be unambiguously determined from the information in Figure 2–5. For any given w/r, by moving horizontally across Figure 2–5, the precise proportions of K and L within both industries are known. But how many units of capital in industry A, or labor in industry B, or output in each industry do these factor proportions represent?

The economy has a limited quantity of K and L. Full employment of the capital stock within the economy requires that:

$$K_A + K_B = K, \tag{2-6}$$

that is, that the quantity of capital employed in industries A and B sum to the entire capital stock. By multiplying the quantity of capital in each industry by the algebraic equivalent of one, this relationship can be reexpressed as:

$$\frac{K_A}{L_A} \cdot L_A + \frac{K_B}{L_B} \cdot L_B = K. \tag{2-7}$$

In other words, the capital-labor ratios in A and B times their respective level of workers employed must sum to the overall capital stock. Dividing equation (2–7) on both sides by the total labor supply L then yields a relationship between the capital-labor ratios in the individual industries and the overall capital-labor ratio of the economy

$$\frac{K_A}{L_A} \cdot \frac{L_A}{L} + \frac{K_B}{L_B} \cdot \frac{L_B}{L} = \frac{K}{L}. \tag{2-8}$$

The expressions L_A/L and L_B/L represent the share or proportion of total labor in the respective industries. So equation (2–8) says that the capital-labor ratios of the individual industries times their shares of overall labor must sum to the overall capital-labor ratio. Substituting in the full employment relationship in the labor market ($L_B = L - L_A$) allows equation (2–8) to be simplified to:

$$\frac{K_A}{L_A} \cdot \frac{L_A}{L} + \frac{K_B}{L_B} \cdot \left(1 - \frac{L_A}{L}\right) = \frac{K}{L}. \qquad (2\text{-}9)$$

From the overall endowment of factors, the values of K and L are known. Similarly, from Figure 2-5 the pair of capital-labor ratios is also known for any given w/r. The only remaining unknown in (2-9) is L_A. Thus for any given w/r, the equilibrium level of L_A can be determined directly from equation (2-9). This value, together with the constraint $L_A + L_B = L$, yields an equilibrium value of L_B. The allocation of labor, together with the known capital-labor ratios in each industry, reveals the amount of capital employed in A and B. This information, together with the production functions or average product relationships, shows the maximum output in each industry. The average product functions are:

$$\frac{Q_A}{L_A} = f_A\left(\frac{K_A}{L_A}\right) \qquad (2\text{-}10)$$

and

$$\frac{Q_B}{L_B} = f_B\left(\frac{K_B}{L_B}\right) \qquad (2\text{-}11)$$

The capital-labor ratios determine the ratio of output to labor in each industry. Average product per worker ratios are then multiplied by the levels of labor employment in each industry to yield the levels of maximum output. Thus, given the levels of K and L in the economy and a description of the production functions f_A and f_B, the levels of maximum output of A and B and the distribution of capital and labor can be determined for varying values of w/r.

As a numerical example, assume that the mythical country of Islandia has 700 units of capital in conjunction with the 1600 workers as factors of production. Furthermore, assume that the relationship between wage-rental ratios and capital-labor ratios described in Figure 2-5 is known. At the wage-rental ratio of 0.2, industry A uses eight units of capital for every sixteen workers. On the other hand, industry B uses only four units of capital per sixteen workers. Industry A may therefore be described as the relatively capital-intensive industry. What we initially want to determine is precisely how many units of capital and labor are employed in industries A and B.

From equation (2-6) we know that if Islandia is employing all of its capital, $K_A + K_B = 700$. From this information and the prevailing capital-labor ratios, equation (2-7) allows us to determine the distribution of factors among industries. In this numerical example equation (2-7) becomes:

$$\left(\frac{8}{16}\right) \cdot L_A + \left(\frac{4}{16}\right) \cdot L_B = 700 \qquad (2\text{-}7')$$

Again, using the full employment relationship for the labor market ($L_B = 1600 - L_A$), equation (2-7') can be transformed into an equation with just one unknown L_A.

$$\left(\frac{8}{16}\right) \cdot L_A + \left(\frac{4}{16}\right)(1600 - L_A) = 700. \qquad (2\text{-}7')$$

Solving for L_A from this equation yields $L_A = 1200$. In other words, 1200 of the 1600 workers in Islandia work in industry A. The remaining 400 must work in industry B. Since the capital-labor ratio in industry A is 8/16 and 1200 workers are employed, 600 units of capital (8/16 · 1200) are used in industry A. From the full employment of capital constraint, the remaining 100 units of capital are employed in industry B. The 100 units of capital and 400 workers derived for industry B are consistent with the capital-labor ratio of 4/16 initially assumed to exist in industry B.

In addition, if we assume a specific relationship in each industry between the capital-labor ratio and output per worker, we can determine the total quantity of production in each industry. For example, if eight units of capital per sixteen units of labor in industry A produces three units of good A per worker, the 1200 workers in industry A mean that 3600 units of A are being produced. Similarly, if the 4/16 capital-labor ratio in industry B produces two units of B per worker, 800 units of good B are being produced.

This numerical example was solved using equation (2-7). Alternatively, equation (2-9) could have been used to determine the quantity of labor and capital in each industry. In fact equation (2-9) will be particularly useful in the next section when we determine how output within the industries changes as the wage-rental and capital-labor ratios change.

FACTOR RETURNS, FACTOR PROPORTIONS, AND THE PRODUCTION POSSIBILITIES CURVE

In this section the effects of varying the wage-rental ratio under the conditions of full employment on the level of output in a given country are discussed in greater detail. The discussion describes the relationship between factor returns, factor proportions, and the various possible combinations of output.

From Figure 2-3 the immediate response to a rise in the wage-rental ratio is a rise in the ratio of capital to labor in both industries. Such a shift makes sense on an intuitive level, because with a rise in the relative price of labor, firms in all industries try to conserve on the now relatively more expensive labor by substituting towards capital. Such substitution also makes sense on an economic level, because with diminishing returns in each production function, reducing the amount of labor relative to capital increases the marginal product of labor MP_L, offsetting labor's higher cost.

From microeconomics, the profit maximizing condition for hiring inputs is:

$$\frac{MP_L}{w} = \frac{MP_K}{r}. \qquad (2\text{-}12')$$

When w and r are expressed in dollars, (2–12′) translates that the additional or marginal product obtained from spending an additional dollar on either labor or capital must be the same. In the present discussion, however, there are no dollars, and relative, rather than absolute, factor rewards are analyzed. Equation (2–12′) can therefore be rearranged as:

$$\frac{MP_L}{MP_K} = \frac{w}{r}, \tag{2–12}$$

which is consistent with the current analysis. If the wage-rental ratio rises, the right side of (2–12) becomes larger. The left side must now also rise. The rise can occur either by raising the marginal product of labor, or lowering the marginal product of capital, or both. The rise in the capital-labor ratio accomplishes both effects. Each unit of labor now has more capital to work with, raising the marginal product of labor, while each unit of capital has less labor to work with, lowering the marginal product of capital. The two sides of equation (2–12) again become equalized.

The positive relationship between wage-rental ratios and capital-labor ratios along the isoquant of one industry was illustrated in Figure 2–3. In Figure 2–8, a rise in w/r from WW to W′W′ leads both industries to use relatively more capital and relatively less labor. As implied by equation (2–12), the new capital-labor ratio is determined by the point where the slope of the isoquant (the ratio of the marginal products) equals the new

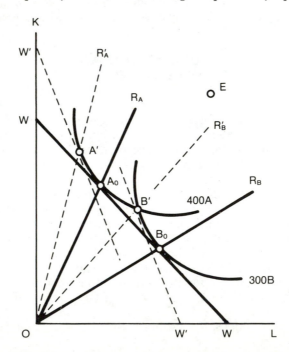

Figure 2–8   The Effects of a Rise in the Wage-Rental Ratio on Capital-Labor Ratios in Both Industries

wage-rental ratio. The capital-labor ratio ray shifts from OR_A to OR'_A in industry A, and from OR_B to OR'_B in industry B. With a constant factor endowment and new capital-labor ratios, it is obvious that output levels must change.

The effect of the rise in the wage-rental ratio on output levels is shown in Figure 2–9, which reproduces the relevant parts of Figure 2–8. Once the wage-rental ratio rises, the capital labor ratios must correspond to those of the rays OR'_A and OR'_B. In Figure 2–8 it initially appears that the change in capital-labor ratios simply shifts production from point A_0 to A' and from point B_0 to B'. Since the new points are along the original iso-quants, such a shift would appear to leave output levels unchanged. However, adding the factor requirements for points A' and B' through vector addition quickly points out why output levels cannot remain constant. With higher capital-labor ratios in both industries and unchanged outputs, the economy's overall factor endowment would have to be point E' in Figure 2–9. Point E' represents more capital and less labor in the economy than the actual endowment at point E. The production mix implied by points A' and B' is therefore clearly impossible.

The actual levels of production of goods A and B which are consistent with higher capital-labor ratios can be easily determined through vector addition. The new levels of production are those whose capital and labor requirements just sum to the overall factor endowment at point E. Hence

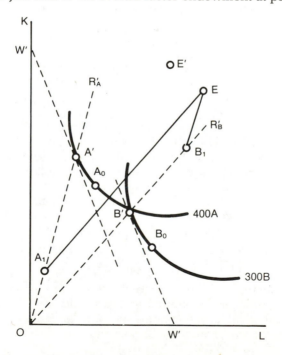

Figure 2–9   The Effect of a Rise in the Wage-Rental Ratio on the Level of Output in the Two Industries

a line parallel to the ray OR'_B is drawn between point E and the ray OR'_A. Similarly the ray OR'_B and point E are connected with a line parallel to ray OR'_A. This parallelogram shows that output now occurs at points A_1 and B_1.

Point A_1 lies along OR'_A between point A' and the origin. Point A_1 therefore lies along an isoquant representing less production than the 400 units produced at point A'. The quantity of good A produced is now less than before the wage-rental ratio rose. Similarly, the point B_1 lies along the ray OR'_B beyond the point B'. The rise in the wage-rental ratio has caused the production of the relatively labor-intensive good B to increase beyond the initial 300 units.

Figure 2–9 also shows what happens to the distribution of factors between the two industries. When the wage-rental ratio rises and equilibrium output in the relatively capital-intensive industry shifts from point A_0 to point A_1, fewer units of both capital and labor are now employed in industry A. Conversely, as the output of the relatively labor-intensive good increases to B_1, additional units of both capital and labor are employed in that industry. Thus the rise in the wage-rental ratio causes a rise in the capital-labor ratio in both industries, and a movement of both factors of employment from the capital-intensive to the labor-intensive industry.

These graphic results are consistent with the implications of the algebraic model. With higher capital-labor ratios in both industries, equation (2–8) shows that the production of the relatively labor-intensive good increases. Since both K_A/L_A and K_B/L_B are now higher, maintaining the relationship with the overall K/L requires that the larger of the two individual ratios be multiplied by a smaller number than before. If good A is relatively capital intensive, then L_A/L, the share of labor used in making A, must be reduced. To reduce L_A/L with a given L, labor must be shifted from industry A to industry B. But since K_B/L_B and L_B both rise, so must K_B. Thus, not just labor, but also capital, shift from A to B. The production of A clearly falls, while the production of B clearly rises. If the shift in production did not occur, then with higher capital-labor ratios in both industries, the economy would not have enough capital to go around.

In the numerical example of the last section, when w/r = 0.2, K_A/L_A = 8/16 and K_B/L_B = 4/16. Under these conditions, 1200 of 1600, or three-fourths of the workers are employed in industry A. Equation (2–8) therefore is:

$$\left(\frac{8K_A}{16L_A}\right)\left(\frac{3}{4}\right) + \left(\frac{4K_B}{16L_B}\right)\left(\frac{1}{4}\right) = \frac{700K}{1600L}. \qquad (2\text{–}8')$$

If the wage-rental ratio were now to rise to 0.4, following the reasoning just outlined, producers in both industries would want to economize on labor, raising the capital-labor ratios in both industries. But what effect does this rise in K_A/L_A and K_B/L_B have on the distribution of factors between industries and the level of output?

Suppose that following the rise in the wage-rental ratio the capital-labor ratio rises to 10/16 in industry A and 6/16 in industry B. From

equation (2–9), we know that the weighted average of the individual capital-labor ratios must equal the overall capital-labor ratio, or:

$$\left(\frac{10}{16}\right)\frac{L_A}{L} + \left(\frac{6}{16}\right)\left(1 - \frac{L_A}{L}\right) = \frac{7}{16}. \qquad (2\text{--}9')$$

Solving equation (2–9'), we find that three-fourths of Islandia's labor
force is now employed in industry B instead of industry A. In other
words, when the wage-rental ratio rose, 800 workers moved from industry A to industry B.

Furthermore, since the capital-labor ratio rose in industry B, capital as
well as labor must have moved from industry A to industry B. Before the
rise in w/r, industry B employed only 100 units of capital. But after the
rise, with 1200 workers and a capital-labor ratio of 6/16, industry B must
now be employing 450 units of capital. Similarly it can be shown that
employment of workers in industry A has fallen from 1200 to only 400,
and employment of capital from 600 to only 250. The increase in both
capital and labor in industry B must raise production of the relatively
labor-intensive good B, while the reduction in both factors of production
in industry A must reduce output of the relatively capital-intensive good
A.

The relationship between the wage-rental ratio and the levels of production can now be generalized. With any small change in the wage-
rental ratio, a slight change in the capital-labor ratio occurs in each industry. Assuming full employment of both capital and labor this change
in each industry's capital-labor ratio requires an increase in the output of
one good and a decrease in the output of the other. In the example where
the wage-rental ratio rises, the capital-labor ratio rises in both industries
causing a reduction in the output of the capital-intensive good A and a
rise in the production of the labor-intensive good B. Alternatively, a decrease in the wage-rental ratio would reduce the capital-labor ratio in
both industries and require a reduction in the production of the labor–
intensive good B and an increase in the production of A.

By computing the levels of maximum output which are consistent with
each w/r, the entire range of production possibilities of the country is
mapped out. This curve or "frontier" of production possibilities is shown
in Figure 2–10. The curve is concave with respect to the origin. This concavity (relative to the origin) reflects the effects on the production function of both constant returns to scale and diminishing marginal
productivity as the quantities of factors in each industry are changed. The
distance of the curve from the origin reflects the limits of total production
imposed by the full use of the two variable factors of production.

An intuitive proof of the concavity of the production possibilities curve
is possible here. A more complete proof using the Edgeworth Box is
shown in the appendix to this chapter. Consider an economy with two
industries with different production functions and a given amount of
capital (say 5000 units) and a given amount of labor (say 1000 units). What
assumptions are necessary for a straight-line production possibilities
curve that is consistent with full employment of both factors? At each

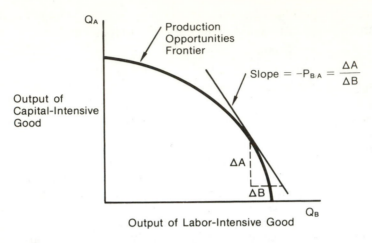

Figure 2–10   Production Opportunities and the Production Terms of Trade

end point of the curve, the total available capital and labor are employed in the industry in which there is positive output, and zero units of either factor are employed in the industry in which there is zero production. The capital-labor ratio in the producing industry is therefore 5. Since the curve is straight-lined, at any point in between, the capital-labor ratios in both industries remain constant and equal to 5. In other words, a straight-lined curve with full employment requires the capital-labor ratios in both industries to be the same and equal to the overall capital-labor ratio.

However, since technology and therefore the production functions differ in the two industries, where the factor ratios are the same in both industries, factors must be employed inefficiently in at least one industry. With constant capital-labor ratios, the marginal product of capital, for example, must be higher in one industry than the other. By employing factors more efficiently, at the very least production can be increased in one industry without reducing production in the second industry. Hence, the straight-lined curve represents a set of minimum production points. Output should never be below these levels. Instead, by more efficiently using factors, outputs at all points except the end points will be above the line, that is, the curve will be concave to the origin.

Just like the straight-line production possibilities curve of the Ricardian model, at any point on the concave production possibilities curve the slope is equal to the marginal rate of transformation in production between products A and B. This rate of transformation is equal to the increase in the output of one good divided by the decrease in the output of the other good, when there is an incremental change in the wage-rental ratio. The marginal rate of transformation is nothing more than the marginal amount of the one product that has to be sacrificed in order to get an incremental amount more of the other.

Again, as in the Ricardian model, in a perfectly competitive economy, profit maximizing firms will ensure that the marginal rate of transformation equals the market price of one product in terms of the other. Thus, if the market quotes the price of a ton of steel as equivalent to 100 bushels of wheat, then producers can be expected to operate at the point on the production possibilities frontier where the marginal rate of transformation in production is equal to 100:1. Were they to operate at any other point, profits could be increased by substituting back to that point.

To summarize the conclusions about supply so far, every point along the production possibilities curve corresponds to:

a. a unique marginal rate of transformation in production,

b. a unique mixture of production between A and B,

c. a unique wage-rental ratio, and

d. a unique set of capital-labor ratios in each industry.

Furthermore, for producers to be producing at their equilibrium or profit-maximizing point along the curve, the marginal rate of transformation in production at that point must be equal to the relative market price of one product in terms of another, that is, $P_{B/A}$. In the international trade literature the market price of one product in terms of another is known as the "terms of trade."

Before discussing the trade implications, it is useful to examine the implications of this supply side analysis for a country in autarky. Autarky, as described in Chapter 1, is the situation a country finds itself in when it does not trade with any other country. All goods supplied to the marketplace must come from domestic production and all demand in the marketplace must come from domestic residents. Therefore the country must be both producing and consuming at one point along the production opportunity frontier in Figure 2–10. The production of good A must be the same as the consumption of good A, and the same is true for good B. The economy therefore chooses the point along the curve where the marginal rate of transformation equals the equilibrium relative price of the goods when that particular bundle is produced. Such a point, in turn, implies unique wage-rental and capital-labor ratios. Further discussion of the determination of such an equilibrium point, however, requires a description of the demand conditions of the country, which is postponed until Chapter 4. Before discussing demand, it is necessary to describe how the opening of trade affects the supply side of the economy.

SUMMARY

A *production function* describes the maximum amount of output that can be obtained from given quantities of capital and labor under current technology. With a limited supply of capital and labor in the economy, output in the economy is therefore limited.

With a *homogeneous* production function, if inputs are doubled, outputs are also doubled. Increasing any one factor by itself, however, produces diminishing returns. Under competitive conditions, each factor is paid a reward equal to its marginal product. In addition, the homogeneous production function assures that, in each industry, each capital-labor ratio is associated with a unique ratio of output per worker and a unique wage-rental ratio. As the capital-labor ratio rises, higher values of output per worker and the wage-rental ratio are also observed.

With specific production functions for the two goods, and limited overall quantities of both factors in the economy, an increase in the maximum quantity of one good produced means that the maximum quantity of the other good that can be produced must fall. It also means that some of both factors must move from the contracting industry to the expanding industry. Increased production in the expanding industry is also associated with a rise in the relative price of that good, and a rise in the relative reward of the factor used intensively in producing it. These relationships are summarized in the *production possibilities curve*.

REFERENCES

JOHNSON, HARRY G., *Two-Sector Model of General Equilibrium*, New York: Aldine-Atherton, 1971. (A geometric approach)

JONES, RONALD W., "The Structure of Simple General-Equilibrium Models," *Journal of Political Economy* 73, No. 6 (December 1965): 557–72. (An algebraic approach)

APPENDIX 2

A. The Edgeworth Box

An alternative way to describe the relationship between relative factor returns, factor proportions, and output of goods is by a diagrammatic technique called the Edgeworth Box. This technique summarizes the production alternatives for a country producing two goods with two factors of production. The basic components of the Edgeworth Box are shown in Figure 2A–1.

The size of the Edgeworth Box is determined by the quantity of the two factors of production, capital and labor, in the economy. The total quantity of labor in the economy is represented by the horizontal distance $O_B Y$ or $O_A X$. The quantity of labor in industry A is equal to the horizontal distance to the left of O_A. The quantity of labor in industry B is equal to the horizontal distance to the right of O_B. Notice that for any point in the box chosen (such as point Q in Figure 2A–1) the quantity of labor employed in industry A $(O_A L_A^0)$ plus the quantity employed in industry B $(O_B L_B^0)$ just sum to the total labor in the economy.

Similarly, the vertical distance of the box represents the total quantity of capital in the economy. The quantity of capital used in industry A is

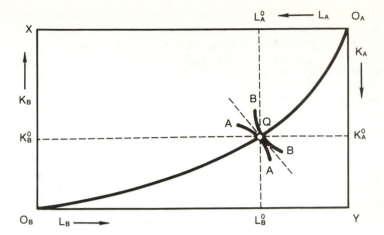

Figure 2A–1 The Edgeworth Box

equal to the vertical distance below $O_A(O_A K_A^0$ at point Q). The quantity of capital used in industry B is equal to the vertical distance above $O_B(O_B K_B^0$ at point Q). Again the quantity of capital in the two industries just sum to the total capital in the economy. Therefore, within the framework of the Edgeworth Box, full employment of both factors is assumed to exist, just as is assumed in Chapter 2.

The curve $O_A Q O_B$ in Figure 2A–1 is called the contract curve. The points along the contract curve represent efficient or maximum combinations of production of goods A and B. At any point along $O_A Q O_B$ the maximum possible quantity of good A is being produced, given the quantity of good B produced, and vice versa. The distance between, say, point Q and origins O_A or O_B represents respectively the quantity of good A or B produced. Thus as point Q moves along curve $O_A O_B$ toward origin O_B, more of good A and less of good B is produced. Conversely, as Q moves toward O_A, less of good A and more of good B is produced.

The points along $O_A O_B$ are determined by the tangency of the isoquants for goods A and B. The isoquants represent the production functions for the two goods. For example, an isoquant for good A shows the combination of capital and labor that just produce a given quantity of good A. Since these isoquants are drawn with respect to O_A, the further an isoquant from origin O_A, the more of both capital and labor employed, and thus the greater the quantity of good A produced. Similarly, the isoquants for good B are drawn with respect to O_B. Thus the quantity of good B produced increases the farther the isoquant BB is from O_B.

The slope of an isoquant at any point represents the ratio of the marginal products of the two factors of production in producing the two goods. Efficient production requires that this ratio be the same in both industries. For example, if the marginal product of capital were relatively greater in industry A than in industry B, the total quantity of both good A and B produced could be increased* by transferring some capital from industry B to industry A and transferring labor from A to B. The ability to increase total production is exhausted only when the relative marginal products of the factors in the two industries are equal. When the relative marginal products are equal, production occurs along isoquants AA and BB at points with the same slopes. Combining the equality of slopes with full employment of both factors in turn implies that efficient production occurs where AA and BB are tangent. Point Q in Figure 2A–1 is an efficient production point.

The curve $O_A Q O_B$ is therefore derived by the points of tangency between the isoquants for good A and for good B. Since as the point Q moves toward origin O_A along curve $O_A Q O_B$ tangency occurs at lower isoquants for good A and higher isoquants for good B, again such a movement represents less production of A and more production of B. Also, since, from equation (2–12) in profit maximizing equilibrium the firm equates the ratio of the marginal products to the wage-rental ratio, the slope of the isoquants represent the wage-rental ratio. Therefore along $O_A Q O_B$ the wage rental ratio is equalized across industries.

As long as the efficiency of capital differs across industries, $O_A Q O_B$ is not a straight line (that is, is not the diagonal). If $O_A Q O_B$ were straight, the efficient capital-labor ratios for every wage-rental ratio would be the same in both industries. Differing efficiencies imply that $O_A Q O_B$ lies to one side of the diagonal. On which side of the diagonal $O_A O_B$ lies depends upon whether capital is used more efficiently in industry A or B. Figure 2A–1 is drawn to conform to the assumption in this book that industry A uses capital more efficiently than industry B. Thus at any given wage-rental ratio, industry A uses relatively more capital than industry B. Industry A is the relatively capital-intensive industry. The greater the difference in relative efficiencies, and therefore intensities of capital use, the greater is the curvature of the contract curve.

The interrelationship of factor returns, factor proportions, and output levels may now be illustrated with the use of the Edgeworth Box. Consider the effect of a rise in the wage-rental ratio. In Chapter 2 such a rise is assumed to raise the capital-labor ratio in both industries. Precisely the same result is obtained from the Edgeworth Box. A rise in the wage-rental ratio is reflected in a steeper slope at the point of tangency between the isoquants AA and BB. For example, in Figure 2A–2, when the wage-rental ratio rises, production shifts from point Q to point Q'. The rise in the ratio provides an incentive for producers to substitute away from the now relatively more expensive labor and toward the now relatively less expensive capital. Producers in both industries therefore move up along their isoquants toward capital and away from labor. At point Q', the new equilibrium, the tangency of the isoquants R'R' is steeper than the initial tangency RR. The steeper slope simultaneously reflects both

---

*At the very least the output of one of the goods could be increased without decreasing the quantity of the second good produced.

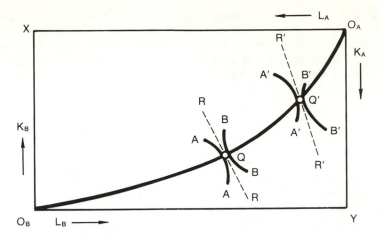

Figure 2A–2   The Relationship Between the Wage-Rental Ratio and Output Levels in the Edgeworth Box

the higher wage-rental ratio and the higher ratio of the marginal products necessary to maximize profits with that relative factor reward.

The effect on the capital-labor ratios of moving to the steeper tangency is shown in Figure 2A–3. A line connecting the origin O_B with the production point Q represents the capital-labor ratio in industry B when production occurs at point Q. This line is the ray O_BN in Figure 2A–3. Similarly, the ray O_BN' represents the capital-labor ratio in industry B when production occurs at the point Q'. Notice that at Q', where the wage-rental ratio is higher, the capital-labor ratio is higher in industry B. In the same way, the capital-labor ratio in industry A is reflected in the

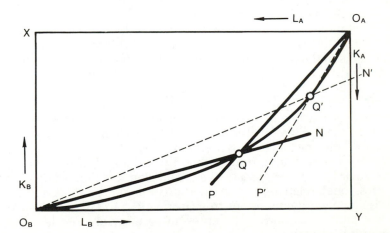

Figure 2A–3   The Relationship Between the Capital-Labor Ratio and Output Levels in the Edgeworth Box

rays $O_A P$ and $O_A P'$. Again, as production moves from point Q to point Q', the capital-labor ratio rises in industry A as well.

The shifting of production from points Q to Q' is consistent not only with producers shifting to higher capital-labor ratios in response to higher wage-rental ratios, but it is also consistent with the maintenance of full employment of both factors of production. The tangency of the isoquants at point Q indicates that all the capital and labor in the economy are employed. Also, since different isoquants are tangent at Q' than at Q, the quantity of both goods produced has changed. Point Q' is the tangency of a lower isoquant for industry A than at point Q, and a higher isoquant for industry B. Thus as the wage-rental ratio rises, producers in both industries increase their capital-labor ratios, and maintenance of full employment requires production of the relatively capital-intensive good A to decrease and production of the relative labor-intensive good B to increase. This relationship between factor rewards, factor proportions and output is precisely the same result discussed in Chapter 2.

The Edgeworth Box can be used to show one other statement in Chapter 2—that the production possibilities curve is concave to the origin. The technique for illustrating this relationship closely follows the technique of Savosnick.[1] As an introduction to this technique, consider what is implied by a straight line, a concave, and a convex production possibilities curve. A straight line implies that there is a constant relationship between the quantity of goods A and B produced. Each time good A is decreased by one unit, the quantity of good B is increased by precisely the same amount. A concave or convex curve, on the other hand, implies a constantly changing relationship between the quantities of the two goods produced. With a convex curve, with successive unit decreases in the quantity of good A produced, the incremental increases in the quantity of good B get larger and larger. Conversely, with a concave curve the additional quantity of B obtained from successive unit decreases in production of good A is smaller and smaller.

Hence, the technique to show that the production possibilities curve must be concave is to consider the effect on good B of two successive unit decrements in the production of good A. The effects are shown in Figure 2A-4. Figure 2A-4 is simply an enlargement of the area around point Q in Figures 2A-2 and 2A-3. The analysis begins at point Q. The line RR at point Q represents the relative factor rewards consistent with efficient or maximum production (the tangency of isoquants) given that the quantity of A produced is the level represented by isoquant AA. Suppose now that the relative factor rewards are held constant, but that the quantity of A produced is decreased or increased by one unit. Since A is produced under constant returns to scale (the production function is homogeneous of degree one), relative factor proportions remain the same and the two new isoquants are equidistant from isoquant AA. Thus in Figure 2A-4 the isoquants $A-1$ and $A+1$ represent respectively one less and one more unit of A than along AA. These two isoquants are tangent respectively to $R_1 R_1$ and $R_2 R_2$, which are parallel to RR, and are equidistant from AA. Therefore, as production moves from left to right in Figure

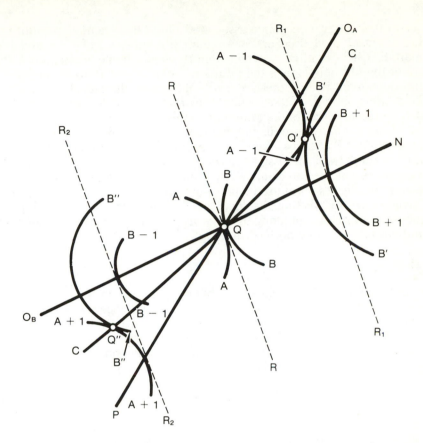

Figure 2A–4   A Demonstration that the Production Possibilities Curve Is Concave

2A–4 along the ray $O_A P$, the level of A output decreases by one unit from isoquants A+ 1 to AA, and by a second unit from AA to A−1. Similarly, since good B is also produced under constant returns to scale, as production moves from left to right along $O_B N$, the output of B increases by one unit from B–1 to BB and by a second unit from BB to B+1.

This exercise shows that if factor prices remain constant as outputs change, the production possibilities curve will be a straight line, since for each unit decrement in good A, good B increases by a constant amount. But in fact, factor prices will not remain constant. While at point Q the supply and demand for each factor are equal, at A+1 and B−1 there is an excess demand for capital and an excess supply of labor and at A−1 and B+1 there is an excess supply of capital and an excess demand for labor. Hence, to preserve factor market equilibrium in these two cases, relative factor prices must change. In the first case the wage-rental ratio falls and in the second case the ratio rises. Retaining the assumption that output of good A decreased by one unit each time, production now occurs along the contract curve at points Q″ and Q′ respectively.

At these production points associated with factor market equilibrium the output of good B occurs at isoquant B″B″ instead of B−1 and isoquant B′B′ instead of B+1. Notice that the new isoquants are both to the left of the old one. Hence the additional quantity of B obtained from a unit decrement in A decreases. Since B″B″ is to the left of B−1, when the production of A decreases one unit from A+1 to AA, the production of B increases by more than one unit. However, since B′B′ is also to the left of B+1, when A production decreases by one more unit to A−1, the production of B increases by less than one unit. The additional quantity of B obtained from successive unit decrements in the production of good A becomes smaller and smaller. This relationship between A and B production implies that the production possibilities curve must be concave. Furthermore, by plotting the level of outputs associated with the isoquants that are tangent along the contract curve CC, the production possibilities curve can be derived directly.

B.   Euler's Theorem

A useful relationship employed in this chapter is Euler's Theorem. This relationship holds that in competition, where homogeneous production functions exist, the returns to factors just exhaust the value of the entire product. A proof of this relationship is now presented.

As shown in the text, since the production function $Q = f(K,L)$ is homogeneous, it may be rewritten:

$$\frac{Q}{L} = g\left(\frac{K}{L}\right) \tag{2A–1}$$

or

$$Q = L \cdot g\left(\frac{K}{L}\right) \tag{2A–2}$$

The partial derivatives $MP_L = \partial Q/\partial L$ and $MP_K = \partial Q/\partial K$ of (2A–2) are:

$$MP_L = g\left(\frac{K}{L}\right) + L \cdot g'\left(\frac{K}{L}\right) \cdot \frac{\partial\left(\frac{K}{L}\right)}{\partial L}$$

$$= g\left(\frac{K}{L}\right) - L \cdot \frac{K}{L} \cdot g'\left(\frac{K}{L}\right)$$

$$MP_L = g\left(\frac{K}{L}\right) \cdot \frac{K}{L} \cdot g'\left(\frac{K}{L}\right) \tag{2A–3}$$

and

$$MP_K = L \cdot g'\left(\frac{K}{L}\right) \cdot \frac{\partial\left(\frac{K}{L}\right)}{\partial K}$$

$$= L \cdot g'\left(\frac{K}{L}\right) \cdot \frac{1}{L}$$

$$MP_K = g'\left(\frac{K}{L}\right).\qquad\qquad (2A\text{--}4)$$

Using these expressions for the marginal product, the sum of the returns to factors is

$$L \cdot MP_L = K \cdot MP_K = L\left[g\left(\frac{K}{L}\right) - \frac{K}{L} \cdot g'\left(\frac{K}{L}\right)\right] + K \cdot g'\left(\frac{K}{L}\right)$$

$$= L \cdot g\left(\frac{K}{L}\right) - K \cdot g'\left(\frac{K}{L}\right) + K \cdot g'\left(\frac{K}{L}\right)$$

$$= L \cdot g\left(\frac{K}{L}\right)$$

or

$$W_i \cdot L_i + r_iK_i = Q_i \text{ for all industries i,}\qquad (2A\text{--}5)$$

which is Euler's Theorem as used in the text.

APPENDIX NOTES

1. See K. M. Savosnick, "The Box-Diagram and the Production Possibility Curve," *Ekonomisk Tidskrift*, Vol. 60, No. 3 (September 1958), pp. 183–97.

CHAPTER 3

The Supply Side of an Open Country

The previous chapter describes the interrelationship between the factors of production and the level of output for a country in isolation. It shows how a country with a given amount of labor and capital and a given level of technology decides upon relative factor distributions among industries, levels of production, and factor rewards for different possible relative prices (terms of trade). This chapter expands the analysis to consider a country which is no longer in isolation. Instead, the country is now assumed to face a given relative price of goods (terms of trade) from abroad and to produce both goods under conditions of full employment of both factors of production. Within this framework three important relationships are shown: (1) that trading in goods can lead to the equalization of factor rewards as well as goods prices among countries, (2) how changes in the relative goods prices affect relative factor rewards, and (3) how changes in relative factor endowments affect output. These three relationships are embodied in (1) the Factor Price Equalization Theorem, (2) the Stolper-Samuelson Theorem, and (3) the Rybczynski Theorem.

RELATIVE GOODS PRICES AND RELATIVE FACTOR PRICES

The previous chapter describes how any point along the production opportunity frontier corresponds to both a unique relative price between products and a unique wage-rental ratio. This section discusses the relationship between these two relative prices within a country, and sets the stage for demonstrating why the opening of trade implies, under certain conditions, that they must both be equal to their counterparts in other countries.

The same production functions f_A and f_B and factor endowments K and L, as before, are considered. Again, for any hypothetical wage-rental ratio $(w/r)_1$, Figure 2-5 indicates which capital-labor ratios involve the most efficient use of technology in the two industries. Given these capital-labor ratios and the full employment of factors, the quantities of goods A and B produced (Q_A and Q_B) are uniquely determined as described in Chapter 2. So any specific wage-rental ratio $(w/r)_1$ chosen is associated with a point along the production frontier such as X_1 in Figure 3–1.

Assume now that the wage-rental ration rises to $(w/r)_2$. From Figure 2–5 we know that the capital-labor ratios must increase in both industries. The rise in each industry's capital-labor ratio along with full employment means that production must fall in the capital-intensive industry and rise in the labor-intensive industry. So both labor and capital are transferred from industry A to industry B. The quantity of B produced rises, while Q_A falls. Production has moved from point X_1 in Figure 3–1 to a point like X_2. The shift in production also means that the marginal rate of substitution in production has changed. From the steeper slope at X_2 it is obvious that the labor-intensive good B is now valued relatively higher than at X_1. In other words, production at X_2 is consistent with a higher relative price of B in terms of A, $P_{B/A}$, than at X_1.

This procedure could be carried out one more time to show that if the wage-rental ratio were to rise to $(w/r)_3$, then production would shift to X_3 with an even higher relative price of good B, $P_{B/A}$. The relationships become clear. The higher the wage-rental ratio, the higher the equilibrium capital-labor ratios in both industries. The higher w/r, with full employment and constant total factor endowments, the greater the production of the labor-intensive product. Finally, the higher w/r, the higher the equilibrium price of the labor-intensive product in terms of the capital-intensive one.

One might wonder about the last point, that the relative price of the labor-intensive good rises when its supply increases. The reason for the positive relationship between output and price is that this discussion deals exclusively with relationships along a constant supply curve. Producers must be given an incentive to coax them into providing more B at

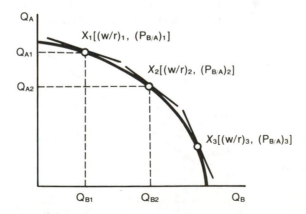

Figure 3–1   The Relationship of Relative Factor Rewards, Relative Goods, Prices, and Production Opportunities

the expense of A along the given curve. The incentives here are simultaneously the rise in the relative price of labor, which reduces the use of labor relative to capital, and the rise in the relative price of B which makes producing B relatively more profitable. Not only is there a positive relationship between w/r and $P_{B/A}$, but for given production functions there is a unique relationship. This relationship is summarized in Figure 3-2.

FACTOR PRICE EQUALIZATION THEOREM

Using the information in Figure 3-2, we can now demonstrate the relationship between factor prices in two trading countries. This relationship is known as the *Factor Price Equalization Theorem*.[1] This theorem states that if two trading countries have identical constant returns production functions, and produce both goods (with no specialization), then the relative and absolute real factor rewards must be the same in the two countries. The equality of factor rewards occurs even though the factors themselves cannot move beyond the national borders and are found in differing abundances in the two countries. The factor rewards remain equal as long as the number of goods traded at least equals the number of factors of production.

"Trading" countries means that both goods A and B are freely traded with no trade restrictions and no transportation costs. "Identical production functions" means that within a given industry the same combination of inputs yields the same output in either country. One way to ensure identical production functions is to assume access to a common set of techniques without cost. This assumption of identical production functions means that the relationship between relative factor rewards, relative factor intensities, and relative goods prices is the same in the two countries. In other words, the relationships in Figures 2-5 and 3-2 are identical in the two countries. Furthermore, free trade means that profit-maximizing producers and utility-maximizing consumers guarantee that

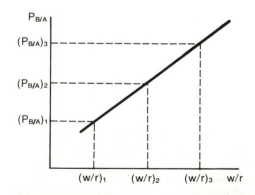

Figure 3-2   The Correspondence between Relative Prices of Factors and Products

$P_{B/A}$ is the same in all countries even if overall factor proportions endowed to each country are quite different. These assumptions therefore indicate that with free trade, $P_{B/A}$ and thus w/r are the same in both countries. Product trade substitutes for factor movements and relative factor prices are equalized.

The logic of this demonstration leads to the conclusion that only relative factor prices are equal. Yet a much stronger result also holds: absolute factor prices are equalized as well. Within countries the equality of absolute factor rewards across industries is a straightforward result. As stated earlier, since labor is mobile between industries, if wage rates were higher in one industry, labor would migrate to that industry. This migration would cause a fall in the wage in the industry into which labor moves, and a rise in the wage in the industry from which labor moves. Similarly, if factors of production were freely mobile between countries, factors would migrate until absolute factor rewards were equalized. However, in the present case equality of absolute factor rewards can be shown to exist even though factors cannot leave the countries where they reside.

An algebraic proof of absolute factor price equalization can be found in the appendix of this chapter. The proof is quite straightforward, employing relationships already described in the book. However, in this section absolute factor price equalization is shown directly from the production function in Figure 3-3 (reproduced from Figure 2-1). Recall that this production function showed how within a given industry the capital-labor ratio is related to the rental rate (marginal product) of capital and the wage-rental ratio. Since under the factor price equalization theorem a particular good is assumed produced by the same techniques in both countries, the production function for good A or good B in one country (as depicted in Figure 3-3) is identical to its counterpart in the other country. Hence, the relationship for industry A, for example, between the capital-labor ratio on the one hand, and the rental rate or wage-rental ratio on the other, is identical in the two countries.

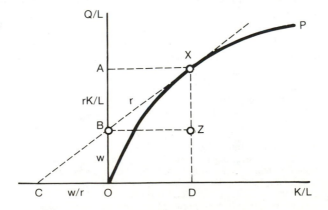

Figure 3-3   The Production Function in One Industry

With this similarity of relationships, the equality of absolute factor rewards across countries can be readily shown. The equality of relative factor rewards across countries has already been shown. With equal wage-rental ratios and identical production functions, the capital-labor ratios in industry A, for example, are the same in the two countries. With equal capital-labor ratios, the absolute rental rate on capital (slope of production function at point X) is equal in the industry across countries. With equal rental rates and wage-rental ratios, the absolute real wage must also be equal. Since with free mobility of factors within a country absolute factor rewards are equated between industries, absolute rewards must be equal in both countries and both industries.

Notice that if only one good were traded between countries, not even relative prices of goods would be equated across countries.* Hence, relative and absolute factor rewards would not be equated either. This conclusion provides an intuitive proof of another important part of the Factor Price Equalization Theorem: factor prices will be equalized only if there are as many traded goods as there are factors of production.

A further intuitive proof of absolute factor price equalization is useful. The crux of the explanation is that while factors of production are not free to cross national boundaries, the work of these factors, embodied in the goods they produce, can cross borders. More specifically, according to Euler's Theorem, the value of a good is simply the sum of the value of labor and the value of capital used to produce the good. Thus, if, say, the autarkic price of labor services were low in Country I, that country would export labor services in the form of the labor-intensive good. Demand for labor would rise in Country I, while in Country II which now produces more of the capital-intensive goods, the demand for labor would fall. Production and trade patterns would continue to shift until factor rewards (and thus production costs) were equalized across countries.

This intuitive argument can also help to explain the other result of the Factor Price Equalization Theorem: factor prices will be equalized only if there are as many traded goods as there are factors of production. If only factors were free to move across countries (and not goods), factor rewards would not be equalized unless both capital and labor moved between countries. Similarly, where only the services of factors (goods) can move between countries, factor prices will not be equalized unless there is a relatively labor-intensive and a relatively capital-intensive good traded between countries. If there were three factors of production (say labor, capital, and land), three different goods would have to be traded (say a relatively labor-, a relatively capital-, and a relatively land-intensive

---

*Trade requires at least two traded goods, or two traded factors, or one of each. However, this one good example is introduced in order to avoid having to introduce a three-factor model to illustrate the point of this paragraph. For an example of one traded good and one traded factor producing factor price equalization, see Robert A. Mundell, "International Trade and Factor Mobility," *American Economic Review*, Vol. 47, No. 3 (June 1957): pp. 321–35, reprinted in *Readings in International Economics*, edited by R. Caves and H. G. Johnson, Homewood, Ill.: Irwin, 1968.

good). Alternatively, if there are three factors but only two traded goods, one of the factors must be free to move between countries in order to guarantee factor price equalization.

While the Factor Price Equalization Theorem is logically correct, some may find its conclusions at odds with what is observed in the world. Auto workers in Detroit seem to be paid higher real wages than those in India. Factor price equality, however, is only assumed to occur in this Theorem under some very specific assumptions. First, goods are assumed to be produced with the same production functions in the two countries. Second, goods are assumed freely traded. If production techniques differ across countries, or goods face barriers such as tariffs, quotas, or transportation costs, the equality of factor rewards is no longer guaranteed. Alternatively, other distortions can cause apparent wage differentials. For example, in countries with higher marginal tax rates, workers may receive substantial compensation in the form of nonmarket, nontaxable benefits. There is also a larger discrepancy between the (net of tax) wage actually received and the (gross of tax) market wage reported. The Factor Price Equalization Theorem is therefore often useful as a point of departure for explaining real wage disparities across countries, and why free trade tends to reduce these disparities.

THE STOLPER-SAMUELSON THEOREM

The effect of a change in relative product prices or the "terms of trade" is now examined. Figures 3-1 and 3-2 already provide some information about the effect. From Figure 3-1 we know that if the terms of trade $P_{B/A}$ decline, the output of product A increases and the output of B decreases. Figure 3-2 shows that the same fall in $P_{B/A}$ implies a reduction in the wage-rental ratio, w/r. In other words, if there is a rise in the relative price of a good, then the factor which is used relatively intensively in the production of that good benefits relative to the other factor. This relationship was first derived by Paul Samuelson and Wolfgang Stolper, and hence became known as the *Stolper-Samuelson Theorem*.[2]

The logic behind this result should be clear from the earlier discussion of how a factor's value is derived from its scarcity in producing some final product. When the relative price of a good rises, the higher relative price reflects an increase in demand by individuals for this good, or in other words, an increase in the relative scarcity of the product. The increased scarcity of the product in turn reflects the increased scarcity of the factors which produce it. So in order to procure higher production of this product, individuals will be willing to offer higher returns to factors used in producing the good in order to bid the factors away from other industries. Since production requires relatively more of the factor used intensively, that factor's return is quite likely to rise by a larger percentage in order to attract that factor in sufficient quantities. The more intensively the factor is used, the more its return will rise relative to the other factor's return. In the extreme intensity case where, for example, very little labor is used relative to capital, increased output would require a large increase in rental rates in order to entice the required capital, but little if any rise in the wages of labor.

The Stolper-Samuelson Theorem can be illustrated in the Lerner-Pearce diagram by reexamining Figure 2–9 (reproduced with additions as Figure 3–4). Recall that the figure was previously used to show how, with a constant overall endowment of factors, a change in the wage-rental ratio changes output in the two industries. In the present section just the reverse effect is examined: how does a change in relative outputs affect the wage-rental ratio?

In Figure 3–4 the economy initially produces 400 units of A and 300 units of B at points A_0 and B_0 respectively. However, the relative price of the labor-intensive good $P_{B/A}$ is now assumed to rise. The rise in price increases the profits from producing good B relative to producing good A. Producers have an incentive to produce more B and less A. But in order to produce more B, factors of production must be bid away from industry A. Since more units of labor per unit of capital are required in industry B than in industry A, and the overall endowment of factors is fixed, labor's rewards must be bid up relative to capital's rewards in order to attract sufficient quantities of labor. The relative rise in labor's rewards also encourages producers to alter equilibrium factor ratios, which permit additional output of B with a constant factor endowment. Thus in Figure 3–4, after the rise in the relative price of B, production occurs at points A_1 and B_1fl Only 100 units of A are produced, while B production has risen to 450 units.

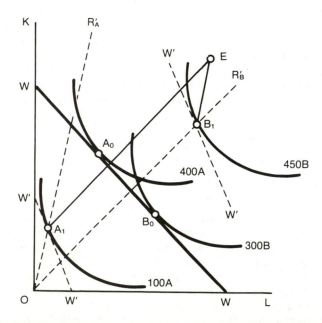

Figure 3–4   The Effect of a Shift in Production on the Wage-Rental Ratio

Notice that at the new production points A_1 and B_1, the slopes of the isoquants are again equal. The new equilibrium wage-rental ratios in the two industries are identical. Notice also that the new wage-rental lines $W'W'$ are more steeply sloped than the initial line WW, implying a higher wage-rental ratio. Hence, the rise in the relative price of the labor-intensive good B results in a rise in the relative reward of the intensively used factor (labor).

This result has been expanded upon by Ronald Jones.[3] Jones showed that not only would a rise in $P_{B/A}$ cause a rise in the wage-rental ratio, but the percentage change in the wage-rental rate would be greater than the percentage change in goods prices which caused it. The change in $P_{B/A}$ therefore results in a "magnified" change in w/r in the same direction. An algebraic derivation of this *magnification effect* is provided in the appendix.

THE RYBCZYNSKI THEOREM

The previous section dealt with the effects of changing the terms of trade while factor endowments were held constant. This section examines the converse proposition: the effects of changing factor endowments with the terms of trade held constant. The results were shown first by T. M. Rybczynski[4] and are therefore referred to as the *Rybczynski Theorem*.

Since the terms of trade are unchanged, the unique correspondence between the terms of trade and the wage-rental ratio is sufficient to assure that the wage-rental ratio is also unchanged. According to the postulates of the model developed so far, the wage-rental ratio depends solely on the terms of trade and the specific characteristics of the production functions. If the production functions of each industry are the same in both countries, with common terms of trade, the wage-rental ratios are the same in both countries regardless of their factor endowments. This result corresponds to the Factor Price Equalization Theorem. Changing the factor endowment of one country therefore has no effect on the wage-rental ratios as long as the terms of trade are assumed unchanged.*

Since the wage-rental ratio remains unchanged, the capital-labor ratios in both industries must also remain unchanged. The exercise is then to find the effect on total output in the two industries when the overall supply of one factor is increased with constant industry capital-labor ratios.

The effects of an increase in the supply of factors can be illustrated in the Lerner-Pearce diagram. In Figure 3–5 the economy is again assumed to initially produce at points A_0 and B_0. By vector addition, the factors of production required for production just sum to the overall factor endow-

---

*Of course, to the extent that increasing factor endowments changes the world supply of goods relative to the world demand, the terms of trade common to the two countries may change. However, that complication is ignored in the present analysis. The country under consideration can be considered too "small" to affect the world relative price of goods.

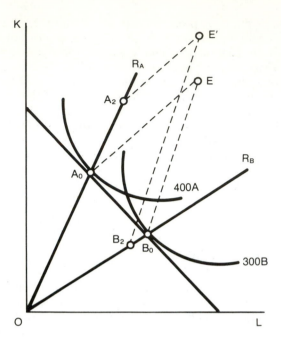

Figure 3–5 The Effect of an Increase in the Supply of Capital on the Levels of Output

ment at point E. Assume now that the supply of capital is increased with the supply of labor remaining unchanged. Under this assumption the economy's endowment point rises vertically by the amount of capital augmentation to E'. How will the shift in the endowment point affect the allocation of factors between the industries and the levels of production?

Under the assumptions of the Rybczynski Theorem, relative prices are constant and capital-labor ratios are constant. The new production point must therefore lie along the initial capital-labor ratios reflected in the rays OR_A and OR_B. The only difference is that the two new output points must sum by vector addition to E' instead of E. As shown in Figure 3–5, the new production points must be A_2 and B_2.

The new production points illustrate the two conclusions of the Rybczynski Theorem. First, the rise in the overall supply of capital has caused the production of the capital-intensive good A to rise absolutely and the production of the labor-intensive good to fall absolutely. An increase in the supply of one factor therefore increases the production of the good which uses it intensively and decreases the production of the other good. Second, points A_2 and B_2 illustrate that the A industry now employs more of *both* factors of production, and the B industry employs less of each. The increase in the supply of one factor therefore causes the migration of both factors to the industry employing the augmented factor intensively.

The effect of an increase in the capital stock on output can also be derived from equation (2–8)

$$\frac{K_A}{L_A} \cdot \frac{L_A}{L} + \frac{K_B}{L_B} \cdot \frac{L_B}{L} = \frac{K}{L}. \tag{2-8}$$

Given K_A/L_A and K_B/L_B, the only way to make the weighted sum of the two industry capital-labor ratios equal a higher overall K/L is to give a larger weight to the industry with a higher K/L. Since the weights in equation (2–8) are the shares or proportions of labor in each industry, the capital-intensive industry needs a bigger weight, which means labor must be transferred from the relatively labor-intensive industry B to the capital-intensive industry A. With constant capital-labor ratios in both industries, this shift in labor (making the denominator in K_A/L_A larger) further implies that capital is also transferred from industry B to industry A (increasing the numerator in the same proportion). Since quantities of both factors employed in industry B fall, output in the labor-intensive industry must clearly fall. Thus with constant terms of trade, the increase in the stock of one factor causes an absolute increase in the production of the good which uses that factor relatively intensively and an absolute fall in the output of the other good.

The same result can also be shown on a more intuitive basis. The objective is to maintain full employment of all factors when the overall supply of capital is increased. The problem is how to employ the increased supply of capital with the constant supply labor in ratios consistent with the individual industries' capital-labor ratios. Since the capital-labor ratios within each industry remain constant, the amount of labor required for the additional capital is known in each industry. Clearly the only way to provide labor for the new capital is to decrease production of the labor-intensive good, and shift those factors to the other industry. Since the capital-labor ratio is lower in industry B, shifting the resources to industry A means that each unit of old capital now has more workers than are required. These extra workers can then be employed with the new capital. Only when the extra workers are sufficient to operate all the new capital at the capital-labor ratio prevailing in industry A will the transfer cease. Output in industry B has clearly fallen, while output in A has risen. But not only does output in A rise, but it rises proportionately more than the increase in the factor itself.

A numerical example can further clarify the theorem. Let us return to the island of Islandia where, at the wage-rental ratio 0.2, eight units of capital are employed with every sixteen units of labor in industry A and four units of capital are employed per sixteen units of labor in industry B. Assume that a boat from some far off country, carrying twelve units of capital, shipwrecks on the rocky shore of Islandia. The Islandians now find that they have twelve additional units of capital to integrate into their production processes. How will they change the distribution of factors of production to accommodate the new capital?

Recall that in the Rybczynski Theorem relative prices are held constant. Thus the capital-labor ratios remain 8/16 and 4/16 in industries A and B respectively. Consider first adding the newly arrived capital with capital and labor from industry A. The capital-labor ratio in that industry rises above 8/16. Since at existing prices no industry in Islandia operates efficiently with a capital-labor ratio above 8/16, such a placement of the capital is not optimal. Alternatively, consider combining the additional capital with capital and labor from industry B. More specifically, consider taking sixteen workers from B and the corresponding four units of capital, and adding to them four units of the additional capital. There is now $4+4 = 8$ units of capital to go with the sixteen workers, precisely the proportions of capital and labor used in industry A! These factors can now be transferred to industry A. Since there are twelve new units of capital, in order to incorporate fully these additional factors of production, a total of twelve units of capital and forty-eight workers must be transferred from industry B to industry A. Thus, with the introduction of additional capital, at constant prices both factors of production leave the relatively labor-intensive industry B and move to the relatively capital-intensive industry A. Production of good B must therefore decrease absolutely, while production of good A increases absolutely.

The implications of the Rybczynski Theorem for production are also shown graphically in Figure 3–6. The figure shows the effect on output when the endowment of capital is increased at constant prices. The curve TT is the original production opportunities frontier, while T'T' is the frontier following the increase in capital. Notice that although potential production of all goods increases, the frontier does not expand proportionately everywhere. The capital-intensive industry benefits more than the labor-intensive industry by the increase in the capital stock.

Constant terms of trade means that production both before and after the increase in capital occurs at points on the two curves which have the

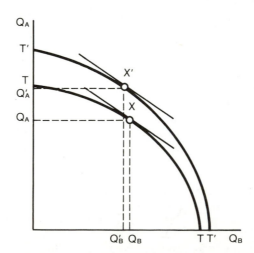

Figure 3–6 The Effect on Output When the Endowment of Capital Is Increased at Constant Prices and Industry B Is Relatively Labor Intensive

same slope. These points are X and X' in Figure 3–6. At these points, the trade-off between A and B, or the terms of trade, are equivalent. Notice that point X' lies to the northwest of point X. The northward movement implies an increase in the production of the capital-intensive good. The movement to the left represents a reduction in the production of the labor-intensive good. Again, the increase in capital is shown to increase the production of the good in which capital is used relatively intensively while reducing the output of the other good. An additional diagrammatic proof of the theorem, employing the Edgeworth Box, is presented in the appendix.

An interesting application of the Rybczynski Theorem is the pattern of growth and trade of Japan during the last two decades (or Germany during the immediate postwar period). During these decades Japan experienced an investment in capital that was great by any standards. As expected, this period was characterized by the output of Japanese capital-intensive products rising even faster than the overall Japanese economy. The share of capital-intensive goods in total output rose sharply. Given demand, one would expect such an explosion of output in these commodities to result in a large increase in their export. Similarly one might also expect a decrease in the export of labor-intensive goods to coincide with the decline in their relative production. This was precisely the pattern found in Japan. Labor-intensive exports soon gave ground to primitive manufactures such as toys and textiles. These were replaced by light manufactured products such as production-line transistors and small business machines. As the capital-labor ratio of the economy continued to increase, automobiles, machinery, steel, ships, and other heavily capital-intensive products rapidly became the leading Japanese exports. As shown in Figure 3–7, over the 1960s and 1970s the share of manufactured goods in total exports declined, while the share of machinery and transport equipment rose sharply. All of these changes in the pattern of Japanese trade are consistent with what one would anticipate using the Rybczynski Theorem.

THE RELEVANCE OF THESE THREE THEOREMS

Why are the Factor Price Equalization, Stolper-Samuelson, and Rybczynski Theorems so important for understanding the basics of international trade? What kinds of relevant information do these theorems provide? The answer is that these theorems provide important information about the effects of the opening of trade, and also about how the pattern or rewards of trade vary as other variables change over time.

For example, the Factor Price Equalization and Stolper-Samuelson Theorems predict what will happen to factor rewards when trade commences. With the opening of trade, the relative prices of goods are equalized across countries. Hence, a country commencing trade finds the relative price of one of its goods tending to rise. Assume the relative price

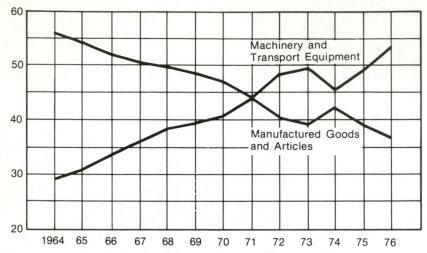

% of
Total
Exports

Machinery and Transport Equipment = SITC Code 7
Manufactured Goods and Articles Combines SITC Code 6, Manufactured Goods
Classified Chiefly by Material and SITC Code 8, Miscellaneous Manufactured
Articles.

Figure 3–7   Exports of Japan—Comparison of the Shares of Total Exports Represented by Machinery and Transport Equipment and by Manufactured Goods and Articles

Data Source: Statistics of Foreign Trade, *OECD*, Series C.

of the labor-intensive good B rises. The Stolper-Samuelson Theorem states that the relative price of good B and the wage-rental ratio move in the same direction. Thus the opening of trade tends to raise wages and lower the rental rate. Trade benefits most the factor which is used relatively intensively in the good for which the country has a comparative advantage. Trade tends to hurt the relative position of the other factor. However, once we introduce demand we will be able to illustrate that the accompanying gains from trade may prevent the other factor from actually being harmed. We will also be able to illustrate some of the pressures for tariffs, quotas, and other trade restrictions which result from changes in relative factor rewards as the level of trade changes. Included will be a discussion of how the presence of factors specific to a given industry can lead to lobbying pressures which are the opposite from those predicted by this basic model.

A similar conclusion concerning the opening of trade can be derived from the Factor Price Equalization Theorem. Under the assumptions of this theorem, when trade commences, relative and absolute factor rewards tend to equalize across countries. In a two-commodity, two-factor model, equalization implies that wages should rise in one country and rental rates should rise in the other. Hence in each country, one factor benefits from trade and the other is hurt. The factor to gain is the one which was relatively cheaper than its counterpart in the other country when the two countries were in autarky. Under the implied assumption of identical production functions in the two countries, this is also the factor used relatively intensively in the good for which the country has a comparative advantage.

As trade continues, these theorems also help us understand what types of changes to expect over time. For example, the Rybczynski Theorem describes how the pattern of trade may change as a country grows. Consider a country undergoing an exceptionally large labor force explosion, but experiencing relatively little investment. The overall capital-labor ratio of the country will be falling steadily. If the country continues to face constant terms of trade, the Rybczynski Theorem predicts that the production of labor-intensive goods will rise proportionately more than in other countries, while the production of capital-intensive goods will rise proportionately less or even fall. Assume the country is initially exporting the labor-intensive good and importing the capital-intensive good. If the composition of demand does not change, then the excess of supply over demand for the labor-intensive good will continue to grow, while the excess of demand over supply of the capital-intensive good will continue to widen. As the country's labor force grows, the country will want to export more and more of the labor-intensive good and import more and more of the capital-intensive good.

Similarly, policy actions within a country which affect the supply of factors in the marketplace are also expected to affect the levels of production and the composition of trade. For example, an increase in marginal tax rates on the wages of labor should reduce the supply of labor to the market. Individuals find they now retain a smaller percentage of the rewards for each additional unit (hour, day, etc.) of labor they provide to the market. The incentive to engage in market production is reduced. Less labor is provided to the market, and the released time is used for such nonmarket activities as home repairs, leisure-time enjoyment, or participating in the "underground" economy. The endowment point E in the Lerner-Pearce diagram moves to the left.

Alternatively, the existence of tax-free municipal bonds, cattle feedlots, and other tax shelters reduce the supply of capital available for market production. While market production may yield a much higher return from the economy's perspective, the individual investor is attracted to the shelters because of higher *after-tax* returns. A rise in marginal tax rates exacerbates this distortion. The factor endowment point E falls vertically.

On the other hand, a cut in marginal tax rates would increase the incentives for market production. Permitted to retain more of what they earn for each additional unit of service to the market, factors will want to supply more of their services to the marketplace. The economy's factor endowment point moves upward and to the right. The precise movement depends on the degree of response of capital and labor to the increased incentives. In any case, the Rybczynski Theorem illustrates the likely initial supply side reaction to any government policy affecting factor rewards.

Over time the demand and supply of goods in all countries may be changing. These changes in turn can produce changes in relative excess demands, and therefore relative goods prices or the terms of trade. As the terms of trade change, the Stolper-Samuelson Theorem predicts which factors benefit more. For example, suppose as countries develop more and more, the world demand for oil rises sharply, while supply rises relatively little. The huge rise in demand increases the excess demand for oil relative to the excess demand for all other goods. The relative price of oil rises. If oil is a relatively capital-intensive good, then the Stolper-Samuelson Theorem predicts that over time the returns to capital should increase relative to the returns from labor. Similarly, as will be described in Chapter 5, if a country attempts to affect its terms of trade by imposing a tariff, a change in the relative returns to factors (and perhaps factor supplies) is an anticipated by-product of this policy action.

SUMMARY

If two countries have identical production functions, then free trade assures that not only relative goods prices, but also relative and absolute factor prices must be the same in the two countries. The equalization of factor prices occurs even though factors are immobile between the countries and the factor endowments proportions of the countries differ substantially. This tendency for factor prices to equalize is known as the *Factor Price Equalization Theorem*. The tendency requires that there are at least as many traded goods as factors of production.

A rise in the relative price of a good benefits the factor used intensively in the production of that good, at the expense of the other factor. This relationship is called the *Stolper-Samuelson Theorem*.

With unchanged relative prices, an increase in the available quantity of one factor causes the output of the good using that factor intensively in production to expand, and the output of the other good to contract. Both factors of production move from the contracting industry to the expanding industry. This conclusion is called the *Rybczynski Theorem*.

These three theorems provide information about the effects of opening trade. Free trade tends to equilibrate relative good and factor prices between countries, benefiting the factor used relatively intensively in the good in which the country has comparative advantage, at the expense of the other factor. Also, growth or government policies can affect the quantities of factors available to the market, affecting the levels of production and the composition of trade.

REFERENCES

JOHNSON, HARRY G. "Factor Endowments, International Trade and Factor Prices," *The Manchester School of Economic and Social Studies*, 25 (September 1957):

270–83; reprinted in Johnson, *International Trade and Economic Growth.* Cambridge: Harvard University Press, 1958.

JONES, RONALD W. "The Structure of Simple General-Equilibrium Models," *Journal of Political Economy* 73, No. 6 (December 1965): 557–72.

LERNER, ABBA P. "Factor Prices and International Trade," *Economica* (February 1952).

MUNDELL, ROBERT A. "International Trade and Factor Mobility," *American Economic Review* 47, No. 3 (June 1957: 321–35; reprinted in *Readings in International Economics*, R. Caves and H. G. Johnson, eds., Homewood, Ill.:Irwin, 1968.

RYBCZYNSKI, T. M. "Factor Endowment and Relative Commodity Prices," *Economica* N.S. 22 (November 1955): 336–41; reprinted in *Readings in International Economics*, R. Caves and H. G. Johnson, eds., Homewood, Ill.:Irwin, 1968.

SAMUELSON, PAUL A. "International Trade and the Equalization of Factor Prices," *Economic Journal* 58 (June 1948): 163–84.

—— "International Factor-Price Equalization Once Again," *Economic Journal* 59 (June 1949): 181–97; reprinted in *Readings in International Economics*, R. Caves and H. G. Johnson, eds., Homewood, Ill.: Irwin, 1968.

STOLPER, WOLFGANG F. AND PAUL A. SAMUELSON, "Protection and Real Wages," *Review of Economic Studies*, 9 (November 1941): 58–73; reprinted in American Economic Association, *Readings in the Theory of International Trade*, Philadelphia: Blakiston, 1949.

NOTES

1. The seminal articles on this subject are Paul A. Samuelson, "International Trade and the Equalization of Factor Prices," *Economic Journal*, Vol. 58 (June 1948), pp. 163–84, and "International Factor-Price Equalization Once Again," *Economic Journal*, Vol. 59 (June 1949), pp. 181–97.

2. See Wolfgang F. Stolper and Paul A. Samuelson, "Protection and Real Wages," *Review of Economic Studies*, Vol. 9, (November 1941), pp. 58–73; reprinted in American Economic Association, *Readings in the Theory of International Trade*, Philadelphia: Blakiston, 1949, Chapter 15.

3. Ronald W. Jones, "The Structure of Simple General Equilibrium Models," *Journal of Political Economy*, Vol. 73, No. 6, (December 1965), pp. 557–72.

4. T. M. Rybczynski, "Factor Endowment and Relative Commodity Prices," *Economica*, Vol. 22, No. 84 (November 1955), pp. 336–41; reprinted in *Readings in International Economics*, edited by R. Caves and H. G. Johnson, Homewood, Ill.: Irwin, 1968.

APPENDIX 3
THE FACTOR PRICE EQUALIZATION
THEOREM

This section demonstrates that under the assumptions given, relative factor rewards are equalized across countries. The next section demonstrates an even stronger result—that absolute factor rewards are equalized as well.

There are at least two ways to demonstrate the equality of relative factor rewards across countries. The first method employs the Edgeworth Box analysis developed in Appendix 2. A slight change in the analysis is required because, since the factor price equalization theorem involves two countries, two Edgeworth Boxes are needed, one to represent each country. These boxes are shown in Figure 3A–1.

Countries I and II are assumed to differ in only one respect, the relative quantities of capital and labor. Country I, with a higher overall ratio of capital to labor than Country II, is assumed to be the relatively capital-abundant country. Country II of course is the relatively labor-abundant country. While relative factor supplies differ, under the assumptions of the factor price equalization theorem, goods are produced by the same homogeneous production functions across countries. Thus the isoquants for good A are identical in the two countries, and the same is true for the B isoquants.

In Figure 3A–1 the Edgeworth Boxes for the countries are superimposed so that the origin for good B in both countries coincides at O_B. However, since the factor proportions differ between countries, the origins for good A differ. The A origin for Country I is O_A and for Country II O_A'. The contract curves $O_A O_B$ and $O_A' O_B$ both bulge to the right below the diagonal. This shape is consistent with the assumption used through-

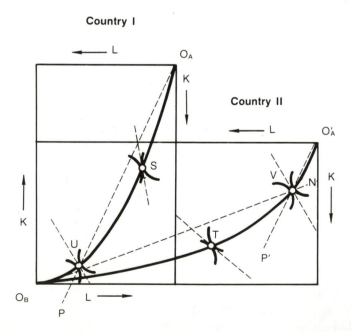

Figure 3A–1   The Effects of Opening Trade on Relative Factor Rewards and Factor Proportions

out the book that A is the relatively capital-intensive and B is the relatively labor-intensive good.

In autarky, the countries produce where domestic supply equals domestic demand, such as points S and T in Figure 3A–1. At these two points the slopes of the tangents differ, indicating that the relative factor rewards differ. Furthermore, since as shown in this chapter, for any production functions there is a unique relationship between relative goods and factor prices, and the production functions in the two countries are assumed identical, relative goods prices $P_{B/A}$ must also differ between the countries.

However, when trade occurs, arbitrage assures that the relative goods prices must be equalized across countries. The equalization of $P_{B/A}$ along with the assumptions of identical production functions and a unique relationship between relative goods and factor prices assures that relative factor rewards must also be equalized. Production in Country I moves to point U, and in Country II to point V. At these two points the capital-labor ratios and therefore relative factor rewards are equal. The equality in industry B can be verified by examining the ray $O_B N$. With homogeneous production functions, along a straight-line ray from the origin, relative factor prices and intensities are constant. Notice that both points U and V lie along $O_B N$. Similarly for industry A, the points U and V lie along the parallel rays $O_A P$ and $O_A' P'$. Again relative factor rewards are equal.

An alternative demonstration of relative factor price equalization employs a diagrammatic technique first used by Lerner, but popularized by Johnson.[1] The technique is shown in Figure 3A–2. The technique relies on two relationships discussed in the main text. For example, the top half

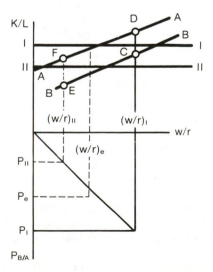

Figure 3A–2 The Effects of Opening Trade on Relative Good Prices, Factor Rewards, and Factor Proportions

of the diagram is simply the relationship between the relative factor rewards in a country and the relative factor intensities in industries A and B (see Figure 2-5). The bottom half of the diagram is simply the positive relationship between relative good prices and relative factor rewards from Figure 3-2 (but drawn upside down). Thus the diagram relates relative goods prices to relative factor intensities through relative factor rewards. This approach is therefore simply a more formal way of describing the approach used in the main text.

Since Countries I and II use the same production functions, they can be drawn on the same graph. As in the Edgeworth Box diagram, the two countries are distinguished by their overall factor intensities. Thus in Figure 3A-2 the overall capital-labor ratio for Country I (the relatively capital-abundant country) is I-I, and the overall ratio for Country II is II-II.

Since from equation (2-8) the overall capital-labor ratio is a weighted average of the individual industries' ratios, the horizontal line for each country representing the overall ratio must lie between the capital-labor ratios for industries A and B (represented by points along AA and BB) at the equilibrium wage-rental ratio. Thus in autarky, in Country I where capital is relatively abundant, the wage-rental ratio is high and the factor intensities are the distances $(w/r)_I C$ and $(w/r)_I D$. Notice that these factor intensities cannot be equilibrium values in Country II because II-II does not lie between these values. Instead, in autarky Country II has factor intensities $(w/r)_{II} E$ and $(w/r)_{II} F$. The corresponding relative goods prices in the lower half of the diagram indicate that the relative price of the labor intensive good B is higher in autarky in the relatively capital-abundant Country I.

When trade occurs, arbitrage assures that relative goods prices converge at equilibrium price P_e. In turn, identical production functions assure that: (a) the wage-rental ratio is equalized between the countries at $(w/r)_e$, and (b) factor proportions are equalized between countries within a given industry.

Absolute Factor Price Equalization

The previous section demonstrated that where production functions are identical across countries and free trade occurs, relative factor rewards are equalized across countries. While the equality of wages relative to rental rates is an important result, an even more powerful result is now shown—the equality of absolute factor rewards across countries.

The proof of absolute factor price equalization requires only relationships that have already been introduced. The goal is to show that the marginal product of factors are equalized across countries. If factor markets are competitive (an assumption of the factor price equalization theorem) then factors are paid their marginal product and absolute factor rewards are equalized.

The first relationship employed in this demonstration is Euler's Theorem from equation (2-2). Consider this equation for industry A in Country I,

$$w_A^I \cdot L_A^I + r_A^I \cdot K_A^I = A^I fl \qquad (3A-1)$$

Recall the equation states that under competition the total wages paid labor (their marginal product times the number of workers) plus the total returns to capital (their marginal product times the number of units of capital) account for the full value of the quantity of good A produced in Country I.

Dividing both sides of equation (3A–1) by the quantity of labor in industry A yields

$$w_A^I + r_A^I \frac{K_A^I}{L_A^I} = \frac{A^I}{L_A^I} \qquad (3A-2)$$

or

$$\frac{A^I}{L_A^I} = w_A^I \left(1 + \frac{r_A^I}{w_A^I} \cdot \frac{K_A^I}{L_A^I}\right). \qquad (3A-3)$$

If the A industry in Country II had been chosen instead, the resulting expression would have been:

$$\frac{A^{II}}{L_A^{II}} = w_A{}^{II}\left(1 + \frac{r_A^{II}}{w_A^{II}} \cdot \frac{K_A^{II}}{L_A^{II}}\right). \qquad (3A-4)$$

Given expressions (3A–3) and (3A–4), the goal is to show that $w_A^I = w_A^{II}$, that absolute wage rates are equal. This demonstration requires only that the three ratios can be demonstrated from previous results.

For example, r_A/w_A is simply the rental-wage ratio. From the conclusions about relative factor rewards, we know that this ratio is equalized across countries. Similarly, K_A/L_A is the capital-labor ratio in industry A. Since industry A uses the same production function in the two countries and the wage-rental ratio is equalized across countries, the capital-labor ratios in industry A must also be the same.

The remaining ratio is A/L_A, or the average output per worker. From equation (2-5), this ratio in any industry is shown to be a function of only the capital-labor ratio in that industry. Again, since the production functions are the same across countries, and the capital-labor ratios are the same, the average output per worker must also be the same. Thus the remaining variable w_A must also be the same across countries. A similar proof can be performed for the absolute rental rate r_A.

The Stolper-Samuelson Theorem

Using either Figure 3A–1 or 3A–2, the basic Stolper-Samuelson result can be shown. In either country, a rise in the relative price of a good benefits the factor used relatively intensively in the good at the expense of the other factor.

For example, consider Country I. The opening of trade raises the relative price of the capital-intensive good A. This price change can be observed directly in Figure 3A–2 as a reduction in the relative price of the labor-intensive good A. The effect of the price change is to lower the wage-rental ratio from $(w/r)_{II}$ to $(w/r)_e$. In other words, the rise in the relative price of the capital-intensive good causes the returns to capital to rise relative to the returns to labor, or capital to gain relative to labor. This change in relative factor rewards is also consistent with Figure 3A–1. In that diagram the opening of trade moves production in Country I from point S to point U. The fact that the wage-rental ratio (tangency of the two isoquants) is less steep with respect to the labor axis at point U indicates that the wage-rental ratio has again fallen as output has changed.

Similarly, the opening of trade raises the relative price of the labor-intensive good and the wage-rental ratio in Country II. In Figure 3A–2 the wage-rental ratio rises from $(w/r)_{II}$ to $(w/r)_e$ when the relative price of the labor-intensive good rises from P_{II} to P_e. In Figure 3A–1, the fact that the relative factor reward line is more steep with respect to the labor axis at point V than at point T again indicates that the factor used intensively gains when the price of a good rises.

While the basic Stolper-Samuelson result can be shown in this straightforward manner, demonstrating the "magnification effect" is much more cumbersome. This effect can be shown only through an algebraic exercise.[2] The algebraic demonstration is derived from two basic assumptions—Euler's Theorem and the fact that producers choose the combination of factors that minimize the cost of production. Again, Euler's Theorem states that the value of rewards paid to factors of production equals the value of total output. For industries A and B this relationship is written:

$$wL_A + rK_A = A = P_A Q_A \qquad (3A–5)$$

$$wL_B = rK_B = B = P_B Q_B. \qquad (3A–6)$$

The form of these relationships can be changed to the cost of producing one more unit of output by dividing both sides by the quantity of output Q. For example, equation (3A–5) for industry A may be rewritten as:

$$w\frac{L_A}{Q_A} + r\frac{K_A}{Q_A} = P_A$$

or

$$wa_{LA} + ra_{KA} = P_A \qquad (3A–7)$$

where a_{LA} and a_{KA} are the respective quantities of labor and capital required to produce one more unit of good A. Similarly, the cost of producing one more unit of B can be derived:

$$wa_{LB} + ra_{KB} = P_B. \qquad (3A–8)$$

Equations (3A–7) and (3A–8) are the form in which Euler's Theorem is employed in this demonstration.

The fact that producers are choosing a combination of factors which minimize cost provides a relationship that permits obtaining the final result more easily. The cost minimizing condition implies that producers hire factors until the ratio of the marginal products in production (the slope of the isoquant) equals the (negative) relative factor rewards (slope of isocost curve) or:

$$-\frac{w}{r} = \frac{MP_L}{MP_K} = \frac{\frac{1}{MP_K}}{\frac{1}{MP_L}} = \frac{da_K}{da_L}. \tag{3A–9}$$

This expression can be rewritten as:

$$wda_L + rda_K = 0. \tag{3A–10}$$

Expanding equations (3A–10) by multiplying each term by the appropriate form of one, and dividing by the cost of production yields (in the case of good A):

$$\frac{wa_{LA}}{P_A} \cdot \frac{da_{LA}}{a_{LA}} + \frac{ra_{KA}}{P_A} \cdot \frac{da_{KA}}{a_{KA}} = 0, \tag{3A–11}$$

or, in the case of good B:

$$\frac{wa_{LB}}{P_B} \cdot \frac{da_{LB}}{a_{LB}} + \frac{ra_{KB}}{P_B} \cdot \frac{da_{KB}}{a_{KB}} = 0. \tag{3A–12}$$

The relationship between the percentage change in factor rewards and the percentage change in the price of the good can now be derived for each industry. These relationships for the two industries are then used to derive the relationship between changes in relative factor rewards and relative good prices. To illustrate how the relationship is derived, consider industry A. Differentiating equation (3A–7) yields:

$$wda_{LA} + a_{LA}dw + rda_{KA} + a_{KA}dr = dP_A. \tag{3A–13}$$

Expanding this expression by multiplying each term by the appropriate form of one and then dividing both sides by P_A yields:

$$\frac{wa_{LA}}{P_A} \cdot \frac{da_{LA}}{a_{LA}} + \frac{wa_{LA}}{P_A} \frac{dw}{w} + \frac{ra_{KA}}{P_A} \cdot \frac{da_{KA}}{a_{KA}} + \frac{ra_{KA}}{P_A} \frac{dr}{r} = \frac{dP_A}{P_A}. \tag{3A–14}$$

From equation (3A–11), the first and third terms on the left side sum to zero. Hence (3A–14) can be simplified to:

$$\frac{wa_{LA}}{P_A} \cdot \frac{dw}{w} + \frac{ra_{KA}}{P_A} \cdot \frac{dr}{r} = \frac{dP_A}{P_A} \tag{3A–15}$$

or

$$\theta_{LA}\%\Delta w + \theta_{KA}\%\Delta r = \%\Delta P_A. \tag{3A–16}$$

Equation (3A–16) states that under competition the percentage change in the price of good A equals a weighted average of the percentage changes in the prices of the factors. The weights θ are the shares or proportions of the respective factors in total production costs. Similarly for good B:

$$\theta_{LB}\%\Delta w + \theta_{KB}\%\Delta r = \%\Delta P_B. \tag{3A–17}$$

The relationship between relative factor rewards and relative prices is derived from these last two equations. Subtracting equation (3A–16) from (3A–17) yields:

$$\% \Delta P_B - \% \Delta P_A = (\theta_{LB} - \theta_{LA})\% \Delta w + (\theta_{KB} - \theta_{KA})\% \Delta r.$$

However, since $\theta_L + \theta_K = 1$ for either good, the expression can be rewritten:

$$\% \Delta P_B - \% P_A = (\theta_{LB} - \theta_{LA})(\% \Delta w - \% \Delta r), \qquad (3A\text{–}18)$$

or

$$\% \Delta P_{B/A} = (\theta_{LB} - \theta_{LA})\% \Delta\left(\frac{w}{r}\right) \qquad (3A\text{–}19)$$

Since good B is assumed to be the relatively labor-intensive good, by definition $\theta_{LB} > \theta_{LA}$ and $1 > \theta_{LB} - \theta_{LA} > 0$. Thus the relationship between the percentage change in the price of the relatively labor-intensive good and the wage-rental ratio is clear. When $P_{B/A}$ rises, w/r rises as well. In addition, since $1 > \theta_{LB} - \theta_{LA}$, the rise in the relative factor rewards is greater than the rise in relative good prices.

The Rybczynski Theorem

The Rybczynski Theorem is easy to demonstrate with the aid of the Edgeworth Box diagram. In Figure 3A–3 Country II is producing initially at point H. The capital-labor ratios in industries A and B consistent with efficient production at point H are $O_B N$ and $O_A P$ respectively. These capital-labor ratios in turn are consistent with a given wage-rental ratio. According to the Rybczynski Theorem, the relative quantity of one factor of production is altered, while all relative prices remain constant. Since a unique relationship between wage-rental and capital-labor ratios is assumed to exist, the constant relative prices imply that capital-labor ratios

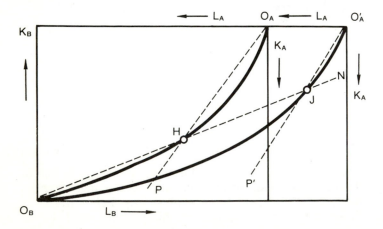

Figure 3A–3   The Rybczynski Theorem

also remain constant. Thus production of goods A and B must remain along rays from the origin with slopes O_AP and O_BN respectively.

In Figure 3A-3, Country II experiences a growth in the number of individuals available to work. This growth in workers increases the potential production of the country. In terms of the Edgeworth Box, the growth is represented by an increase in the length of the labor axis. Figure 3A-3 now extends farther to the right than before. The increased size of the box also affects the origin for good A. This origin is now farther to the right at point O_A'. Production of good A therefore occurs along ray O_A 'P', which is parallel to O_AP. More specifically, production occurs at point J where $O_A'P'$ intersects the ray O_BN. The ray O_BN of course remains the same as before since the origin O_B is undisturbed.

At point J, the quantity of goods A and B produced have changed as compared with point H. The quantity of good B produced has clearly increased. The length of ray cut off by $O_A'P'$ is clearly longer than at point H, indicating that B production occurs at an isoquant farther to the right than before. Such an isoquant represents a higher level of output. Similarly, $O_A'J$ is much shorter than O_AH, indicating that the production of good A occurs at a lower isoquant. Thus the basic proposition has been shown. The increase in one factor of production (labor) has increased the absolute production of the good using that factor intensively (good B) and decreased the absolute production of the other good (good A). This same Edgeworth Box technique could also be used to show that an increase in capital increases the absolute production of A and reduces the absolute production of B, or that if both factors increase, there will be a relative increase in the production of the good which uses the factor that increases relatively more.

APPENDIX NOTES

1. See Abba P. Lerner, "Factor Prices and International Trade," Economics, Vol. 19, No. 1 (February 1952) pp. 1-15, and H. G. Johnson, "Factor Endowments, International Trade and Factor Prices," in his International Trade and Economic Growth, Cambridge: Harvard Univ., 1967.

2. This demonstration is based on the original derivation by Ronald Jones in "The Structure of Simple General Equilibrium Models," Journal of Political Economy, Vol. 73 (December 1965), pp. 557-72.

CHAPTER 4

Introducing Demand and the Gains from Trade

The discussion to this point has been confined to the adjustment of supply. Trade and the terms of trade are determined, however, by the interaction of supply with demand. This chapter introduces demand. A measure of the economic gains from trade can be obtained by first examining the interaction of supply with demand where trade does not exist and then in situations where trade occurs. A measure of the effect of a trade barrier such as tariffs on the overall economy is then obtained by determining how the gains from trade are affected. The chapter concludes with a discussion of the Heckscher-Ohlin model of international trade and the incentives for free trade.

A REPRESENTATION OF DEMAND

To show the effects of demand as simply as possible, we need a graphical representation of demand choices. The use of *indifference curves* for the economy serves this purpose. The concept of indifference curves should be familiar from microeconomics where they are used to describe the relative preference for two goods by an individual consumer. A *community indifference curve* represents the same relative preferences, only for the aggregate of all individuals in the economy. The community indifference curve has the same properties as the individual indifference curve. A given curve represents those combinations of two goods in question for which the economy as a whole is indifferent. The slope of each indifference curve shows the economy's marginal rate of substitution in consumption, that is, how many units of one product the economy needs to compensate it precisely for the loss of one unit of the other product.

A set of indifference curves for a given economy is shown in Figure 4-1. An obvious characteristic of the curves shown is their convexity; they slope downwards from left to right, bulging towards the origin. This convexity is caused by the assumption of a diminishing marginal rate of

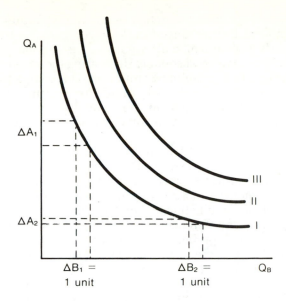

Figure 4–1   Community Indifference Curves

substitution. The greater the consumption of a given product, holding the other constant, the less its relative value per unit. Thus as the quantity of B consumed increases, the economy is willing to give up less A to get one unit of B (or give up more B in order to obtain one more unit of A). For example, in Figure 4–1, ΔB_1 and ΔB_2 are one unit increases in the consumption of B. However, the economy is willing to give up more units of A (ΔA_1) when B consumption is relatively low than when B consumption is high (ΔA_2) in order to obtain the additional unit of B. Thus, each indifference curve assumes that the marginal rate of substitution of A for B decreases as the quantity of B consumed increases, and each indifference curve has a convex shape.

Another property of community indifference curves is that they can be ranked in terms of level of preference. The further to the right a curve is, the more it is preferred since the rational individual (and by analogy the rational economy) prefers more to less. A curve further to the right represents opportunities for more of both A and B. Thus, in Figure 4–1 the indifference curves are given a higher ranking as they move up to the right. The higher the order of rank, the higher the level of community satisfaction assumed.

This positive relationship between the ranking of an indifference curve and the level of satisfaction is generally accepted to hold for an individual's set of preferences. However, the positive relationship for the community as a whole has some conceptual problems and may not always hold. Our assertion that community indifference curves can be ranked in this way, therefore, rests on some common simplifying assumptions.

The major problem with the notion of community indifference curves is how to handle redistributions of income. For example, the increase in the community's income which allows it to achieve a higher order indifference curve may involve absolutely decreasing the income of one individual. According to the Stolper-Samuelson Theorem, such a situation would result from the opening of trade. The question then becomes whether the loss of satisfaction to the individuals whose incomes decrease is greater than the gain in satisfaction to the individuals whose incomes rise.

However, if the tastes and preferences of the two groups differ, no direct comparison may be possible. The redistribution of income among people with different tastes produces a new set of indifference curves whose contours intersect those of the original curves. The current and initial consumption combinations cannot be compared in terms of satisfaction. Intersecting indifference curves mean that sometimes the initial consumption bundle is preferred, and sometimes the current bundle is preferred. No clear welfare distinction exists between the two points.

Community indifference curves must therefore be used with caution. However, these curves are very useful for simplifying the illustration of fundamental economic principles such as the gains from trade, the effects of tariffs or other government imposed taxes, or just deriving aggregate demand curves. Community indifference curves are used in this text to represent a unique set of clearly defined preferences for the community as a whole. The problem of income redistribution can then be overcome in one of three ways.

First, the problem of income redistribution can be ignored completely. For example, a rise in the community's income can be assumed to raise one person's income and leave all other persons' incomes the same as before. If the satisfaction levels of two individuals can be assumed independent so that a rise in one person's income does not affect the satisfaction level of the second person, the community is better off. Alternatively, a rise in aggregate income can be assumed to represent a rise in each individual's income so that all inhabitants are clearly better off. Again, if individuals' satisfaction levels are assumed independent, the economy is better off.

Second, specific assumptions about indifference curves and income which eliminate the redistribution problem can be made. This method of justification requires that at least two of the following conditions hold:

1. All individuals in the country must have the same tastes and preferences;
2. All individuals must have the same incomes; and
3. All individuals must have homogeneous indifference curves (just like production functions).

For example, if all individuals have the same, homogeneous indifference curves, then if a given amount of income is transferred from one person to another, the first person's loss of satisfaction is just equal to the second person's gain. Income redistributions are neutral for the economy as a whole.

Third, the compensation or "bribery" principle can be invoked. This principle simply assumes that if the incomes of those who gain rise more than the loss of income to the losers, the economy is better off. The operating assumption is that those who gain can compensate or bribe the losers into accepting the change. The losers are no worse off than before, and the gainers still have additional income remaining with which to raise their satisfaction. As long as such a bargaining process operates reasonably efficiently, any rise in overall community income must raise the level of community satisfaction.

EQUILIBRIUM IN AUTARKY

Autarky, as noted earlier, is a state in which a country does not trade; imports and exports are both equal to zero. In autarky the country must produce any goods it consumes, that is, the domestic supply of each good just equals domestic demand. How is the level of production determined in such an isolated country?

The supply constraint for a country, as described in Chapter 3, is given by the production possibilities curve that represents the frontier combinations of goods which can be produced given factor endowments and existing technology. Under autarky this production frontier serves as a constraint to both demand and supply. The economy would like to reach the highest community indifference curve possible, and without a budget constraint the economy would certainly be on some curve off to the right into the horizon. But with given technology and limited factors, the economy can only produce so much. Given the production possibilities frontier, the economy chooses to produce that combination of A and B which will allow it to reach the community indifference curve that is farthest up and to the right. That indifference curve is the one tangent to the production possibilities curve.

In an earlier chapter we saw that the slope of the production possibilities curve is equal to the marginal rate of substitution in production, that is, the rate at which good A can be substituted for good B while maintaining full employment. Similarly, we have just seen that the slope of an indifference curve is the marginal rate of substitution in consumption, that is, the rate at which the community is willing to substitute A for B and maintain the same level of satisfaction.

If the economy produced at a point where these two marginal rates were not equal, then individuals could obtain either A or B for less than they were paying. For example, assume consumers are willing to give up five units of good A for every unit of good B they receive, but producers only have to forego the production of three units of A to produce a unit of B. Consumers should then be able to obtain another unit of B for less than five units of A, and producers should be able to receive more than three A units. Both groups can be made better off. Production and consumption of good B rises and good A falls as both groups take advantage of the opportunity to increase their welfare.

However, the shift in production and consumption lowers the price consumers are willing to pay for good B and raises the costs of producing good B. The difference between consumer and producer prices is reduced, reducing the incentive to shift production towards more B. Only when the two values are equal do the incentives disappear completely, and the economy is in equilibrium. Such a position is shown by point M in Figure 4–2. At point M the indifference curve I is just tangent to the production possibilities curve TT. Given the output constraints and preferences of the community, the economy is producing and consuming A_0 of the capital-intensive good A and B_0 of the labor-intensive good B.

EQUILIBRIUM WITH TRADE

Now assume that the same economy is free to trade with any other nation. The opening of trade affects both equilibrium supply and demand.

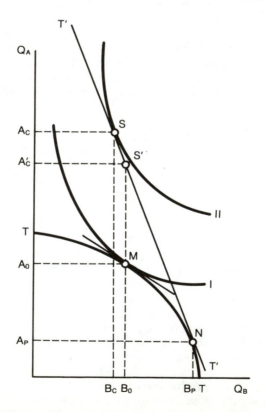

Figure 4–2   The Effects of Trade on Production and Consumption

Domestic production is still constrained by the production possibilities curve TT. However, domestic production no longer takes place at point M, as in autarky. The point of production shifts because the relative prices received by producers for their goods have changed. In autarky the relative price of goods was determined solely by the interaction of domestic production with domestic demand. But with free trade, not only can domestic residents consume the goods produced domestically, but so can foreign residents. Similarly, domestic demand can be satisfied by foreign production. Relative prices or the terms of trade are now determined by the interaction of world demand and world supply.

To describe precisely how the terms of trade are determined would require a precise representation of aggregate world demand and supply. But one thing about the terms of trade is known for certain—in the absence of trade barriers, after trade the terms of trade must be the same in all countries. If the terms of trade differed in two countries, individuals could purchase good A relatively more cheaply in one country. Residents of both countries would immediately try to purchase good A from that country (and good B from the other country). The excess demand for good A in the country where it is relatively cheaper would drive up the relative price of A there. The excess demand for B in the other country would drive up its relative price there. These relative price movements cease only when the terms of trade are the same in both countries.

So while the determination of the terms of trade is not shown in Figure 4–2, particular terms of trade are assumed to exist. The terms of trade simply represent the relative goods price at which the sum of the goods demanded across all countries in the world equals the sum of the goods supplied. Further, by assuming that the country in question is small relative to the world, the terms of trade are assumed exogenous and constant. In other words, the small open economy is assumed to be a "price-taker."

In Figure 4–2 the terms of trade with trade are assumed to be $P_{B/A}$ (slope of the line T'T'), which differ from the autarky terms of trade. In order again to equate the marginal rate of substitution in production with the relative prices that can be received for the goods, domestic production shifts to point N on the production frontier. The economy increases the production of B to B_p and reduces the production of A to A_p, as the assumed terms of trade imply a higher relative price of B than in autarky.

The higher relative price of B also affects domestic demand. Regardless of which indifference curve the community is on, consumption now occurs further to the left (consuming more A and less B) compared with autarky. An important question, however, is which indifference curve the community is now on. Is it still on the indifference curve achieved in autarky, or has a new level of satisfaction been reached?

While production now occurs at point N, consumption is certainly not constrained to that point. The country is now free to trade any domestically produced goods at the world terms of trade. Under autarky the demand for either good must be exactly equal to the domestic supply. However, trade requires only that the value of total domestic demand equal the value of total domestic supply, or

$$C_A + P_{B/A} \cdot C_B = Q_A + P_{B/A} \cdot Q_B \qquad (4\text{-}1)$$

where C_A and C_B are the quantities of goods A and B consumed.

The composition of consumption is free to differ from the composition of production. The set of consumption opportunities is therefore now defined by the terms of trade line T'T'. The country is free to trade any of the good B (or A) produced for foreign produced A (or B) at the prevailing world price $P_{B/A}$. Again the economy wants to maximize its level of satisfaction by achieving the highest indifference curve, subject to the supply or income constraint T'T'. Thus, consumption occurs in Figure 4–2 at point S where T'T' is tangent to indifference curve II. Since indifference curve II lies upward and to the right of indifference curve I, trade has clearly raised the level of the country's satisfaction. Alternatively, the rise in satisfaction can be demonstrated by the fact that there exists at least one point between S and N along T'T' where the economy can consume more of both A and B than it could at the autarky consumption point M.

At point S the economy is consuming A_C of A and B_C of B. Part of this consumption bundle is being supplied from abroad. In particular $(B_P - B_C)$ of B is being exported in exchange for $(A_C - A_P)$ imports of A. Notice that since the slope of the line NS represents the world terms of trade $P_{B/A}$, the value of these exports is exactly equal to the value of imports when both goods are measured in terms of either good B or good A.

THE GAINS FROM TRADE

In moving from autarky to a free trade position, the levels and proportions of the consumption and production of each good change, and the economy is made better off. This increase in satisfaction is known as the *gains from trade*. In this section these gains are divided into the portion due to changes in production, and the portion due to changes in consumption.

Why should there be gains from trade? On the production side the gains occur because the real value of production has increased. Facing different terms of trade than under autarky, firms are able to increase the value of total income or production by altering their production mix. In Figure 4–2 the opening of trade leads to an increased relative price of good B. By shifting production from point M to point N, and trading at world prices, the same amount of B can be consumed as before (B_0). Such a consumption point is represented by the point S' in Figure 4–2. In addition the excess production of B above B_0 (B_0B_P) can then be traded for units of A. Notice that at the world terms of trade, the quantity of A received for the additional $B(A_PA_C')$ is greater than the amount of A lost through the shift in production (A_PA_0) as the country moved from its autarky production point. Production at point N therefore equals the value of production at point M, plus some additional units of A. The value of production has clearly risen.

On the consumption side the gains occur because the economy can now consume goods at a different price ratio than at point M. Under autarky, the resulting domestic terms of trade are precisely those which maximize welfare subject to the constraint of no trade. Even if the autarkic production of each good were unchanged, opening trade increases the country's level of satisfaction or welfare. At the autarkic terms of trade people were content with the combination of goods they had. With free trade, the terms of trade change, permitting people the option of acquiring a different bundle of goods. Since they can always keep what they had under autarky, they will never be worse off, but with a change in prices they can now make themselves better off. These are the consumption gains from trade.

In Figure 4–2 the opening of trade has raised the relative price of good B. Thus, even if production remains at point M, the level of satisfaction of the community can be increased because the marginal rate of substitution in consumption in the world now differs from the initial marginal rate of substitution in consumption at home. Good B is valued relatively more on the world market than in the domestic economy, which implies that foreigners are willing to give up more units of A for a unit of B than domestic individuals would demand in autarky. Thus, domestic residents have an incentive to give up some units of B in exchange for some units of A. Alternatively, domestic residents can now acquire units of A in exchange for fewer units of B than possible in autarky, again creating an incentive to trade good A for good B.

As more units of B are exported to foreigners, the quantity of A that foreigners are willing to exchange for another unit of B falls, while the quantity of A demanded by domestic residents to part with another unit of B rises. Units of B are therefore exported in exchange for units of A until the rates of substitution at home and abroad are equal. The economy would not exchange goods if the exchange reduced satisfaction, nor would it have an incentive to exchange if satisfaction remained constant. That the incentive exists and exchange takes place is evidence that satisfaction has increased.

The division of the gains between production and consumption is displayed in Figure 4–3, a modification of Figure 4–2. The total gains from trade are represented by the movement from point M to point S. In order to identify the consumption proportion of this total, assume production initially remains at the autarky level, point M. Consumption, however, is allowed to respond to the world terms of trade. The consumption opportunities available at the world terms of trade are described by the line RM. The economy moves along this line until the marginal rates of substitution in the world and the economy are equilibrated. The equilibrium occurs at point R on community indifference curve I'. The level of satisfaction of the community has risen, and the entire rise is due solely to changes in consumption opportunities. The consumption gains from trade can therefore be described as either the movement from M to R or from the indifference curve I to I'.

In fact, however, production does not remain at point M when trade opens. Rather, it moves to point N. The shift in production produces a

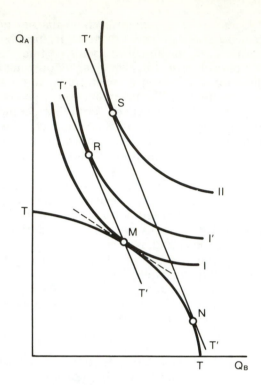

Figure 4–3   The Gains from Trade

further increase in satisfaction. In Figure 4–3, the shift in production moves the terms of trade line until it is tangent to the production possibilities curve at point N. This rightward movement allows the economy to reach the even higher indifference curve II. So the proportion of total gains due to production can be described as either the movement from point R to S, or the movement from indifference curve I′ to indifference curve II.

As an example of the importance of these production and consumption gains, suppose that for military reasons the United States feels obliged to produce more oil domestically than it would under uninhibited free trade. This argument is similar to the oil independence arguments that have been prominent since the 1973 oil embargo. The conventional solution to induce increased domestic production is to impose barriers against imports of oil from overseas in order to drive up the domestic relative price of oil. If such a policy were instituted and successfully eliminated oil imports, the United States would return to autarky in oil. But returning to autarky such as at point M in Figure 4–3 means that the U.S. loses both the production and the consumption gains from trade. Thus, oil independence is achieved at a price in terms of economic satisfaction.

If the original desire were only to raise domestic output and not affect consumption, then a barrier against imports would be inefficient. As was shown earlier, changing the relative price at which goods are traded affects both production and consumption. The original objective was defined solely in terms of production. The economy was aiming for a point like point R, but the tariff brought the economy to point M. The consumption gains from trade were lost unnecessarily, because consumption patterns were distorted in an effort to conform to a false relative price for oil. The process of choosing proper policies to correspond to different goals is discussed further in Chapter 6 on distortions.

THE HECKSCHER-OHLIN MODEL

A traditional trade model for analyzing the effects of free trade on factor rewards and production patterns is the *Heckscher-Ohlin* model. The model is named after the twentieth-century Swedish economist Eli Heckscher and his student Bertil Ohlin, who developed the framework. Bertil Ohlin received the 1977 Nobel Prize in economics in recognition of his contribution to the field of international trade theory.

The Heckscher-Ohlin model of international trade, as usually formulated, starts with two countries initially in autarky. These two countries produce the same two goods with the same two factors of production, but differ in some relevant aspect. Trade is then opened and the ensuing changes in the terms of trade and trade patterns are analyzed.

Three possible differences between the countries exist. First, the technology used in producing the goods may differ even though the countries produce the same two goods with the same two factors. This difference is equivalent to assuming different production functions in the two countries. Different production functions can cause different relative prices in autarky even if the countries are the same in all other respects. Second, tastes and preferences can differ in the two countries. Thus, even if production is identical in the two countries, differing demands can produce differing relative prices in autarky. Finally, the relative endowments of factors of production may differ. One country would then have more capital per unit of labor, which would make capital and the capital-intensive good relatively cheaper.

The Heckscher-Ohlin model, as in the case of the Ricardian model, is a model of only the supply or production side. Divergent tastes and preferences are not the traditional source of differences between the two countries in the model. The remaining choices for the source of differences are technology and relative factor endowments. Technology is commonly assumed to be the same across countries, leaving factor endowments as the usual source of differences. Identical factor endowments and differing technology are just as easily analyzed, nonetheless. Each of these assumptions produces a different autarkic relative price in the two countries and thus allows production gains from trade.

With identical tastes and production technology, but differing factor endowments, the country that is relatively capital-abundant has a lower autarkic relative price for its capital-intensive product. For any given relative price, the Rybczynski Theorem implies that the relatively capital-abundant country produces relatively more of the capital-intensive good. With relatively more capital-intensive goods, yet similar tastes, the autarkic relative price of the capital-intensive good must fall in the capital abundant country. Hence, the autarkic price of the capital-intensive good is lower there. Alternatively, the country where labor is relatively abundant has a lower autarkic relative price of the labor-intensive good.

Since autarkic relative prices differ in the two countries, there are potential gains from trade. When trade commences, prices are equilibrated between the countries. Production changes in each country. Each country specializes in producing and exporting the good which it can produce comparatively cheaper. In this example, the relatively capital-abundant country therefore exports the capital-intensive good. This is the general conclusion of the Heckscher-Ohlin model: *a country will export the good which uses its most abundant factor relatively intensively.*

Several attempts have been made to measure the empirical relevance of the Heckscher-Ohlin model. One such study authored by Wassily Leontief had an enormous initial impact.[1] Leontief used input-output tables to compare the relative factor intensities of a million dollars worth of U.S. exports and a million dollars worth of U.S. import-competing goods. Leontief used U.S. import-competing goods instead of actual U.S. imports because the input-output tables were available only for U.S. industries. This comparison is equivalent to assuming that production functions for U.S. imports are the same at home and abroad, which is consistent with the Heckscher-Ohlin theory. Since the U.S. is a relatively capital-abundant country, U.S. exports were expected to be capital intensive. Leontief's analysis showed, however, that U.S. import-competing goods were 30 percent more capital intensive than U.S. exports. Additional tests failed to reverse these findings, which became known as the *Leontief Paradox.*

Much attention has been given to explaining this paradox. Many explanations have been posited, most suggesting that a multi-factor trade model is more appropriate. One explanation is the possible superior efficiency of American labor. If American workers are three times as efficient as foreign workers, then the apparent capital abundancy in the U.S. could be an illusion. Each U.S. worker effectively represents three foreign workers, making the U.S. a labor-abundant country.[2]

A second explanation is that Leontief's measure ignored the importance of natural resources endowments.[3] The U.S. imports many minerals and forest products which are produced in the U.S. using relatively capital-intensive techniques. On the other hand, U.S. exports of natural resources are primarily farm products, which are produced by relatively labor-intensive techniques. The Leontief Paradox could therefore be caused by measuring only the value of the labor and capital, not the value of the natural resources. Further, the large quantitites of imported natural resources appear to be consistent with the concept of importing goods embodying scarce factors of production.

A third argument is that tariff or other trade barriers distorted the pattern of trade. A fourth suggestion is the possible existence of factor intensity reversals in the production function.[4] The Heckscher-Ohlin model assumes that if a good is relatively capital intensive at one ratio of factor prices, it is relatively capital-intensive at all factor price ratios. However, it is conceivable that as the wage-rental ratio rises, the capital-intensive good could become relatively labor-intensive, and the labor-intensive good relatively capital intensive. Thus, if for some reason the wage-rental ratio differed in the U.S. and the rest of the world, what appears as a capital-intensive import in terms of U.S. production might actually be a labor-intensive export of the rest of the world.

A fifth explanation is the failure of the Heckscher-Ohlin theory to include the demand side.[5] Demand is implicitly assumed similar in all countries. However, if the U.S. has a strong preference for capital-intensive goods and the rest of the world strongly prefers labor-intensive goods, a capital-abundant country like the U.S. could quite likely have the trading pattern observed by Leontief.

A more interesting argument has questioned Leontief's division of factors into only two groups, labor and capital. In particular, the grouping "labor" may consist of many different types of labor, each possessing a different amount of capital in the form of skills or human capital. This possibility was examined by Keesing,[6] who demonstrated that U.S. exports of manufactured goods are considerably more skill-intensive than U.S. imports would be if produced by American firms. In a later study[7] Keesing also examined the effect which the particular capital input, research and development, has on exports. As shown in Table 4–1, the indicator of research and development activity selected for the analysis was the number of scientists and engineers engaged in research and development expressed as a percentage of the labor force in each industry. Export performance in the eighteen industries was measured by the proportion of U.S. exports in the total exports of the group of ten nations in 1962. Keesing found that while the share of U.S. exports within a given export category was inversely related to the measured capital intensity of the industry, there was a strong, positive relation between the export share and the amount of research and development. U.S. exports therefore appear to be human capital or research and development intensive.

More recently, Harkness and Kyle[8] have questioned the procedures which have been used in previous multi-factor studies to measure the effect on exports. They point out that the Heckscher-Ohlin model does not claim, as for example Keesing attempted to measure, that across industries either the absolute or relative share of exports is positively related to the capital-labor ratio. The Heckscher-Ohlin model predicts only that industries with relatively high capital-labor ratios tend to be exporters, and those with low capital-labor ratios tend to be importers. So using logic analysis, they simply measure whether several factors, including capital-labor ratios, four different levels of human capital, and resources intensity, have a positive impact on comparative advantage. The results support the Heckscher-Ohlin model. The principal conclusion is

Table 4–1 Competitive U.S. Trade Performance in Comparison with Research and Development, for Eighteen Industries

Industry	U.S. Exports as % of Group of Ten Exports, 1962	Scientists and Engineers Engaged in R&D as % of Employment, January 1961
Aircraft	59.52	7.71
Office machinery	35.00	5.09
Drugs	33.09	6.10
Other machinery	32.27	1.39
Instruments	27.98	4.58
Chemicals, except drugs	27.32	3.63
Electrical equipment	26.75	4.40
Rubber	23.30	0.95
Motor vehicles	22.62	1.14
Petroleum refining	20.59	2.02
Fabricated metal products	19.62	0.51
Nonferrous metals	18.06	0.69
Paper and allied products	15.79	0.47
Stone, clay, glass products	15.22	0.60
Other transport equipment	13.71	0.46
Lumber and wood products	11.68	0.03
Textile mill products	10.92	0.29
Primary ferrous metals	9.14	0.43

Sources: U.S. exports as % of Group of Ten exports computed from United Nations *Commodity Trade Statistics 1962;* scientists and engineers engaged in R&D as percentage of employment computed from data in National Science Foundation. *Scientific and Technical Personnel in Industry,* NSF 63-32 (Washington, D.C., 1963). Adapted from: Donald B. Keesing, "The Impact of Research and Development on United States Trade," *The Open Economy: Essays on International Trade,* edited by P. B. Kenen and R. Lawrence, New York: Columbia University Press, 1968, pp. 175–89.

that capital intensity has a significant positive impact on the export activity of U.S. manufacturing industries. Within their multi-factor model, Harkness and Kyle can conclude that capital-intensive U.S. industries tend to be exporters, that research and development has a positive impact on exports, and that the U.S. is relatively capital rich with respect to its trading partners.

THE INCENTIVES FOR FREE TRADE

The analysis in this chapter has shown that a country as a whole gains from trade, and thus is better off. It can also be shown that the welfare of the world as a whole is also improved by free trade because more goods are available in the world economy for consumption. Can we then expect that all rational inhabitants of all countries will support free trade? The answer is no. Labor and capital in each country will support policies which further their own interests in the short run. Free trade, as shown in

Chapter 3, implies that one group in the country benefits at the expense of another group, while it simultaneously implies a gain for the country as a whole. More specifically, free trade tends to benefit the factor used relatively intensively in the good for which the country has a comparative advantage. If that good is capital intensive, free trade benefits capital more than it harms labor.

According to the Heckscher-Ohlin model, a country has comparative advantage in the good which uses the abundant factor intensively. Thus, the capital-abundant country has a comparative advantage in the capital-intensive good. Free trade raises the relative price of this good. The Stolper-Samuelson Theorem states that the return to capital increases and the return to labor falls. Furthermore, the magnification effect indicates that the percentage rise in the relative return to capital is even larger than the percentage rise in the relative price of the capital-intensive good. Thus, although the country as a whole is better off, the absolute returns to labor can actually fall. Clearly the owners of capital in the capital-abundant country will support free trade. However, labor in the country will oppose free trade. Only through protection will the relative price of the labor-intensive goods and the unit return to labor rise.

The effects of trade restrictions are important to understand the motivation of certain groups in a country, and the basic trade model provides the first insights into the politics of international trade. Additional insights are presented in the next chapter on tariffs, among them a discussion of why some owners of capital in a capital-abundant country like the U.S. are observed lobbying for trade restrictions.

SUMMARY

Community indifference curves, like individual indifference curves, are intended for ranking levels of satisfaction. Community indifference curves present some conceptual problems, primarily related to the redistribution of income. However, with any of several simplifying assumptions, the curves can be used to illustrate fundamental economic principles such as the gains from trade.

A country in autarky consumes just what it produces. With the opening of trade, alternative production and consumption opportunities are available to the country. The increased opportunities produce production and consumption gains which permit a country to reach a higher level of satisfaction. These production and consumption gains are the *gains from trade*.

The *Heckscher-Ohlin* model describes only the production side of economies, just like the Ricardian model. As often formulated, the Heckscher-Ohlin model predicts that a country will export the good which uses its most abundant factor relatively intensively. This implication was at odds with Leontief's data for exports and import-competing goods in the U.S., initiating the search for an explanation of the *Leontief Paradox*.

Although free trade makes countries and the world better off, individual factors of production, such as labor, pursuing their own interests, may encourage the adoption of trade restrictions.

REFERENCES

HARKNESS, JON and JOHN F. KYLE, "Factors Influencing United States Comparative Advantage,"*Journal of International Economics*, 5 (1975): 153–165.

HECKSCHER, ELI, "The Effect of Foreign Trade on the Distribution of Income," *Ekonomisk Tidshrift* 21 (1919): 497–512 (in Swedish); for an English translation see American Economic Association, *Readings in the Theory of International Trade*, Philadelphia: Blakiston, 1949.

HODD, MICHAEL, "An Empirical Investigation of the Heckscher-Ohlin Theory," *Economica*, 34 (February 1967): 20–29.

JONES, RONALD, "Factor Proportions and the Heckscher-Ohlin Theorem," *Review of Economic Studies*, 24 (October 1956): 1–10.

KEESING, DONALD, "The Impact of Research and Development on United States Trade," *The Open Economy: Essays on International Trade*, P. B. Kenen and R. Lawrence, eds., New York: Columbia University Press, 1968: 175–89.

——"Labor Skills and Comparative Advantage," *American Economic Review, Proceedings*, 56 (May 1966): 249–58.

KREININ, MORDECHAI E., "Comparative Labor Effectiveness and the Leontief Scarce-Factor Paradox," *American Economic Review*, 55 (March 1971): 126–46.

LEONTIEF, WASSILY, "Domestic Production and Foreign Trade: The American Capital Position Re-examined," Proceedings of the American Philosophical Society (September 1953); reprinted in *Readings in International Economics*, R. Caves and H. G. Johnson, eds., Homewood Ill.: Irwin, 1968.

—— "The Use of Indifference Curves in the Analysis of Foreign Trade," *Quarterly Journal of Economics* (May 1933).

MAGEE, STEPHEN P., *International Trade and Distortions in Factor Markets*, New York: Marcel Dekker, 1975.

MEADE, JAMES E., *A Geometry of International Trade*, London: Allen & Unwin, 1952.

MINHAS, B.S., "The Homohypallagic Production Function, Factor Intensity Reversals and the Heckscher-Ohlin Theorem," *Journal of Political Economy*, (April 1962).

NAYA, SEIJI, "Natural Resources, Factor Mix, and Factor Reversal in International Trade," *American Economic Review*, 57 (May 1967): 561–70.

OHLIN, BERTIL, *Interregional and International Trade*, Cambridge, Mass: Harvard University Press, 1933.

VANEK, JAROSLAV, "The Natural Resource Content of Foreign Trade, 1870–1955, and the Relative Abundance of Natural Resources in the United States,"*Review of Economics and Statistics*, 41 (May 1959): 146–53.

NOTES

1. Wassily Leontief, "Domestic Production and Foreign Trade: The American Capital Position Re-examined," *Proceedings of the American Philosophical Society*, September 1953, reprinted in *Readings in International Economics*, edited by R. Caves and H. G. Johnson, Homewood, Ill.: Irwin, 1968.

2. Leontief, op. cit. Leontief's conjecture that American labor is three times as efficient as foreign labor is questioned in Mordechai E. Kreinin, "Comparative Labor Effectiveness and the Leontief Scarce-Factor Paradox," *American Economic Review*, Vol. 55 (March 1971), pp. 126–46.

3. Jaroslav Vanek, "The Natural Resource Content of Foreign Trade, 1870–1955, and the Relative Abundance of Natural Resources in the United States," *Review of Economics and Statistics*, Vol. 41 (May 1959), pp. 146–53.

4. Stephen P. Magee, *International Trade and Distortions in Factor Markets*, New York: Marcel Dekker, 1975. Empirical tests for factor intensity reversals have included Michael Hodd, "An Empirical Investigation of the Heckscher-Ohlin Theory," *Economica*, Vol. 34 (February 1967), pp. 20–29; Seiji Naya, "Natural Resources, Factor Mix, and Factor Reversal in International Trade," *American Economic Review*, Vol. 57 (May 1967), pp. 561–70; and B. S. Minhas, "The Homohypallagic Production Function, Factor Intensity Reversals and the Heckscher-Ohlin Theorem," *Journal of Political Economy*, (April 1962).

5. Ronald Jones, "Factor Proportions and the Heckscher-Ohlin Theorem," *Review of Economic Studies*, Vol. 24 (October 1956) pp. 1–10.

6. Donald Keesing, "Labor Skills and Comparative Advantage," *American Economic Review*, Proceedings, Vol. 56 (May 1966), pp. 249–58.

7. Donald Keesing, "The Impact of Research and Development on United States Trade," in *The Open Economy: Essays on International Trade*, edited by P. B. Kenen and R. Lawrence, New York: Columbia University Press, 1968, pp. 175–89.

8. Jon Harkness and John F. Kyle, "Factors Influencing United States Comparative Advantage," *Journal of International Economics*, Vol. 5 (1975) pp. 153–165.

CHAPTER 5

The Effects of Tariffs on Trade and Relative Prices

This chapter deals exclusively with the effects of tariffs and quotas and, by analogy, other forms of trade barriers. First, general equilibrium or *mutatis mutandis* supply and demand schedules are derived from the production possibilities curve and indifference curves in order to facilitate an in-depth analysis of trade barriers. These schedules permit the description of quantity and price effects tariffs have on trade if supply and demand adjust fully. Second, a precise symmetry between tariffs and export taxes is described; this is *Lerner's Symmetry Theorem*. Third, the similarities and differences between tariffs and quotas are analyzed. Basically, in a static or unchanging world there is an exact correspondence between tariffs and quotas. However, in a world where supply or demand changes over time, tariffs and quotas have substantially different effects. Finally, this chapter addresses some related issues such as the degree of factor specificity, political pressures for tariffs, the effects of trade barriers on the trade balance, and a "Laffer Curve" for tariff revenue.

Recall from Chapter 3 that the obvious immediate effect of a trade barrier such as a tariff or quota is to retard the tendency of prices to equilibrate among countries. With these barriers, relative goods prices are no longer expected to be equal in two countries. Since arbitrage transactions are taxed by a tariff or prohibited by an import quota, arbitrage can no longer guarantee price equality. It follows that the tendency for factor prices to equalize across countries, discussed in the Factor Price Equalization Theorem, is also reduced. Unless the trade of the good which is now taxed by the tariff or quota is replaced by trade in another good or factor, factor prices should diverge more than under free trade. Trade barriers, then, move a country's consumption, production, and prices away from their free trade values and toward their autarky values.

The discussion in this chapter centers on the effects of trade barriers in a two-good, two-factor, two-country context. Again, the framework is merely an abstraction employed to illustrate basic economic principles. Richer implications could be developed in a multi-good, multi-factor, multi-country framework, but only at the cost of additional complexity. With the introduction of a tariff, the expanded model would allow for increased trade in substitute products, additional restrictive effects in complementary goods, trade in intermediate products, and a host of price changes. The model used in this chapter remains uncomplicated solely to illustrate basic economic principles. We have seen that the Factor Price Equalization Theorem illustrates a basic principle, although the assumptions underlying the theorem appear far too restrictive to approximate the world. Similarly, the principles illustrated in this chapter are far more broadly applicable than it appears from the use of an illustrative and restrictive model. The response in either framework follows La Chatelier's principle in physics: when disturbances are introduced into optimizing systems, the systems invariably attempt to adjust in the least costly fashion. Economic systems respond similarly when disturbances such as tariffs are introduced.

DERIVING *MUTATIS MUTANDIS* DEMAND
AND SUPPLY SCHEDULES

The focus now turns to what happens to the level of trade, the relative price of goods, and relative factor rewards when one country imposes a tariff of t percent on the value of its imports. Although the analysis continues within the framework of the two-country, two-goods model, as noted above, it could be expanded to include several countries or a number of commodities. The present analysis differs from many other treatments of this subject in its use of general equilibrium supply and demand curves rather than indifference curves or partial equilibrium supply and demand curves. Although general equilibrium curves are easy to use, their usefulness is not fully appreciated without a fairly complete understanding of their implications; therefore we now describe the derivation of these curves.

The general equilibrium demand and supply curves are derived directly from the indifference and production possibilities curves employed earlier. Given a set of indifference curves and a production frontier, a change in the relative price of goods simultaneously affects production, consumption, and trade. All of these responses can be summarized in the demand and supply curves.

The transformation from indifference and production possibilities curves to supply and demand curves is shown in Figure 5–1. At the initial terms of trade $(P_{B/A})_2$, domestic production just satisfies domestic demand, as shown by point A in the upper part of the graph. At point A the community indifference curve is just tangent to the production frontier. Point A is then transformed into an equivalent point on a graph which relates the relative price $P_{B/A}$ to the quantity of just good B demanded and supplied. Since the demand is just being satisfied at home at point A,

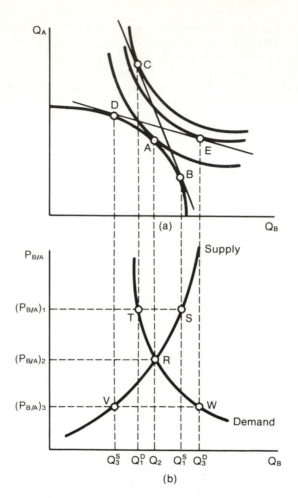

Figure 5–1   Derivation of General Equilibrium Supply and Demand Schedules

the corresponding point R in Figure 5–1(b) shows that at relative price $(P_{B/A})_2$ demand just equals supply.

If the relative price of B were higher, say $(P_{B/A})_1$, domestic production would shift toward good B, while the community would shift its consumption toward good A. The new combinations of production and consumption are described by points B and C respectively. These combinations are then translated into points S and T in Figure 5–1(b), which show the quantities of only good B supplied and demanded at price $(P_{B/A})_1$. Similarly, at a lower relative price of B, $(P_{B/A})_3$, the quantity of B demanded rises and the quantity supplied falls. The changes in demand and supply are reflected in points W and V in Figure 5–1(b).

By determining the quantities of B demanded and supplied at all possible relative prices $P_{B/A}$, the demand and supply schedules are traced.

These are not the familiar Marshallian schedules traditionally presented in textbooks. Note first that the vertical axis represents not the money price of product B, but the price of B in terms of A. Furthermore, unlike the Marshallian schedules, those in Figure 5–1(b) do not hold income constant, but rather directly embody all the effects of moving along both the production frontier and social preference patterns. The schedules therefore represent the quantities of B that are consumed or produced in general equilibrium, that is, when income and the prices of all other products are allowed to change. Because all other variables are allowed to change, these schedules are referred to as *mutatis mutandis** supply and demand schedules.

While the analysis proceeds in terms of the quantities of good B supplied and demanded at various relative prices, obviously a corresponding and consistent analysis is possible in terms of good A. Given the factor endowments and the production functions in the country, the quantity of good B produced at a particular relative price is also associated with a certain quantity of good A produced. The corresponding quantity of A can be derived from Figure 5–1(a) by examining the vertical axis at each relative price. Similarly, given the income constraint of the country at each relative price, a certain quantity of good A as well as good B corresponds to the maximum level of satisfaction of the economy. So the demand and supply curves derived for good B imply a corresponding set of curves for good A. Hence, using the supply and demand curves for either good should provide the same results.

THE EFFECTS OF A TARIFF

Assume the schedules derived in Figure 5–1(b) represent the supply and demand curves of Country I. Now assume that there exists a second country (Country II) whose supply schedule or demand schedule (or both) differs from those in Country I.** These two sets of schedules are shown in Figure 5–2.

For either country the amount of B exported or imported at a given price can be determined by the difference between supply and demand. If the supply curve lies to the right of the demand curve at a given price, more B is produced domestically than consumed, and there are units of B available for export. Alternatively, if the demand curve is to the right of supply, there is an excess demand for B at that price, and B has to be imported. Where the supply and demand schedules meet represents autarky.

---

*Literally "with the necessary changes." Marshallian schedules in contrast are drawn *ceteris paribus,* "other things being equal."

**At least one curve must differ in the two countries. If they do not, then autarky relative prices will be the same in both countries and there will be no incentive to trade, i.e., no consumption or production gains from trade.

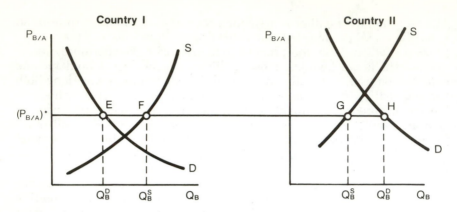

Figure 5–2   Exports and Imports under Unrestricted Trade

Since only two countries are being considered, any amount of B imported by, say, Country II must be supplied by Country I. Thus, world trade equilibrium occurs at that relative price where the quantity of B exported by one country equals the quantity of B imported by the other country. The equilibrium occurs at relative price $(P_{B/A})^*$ in Figure 5–2. Country I exports EF of B, which is equal to imports of GH in Country II.

Now suppose that Country II decides to impose an *ad valorem* tariff. An ad valorem tariff is a percentage of the value of the imported good. In this example it is assumed to equal t percent on imports of B. What effects will this tariff have? The immediate effect of the tariff is to create two separate prices for B, one for Country I, $(P_{B/A})_I$, and one for Country II $(P_{B/A})_{II}$. These two prices differ precisely by the value of the tariff. While B costs only $(P_{B/A})_I$ when it arrives on the shores of Country II, consumers within Country II have to pay a premium of t percent to purchase B in a store. The price of B in Country II is therefore

$$(P_{B/A})_{II} = (1 + t)(P_{B/A})_I. \tag{5-1}$$

The determination of the new equilibrium price in both countries is shown in Figure 5–3. The tariff drives a *wedge* equal to t percent between the prices paid in the two countries. The relative price of B is therefore forced to change in both countries. If it remained at $(P_{B/A})^*$, while Country I would still be willing to supply the quantity EF of B, Country II would demand a much smaller quantity. So the relative price of B rises in Country II and falls in Country I until the exports again equal imports. In Figure 5–3 the quantity E'F' exported at $(P_{B/A})_I$ equals the quantity G'H' imported at $(P_{B/A})_{II}$.

Figure 5–3 illustrates two effects of the tariff. First, the relative price of the taxed good rises in the importing country. Second, the level of trade in the world falls as less B is exchanged between the countries. Reduced trade implies the gains from trade are reduced.

The precise change in the relative price and the level of trade de-

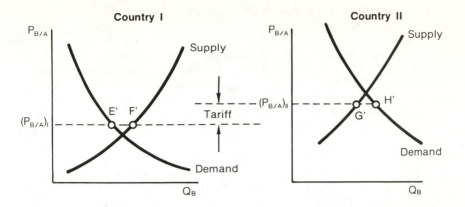

Figure 5-3   Exports and Imports with a Tariff

pends on the slopes of the supply and demand curves.* The heights of
the supply curves illustrated in Figure 5-3 represent the marginal rates of
transformation in production in each country. Thus, the slope of the supply curve corresponds to the change in price necessary to induce a
change in quantity supplied, and thus to the degree of concavity of the
production possibilities curve. The less the marginal rate of transformation in production is required to change, the less the concavity of the
production possibilities curve, and finally the more elastic (flatter) is the
supply curve. A correspondence therefore exists between the production
possibilities curve and the supply curve. Similarly, the slope of the demand curve corresponds to the slope of the community indifference
curves. The more elastic the demand curves, the less convex the indifference curves.

While the tariff affects the level of trade, it does not affect the trade
balance. The value of good A exported by Country II must still equal the
value of good B imported. In this barter model, the trade balance remains
zero. The constant zero trade balance follows from the fact that each
country's current aggregate demand is literally restricted to the value of
its current income from production. The budget constraint requires total
expenditure to equal total income. This budget constraint in turn implies
that the value of a country's exports must equal the value of its imports.
By assumption, therefore, trade must be balanced and the trade balance
must equal zero. These assumptions seem eminently reasonable, yet they
do force the result that trade barriers do not affect the trade balance.
Hence, for a tariff to have an effect on the trade balance, it must somehow affect the demand for one of the financial assets, money or bonds.
The relationships among the money, goods, and bond markets are discussed in the second section of this book.

*It also depends on how the tariff revenue collected is redistributed. For ease of exposition,
the government is assumed to dispose of the tariff revenue in some neutral fashion.

THE COSTS OF A TARIFF FOR A SMALL COUNTRY

The previous section shows in terms of *mutatis mutandis* demand and supply curves that a tariff raises the relative price of the taxed good to both consumers and producers. A tariff therefore changes both the domestic relative price in production and the domestic relative price in consumption from their free trade levels. The effects of a tariff on a small country which faces fixed foreign terms of trade are shown in Figure 5–4. The country is producing initially at point M and consuming at point P. At the initial points, the domestic and foreign relative prices are equal.

Suppose the country imposes a tariff on its imported good A. Since the small country has no power to affect the terms of trade, imposing a tariff does not affect the slope of the FF curve. But the tariff creates a wedge between the terms of trade and the domestic relative prices in production and consumption. Thus, post-tariff production moves to point N and consumption to point Q.

Notice that the tariff causes a loss of satisfaction for the community from indifference curve I to I'. This loss can be divided into the usual two

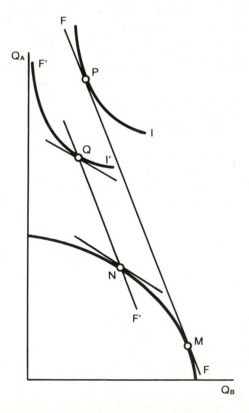

Figure 5–4   Effects of a Tariff on Production and Consumption

parts, a *production loss* and a *consumption loss*. The production loss occurs because the tariff has raised the domestic rewards for producing A above its opportunity cost in the world by raising the relative price of A in production. Domestic producers naturally switch to producing more A, since it is now more profitable for them compared with producing B. But the relative value of A in international trade has not changed, and thus the value of total domestic production is reduced on the world market.

Similarly, the rise in the domestic relative price of A causes the community to shift consumption towards B. But again there is a wedge between the domestic and world terms of trade in consumption, which means that in order to achieve a given level of satisfaction the country consumes a bundle of goods which is more expensive than necessary at world prices. Given the budget constraint of the country (either FF or F'F'), the level of satisfaction must be reduced by consuming a more expensive bundle. Thus, the second loss from the tariff is a consumption loss.*

In terms of the *mutatis mutandis* demand and supply curves, the imposition of the tariff causes the domestic relative price to rise t percent above the world terms of trade. As shown in Figure 5-5(a), this wedge produces a net loss to the economy as a whole. The wedge produces a net loss to consumers equal to the sum of areas A + B + C + D. This sum represents a loss of *consumer surplus*. Before the tariff, consumers purchased D_0 of good A at the world terms of trade. After the tariff is imposed, they purchased only D_1 at t percent above the world price. Two losses of welfare occur. One, represented by areas A + B + C, is the fact that consumers pay a higher price for D_1 units they previously purchased. Consumers were willing to pay up to $(1+t)(P_{A/B})_0$ for D_1 units before, but only had to pay $(P_{A/B})_0$. Their satisfaction from the D_1 units exceeded the price. The excess of satisfaction over price is consumer surplus. But at the tariff-inclusive price, the difference between satisfaction and price is less. In fact, the satisfaction from the last of the D_1 units just equals the price. Consumer surplus is reduced.

Second, all the consumer surplus on the D_0–D_1 units no longer consumed is lost. This loss is the area D. At price $(P_{A/B})_0$, the satisfaction on each of the D_0–D_1 units equaled or exceeded the price. But the satisfaction on these units was also less than $(1+t)(P_{A/B})_0$. So when the tariff is applied, these units are no longer consumed. Consumer surplus falls by area D.

The rise in price does raise *producer surplus*. Producers, who initially received $(P_{A/B})_0$ on the initial S_0 units produced, now receive t percent more on those units. In addition, they now produce an additional S_1–S_0 units whose cost of production is less than or equal to the tariff-inclusive price. The total gain to producers is the area A.

---

*We are assuming that the proceeds of the tariffs are redistributed back to the economy by the government in a neutral fashion. We are also analyzing the effects of tariffs within the conventional fixed factor endowments model. We have ignored the effects of changing marginal factor rewards on total factor supplies.

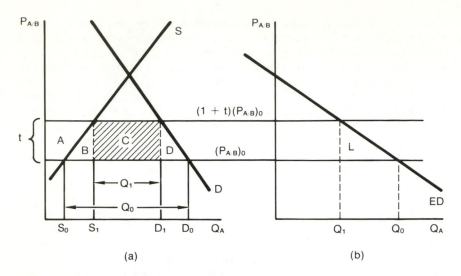

Figure 5-5   The Production and Consumption Distortions of a Tariff in Terms of *Mutatis Mutandis* Demand and Supply Curves

The area C represents tariff revenue collected on the remaining $D_1 - S_1 = Q_1$ units of imports. These revenues of the government are assumed to be returned to the private sector in some neutral fashion.

What are the net losses to society? Consumers lose A + B + C + D. Producers gain area A, offsetting some of the loss. In addition, the tariff revenue, equal to area C, is returned to the private sector. The remaining losses equal areas B + D. This sum is the loss from imposing the tariff.*

Alternatively, subtracting the level of supply at each relative price in Figure 5-5(a) from the level of demand at each price yields the excess demand curve for the country shown in Figure 5-5(b). Again the tariff causes the domestic relative price to rise by t percent, the quantity imported to fall from Q_0 to Q_1, and a loss of domestic welfare equal to the triangle L. The area of that triangle L in 5-5(b) is simply the sum of the triangle distortions B + D in 5-5(a).

The above analysis illustrates an important theorem about tariffs: *a small country which has no power to affect the terms of trade is always economically worse off by imposing a tariff.* Since a small country's tariff cannot be justified on economic efficiency grounds, these tariffs must be

---

*Figure 5-4 shows both a production and consumption loss from the tariff, while Figure 5-5 shows only a net consumption loss. The reason is that Figure 5-4 considers both goods A and B simultaneously, while Figure 5-5 considers only good A. If good B were considered in terms of *mutatis mutandis* demand and supply curves, a net production loss could be shown. A tariff lowers the domestic relative price of the exported good B. The lower relative price reduces producer surplus, but raises consumer surplus. A diagram similar to Figure 5-5 would show that the loss in producer surplus exceeds the gain in consumer surplus. Thus, considering the demand and supply curves together yields both the production loss and consumption loss shown in Figure 5-4. The loss measured in either good, however, is the same and equal to the area B + D in Figure 5-5(a).

imposed for other reasons. Presumably the tariffs are imposed as part of an international or domestic political goal, such as appeasing a very vocal domestic pressure group. The appeasement is not achieved, however, without a cost to the economy as a whole.

THE LERNER SYMMETRY THEOREM

An interesting relationship between import tariffs and exports taxes has been described by Abba Lerner.[1] Professor Lerner showed how the same level of trade could be achieved by an equivalent tariff or export tax. For example, consider the t percent tariff in Figure 5-3. The tariff imposed by Country II causes the relative price of B to be higher in Country II than in Country I and the level of imports to fall to G'H'. The same result could be achieved alternatively by Country II imposing instead a t percent tax on its exports of A. By having Country II impose both taxes the revenues accrue to the same entities. Symmetry, of course, requires that the revenues accrue to the same entities.

Consider first the price effect of the tax. Taxing exports raises the price of A to Country I and causes the relative price of A in terms of B, $P_{A/B}$, to be higher there. If $P_{A/B}$ is higher in Country I, then the price of B in terms of A must be lower. Thus, the final price effect is the same as in Figure 5-3 with a lower $P_{B/A}$ in Country I than in Country II. Equation (5-1) becomes

$$(P_{A/B})_I = (1 + t)(P_{A/B})_{II} \qquad (5\text{-}2)$$

where t now represents an export tariff of t percent. Since neither demand nor supply curves have changed, with a t percent wedge between relative prices, Country II must again be importing G'H' of B.

A third possibility is that Country I imposes the tax instead of Country II. For example, suppose Country I imposes a tariff of t percent on A. Again a wedge of t percent is created between domestic and foreign prices. With only two goods and one relative price, again the relative price of B is lower in Country I. In fact, this situation is also described by equation (5-2), but now t represents the tariff. The equilibrium relative price and level of imports must be the same as before. The only difference is that Country I now receives the tax revenue instead of Country II. In a similar way it can be shown that these taxes are also equivalent to Country I imposing an export tax.

TARIFFS AND QUOTAS AS ALTERNATIVES

In the case of any economic restriction, there is usually a choice between a price restriction and a quantity restriction. In the case of trade, a *tariff* is the price restriction, and a *quota* is the quantity restriction. A tariff drives a wedge between the world price of a good and its domestic price, while a quota drives a wedge between the quantity that can be supplied from abroad and the quantity demanded. Both policies raise the domestic price of the protected good, increase its domestic production, and reduce the quantity consumed domestically. A tariff produces these effects directly by raising the price, while a quota accomplishes the same effects by setting a ceiling on the quantity of the commodity that can be imported.

In a static economy where the demand and supply curves remain constant, it is always possible to find a quota whose effects now and in the future are precisely identical to those of any given tariff. However, such a static world is quite unrealistic. Over time, the demand curve, the production possibilities curve, or both may fluctuate, implying different patterns of price and quantity movements under initially equivalent tariffs and quotas.

It is important to understand the effects of both tariffs and quotas in a changing economy. An analysis of the differences is presented after a brief discussion of the specifics of the quota. In order to highlight the price and quantity differences, it is assumed that the quota privileges are auctioned to the highest bidders. Although such auctioning occurs rarely, this assumption permits us to ignore the different income effects and distribution effects associated with the proceeds of the tariff. Later these differences are discussed explicitly.

The Equivalence of a Tariff and a Quota in a Static World

The equivalence of a tariff and quota where demand and supply conditions do not change over time can be easily shown. Consider the tariff imposed by Country II in Figure 5-3 on the importation of good B. The tariff raises the domestic relative price of good B, reduces imports to G'H' and lowers the world relative price of B (improves the country's terms of trade). The higher the tariff rate t, the higher the domestic relative price, the lower the level of imports and the more the country's terms of trade improve. These relationships continue until a tariff is reached at which good B is no longer imported. At this *prohibitive* tariff, trade ceases, and the country returns to autarky.

Similarly, the country could choose a quota which yields exactly the same results. For example, instead of the tariff t in Figure 5-3, the country could have simply instituted a quota equal to G'H' of good B. Again, the domestic relative price of B would have risen to $(P_{B/A})_{II}$, and the country's terms of trade would have improved to $(P_{B/A})_I$. Further lowering the quota produces the same results as raising the tariff. The lower the quota, the higher the domestic relative price of good B, the less of good B that can be imported, and the more the country's terms of trade improve. And just as there is a prohibitive tariff, there is an equivalent prohibitive quota. The prohibitive quota is simply where no units of good B are permitted to be imported. The country again returns to autarky and the domestic relative price of B is the same autarkic price as with the prohibitive tariff.

The Effects of Tariffs and Quotas in a Changing World

While there is always an equivalent tariff and quota in a static world, differences between tariffs and quotas arise where income, tastes, and technology change frequently. Under these circumstances, a quota insulates domestic markets from world markets more than a tariff does. The constant quantity of imports is the only link between the domestic markets and the outside world. A surge or decline in domestic demand must be relieved through domestic price and quantity adjustments. Domestic price fluctuations therefore do not coincide with world price fluctuations. Tariffs, on the other hand, maintain a constant ratio between domestic and foreign prices. A surge or decline in domestic demand can be relieved, in part, through an adjustment in the level of trade. Domestic price fluctuations coincide with foreign price fluctuations when there are tariffs. Thus, the degree of reliance on foreign markets responds to changing economic conditions. In summary, when demand and supply curves are deterministic or known with certainty, quotas have tariffs as precise equivalents. Under stochastic or changing conditions, quotas insulate the country from the rest of the world while tariffs integrate the markets.

As an example of how quotas and tariffs may differ where there is change over time, consider the effect of a supply curve that is shifting to the left over time. For example, suppose that due to the lack of reinvestment, the U.S. steel industry is expected to become less and less efficient over time, while foreign steel producers maintain their current level of efficiency. This example is illustrated in Figure 5–6(a). For simplicity the diagram assumes a small country case, since the foreign price is not affected by domestic supply and demand. Initially the U.S. places a tariff of t percent or an equivalent quota of G'H' on steel imports. With either import restriction, the domestic price of steel equals $P_f(1+t)$, where P_f is the foreign price of steel, and imports equal G'H'. So both import re-

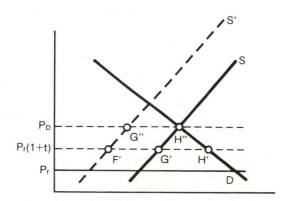

Figure 5–6(a)   The Nonequivalence of Tariffs and Quotas with Increasingly Inefficient Production

strictions help the domestic production of steel by raising the domestic price of steel above the world price.

However, while the effects of the two restrictions are initially the same, over time the effects diverge. With a tariff, the difference between the domestic and world price of steel, and thus the degree of assistance, remains constant over time. As the domestic supply curve shifts to the left, the world price remains P_f and the domestic price remains $P_f(1+t)$. The country responds to the changing supply conditions by simply importing more steel as production falls. Hence in Figure 5–6(a), when the supply curve shifts from S to S', under a tariff, imports increase from G'H' to F'H'.

However, with a quota, as domestic costs rise, additional tons of steel cannot be imported to replace domestic steel. Therefore, in order to obtain given amounts of steel, domestic consumers have to pay higher and higher prices. Thus, over time, the difference between the domestic and world prices of steel becomes larger and larger. In Figure 5–6(a), as the supply curve shifts from S to S' and the quota remains at G'H' = G''H'', the domestic price of steel rises to P_D. As the price divergence increases over time, so does the implicit subsidy to the steel industry, and, as is discussed in the next chapter, so do the resulting inefficiencies.

Where an industry is becoming increasingly inefficient, a tariff provides more incentive for the industry eventually to phase out of production. A quota, with its ever increasing assistance, provides no incentive for the inefficient industry to stop production. If, on the other hand, the U.S. steel industry were becoming more and more efficient relative to the foreign competition, just the opposite conclusion would hold. Increasing efficiency is represented by a rightward shift in the supply curve over time. Under a tariff, as the supply curve shifts to the right, the domestic price of steel still remains at $P_f(1+t)$. The assistance to domestic producers remains constant at tP_f. But since domestic producers are becoming more and more efficient, they are willing to supply more and more steel at the subsidized price, and the level of imports falls. Alternatively, under a quota, as domestic producers supply more and more steel at prevailing prices, the increase in supply relative to demand causes the domestic price of steel to fall. The divergence between domestic and world steel prices is diminished, which in turn implies that the subsidy to the increasingly efficient industry is reduced. Thus, with increasing efficiency, a quota is preferable to a tariff since the quota automatically leads to phasing out the eventually unnecessary subsidy.

If the demand curve is shifting over time, a tariff is preferable for a rightward shift and a quota is preferable for a leftward shift. For example, if income in the country grows over time, demand will increase and the demand curve will shift to the right. The demand curve shifts to the right because demand is increasing, say, because income in the country is growing over time. This case is illustrated in Figure 5–6(b). Initially the country has a tariff of t percent or the equivalent quota equal to EF. If the country maintains a quota equal to the initial level of imports, as demand rises the domestic price of steel also rises. When the demand curve shifts

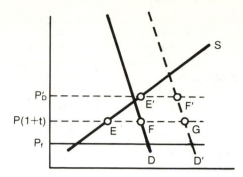

Figure 5–6(b)   **The Nonequivalence of a Tariff and Quota as Domestic Demand Increases**

to D′ in Figure 5–6(b), if the country continues to import only E′F′ = EF, the domestic price of steel rises to P'_D. The reason for the price rise is quite obvious. The domestic demand for steel rises, yet only the constant amount of the domestic demand E′F′ can be satisfied by foreign supply. All additional demand must therefore be satisfied by coaxing domestic producers to increase their supplies of steel. But domestic production will increase only if the domestic price rises.

Alternatively under a tariff, the additional demand for steel can be satisfied simply by importing more from abroad. There is no reason for the domestic price of steel to rise. By this same reasoning it follows that with a leftward shift or decrease in demand, a quota is preferable to a tariff. With a tariff, the degree of protection to an industry whose products are demanded less and less remains at a constant level. However, with a constant quantity of steel imports, as demand for steel falls, the domestic price of steel falls, and thus the artificial assistance to the industry falls. The quota, therefore, provides an incentive for phasing out an industry whose product faces declining demand.

TARIFF VERSUS QUOTA—
SOME OTHER CONSIDERATIONS

Since either form of import restriction artificially raises the domestic price of the protected good and thus provides a subsidy to the protected industry, it is not surprising that the industry would favor protection. However, the choice between a tariff and a quota may be almost as important to an industry as the overall question of import restrictions. This is especially true for an industry which finds its relative position in the world changing over time.

For example, in the previous section the steel industry found itself becoming less and less efficient relative to its foreign competitiors. Thus a subsidy large enough to allow the industry to compete with foreign imports this year will not be large enough in the future. As shown in the previous section, this is at least part of the reason that in recent years the steel industry in the United States initially favored import quotas against steel products from Japan, but settled for a "trigger price" mechanism based on the cost of production rather than a simple ad valorem tariff.

The choice of a quota versus a tariff is also important to three other groups: domestic importers, foreign exporters, and the government. Under a tariff, all revenue from the wedge imposed on imports accrues to the government. However, under a quota, the equivalent revenue could accrue to any one of the three groups, depending upon how the quota is administered. For example, if rights to import the limited quantities are given to domestic importers, this group receives benefits from the restriction. In this case, the importer buys the protected good at the world price, yet sells the good at the same higher price as the domestic producers. The difference in price is additional revenue for the importer. Thus, a quota represents more profit to the importer than does the equivalent tariff.

Alternatively, as occurred in 1977 in the case of color televisions from Japan or earlier in beef quotas, the U.S. could instruct the foreign country simply to limit its exports to the U.S. In this case, foreigners must decide how to distribute the limited rights to sell goods in the United States. Those fortunate foreigners who receive these rights reap benefits from the export quota. Since foreigners receive the benefits, this case is equivalent to foreigners imposing tariffs on the U.S.

Finally, the United States government could choose to implement the quota by auctioning off import rights to the highest bidder. Competition for the import rights would then drive down the net profits of domestic importers or foreign exporters until they were the same as in the absence of the quota. The government's total revenues from this policy should be approximately equal to the revenues from imposing the equivalent tariff.

POLITICAL PRESSURES FOR TRADE RESTRICTIONS—THE SPECIFICITY OF FACTORS

A question related to the economics of trade restrictions is what political pressures for and against protection can be expected from various economic groups. While the tariff versus quota considerations remain pertinent, the discussion of pressures for trade protection in this section will be in terms of tariffs.

In the closing discussion in Chapter 4 of the Stolper-Samuelson and Factor Price Equalization Theorems, it was stated that for the country as a whole, pressure for tariffs will tend to come from groups representing the factor used relatively intensively in the good for which the country does not have a comparative advantage. For example, suppose the United States has a comparative advantage in capital-intensive goods. Free trade raises the relative price of these goods, benefiting capital at the expense of labor. Imposition of a tariff, however, would then raise the do-

mestic relative price of the imported good and thus the price of domestic import-competing goods. From the Stolper-Samuelson Theorem, the factor used intensively in the production of the import-competing good benefits when the relative price of that good rises. So in this example, the imposition of a tariff benefits labor which is used relatively intensively in the import-competing good.

The argument that labor favors tariffs has been made in terms of the country as a whole. However, a similar argument can be made at the industry level as well. For example, if the shoe industry is relatively labor intensive, then from the Stolper-Samuelson Theorem, labor is expected to favor shoe tariffs and owners of capital are expected to oppose the tariffs. A tariff raises the relative price of shoes, benefiting the intensive factor labor at the expense of capital.

Yet, while at both levels basic economic theory predicts that the owners of capital will oppose tariffs, it is not uncommon to find the owners of shoe factories or steel mills lobbying for restrictions against competing imports. How can this paradoxical behavior be reconciled with the economic theory? The answer lies in the concept of *factor specificity*.[2]

Until this point it has been assumed that factors of production are freely mobile among industries. In other words, it is assumed that a worker in a shoe factory or steel mill can easily switch to being an autoworker or a farmer, or that a shoe stitching machine or blast furnace can be easily transformed into an autombile stamping machine or farm machinery. Obviously such an assumption may not be plausible in the short run. In the short run both capital and labor may tend to be specific to particular uses.

Consider the case where in the short run capital cannot be transferred at all between industries A and B. Labor, however, is still completely mobile between the two industries. The model of trade now contains three distinct factors of production: labor and capital in industry A, and capital in industry B. Because labor is still mobile between the two industries, labor still receives the same wage (equal to its marginal product) in both industries. However, there is no longer any force to equate the returns to capital in the two industries, since capital can no longer move from one industry to the other. Thus, it is quite likely that the returns to capital in the two industries will differ and move in opposite directions when relative prices change.

How are the returns to capital in the two industries expected to change? The returns to capital in a specific industry are expected to be positively related to the relative price of the output. When the price of the output rises, the returns to capital in that industry rise, and when prices fall, so do the rental rates. Recall from the discussion of the production function in Chapter 2 that the scarceness of resources makes final products scarce. Thus, the demand for factors is a *derived demand*, that is, derived from the fact that people demand the products the factors produce. When a particular product, for example automobiles, is suddenly in heavy demand, the factors of production that make automobiles are also in heavy demand. Alternatively, if OPEC (Oil Producing and Exporting Countries) again cuts off the supply of oil and the demand for automobiles falls, then factors used in automobile production will find the demand for their services falling.

However, when the demand for automobiles falls, which factor's return will fall by more, the return to capital which is specific to the industry or the return to labor which can move between industries? The answer lies in the fact that labor has a "safety valve" and capital does not. Thus, when the demand for automobiles falls, labor can migrate to other industries, but in the short run, capital cannot. Because of competition for the labor, labor in the automobile industry continues to receive the same wage that it would in other industries. The returns to labor are therefore not expected to fall very much. However, most of the capital is specific to the automobile industry even if the automobile industry goes completely out of business. The specific capital earns economic rents whose size varies positively with automobile demand. When automobile demand falls, the returns to capital are therefore expected to fall by much more than the returns to labor. Conversely, if demand for automobiles should suddenly experience a rise, the owners of capital would probably gain more than the autoworkers. A premium will be paid for automobiles, and that premium will tend to accrue to the factor specific to the industry in the form of an economic rent. Thus, the returns to capital will tend to rise and fall with the relative price of automobiles.

Returning to the original question, factor specificity can explain why the owners of capital in the shoe industry favor import restrictions on shoes, even though the United States has a comparative advantage in capital-intensive goods and shoe production is relatively labor intensive. Since much of the capital employed in the shoe industry is specific to producing shoes, the capital cannot easily move to another industry. Thus, the assumption of the basic trade model that factors are mobile among industries is violated at least in the short run. There is now an industry specific factor whose return rises and falls with the relative price of shoes. The owners of this factor (the factory owners), interested in protecting their investment, therefore favor protective legislation which causes the relative price of shoes to rise.

IMPORT RESTRICTIONS AND THE TRADE BALANCE

One argument repeatedly used to support the concept of import restrictions is that they improve a country's trade position. If a tariff is imposed, the domestic price of imported goods rises, and domestic consumers substitute domestically produced goods for the foreign imports. If a quota is imposed, there are simply fewer foreign goods permitted into the country. So either policy reduces imports, and, by changing the composition of current period consumption and production, supposedly improves the trade balance. This reasoning, however, neglects two important facts:

a. The trade balance is the difference between the level of exports and the level of imports, and if one component is affected the other component is usually affected as well;

b. resources are often mobile between industries, permitting changes in the quantities of imported or exported goods produced in the domestic country.

Thus, while an import restriction reduces the quantity of imports, it simultaneously reduces the quantity of exports. In general, a restriction is expected to reduce both exports and imports by the same amount, and no change in the trade balance will be observed. This is directly implied by Lerner's Symmetry Theorem. If a tax on imports is expected to improve the trade balance, a tax on exports should worsen the balance. But as shown by Lerner's Symmetry Theorem, the effects of the two taxes are equivalent. Obviously there is no reason on the grounds of consumption or production switching to expect tariffs always to improve the trade balance.

For example, in 1977 the United States negotiated an "orderly market agreement" restricting the number of assembled color television sets that could be imported from Japan. This restriction was expected to reduce United States imports and simultaneously increase the quantity of color television sets assembled in the United States. But in order to increase the domestic production of television sets, resources that could be used to produce other goods must be attracted into television production. Labor, capital, and components which could be used to produce radios, phonographs, black and white televisions, computers, or similar products are now used to produce color televisions. Naturally, with these resources being used for color televisions, the domestic production of these other goods must decrease. Given the domestic demand for these other goods, the lower domestic production means fewer of these goods are available for export or more have to be imported. So while the imports of color televisions may decline, the competition for resources means that the imports of some other goods are rising and the exports of still others are falling, eliminating any anticipated improvement in the trade balance.

An opposite process occurs in Japan. With the United States trade restriction, the production of Japanese color televisions declines. However, this decline in television production releases resources for other types of production. Thus, Japanese production of radios, phonographs, video recorders, and black and white televisions should be increasing. Given the Japanese demand for these products, the increased production means that more of these alternative goods are available for export.

This shifting of resources in the two countries makes plausible the sharp rise in the export of radio, stereo, video recorders, picture tubes, and other electronic equipment from Japan to the United States during 1977 and 1978. The Japanese simply substituted other products for the color televisions that could no longer be exported, and little if any change in the overall trade balance resulted from the import restriction. Obviously policies which attempt to affect the current period composition of consumption and production of traded goods should have little effect on the trade balance. Instead, as described in Chapters 8 and 14, changes in a country's overall trade balance are related to factors which affect the current aggregate level of expenditure relative to current aggregate income (borrowing and lending), such as the relative change in a country's rate of income growth. Furthermore, a nonzero trade balance involves exchanging goods for financial assets, such as money or bonds, which are introduced in the second section of the book.

TARIFFS AND THE LAFFER CURVE

As will be described in Chapter 8, the *Laffer Curve* is usually employed to show the relationship between marginal income tax rates in an economy and the amount of income tax revenue the government actually receives. The basic concept underlying the Laffer Curve is that the higher are *marginal* tax rates, the more incentive individuals have to avoid them. In the case of income taxes, paying taxes can be avoided by such methods as working in the *underground* economy instead of in the marketplace, putting capital in tax shelters, paying accountants and lawyers to prepare tax returns, and working fewer hours in a market job in order to spend more time at home personally producing one's desired services. In addition to reducing tax revenues, these activities also imply economically inefficient uses of resources which reduce the country's output.

The same concept of the relationship between tax rates and tax revenues can also be applied to tariffs. A Laffer Curve for tariffs is shown in Figure 5–7. A characteristic of any Laffer Curve is that there are two tax rates at which the government's tax revenues are zero. One tax rate is zero percent. In other words, if the government applies no tariff, it receives no tariff revenue. The other tax rate is the prohibitive tariff. At this sufficiently high tax rate, no goods are imported, so no tariff revenues are collected. In between these rates, tariff revenues are positive.

As tariff rates rise above zero percent, tariff revenues initially increase, peak, and then decline. Why does the decline occur? The simple answer is that tariff revenues are the product of two factors, the tax rate and the quantity of imports. As tariff rates are increased, the amount of revenue received from a constant amount of taxable imports increases. But typically, as tariffs rise, taxable imports do not remain constant. The private sector begins to find ways to avoid the tariff.

One way to avoid the tariff is, of course, to substitute domestically produced goods for imports. The higher the tariff, the higher the domestic relative price of importables, and the more attractive domestic import-competing goods become. Fewer goods are imported (and exported), and tariff revenues fall. Another way to avoid tariffs is again to hire accountants and lawyers to investigate how to exempt imports from particular customs duties. The higher the duties, the more incentives to employ these specialists. A third way to avoid tariffs is to engage in underground economy activities. In the case of imports, the underground economy involves exchanging goods with foreigners outside the marketplace—smug-

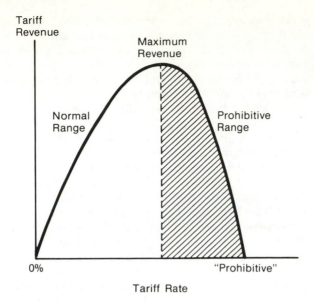

Figure 5-7   A Laffer Curve for Tariff Revenue

gling. There are numerous historical accounts of how countries have responded to higher tariffs with increased smuggling. For example, in pre-Revolution America, colonists responded to higher tariffs on English tea by smuggling more tea from Dutch traders.

These reactions have not gone unnoticed by economists. Observing the eighteenth-century world, Adam Smith could not have been more explicit in *The Wealth of Nations*:

> High taxes, sometimes by diminishing the consumption of the taxed com-
> modities, and sometimes by encouraging smuggling, frequently afford a
> smaller revenue to government than what might be drawn from more mod-
> erate taxes.[3]

The point is clear. The higher the tariff rate, the lower the level of imports qualifying for customs duties. While higher tariffs initially raise tariff revenues, at some point the *prohibitive range* is reached. Within that range, higher tariff rates are associated with even larger percentage declines in taxable imports. Total tariff revenue declines.

SUMMARY

Mutatis mutandis, or general equilibrium, demand and supply curves of a country are derived directly from the indifference and production pos-sibilities curves of the country. They show how demand and supply for a particular good respond to changes in relative prices, when income and the prices of all other products are allowed to change.

A tariff is a tax which drives a *wedge* between prices paid in two countries. Tariffs therefore retard the tendency for prices to equilibrate among countries. An import tariff imposed by a large country turns the world terms of trade against the imported good.

By creating a wedge between domestic and foreign relative prices, a tariff reduces the gains from trade. This welfare loss can be partitioned into a *production loss* and a *consumption loss*. A small country experiences these losses without any improvement in its terms of trade. A tariff therefore always reduces the welfare of a small country.

Lerner's Symmetry Theorem describes how a tariff in a country has effects on relative prices and the level of trade equivalent to those of an export tax. It can also be shown that in a static economy there is a unique quota which corresponds to any tariff. In a changing economy, however, demand and supply curves shift over time, and initially similar tariffs and quotas eventually have different effects.

Political pressure for protection often comes from the factor used intensively in an industry, and is opposed by the other factor. Where factors are specific to a given industry, however, both factors may support protection for that industry.

When all markets are allowed to adjust, an import restriction should not be expected to improve a country's trade balance. Also, raising tariff rates may not increase tariff revenues, as the private sector begins to find ways to avoid the tariff. The relationship between tariff rates and tariff revenues can be summarized in a *Laffer Curve*.

REFERENCES

BHAGWATI, JAGDISH, "On the Equivalence of Tariffs and Quotas," Chapter 9 in his *Trade, Tariffs and Growth*, Cambridge, Mass: MIT Press, 1969.

JOHNSON, HARRY G., *Aspects of the Theory of Tariffs*, Cambridge, Mass: Harvard University Press, 1972.

LERNER, ABBA P., "The Symmetry Between Import and Export Taxes," *Economica* 3, No. 11 (August 1936): 306–13; reprinted in R. Caves and H.G. Johnson, eds., *Readings in International Economics*, Homewood, Ill.: Irwin, 1968.

METZLER, LLOYD, "Tariffs, the Terms of Trade, and the Distribution of National Income," *Journal of Political Economy*, 57 (February 1949): 1–29; reprinted in Caves and Johnson, *Readings in International Economics*.

MUSSA, MICHAEL, "Tariffs and the Distribution of Income: The Importance of Factor Specificity, Substitutability and Intensity in the Short and Long Run," *Journal of Political Economy*, 82, No. 5 (November/December 1974): 1191–1203.

STOLPER, WOLFGANG F. and PAUL A. SAMUELSON, "Protection and Real Wages," *Review of Economic Studies*, 9 (November 1941): 58–73; reprinted in American Economic Association, *Readings in the Theory of International Trade*, Philadelphia: Blakiston, 1949.

NOTES

1. Abba Lerner, "The Symmetry Between Import and Export Taxes," Vol. 3, No. 11 (August 1936): pp. 306–13, reprinted in *Readings in International Economics*, edited by R. E. Caves and H. G. Johnson, Homewood, Illinois: Irwin, 1968: pp. 197–203.

2. See for example, Michael Mussa, "Tariffs and the Distribution of Income: The Importance of Factor Specificity, Substitutability and Intensity in the Short and Long Run," *Journal of Political Economy*, Vol. 82, No. 5 (November/December 1974): pp. 1191–1203.

3. Adam Smith, *The Wealth of Nations*, Book 5, Chapter 2.

CHAPTER 6

Trade Barriers and Alternatives: Policy Interventions to Correct Distortions

Chapters 4 and 5 dealt with the effects of opening a country to free trade and how imposing trade barriers alters free trade relative prices, the level of trade, and welfare. Under free trade a country exchanges goods in the world market in order to maximize utility. As shown in Figure 4–2, the country shifts production along the production possibilities curve until the marginal rate of transformation in production equals the world terms of trade. Given factor endowments this shift in production maximizes income at the world terms of trade. The country also shifts consumption along the budget constraint until the marginal rate of substitution in consumption equals the terms of trade. The community's production frontier and indifference curve are then both tangent to the budget constraint line which has the terms of trade as its slope. The highest possible level of satisfaction has been reached.

Conditions can arise, however, in which this *Pareto optimal* position cannot be reached by free trade alone. Distortions can exist which keep the economy from reaching the maximum potential output or satisfaction through normal market transactions. This chapter enumerates several possible distortions and discusses optimal methods for their removal. The optimal policy for dealing with a distortion will always be defined as that policy which allows the economy to attain the highest level of satisfaction. A major conclusion of the analysis is that despite the distortion involving traded goods, a trade barrier is usually not the optimal policy.

TYPES OF DISTORTIONS

Before analyzing distortions directly, we must define certain terms. In the following sections, all price ratios are referred to as terms of trade, but we no longer refer generally to the terms of trade without qualification. The rate at which goods may be exchanged domestically in production (the marginal rate of transformation in production) is referred to as the *terms of trade in production,* or TTP. The rate at which goods may be exchanged domestically in consumption (the marginal rate of substitution in consumption) is referred to as the *terms of trade in consumption,* or TTC. Finally, the rate at which goods may be exchanged through international trade is referred to as the *foreign terms of trade,* or FTT.

Following Bhagwati, et al,[1] possible distortions can be summarized into three categories: production distortions, consumption distortions and trade distortions. A *production distortion* results when the marginal cost to individuals of producing a good differs from the marginal cost to society. In terms of the current set of abbreviations, TTP $\neq$ FTT = TTC.

One such production distortion is shown in Figure 6–1. There the community continues to maximize satisfaction given the consumption constraint by trading until the foreign terms of trade line FF is tangent to a community indifference curve at point R (FTT = TTC). Notice, however, that the line is not tangent to the country's production possibilities curve, but rather crosses it at point S. The production possibilities curve here measures the relative cost of production from society's viewpoint. At point S the true terms of trade in production for society are DD, but individuals can achieve only FF through the marketplace. The angle between DD and FF therefore measures the rate of distortion in production.

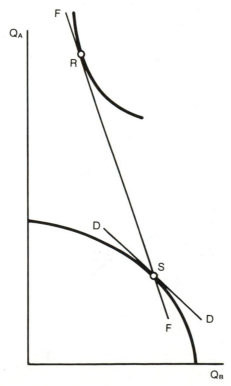

Figure 6–1   A Production Distortion

A production distortion occurs where production of a particular good is accompanied by negative externalities. For instance, if the production of good A illustrated in Figure 6–1 creates pollution which harms society, but is imperceptible to individual producers, the total cost of producing another unit of good A is higher to society than to private producers. Positive externalities are also a possibility. If there are economies of scale in industry B, then the cost falls as output increases. The reduction in cost to a single producer, however, may be small. If one producer increases production, the costs to him and every other producer are reduced. In other words the producer confers benefits on other producers. Thus, the marginal cost of producing B is perceived to be represented by FF to the individual producer, when in fact it is DD.

If there is a *consumption distortion*, the terms of trade in consumption to the community differ from the rate at which goods can be exchanged in the world market, that is, TTC ≠ FTT = TTP. Such a distortion is illustrated in Figure 6–2. In this graph the indifference curves represent preferences from the viewpoint of the country as a whole. Again the country faces the foreign terms of trade line FF. Production occurs at point G where FTT = TTP, but consumption occurs at point H where FF is not tangent to the community indifference curve. The reason for con-

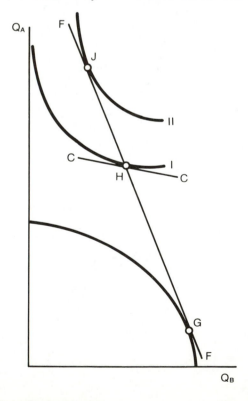

Figure 6–2   A Consumption Distortion

suming at point H is that the price ratio facing the community as a whole differs from the relative value to individuals.

A pollution example again clarifies the distinction. Suppose that good B in Figure 6-2 is leaded gasoline. People can purchase this gasoline under free trade for the relative price $P_{B/A}$ implicit in line FF. But leaded gasoline is known to produce hydrocarbons which in turn cause air pollution and raise the cost of consumption to the community. Thus good B has a lower relative value to society than is reflected in $P_{B/A}$. The value is now the resource cost $P_{B/A}$ minus the air pollution, which together equal $P'_{B/A}$, the relative value implicit in line CC. Notice that because the market price differs from the value to the community, the economy as a whole is below its potential satisfaction level. If the two prices were equalized, the community could reach indifference curve II at point J.

A *trade distortion* is just a combination of both production and consumption distortions. In this case the distortion drives a wedge between the free trade price and the domestic prices in production and consumption, that is, FTT $\neq$ TTP = TTC. An example of a trade distortion is a country which has market power in its export good, as considered in the following section.

THE EFFECTS OF TARIFFS
IN A LARGE COUNTRY

Chapter 5 illustrated an important theorem about tariffs: a small country that has no power to affect the foreign terms of trade is always economically worse off by imposing a tariff. But if a country is worse off with a tariff, why should any country use one? The economic answer lies in the phrase "no power to affect the foreign terms of trade." Recall that in the two-country analysis in Figure 5-2 and 5-3 in Chapter 5, when Country II imposes the tariff the foreign terms of trade change from $(P_{B/A})^*$ to $(P_{B/A})_I$. The reason is that Countries I and II are considered to be similar in size and thus neither can be considered a "small" country. When Country II undertakes a policy such as imposing tariffs, its effects are definitely felt in Country I. While a small country also affects the rest of the world when it imposes a tariff, the effects are so minute that they can be ignored.

The remaining question is to what extent and under what conditions should "large" countries (which are assumed capable of affecting the foreign terms of trade) impose tariffs. *Market power* in a good is what allows a country to affect its terms of trade and make its export good worth relatively more. By raising the relative price of the export good, the country can now consume more imports per good exported. But even countries with this market power suffer the same potential production and consumption losses as the small country. The tariff still creates the wedge in consumption and production. Imposing a tariff therefore makes economic sense only to the extent the gains from changes in the terms of trade outweigh the production and consumption losses.

Such a situation is depicted in Figure 6–3. Initial production and consumption occur at points P and C where the foreign and domestic terms of trade in production and consumption are equal. When the tariff is imposed on the imported good A, a wedge is driven between the foreign terms of trade and the terms of trade in production and consumption. If the foreign terms of trade did not change, production and consumption would move to points P″ and C″, and the level of satisfaction of the community would fall from curve II to I. But because the country has market power in its export good,* the tariff causes a rise in the foreign relative price of that good. The foreign terms of trade line rotates clockwise to F′F′, and production and consumption move to points P′ and C′. In the particular example shown, the terms of trade improve sufficiently to more than offset the production and consumption losses. The level of satisfaction of the community is III compared to II before the imposition of the tariff.

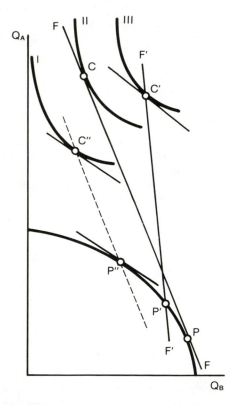

Figure 6–3   Effects of a Tariff on Production and Consumption in a Country with Monopoly Power in Its Export Good

*A country which has market power in its export good also has market power with respect to its imported good. Thus the country can achieve the same economic objectives through either an import tariff or export tax, as Lerner's Symmetry Theorem would imply.

Of course, to the extent that the potential retaliation of other countries against the imposition of a tariff is not accounted for in the change in the world terms of trade, these conclusions are misleading. If other countries respond to the imposition of the domestic tariff by imposing a tariff of their own, the terms of trade deteriorate for the domestic country, and the net gain to the domestic country may disappear. The domestic country may then choose to retaliate for the second tariff, and so on. While one country may end up benefiting relative to its trading partners from the tariffs, with each successive tariff, the level of trade in the world falls.

The discussion of whether a tariff increases the satisfaction level of an individual country is known in the international trade literature as the *optimum tariff* argument. It has been shown in this literature that while such a tariff increases the satisfaction level of the domestic country, it reduces the satisfaction of the foreign countries by even more.[2] Thus, such a tariff reduces overall world satisfaction. The economic argument for a tariff therefore can be made only in terms of one country's special interests, not from a global viewpoint.

A *MUTATIS MUTANDIS* DERIVATION
OF THE OPTIMUM TARIFF

A concise analysis of the determination and effects of the optimum tariff can be made in terms of the *mutatis mutandis* demand and supply curves. The analysis employs the excess demand curve for the domestic country developed in Figure 5–5(b). It also uses an excess supply curve for the rest of the world, which is derived by subtracting the level of demand in the rest of the world from the level of supply. These are shown in Figure 6–4, along with a third curve which is the marginal cost curve (MC) associated with the rest-of-world excess supply curve.

Since the domestic country has market power, as more and more of the good is demanded from the rest of the world, total world demand for the good rises significantly, as does the world equilibrium relative price which clears the world market for this good. The price of all units of the good, not just the last one, rises. The marginal cost of consuming the last unit is therefore equal to the price of the last unit plus the amount by which the price of all previous units is raised. These marginal costs are shown by the line MC in Figure 6–4.

In microeconomic theory, a seller or buyer maximizes the gains from his market power by selling or buying at the quantity which equates his marginal cost and marginal revenue. The marginal revenue curve in the case of this country with market power in its import good is the country's excess demand curve. The excess demand curve shows how much each additional unit of good A is worth to the country, or how much the country is willing to pay for each extra unit. So in the case of the optimum tariff, the country also equates the marginal revenue with the marginal cost by imposing a tariff which makes the domestic relative price P_D and the quantity imported Q_T, as in Figure 6–4. The world terms of trade, or

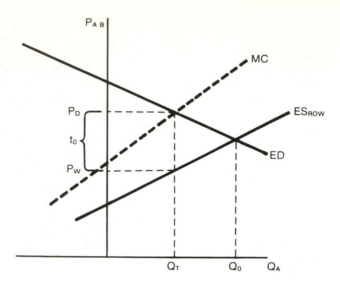

Figure 6–4 The Optimum Tariff

relative price of good A, fall from P_0 at free trade to P_W with the tariff, and the optimum tariff is t_0.

One effect of the trade restriction is to cause production and consumption inefficiencies in both countries. The sum of these two types of inefficiencies for the home country is represented by the triangular area I in Figure 6–5. This area is the same as the one described in Figure 5–5 (b). Similarly, the sum of the losses due to production and consumption inefficiencies in the rest of the world is represented by the triangular area II.

The second effect of the tariff is a transfer of expenditure power from the rest of the world to the domestic country. The domestic country collects tariff revenues on the imports Q_T equal to $t_0 \cdot Q_T$. This quantity is represented by the rectangle P_DTRP_W in Figure 6–5. Part of the tariff revenue is collected from domestic residents, and part from foreigners. The rectangular area D represents the additional cost due to the tariff that domestic residents pay in order to consume the quantity Q_T. Prior to the tariff, the domestic relative price of the imported good was P_0, the initial world terms of trade. However, the tariff raises the domestic relative price to P_D, and $(P_D - P_0)Q_T$ is that part of the tariff revenue collected from domestic consumers. Similarly, the rectangular area F represents that part of the tariff revenue paid by foreigners. Prior to the tariff, foreign importers received P_0 for each of the Q_T units imported by the domestic country. However, due to the domestic country's market power, the imposition of the tariff causes the world market relative price of the imported good to fall to P_W. The difference in revenue $(P_0 - P_W)Q_T$ that used to accrue to foreign producers now is collected by the domestic government as tariff revenue. Hence, the area F represents a transfer of expenditure power from the foreign to the domestic country.

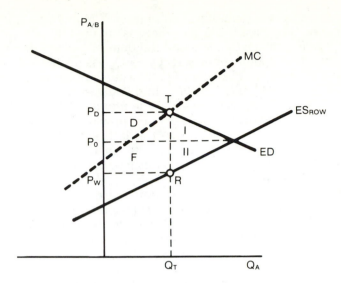

Figure 6–5 The Revenue and Efficiency Effects of the Optimum Tariff

The net effect of the domestic optimum tariff t_0 on the domestic and foreign countries and the world as a whole can now be shown. From the domestic country's viewpoint, only areas I and F are important. Area D represents revenue which is removed from the domestic country and then returned. There is no net loss to the domestic country.* Area II represents the loss to the rest of the world due to production and consumption inefficiencies, and therefore does not affect the domestic country. However, area I is the production and consumption inefficiencies which occur in the domestic country, and therefore represents a net loss to the domestic country. In contrast, area F represents a net gain to the domestic country equal to the transfer of expenditure. Thus, to the extent that area F exceeds area I, the domestic country benefits from the optimum tariff.

The foreign countries and the world are clearly worse off from the domestic optimum tariff. The rest of the world suffers two losses. The Area II represents the loss due to the inefficiencies in consumption and production. Area F represents the loss due to the transfer of expenditure to the domestic country. The net effect on the foreign countries is therefore the sum of these two losses. The net loss to the world as a whole is equal to the sum of areas I and II. Neither area D nor F enters into the change in world welfare, since both represent simply a transfer of expenditure from one country to another country, or back to the initial country. However, both areas I and II represent net losses due to inefficiencies. Hence, the tariff causes a net loss to the world equal to the sum of these areas.

---

*Again it is assumed that the revenues are returned to the economy in a neutral fashion, and effects of changing factor rewards on factor supplies are ignored.

The net gain to the domestic country (area F minus area I) is summarized in area G in Figure 6–6. This area is simply the vertical distance between the marginal cost curve and the domestic excess demand curve over the reduced quantity of imports $Q_0 - Q_T$. As the tariff is raised and the quantity of imports falls below Q_0, the country experiences both costs and benefits. The benefits are the additional resources or expenditure power released because the terms of trade improve. These additional resources are the additional exports paid on previous and additional units of imports in order to consume just the last units. The additional resources equal the vertical distance under the marginal cost curve at those quantities. The cost of the reduced consumption is the lost satisfaction from consuming fewer units. This loss is equal to the vertical distance under the domestic country's excess demand curve at these lost units. Therefore, the net gain is the vertical distance between the marginal cost and the excess demand curve for all lost units, the area G. As long as this area is positive (MC exceeds the excess demand curve), the possibility of an optimum tariff exists. The objective of the optimum tariff is to maximize the size of the area G.

The size of the tariff which maximizes the area G can be derived algebraically from the basic relationship between average and marginal cost

$$MC = AC\left(1 + \frac{1}{\epsilon}\right) = P_W\left(1 + \frac{1}{\epsilon}\right)* \qquad (6-1)$$

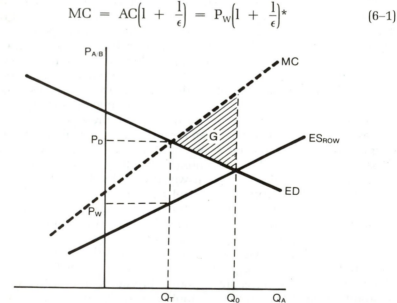

Figure 6–6   The Domestic Gains from the Optimum Tariff

*This formula is easily derived by differentiating total cost with respect to quantity:

$$\frac{dTC}{dq} = \frac{dPq}{dp} = MC = P + q\frac{dP}{dq} = P\left(1 + \frac{q}{P}\frac{dP}{dq}\right) = P\left(1 + \frac{1}{\epsilon}\right).$$

where ϵ is the elasticity of the supply curve at the average cost or world price P_W. At the optimum tariff, marginal cost equals the domestic price, or

$$MC \; = \; P_D \; = \; P_W(1 \, + \, t). \tag{6-2}$$

Substituting (6–2) into (6–1) yields

$$P_W(1 \, + \, t) \; = \; P_W\!\left(1 \, + \, \frac{1}{\epsilon}\right), \tag{6-3}$$

or solving for the optimum tariff t

$$t \; = \; \frac{1}{\epsilon}. \tag{6-4}$$

Hence, the optimum *ad valorem* tariff which maximizes the domestic country's gain is equal to the reciprocal of the elasticity of the rest-of-world's excess supply curve at the optimum quantity of imports.

OPTIMAL INTERVENTION

The previous two sections show that if a country has market power in its exports, the proper government policy may be a tariff. But what if a production or consumption distortion exists? Is the optimal policy still a tariff? The answer is no. The implication of the analysis is that before a proper policy can be chosen, the nature of the distortion must first be determined.

Illustrations of production and consumption distortion are shown in Figures 6–1 and 6–2 respectively. Notice that in each case there is a wedge between the foreign terms of trade and only one of the other terms of trade. To offset that distortion and maximize community welfare, a policy is needed which creates an equal size wedge in the opposite direction. Why a tariff is not an optimal policy should therefore be obvious. While a tariff may create an equal size wedge in the opposite direction from the distortions, it also adds an entirely extraneous wedge.

Figure 6–7 illustrates the argument for a production distortion. The economy is initially producing and consuming at points P and C under free trade. But such a position does not maximize the economy's welfare, because there is a production distortion which causes production to remain at P rather than P', where the foreign terms of trade are tangent to the production possibilities curve. A policy is needed which increases the production of the export good B.

A trade policy can be found which encourages the production of exports. For example, suppose the government decides to undertake an export subsidy program. Any unit of B which is sold abroad now receives a subsidy equal to the wedge at point P. Given the foreign terms of trade, this action has two effects. First, producers now receive more for produc-

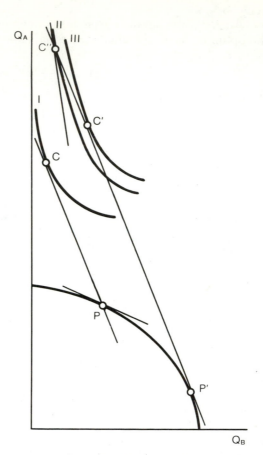

Figure 6–7   Optimal Intervention with a Production Distortion

ing a unit of B for export, which now causes them to produce at point P′, the optimal production point. Second, consumers in the domestic country find that they now have to pay more for B. Before the subsidy program they paid only the foreign terms of trade FTT. But domestic producers now receive FTT plus a subsidy for each unit of B exported. In order to get domestic producers to sell some of the B at home, domestic consumers now also have to pay FTT plus the subsidy. So the domestic terms of trade in consumption now exceed the foreign terms of trade by the subsidy. Consumption occurs at point C″, not C′. The trade policy has produced not only an offsetting wedge in production, but also a wedge in consumption. In this specific instance the economy's welfare level is less than if the country could consume at the foreign terms of trade.

What type of policy produces a better solution? Such a policy offsets only the production wedge without simultaneously producing a consumption wedge. A simple domestic production subsidy would produce such a result. If the government agrees to subsidize the production of all units of B, regardless of whether they are exported, production of B can be increased to point P'. But since all producers receive the same compensation regardless of the nationality of the consumers, there is no divergence between the prices domestic and foreign consumers pay. Consumption occurs at point C' and welfare is maximized.

The important conclusion from this analysis is that the best way to deal with a problem is to solve it directly. If there is a production distortion, welfare is maximized by using a production solution, that is, a production tax or subsidy. Similarly, if there is a consumption distortion, the best policy is to add a consumption tax or subsidy at the source of the distortion. A trade intervention action such as a tariff or export subsidy can be used to solve either a production or consumption problem. It cannot, however, maximize welfare, because it produces both production and consumption effects of its own.

The process for deciding which policy to use in a given situation can therefore be divided into two steps. First, the problem must be analyzed to determine what type of distortion is being faced. Second, the proper intervention for that type of distortion must be determined. To illustrate the two-step process, let us return to the oil example introduced in Chapter 3.

Say, for military reasons, the United States wants to reduce its dependence on foreign oil. The question arises as to the best economic way of achieving the military goal. The first step is to determine precisely what that goal is. One possibility is to raise only domestic production of oil. Given the domestic demand, oil imports fall. Another possibility is just to reduce domestic consumption of oil. Given domestic production, a fall in domestic demand also reduces imports. Each goal has a different effect on the economy.

Once the desired policy goal has been determined, the proper policy action becomes clear. If only domestic production is to be increased, a subsidy on oil production or a reduction in oil producers' marginal taxes is required. If only domestic demand is to be reduced, a tax on oil consumption is in order. For both a production increase and consumption reduction, a tariff on oil imports or allowing domestic oil prices to rise is the proper policy. Each goal requires a different optimal intervention.

CASE 1—STEEL IMPORTS 1977

In 1977 the increasing difficulties of the United States steel companies in competing with foreign produced steel received increased attention. Foreign steel manufacturers were capturing larger and larger shares of the U.S. steel markets, and domestic steel manufacturers began closing plants and laying off workers. A protectionist atmosphere began building in the country as elected representatives, stock owners and steelworkers began clamoring for aid to the troubled industry. Since the apparent threat to the steel industry came from imported products, attention was focused on this symptom as the root of all steel industry problems. Foreign steel was produced more efficiently, was produced with "cheap labor," or was being sold in the U.S. below cost. To offset these alleged inequities caused by trade, various trade policies were demanded, such as tariffs, quotas, and finally "trigger prices." Yet, as this chapter describes, finding the proper policy to deal with a problem is a two-step process. First, the type of distortion (if in fact one exists) must be determined, and second, the type of policy tool that deals most directly with that distortion must be chosen. Only then can the problem be solved effectively.

Simply because a particular problem involves imported or exported goods does not mean that a trade restriction is the proper policy. Recall that a trade restriction creates both a production and a consumption wedge, so a trade policy is justified only if both a production and a consumption distortion of equal magnitudes must be remedied. In the case of the U.S. steel industry, only a possible production distortion was claimed to exist. The fears that U.S. steel producers were losing the U.S. steel market to foreign competition and that steelworkers were losing their jobs essentially reflected a belief that the domestic production of steel was somehow not sufficiently high. If these beliefs were justified, the proper policy for solving the steel problem should therefore have encouraged more domestic production of steel.

While a possible production distortion existed, no apparent consumption distortion could be found. The proponents of steel industry protection did not argue that domestic consumption of steel must be reduced. In fact, if anything, these proponents desired to have the level of steel consumption rise in order to induce more output by domestic producers. A policy which would reduce domestic demand by creating a tax on consumption was therefore not the proper policy. Thus, a trade intervention could be ruled out as the optimal policy for dealing with the problems of steel. While that trade policy encourages production of domestic steel, it simultaneously reduces the overall demand for steel. A consumption tax could also be excluded from consideration, since it produces only an undesirable consumption effect without the desirable production effect. Thus, the conclusion here is that the proper policy for dealing with what was essentially a production problem of the steel industry would have been some type of production solution. Yet the precise type of production solution is still very important.

While the primary symptom of the steel industry's illness was a reduction in efficiency as compared with foreign producers, the cause of the symptom was really much deeper. It is hard to believe that owners and managers passively allowed their investments to depreciate to the point of noncompetitiveness without some external incentives. What are some of these incentives? Why have steel executives failed to invest more resources into the modernization of production processes and thus failed to remain competitive with, say, Japanese producers?

There are at least two reasons for the lack of new investment.[3] One reason is pollution controls. Steel production is a relatively dirty process. Adapting steel plants to conform to local pollution standards therefore requires huge outlays of capital. Given the limited quantity of investment capital, the capital for pollution control must subtract from other capital investments, such as expenditures budgeted for modernization of production techniques. Also, given the huge capital requirements for pollution control, the steel producers have a direct incentive for closing down older plants.

A second reason for the lack of incentive to incorporate more efficient production techniques is the interaction of inflation, corporate taxation, and financial accounting. Specifically, corporations for tax purposes are only permitted to depreciate the value of their investments on the basis of the original cost rather than the current replacement value. During periods of inflation, actual depreciation allowed for tax purposes is less than the replacement cost of the physical plant being depreciated. The taxes on steel corporations because of historical cost depreciation therefore are higher, thus restricting the company to finance a smaller part of the cost of replacement or modernization. Steel corporations, especially because of their great capital stock, therefore have less incentive to reinvest.

Furthermore, during periods of inflation, the more years over which the investment is depreciated, the greater the disparity between original and replacement costs, and the smaller the incentive to reinvest. Thus, during periods of inflation, as replacement costs for fixed capital rise, industries with the longest-lived capital have the least incentive to reinvest. The steel industry, with machines built to last fifty or more years, has among the longest-lived capital. The steel industry in the U.S. therefore bears a real burden under the existing tax laws. The Japanese tax system does not impose such a burden on long-lived capital. Japanese steel producers therefore have a much greater incentive to reinvest and modernize their production processes.

The two-step process for finding the proper policy response to a problem therefore shows that a trade policy should not be used to remedy the plight of the U.S. steel industry. Rather, the problems of steel stem primarily from a distortion of the tax laws. The most direct and efficient policy for dealing with the problems of steel is to reform the tax laws.*

Of course, before even this direct solution should be undertaken, the legitimacy of the steel companies' complaints must be analyzed from the viewpoint of the economy as a whole. The lobbyists for the steel companies obviously press for aid from the steel companies' perspective. The owners of steel companies see their market shares falling, and they want to protect their investment. But while pollution control laws reduce the

---

*In a strict sense, the required tax reforms are not a production solution. Instead, by making the employment of capital relatively more expensive than the employment of labor, the existing tax laws create a distortion in the market for factors of production. The factor market distortion causes the production possibilities curve to move in towards the origin, in addition to causing production to occur at an inefficient point along the production curve. So eliminating the factor market distortion causes both a movement to an efficient production point along the curve as well as a shifting of the curve outwards to higher potential production levels. For a more detailed discussion of factor market versus production distortions, see Albert Fishlow and Paul David, "Optimal Resource Allocation in an Imperfect Market Setting," *Journal of Political Economy*, Vol. 59, No. 6 (December 1961), pp. 529–46.

value of the capital stock of steel companies, they do represent a legitimate way of dealing with the divergence between private and social cost created by the pollution. What must be determined is whether the value of the lost steel production to the economy under current pollution control laws exceeds the benefits to the economy from cleaner air and water. If the costs exceed benefits, then pollution laws should be relaxed.

Also, before any special tax legislation is passed for the steel industry, it should be determined if even such legislation would permit the U.S. steel companies to compete on world markets. It may be that the U.S. comparative advantage is no longer in steel production. If so, free importation of cheaper foreign steel provides gains to consumers and prevents a misallocation of U.S. resources in production. In that case, on the grounds of economic efficiency, the U.S. steel industry should be encouraged to contract.

CASE 2—INFANT INDUSTRY ARGUMENT

One particular type of argument for intervention (especially heard in the context of developing countries) is the *infant industry argument*. The argument usually consists of a statement that an industry could potentially provide valuable jobs and products for an economy, but it stands no chance of establishing itself unless it is protected. The protection often recommended is a tariff. But just as in the other cases where distortions exist, prescribing a type of intervention is a two-step process. First the exact nature of the distortion must be determined, and only then can the precise policy recommendation be made.

There is more than one argument for protecting an infant industry, but the important part of each argument is why there is no incentive for the industry to develop by itself.[4] The fact that development requires large outlays now with no return for several years is not by itself sufficient reason for protection. Most investment projects do not repay their investments immediately. The important question is what the rate of return will be over the life of the entire project. If the rate of return is greater or equal to the return on other investment projects, then the private markets should have an incentive to undertake it. But the incentive may not exist for two reasons. First, capital markets may be inefficient so that private financing is difficult even if the project has a reasonable return. Second, while the private rate of return may not be sufficiently large to induce private investment, the social return may be sufficiently higher to make it comparable to other investment projects.

Why should private and social returns diverge? The reason usually centers around some knowledge, skill, or production technique created by the industry which makes the country better off, but whose returns are not captured directly by the industry itself. For example, the technique pioneered by this industry may be employed by other industries after it is developed. Thus, the developing industry cannot get all the future returns from its technique. Or labor in the industry may gain skills which can be transferred later to other industries. Again, all the returns are not captured by the investing firms.

If any of the above problems is determined to exist, there may be grounds for the government to intervene. Notice, however, that in none of the cases is a trade restriction the optimal intervention, because none involves both a product consumption distortion of equal magnitude. If capital markets are inefficient, the optimal policy is for the government to increase the market efficiency, say by increasing the flow of information between borrowers and lenders. If the problem is that other industries will use free of charge the techniques developed, the government should subsidize domestic production in the industry in question. More precisely, the government should subsidize only those firms initially in the industry, because if all firms are subsidized the only effect is to attract more marginal firms, not to encourage investment in the existing ones. Finally, if workers are the ones to gain the transferable skills, the government should just subsidize on-the-job training programs. The theory of human capital implies that even that subsidy may be unnecessary, since workers should be willing to accept less than market wages while gaining an on-the-job skill which will provide higher income in the future. In any case, none of these arguments represents a trade distortion, so no trade policy such as a tariff is the best alternative.

One final point is that any of the above arguments is still only an argument for temporary intervention. Whether the government chooses a tariff, a production subsidy, or a job training subsidy, the program is needed only while the industry is developing the particular technique. Once the industry has passed the development stage it should be able to compete without further assistance. If an industry requires additional government intervention, it is likely that the project should not have been undertaken in the first place.

SUMMARY

There are three possible types of distortions: a *production distortion*, a *consumption distortion*, and a *trade distortion*. Each involves at least one inequality among the terms of trade in product consumption, and the foreign terms of trade. The most economically efficient way to deal with any of these distortions is to eliminate the inequality directly. Any other policy cannot maximize the country's welfare.

Tariffs imposed by a large country can improve the country's terms of trade. Simultaneously they create production and consumption losses. As long as the gain in welfare from the improvement in the terms of trade exceeds the reduction in the gains from trade, the country is better off. The tariff which maximizes this net gain to the country is called the *optimum tariff*. This tariff, however, reduces world welfare by reducing the level of satisfaction of foreign countries more than the satisfaction gain to the domestic country.

REFERENCES

BALDWIN, ROBERT E., "The Case Against Infant Industry Tariff Protection," *Journal of Political Economy* 77, No. 3 (May/June 1969): 295–305.

BHAGWATI, JAGDISH, "The Generalized Theory of Distortion and Welfare," *Trade, Balance of Payments, and Growth: Papers in International Economics in Honor of Charles P. Kindleberger*, J. Bhagwati, et al., eds., Amsterdam: North Holland, 1971.

—— and V. K. RAMASWAMI, "Domestic Distortions, Tariffs, and the Theory of Optimum Subsidy," *Journal of Political Economy* 71, No. 1 (February 1963): 44–50; reprinted in J. Bhagwati, *Trade, Tariffs and Growth*, Cambridge, Mass: MIT Press, 1969.

FISHLOW, ALBERT and PAUL DAVID, "Optimal Resource Allocation in an Imperfect Market Setting," *Journal of Political Economy* 59, No. 6 (December 1961): 529–46.

GRAAF, J.V. DE, *Theoretical Welfare Economics*. Cambridge: Cambridge Press, 1957.

JOHNSON, HARRY G, "Optimal Trade Intervention in the Presence of Domestic Distortions," *Trade, Growth and the Balance of Payments: Essays in Honor of Gottfried Haberler*, Baldwin, et al., eds., Chicago: Rand-McNally, 1965; reprinted in H.G. Johnson, *Aspects of the Theory of Tariffs*, Cambridge, Mass: Harvard University Press, 1972.

SCITOVSKY, T. DE, "A Reconsideration of the Theory of Tariffs," *Review of Economic Studies*, 9, No. 2 (Summer 1942): 89–110; reprinted in American Economic Association, *Readings in the Theory of International Trade*, Philadelphia: Blakiston, 1949.

NOTES

1. Jagdish Bhagwati and V. K. Ramaswami, "Domestic Distortions, Tariffs, and the Theory of Optimum Subsidy," *Journal of Political Economy*, Vol. 71, No. 1 (February 1963), pp. 44–50. Also Jagdish Bhagwati, "The Generalized Theory of Distortions and Welfare," Chapter 4 in *Trade, Balance of Payments, and Growth: Papers in International Economics in Honor of Charles P. Kindleberger*, edited by J. N. Bhagwati, et al., Amsterdam: North Holland, 1971.

2. T. de Scitovsky, "A Reconsideration of the Theory of Tariffs," *Review of Economic Studies*, Vol. 9, No. 2 (Summer 1942), pp. 89–110, reprinted in *Readings in the Theory of International Trade*, (Philadelphia: Blakiston), 1949. Also J. V. de Graaf, *Theoretical Welfare Economics*, (Cambridge: Cambridge Press), 1957.

3. For a discussion of the problems of the steel industry, see "Helping American Steel," *Wall Street Journal*, October 17, 1977, p. 30.

4. For more elaborate discussion of arguments concerning infant industries see Harry G. Johnson, "Optimal Trade Intervention in the Presence of Domestic Distortions," in *Trade, Growth and the Balance of Payments: Essays in Honor of Gottfried Haberler*, edited by Baldwin, et al., Chicago: Rand-McNally 1965, pp. 3–34 and Robert E. Baldwin, "The Case Against Infant Industry Tariff Protection," *Journal of Political Economy*, Vol. 77, No. 3 (May/June 1969), pp. 295–305.

CHAPTER 7

Transfers, Growth, and the Terms of Trade

We have discussed the equilibrium world trading patterns and relative prices resulting when two countries consume, according to their tastes and preferences, an amount of goods equal to the value of what they produce. In terms of the *mutatis mutandis* curves like Figure 6–4, the world equilibrium relative price of a good under free trade occurs where the excess demand for, say, good B of Country II equals the excess supply of Country I. The equilibrium relative price can also be described as the one where the total world supply of good B (the sum of the supplies in Country I and Country II) equals the total world demand (the sum of demands in the two countries). Such a determination of free trade equilibrium is shown in Figure 7–1. The demand curve for the world D_{world} is the horizontal sum at each relative price of the demand for good B along the *mutatis mutandis* demand curves of the two countries. Similarly, the world supply curve S_{world} is the sum of supplies of B at each relative price as represented by the *mutatis mutandis* supply curves. Under the initial assumption of free trade, the world equilibrium terms of trade are $(P_{B/A})_0$.

THE TRANSFER PROBLEM

A question of interest in international trade theory is how this equilibrium relative price is likely to change if, for example, Country I transfers purchasing power to Country II. Such a transfer of purchasing power has been of international economic significance from time to time as military victors have demanded reparations from losers, as countries have provided foreign aid to other countries, and more recently, as the rising relative price of oil has transferred real resources from oil-consuming to oil-producing countries. The change in the terms of trade following the transfer is of importance because a movement in the terms of trade in the transferor's favor can lessen the burden of the transfer, while a movement against the transferor exacerbates the problem. The question

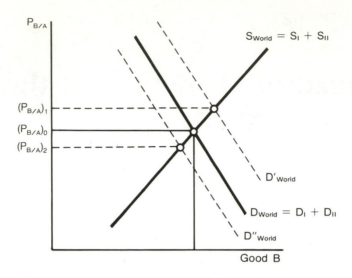

Figure 7–1   The Effects of a Transfer on the Terms of Trade

of which way the terms of trade are likely to move became known in the international trade literature as the *transfer problem*.[1]

The basic focus of the transfer problem can be described in terms of Figure 7–1. Suppose that Country I transfers an amount X of purchasing power to Country II. The transfer begins by Country I cutting its expenditures, say through neutral taxes, to X below current income. The tax revenue of X is then transferred to Country II where it is allocated, again in some neutral fashion. Expenditure in Country II exceeds current income by an amount X. Both countries are assumed to split any additional income between expenditures for good A and good B. In Figure 7–1, then, the reduction in purchasing power reduces demand for good B in Country I, shifting the D_{world} curve to the left. On the other hand, the increased purchasing power in Country II increases the demand for good B in that country. The question is: which expenditure change has a larger effect on the world demand for good B?

The answer lies in part in the marginal propensities to spend on good B in the two countries. The marginal propensities to spend represent how much consumption of good B rises when purchasing power rises. If Country II has a higher marginal propensity to spend on good B, the shifting of purchasing power increases the demand for B more in Country II than demand falls in Country I. In terms of Figure 7–1 the total world demand for B increases at each relative price, shifting D_{world} rightwards to D'_{world}. The terms of trade move in favor of Country I as the relative price of its exported good rises to $(P_{B/A})_1$. Conversely, if Country I has a higher propensity to spend on B, the transfer of income reduces the net world demand for B. The world demand curve shifts leftwards to D''_{world}. The relative price of Country I's exported good falls to $(P_{B/A})_2$.

A rise in Country I's terms of trade reduces the real burden of the transfer. Country I is effecting the transfer by exporting units of B to Country II. So if, for example, the size of the transfer X is defined as 100 units of B and 100 units of A, the total quantity of B which must be exported depends on the relative price $P_{B/A}$. If $(P_{B/A})_0 = 1$, then the initial transfer means 200 units of B must be exported to Country II. If the transfer causes the terms of trade to move in the transferor's (Country I) favor, raising the relative price to $(P_{B/A})_1 = 2$, then the 100 units of A are now equivalent to only 50 units of B. The size of the transfer is reduced to only 150 units of B. Conversely, if the terms of trade move against the transferor country, so that $(P_{B/A})_2 = 1/2$, the transfer rises to 250 units of B. The change in the terms of trade have created a *secondary burden*, increasing the quantity of Country I's output which must be given up to complete the required transfer.

More formally, let m_{II}^B represent the marginal propensity of Country II to spend (import) on good B, and c_I^B represent the marginal propensity to spend on B in Country I. A transfer T of purchasing power from Country I to Country II reduces the demand for B by $c_I^B \cdot T$ and raises the demand by $m_{II}^B \cdot T$. The terms of trade turn against the transferor only if $m_{II}^B \cdot T < c_I^B \cdot T$, that is, total world demand for B falls. Since only two goods (A and B) are consumed in Country I, then by definition $c_I^B = (1 - m_I^A)$, since what is not spent on B is spent (imported) on A. The condition for a secondary burden therefore becomes

$$m_{II}^B \cdot T < (1 - m_I^A) \cdot T$$

or

$$0 < (1 - m_I^A - m_{II}^B) \cdot T.$$

The secondary burden occurs if the value in the parentheses is positive, or in other words, if the marginal propensities to import in the two countries sum to less than one. Conversely, the burden of the transfer is lessened if the propensities to import sum to more than one.

Notice that an important conclusion from this condition is that there is no presumption that a transfer will improve or worsen the terms of trade. On theoretical grounds, either result is equally likely. The actual change depends upon the values of the marginal propensities in the individual countries.

This condition involving the marginal propensities to import is a traditional result of international economics. As stated here, however, the condition involves only income effects. But if the terms of trade change, the transfer should also produce substitution effects in demand (and supply) in both countries. These substitution effects could conceivably change the results under certain conditions. The appendix to the chapter shows explicitly how to incorporate the substitution effects into the results. The appendix concludes that as long as a fall in the relative price of B produces a world excess demand for B, the qualitative conclusions from analyzing only the income effects hold. In terms of Figure 7–1, if the world equilibrium price is $(P_{B/A})_0$ and the relative price of B fell to $(P_{B/A})_2$, the conclusion would hold as long as an excess demand for B was created. An excess demand for B, of course, would cause the relative price of B to rise again. In other words, the conclusion holds as long as the equilibrium at $(P_{B/A})_0$ is stable. A sufficient condition for such stability is simply that the demand curve is downward sloping and the supply curve is upward sloping, the normal shapes of those curves.

Perhaps the best known historical application of the transfer problem concerned the German reparations following World War I. After its defeat in the war, Germany was required to pay large sums to France and other Allies. These payments represented the transfer of wealth, and the question arose whether the German terms of trade would deteriorate as demand fell in Germany and rose elsewhere.

If the terms of trade were unaffected by the transfer of purchasing power, then a certain quantity of goods would have to be transferred from Germany to the other countries to settle the claims created by the initial transfer to the Allies. However, if the change in world demand produced by the transfer caused the German terms of trade to deteriorate, German exports would be worth less on world markets, and more of these goods would have to be exported to offset the initial financial transfer. In other words, a deterioration of the terms of trade would create an additional or secondary burden for the transferor country. The question for Germany was therefore whether the terms of the reparations would cause Germany's terms of trade to deteriorate, and thus make the burden on Germany substantially larger than the Dawes Committee had planned.

The German reparations issue became the subject of a famous debate between John Maynard Keynes and Bertil Ohlin.[2] Keynes argued that the German reparations would cause demand for German goods to fall by more in Germany than they would rise elsewhere. The resulting deterioration in the German terms of trade would mean that canceling the claims that the Allies had on Germany would require even larger quantities of German exports. Ohlin, on the other hand, argued that there was no particular reason for the German terms of trade to deteriorate, and hence the transfer could quite possibly be accomplished without a secondary burden.

The analysis of the transfer problem tends to support Ohlin's position that while it was possible for Germany's terms of trade to fall because of the reparations, it was by no means certain. The final outcome depended largely on the value of the German and Allied marginal propensities to import. In fact what happened was that the terms of trade turned against Germany, and Germany experienced a large secondary burden. The unfavorable movement in the terms of trade, however, can be traced to more than just the values of the import propensities. As Germany began effecting the transfer, and German goods began appearing in large quantities in Allied countries, the recipient countries began worrying about unemployment and other problems these imports might create. The recipient countries therefore responded by raising tariffs and imposing other trade barriers to German goods. As the analysis of tariffs has shown, these measures should have caused Germany's terms of trade to deteriorate. Germany's secondary burden can be explained largely by these measures.

Another possible transfer which could be analyzed within this framework is the U.S. aid program for Europe following World War II, known as the Marshall Plan. Also, one can interpret the large rise in OPEC oil prices as representing an additional transfer of wealth from oil consuming countries to oil producing countries. At first glance it appears that the oil consumers have a sizable marginal propensity to import oil from OPEC. It also appears that OPEC countries spend a large proportion of their revenues to import food, machinery, and consumer goods from non-OPEC countries. Hence, from the analysis of the transfer problem this recent transfer should not be expected to produce a secondary burden.

LIMITATIONS TO THE TERMS OF TRADE EFFECT

As Figure 7–1 shows, a transfer of purchasing power to a foreign country can improve the domestic country's terms of trade. The improvement in the terms of trade in turn reduces the burden of the transfer for the domestic country. The logical question to then ask is whether the terms of trade can improve sufficiently to offset the transfer burden completely, or better still, make the domestic country better off than before the transfer. The answer to this question is no, and the reasoning behind the answer is quite easy to show in terms of the *mutatis mutandis* curves.

Consider the initial world supply and demand curves from Figure 7–1. These curves are reproduced in Figure 7–2. The transfer from Country I to Country II shifts the world demand curve to the right, improving Country I's terms of trade from $(P_{B/A})_0$ to $(P_{B/A})_1$. Can the terms of trade rise sufficiently to offset the transfer?

Suppose that $(P_{B/A})_3$ represents the terms of trade at which the transfer is just offset. In other words, if the terms of trade rose to $(P_{B/A})_3$, purchasing power would be the same in both countries as it was prior to the transfer. If the distribution of purchasing power is the same as before, the world demand curve shifts back to D_w. There are no income effects in demand produced by the transfer, only substitution effects. These substitution effects require that at higher relative prices for good B, the demand for B will fall in both countries. Supply side substitution effects, however, imply that output of B will be greater at higher relative prices. Supply clearly exceeds demand at $(P_{B/A})_3$, and the equilibrium terms of trade must lie somewhere below. The transfer cannot be offset.

The argument of improved terms of trade has been used in the past in an attempt to justify foreign aid. It has been argued that foreign aid, by increasing foreign demand, improves the donor country's terms of trade and makes the donor country better off. As just described, such an argument has no economic validity. In addition, any gain to the donor country would come at the expense of the recipient, and we certainly would not expect a country to accept aid if it were made worse off.

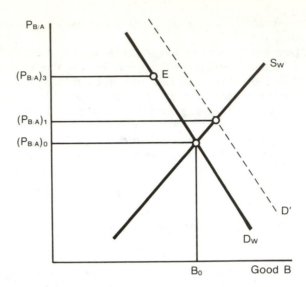

Figure 7–2   The Burden of Transfer

Therefore, although foreign aid can certainly be justified on humanitarian grounds, it cannot be justified on economic grounds. If a country has, say, excess food at prevailing world prices, and all it wants is to improve its terms of trade, the food should not be given away as aid. A sufficient rise in the terms of trade to increase the country's purchasing power cannot be achieved by simply shifting the world demand curve. All a transfer can do is shift the world demand curve. A sufficient rise in the terms of trade also requires that the world supply curve shift to the left. The analysis suggests the rather cold conclusion that if a country with excess food is concerned only with its own economic welfare, it should burn its excess production rather than feed starving people in other countries.

THE INVERSE PROPOSITION: CHANGES IN THE TERMS OF TRADE AND THE TRADE BALANCE

It has already been demonstrated how there can be no *a priori* presumption that a transfer will either improve or worsen a country's terms of trade. As shown algebraically in the appendix, the inverse relationship is the same: there is no presumption that a deterioration in a country's terms of trade will generate a transfer in either direction. The transfer in this context is a trade balance surplus. So there is no guarantee that the deterioration of a country's terms of trade will generate a trade balance surplus.

Much confusion surrounds this point in discussions of devaluations. It is often presumed that the terms of trade of a country which devalues deteriorate, in turn generating a trade surplus. However, this reasoning has several flaws. First, devaluation refers to the change in the relative values of two monies, not two goods. The relative price of monies and the relative price of goods are two separate and distinct concepts, and a specific change in one does not directly imply a specific change in the other. Second, even if the terms of trade deteriorate, there is no reason to expect a specific transfer to result.

To see this second point, consider the initial equilibrium at relative price $(P_{B/A})_0$ in Figure 7–2. Suppose the relative price of B falls, causing Country I's terms of trade to deteriorate. What reactions are generated in the two countries? The devaluation scenario usually concentrates on the substitution effects. A lower relative price of good B increases the demand and reduces the supply of B. If the increased demand and reduced supply occur in (foreign) Country II, a trade balance surplus is generated for Country I. Figure 7–2, however, shows that a fall in $P_{B/A}$ increases *world* demand and decreases *world* supply of B. In both countries individuals and firms substitute down along their demand and supply curves for B. The result is a world excess demand for B, but no identifiable excess supplies or demands in particular countries of the world. The only certain result is a tendency for the relative price of B to return towards $(P_{B/A})_0$, but no tendency for units of B to flow from one particular country to another. Hence the substitution effects do not generate *a priori* a trade surplus in the country whose terms of trade deteriorate. The discussion of why changes in relative prices do not imply particular trade balance effects is further expanded in Chapter 17, the chapter on devaluation.

GROWTH AND THE TERMS OF TRADE

Growth, like transfers, can have an effect on a country's terms of trade. Unlike transfers, however, growth causes a rightward shift in both the country's supply curve and its demand curve. Growth simultaneously increases both the production and consumption of a country's goods. An important question then is whether the supply curve or the demand curve shifts by more. Assuming similar absolute slope magnitudes, if the demand curve for the exported good shifts more than the supply curve, the country's terms of trade improve. If the supply curve shifts more than the demand curve, the terms of trade deteriorate. The potential deterioration in the terms of trade creates the possibility that a country could actually be made worse off by growth. This particular case is known in the international trade literature as *immiserizing* growth.

It is not difficult to imagine a case where individuals within a country are made worse off by growth. If, for example, growth occurs because of a population explosion in a country, it is quite possible that although aggregate income increases, per capita income falls. Even in this case, however, while individuals are worse off, more is being consumed in aggregate than before. For immiserizing growth to occur, aggregate consumption would have to fall also.

The deterioration in the terms of trade which produces immiserizing growth requires two events: (a) a large increase in the supply of a country's export good, and (b) a small increase in the good's demand. To see how these two effects can occur, consider a country whose population is constant, but whose capital stock is increasing. In this case aggregate and per capita income move together. From the Rybcyznski Theorem, an increase in the capital stock causes, at initial prices, an increase in the production of capital-intensive goods and a reduction in the production of labor-intensive goods. If the country exports capital-intensive goods, as it grows as described, more and more of its exports appear on world markets. The world supply curve for the country's export good shifts to the right, causing a drop in the good's value. Similarly, if the country in question has a low income elasticity of demand for its exported good, domestic demand for the good rises very little with growth. The world demand curve for the exported good hardly moves, reinforcing the excess supply on the production side and the deterioration in the country's terms of trade. So immiserizing growth is more likely to occur the more the factor used intensively in the exported good increases, and the smaller is the country's demand elasticity for its exports.

An example of immiserizing growth is shown in Figure 7–3. A country exporting the capital-intensive good A experiences growth in its capital stock. The country initially produces at point D and consumes on point F of community indifference curve I. The increased capital shifts the production possibilities curve outward from TT to T'T'. However, the implied increase in the supply of good A and the small increase in demand

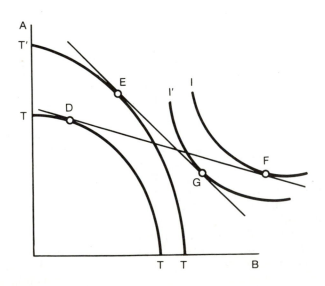

Figure 7–3   Immiserizing Growth

causes the country's terms of trade to deteriorate. While the country now produces more of both goods at point E, consumption occurs at point G on the lower community indifference curve I′. The growth has made the country worse off.

At the other extreme, if the country experiencing capital growth exports the labor-intensive good, or if the country has a high demand elasticity for the exported good, the terms of trade are likely to improve. In this case the terms of trade effect augments the gains from growth. In the middle are the cases of more balanced growth. For example, if labor and capital are increasing in proportion to the ratio in which they already exist in society, supplies of both goods should increase at similar rates. If higher income in turn leads to increased demand for the goods in proportions similar to which their productions expand, growth is expected to have very little if any effect on the terms of trade. The full effects of growth can therefore be evaluated only after considering its effects on supply and demand in all countries.

FACTOR MOBILITY

Growth in an economy is facilitated by the increase or decrease in the quantity of labor or capital available for work. One source of additional factors of production is foreign countries. As labor or capital flows in from abroad, the production possibilities curve of the country shifts outward. Changes occur in the absolute and relative quantities of goods produced and consumed. Changes also occur in the welfare of the country as a whole, as well as in the welfare of specific groups.

That factor mobility changes production and welfare should not be surprising. Previous discussions of changes in production and welfare centered around the gains achieved when a country trades at relative prices differing from those initially prevailing in autarky. Factor mobility involves a similar phenomenon. Presumably capital and labor do not choose to move from one country to another without incentives. The incentives are factor rewards in excess of those initially prevailing in the country of origin. So, by responding to their personal incentives and migrating, factors of production can produce changes in world production patterns and the distribution of income.

Since the movement of goods and the movement of factors in response to new relative price opportunities are similar phenomena, they should also produce similar final distributions of production and income. In fact, it is easy to show that factor movements are a substitute for trade in goods in maximizing the efficiency of the world economy, and in producing goods and factor price equalization.

Consider two countries (I and II) initially in autarky. The relative prices of goods A and B initially differ between the two countries, as do relative factor rewards. The traditional analysis is to assume that these two countries decide to engage in free trade of goods, which results in relative goods price equalization between the countries. Under the assumption of similar production techniques in the two countries, and given the unique correspondence between relative goods prices and relative factor rewards, the free trade equalizes relative and absolute factor prices between the countries.

Alternatively, instead of trade in goods, the two countries could be assumed to trade the services of factors of production. Labor would be assumed to migrate to the country where wages are initially relatively higher, while capital would migrate in the opposite direction. Free trade in factor services, given demand in the two countries, should produce the same free trade equilibrium wage-rental ratio as did the trade in goods. Again, given similar production techniques and the unique relationship between relative factor and relative goods prices, the same equilibrium relative price of goods prevails as before in the two countries. Hence, perfect mobility of capital and labor is a substitute for free trade in goods.

An interesting application of this substitution relationship has been shown by Mundell.[3] He showed how free mobility of a factor of production could be used to circumvent a trade barrier, such as a tariff or quota, and prevent the loss of the gains from trade. The example is shown in Figure 7-4. Country II is initially engaged in free trade with Country I. Following the opening of trade, Country II produces at point P on its production possibilities curve TT and consumes at point S along line FF. With free trade, therefore, Country II is a net exporter of the capital-intensive good A and a net importer of the labor-intensive good B.

Under the condition of similar production techniques and no transportation costs, free trade equilibrates both relative goods and relative factor prices in the two countries. So even if labor is assumed perfectly mobile between the two countries, once free trade has occurred, labor has no incentive to migrate from one country to the other. However, con-

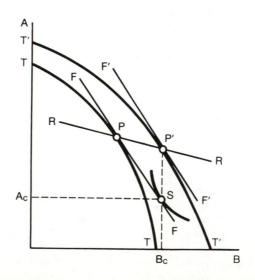

Figure 7-4   The Response to a Tariff on Good B with Labor Mobility

sider what would happen if Country II suddenly decided to impose a prohibitive tariff on its imports of B. Initially, without any imports of good B, the domestic relative price of B in Country II would rise. The higher relative price of the labor-intensive good in turn implies that the reward to labor in Country II rises. Now labor has an incentive to migrate!

As labor migrates from Country I to Country II, the level of production is affected. The Rybczynski Theorem states that at constant relative goods prices, as the supply of labor increases, production of the labor-intensive good rises and production of the capital-intensive good falls. So Country II produces more B (which it can no longer import) and less A. The change in production is shown by the Rybczynski line RR.

As long as the return to labor differs in the two countries, labor continues to migrate. The factor price differential ceases when Country II produces enough of good A and good B, without trade in goods, to consume as much of each as it did under free trade. Production therefore moves out to point P', directly above the free trade consumption bundle, point S. At P' Country II produces exactly the amount of good B it previously imported. It produces, however, more of good A than it consumes. The additional units of A represent goods that will be sent to Country I as payment for the services of the imported labor.

Notice that in the final equilibrium, relative goods prices are the same as initially. Relative factor rewards must therefore also be the same as they were initially. Country II is producing and consuming at its free trade level. While the tariff prevented trade in good B, labor mobility made trade in B unnecessary. No tariff revenue is collected, and no gains from trade are lost. Trade in factors has been substituted for trade in goods.

The migration of labor has affected the Gross Domestic Product of both countries. More production takes place in Country II than initially, and less in Country I. The imported labor in Country II, however, is being paid its marginal product each period, so, under the assumption that the workers do not change their citizenship, a periodic payment goes from Country II to Country I for factor services. Under this assumption, Gross National Product [which subtracts (adds) net payments to (net receipts of) foreign factors] is unchanged in the two countries.

This example has shown that with mobility of factors between countries and between industries, a tariff is unsuccessful at raising the relative reward of the domestically abundant factor. Accomplishing that goal requires not only a tariff, but also a national barrier to factor entry or exit. So in the relatively labor-abundant country (Country II), not only will labor favor a tariff on good B, but it should also be expected to support efforts limiting the inflow of workers from abroad. Similarly, in the capital-abundant country, the owners of capital will favor both tariffs on capital-intensive imports and restrictions on foreign investment in their country.

If factor specificity is assumed, then both factors will favor restricted entry to competing foreign factors, regardless of which factor is relatively abundant. For example, assume industry A is the automobile industry and industry B is wheat farming. Capital in the automobile industry is assumed to be automated welding robots, and is assumed to be specific to that industry. The specific capital in the wheat industry is land. Assume that there is a sudden influx of welding robots. Output expands in the automobile industry, but the marginal product of welding robots is lowered. The owners of this capital receive a lower rental rate and are unhappy.

The owners of wheat land are also unhappy, because the expanded automobile production attracted workers from wheat farming to automobile assembly. Under the assumption of a constant domestic supply of labor, fewer people now work at farming wheat, and the marginal product of land also falls. Similarly, a wave of labor immigration would drive down the marginal product of the domestic labor force. Both labor and capital therefore lobby to restrict entry of foreign competing factors of production.

FACTOR MOBILITY AND NATIONAL WELFARE

An issue related to the migration of labor is whether the migration makes the country of emigration worse off and the country of immigration better off. Under some simplifying assumptions, the migration can be shown to produce no welfare effects at all. The assumptions are that the migration is marginal, there are no externalities associated with the migrant's work, and the government has not been subsidizing the migrant.

Marginal means that only a small fraction of workers migrate. Consider, for example, the migration of one worker. In the country he leaves, he had been paid his marginal product. In other words, his reward from society had been precisely his contribution. So the factors of production left behind find their welfare unchanged, because they have the same output remaining to divide among themselves as before. Also, when the migrant comes to his new country, his pay is again equal to his marginal product. Again, his reward is precisely equal to his contribution. While Gross Domestic Product rises in the country of immigration, the additional income accrues to the immigrant. The initial factors of production still have the same income to divide among themselves.

What separates marginal from nonmarginal migration is what happens to the wage rate in the two countries. In the marginal migration example above, it is implicitly assumed that wage rates in the two countries are the same before and after migration. Thus, not only is the quantity of output remaining for the nonmigrant factors the same before and after migration, so is the distribution. With unchanged wage rates and rental rates, both capital and labor receive the same total rewards as before.

However, if migration were nonmarginal, factor returns would be affected. Specifically, wage rates would rise in the country of emigration, where fewer workers remain, and fall in the country of immigration. The change in factor rewards in turn produces distributional effects. In the emigration country, higher wages imply that workers are gaining at the

expense of owners of capital. The lower wages in the immigration country imply that workers receive less and capital receives more. So, even if
the migrating workers took only their marginal products with them, their
migration would change the distribution of income among factors in both
countries. However, it can be shown that in this case the migrating workers take more than their marginal product with them, and that aggregate
incomes available to other factors can also change.

The assumption of no externalities is necessary to eliminate the possibility of such things as increasing returns to scale. If one worker were to
leave, and he had been supplying positive externalities to his country,
then his departure would cause aggregate income to fall by more than his
marginal product. In other words, with positive externalities, even marginal migration leaves the remaining factors in the country of emigration
worse off. Of course, if the migrant had been providing negative externalities to the country, the remaining factors would be better off. Negative externalities can include such activities as mugging, stealing, and
murder, and presumably can provide a rationale behind the eighteenth-
century British practice of exiling certain convicted criminals to Australia.

The assumption that the government has not been subsidizing the migrant is made to eliminate the possibility that the worker takes capital
other than his own with him. The subsidization issue usually revolves
around education. Who paid for the worker's education, his parents or
his country? If the worker or his parents financed his education, then any
pay he receives above the wages of unskilled labor is a return to the
family's investment. When the worker emigrates, he takes his own investment, embodied in his human capital, with him. If the government
financed his education, however, the investment was undertaken by the
country, presumably in anticipation of some future benefits. Perhaps the
country anticipated positive externalities from an educated work force.
Now if the worker emigrates, he takes with him capital which belongs in
part to the remaining factors. In this case, even the marginal worker
makes the country of emigration worse off.

SUMMARY

The transfer of wealth from one country to another reduces the demand
for both goods in the first country and increases demand in the second.
This change in demand can produce changes in the terms of trade which
augment or reduce the size of the transfer. A well known historical transfer was the German war reparations following World War I. The actions
of the Allies turned the terms of trade against Germany, increasing the
real burden of the reparations. While an improvement in the terms of
trade can reduce the burden of a transfer, it cannot offset the burden
completely, much less make a country better off.

Just as a transfer can either improve or worsen the terms of trade, a
deterioration in the terms of trade can generate either a trade surplus or

deficit. A deterioration in the terms of trade is therefore not an automatic solution to a trade deficit.

Growth affects both supply and demand, and therefore can affect the terms of trade. A growth-induced improvement in the terms of trade makes a country better off. A deterioration makes a country worse off. A sufficiently large deterioration in the terms of trade can produce *immiserizing* growth, where a country finds itself worse off than if no growth had occurred.

Factor mobility represents a substitute for trade of goods. By responding to their personal incentives and migrating, factors of production can produce the same changes in world production and consumption patterns, and the distribution of income, as trade in goods. Also, when barriers to the flow of goods are raised, factor mobility enables circumvention of the barriers. Where the migration is marginal, the migrant produces no externalities, and the migrant takes with him only capital for which he paid, neither country is worse off than in the absence of migration.

REFERENCES

Bhagwati, Jagdish. "Immiserizing Growth: A Geometrical Note," *Review of Economic Studies* 25, No.3 (June 1958):201–5; reprinted in *Readings in International Economics*, R. Caves and H.G. Johnson, eds., Homewood, Ill.: Irwin, 1968.

Johnson, Harry G. "The Transfer Problem and Exchange Stability," *Journal of Political Economy* 64, No.3 (June 1956):212–25; reprinted in *Readings in International Economics*, R. Caves and H.G. Johnson, eds., Homewood, Ill.: Irwin, 1968.

Keynes, John Maynard, "The German Transfer Problem," 39 *Economic Journal* (March 1929):1–7: reprinted in American Economic Association, *Readings in the Theory of International Trade*, Philadelphia: Blakiston, 1949.

Metzler, Lloyd. "Tariffs, the Terms of Trade, and the Distribution of National Incomes," *Journal of Political Economy* 57 (February 1949): 1–29; reprinted in *Readings in International Economics*, R. Caves and H. G. Johnson, eds., Homewood, Ill.: Irwin, 1968.

Mundell, Robert A., *International Economics*, New York: Macmillan, 1968.

—— "International Trade and Factor Mobility," *American Economic Review* 47, No.3(June 1957):321–35; reprinted in *Readings in International Economics*, R. Caves and H.G. Johnson, eds., Homewood, Ill.: Irwin, 1968.

Ohlin, Bertil. "The Reparations Problem: A Discussion," *Economic Journal* 39 (June 1929):172–73; reprinted in American Economic Association *Readings in the Theory of International Trade*.

Samuelson, Paul A. "The Transfer Problem and Transport Costs," in *Readings in International Economics*, R. Caves and H.G. Johnson, eds., Homewood, Ill.: Irwin, 1968.

NOTES

1. See for example, Paul A. Samuelson, "The Transfer Problem and Transport Costs," and Harry G. Johnson, "The Transfer Problem and Exchange Stability," reprinted as chapters 8 and 9 of R. Caves and H. Johnson, *Readings in International Economics*, op. cit.

2. See John Maynard Keynes, "The German Transfer Problem," *Economic Journal*, Vol. 39 (March 1929), pp. 1-7, and B. Ohlin, "The Reparations Problem: A Discussion," *Economic Journal*, Vol. 39 (June 1929), pp. 172-73. Both articles are reprinted in *Readings in the Theory of International Trade*, Philadelphia: Blakiston, 1949.

3. Robert A. Mundell, "International Trade and Factor Mobility," *American Economic Review* 47, No. 3 (June 1957):321-35; reprinted in *Readings in International Economics*, edited by R. Caves and H.G. Johnson, Homewood, Ill.: Irwin, 1968.

APPENDIX 7

The barter model[1] in this appendix consists of two countries, I and II which each produce two goods, A and B. Country II is assumed to produce more A than it consumes, so it exports A, while Country I exports B. The relative price of goods, or terms of trade are defined in terms of A as

$$P_{B/A} = \frac{A}{B},\qquad(7A-1)$$

that is, the number of units of A necessary to obtain a unit of B. A rise in this number means B is worth more units of A, or A is worth fewer units of B, and represents *ceteris paribus* an increase in wealth for Country I. Similarly a fall in $P_{B/A}$ means Country II can buy more units of its imports B for each unit of its export A.

A comparative statics approach is used in the analysis. The countries are assumed initially in equilibrium. A shock then occurs which causes an excess demand for one good and an excess supply of the other. Disequilibrium is then assumed eliminated by a change in another variable, creating a relationship between changes in the two variables.

The Terms of Trade and the Trade Balance— Stability Conditions

An important question that must be considered is whether the equilibrium situations in our analysis are stable. An equilibrium is stable if a small movement away from equilibrium is followed by forces which return the system to that equilibrium. For the trade balance, the equilibrium is stable if a rise in the relative value of the exported good leads to an excess supply of that good.

Using Country I as an example, the trade balance can be expressed as the difference between foreign and domestic imports (M), both expressed in terms of good A, that is,

$$TB = PM_{II}[P] - M_I\left[\frac{1}{P}\right].$$ (7A-2)

Notice that the demand for each imported good is assumed negatively related to its relative price. Differentiating (7A-2) with respect to P yields

$$\frac{dTB}{dP} = M_{II} + P\frac{\partial M_{II}}{\partial P} - \frac{\partial M_I}{\partial\left(\frac{1}{P}\right)}\frac{d\left(\frac{1}{P}\right)}{dP}$$

$$= M_{II} + \left(\frac{P}{M_{II}} \cdot \frac{\partial M_{II}}{\partial P}\right)M_{II} + \left(\frac{\frac{1}{P}}{M_I} \cdot \frac{\partial M_I}{\partial\frac{1}{P}}\right)PM_I$$ (7A-3)

since

$$\frac{d\left(\frac{1}{P}\right)}{dP} = -1.$$

The terms in the parentheses are the elasticities of demand for imports in II and I respectively. Replacing these expressions with the more familiar elasticity notation of η_I and η_{II} (which are assumed negative) yields

$$\frac{dTB}{dP} = M_{II} - \eta_{II}M_{II} - \eta_I PM_I$$

$$= M_{II}\left(1 - \eta_{II} - \eta_I\frac{PM_I}{M_{II}}\right).$$ (7A-4)

If trade is initially balanced ($M_1 = M_1P$) and P is assumed equal to one, the stability condition for an increase in P (a rise in Country I's terms of trade) is

$$\frac{dTB}{dP} = (1 - \eta_{II} - \eta_I) < 0$$ (7A-5)

This condition involving a rise in P may be interpreted in terms of either Country I or Country II. A rise in Country I's terms of trade creates an excess supply (negative excess demand) of B (Country I's export), worsening Country I's trade balance. Equivalently, a fall in Country II's term of trade creates an excess demand for its export A, improving its trade balance. In either form the condition in (7A-5) may be familiar to some as the *Marshall-Lerner* condition. As sometimes applied, the condition is used to establish the conditions under which devaluation will be successful. But devaluation represents the change in the relative value of two currencies, not goods. As pointed out in the text, such a use of the condition is therefore clearly a misapplication. At most, all the Marshall-Lerner condition shows is the condition for stability in the goods market when the relative price of goods changes. As developed here, the Marshall-Lerner condition is of questionable value even as a determinant of stability conditions, because it ignores both supply elasticities and the cross substitution effects between goods.

THE TRANSFER PROBLEM

The trade balance represents the transfer of goods from one country to another. There are two ways in which the relationship between the trade balance and the terms of trade may be discussed. One way is to start with a change in the terms of trade and observe what transfer of goods is necessary in order to restore equilibrium (see the next section). A more traditional approach in the barter model, however, is to start with a transfer of assets from one country to another and observe the change in the terms of trade necessary to restore equilibrium. This latter approach is known in classical international trade literature as the *transfer problem*.

If the terms of trade remain unchanged following the transfer, a certain quantity of goods have to be transferred from the transferor to the recipient country to offset the initial transfer of assets. But if the domestic terms of trade deteriorate, the domestic exports become worth less on the world market, and more of these goods have to be exported to offset the financial transfer. In other words, a deterioration of the terms of trade creates an additional burden for the transferring country. Conversely, if the terms of trade improve, the real burden of the transfer is reduced for the transferor country.

In order to develop a framework for analyzing this problem, first examine the effect of a transfer on the excess demand for B in both countries under the assumption that the terms of trade do not change. Assume that Country I transfers purchasing power ΔT to Country II. In Country I total expenditure falls by ΔT, but expenditure or demand for B falls only by $c_I \Delta T$ where c_I is the marginal propensity to spend on home goods in Country I. In Country II total expenditure rises by ΔT, and total demand for B rises by $m_{II} \Delta T$, where m_{II} is the marginal propensity to spend on imports in Country II. Since there are only two goods in each country and the entire amount of any additional purchasing power is assumed spent, the relationship between the m's and c's can be expressed

$$m_I + c_I = 1 = m_{II} + c_{II}. \qquad (7A\text{--}6)$$

The change in demand for B in Country I may therefore be expressed alternatively in terms of Country I's marginal propensity to spend on imports as $(1-m_I)\Delta T$.

The net change in total demand for B may then be expressed as the sum of the changes in the two countries, or

$$-(1 - m_I - m_{II})\Delta T \qquad (7A\text{--}7)$$

where the change in demand in Country I is negative because expenditure falls there. This expression states that a transfer of expenditure creates an excess demand or excess supply for B depending on whether the sum of the marginal propensities to import is greater or less than one.

Since the transferrence is assumed to occur through the trade balance in this model, the term ΔT in (7A–7) may be replaced by ΔTB. The trade balance in Country I is always the negative of the trade balance in II, and is equal to the transfer of expenditure power or wealth.

To correct the excess demand created by the transfer, the terms of trade must change. From equation (7A–5) it is known that the stability condition requires an increase in the terms of trade P to produce an excess supply of B (or in other words, worsen I's trade balance) by

$$-(1 - \eta_{II} - \eta_I)M\Delta P. \qquad (7A–8)$$

In order for the market for good B to return to equilibrium, the excess demand for B created by the transfer at constant terms of trade must be equal to the excess supply created by the change in the terms of trade. Equating (7A–7) and (7A–8) and rearranging the terms yields a general criterion for the change in the terms of trade following a transfer

$$\frac{\Delta P}{\Delta TB} = \frac{1 - m_I - m_{II}}{(1 - \eta_{II} - \eta_I)M}. \qquad (7A–9)$$

Equation (7A–9) shows that while the transfer may cause the terms of trade to deteriorate, the actual change depends upon the value of the individual parameters for the two countries.

THE EFFECT OF PRICES ON THE TRADE BALANCE

The expression derived above can be inverted to provide a relationship describing the changes in the trade balance that should follow a change in the terms of trade. The relationship is now

$$\frac{\Delta TB}{\Delta P} = \frac{(1 - \eta_{II} - \eta_I)M}{1 - m_I - m_{II}}. \qquad (7A–10)$$

Recall that P above is $P_{B/A}$ or Country I's terms of trade, while TB represents a transfer of goods from I to II. Notice that there is no assurance that a fall in I's terms of trade (fall in P) will create an excess demand for good B and improve I's trade balance. Stability requires the numerator to be negative, and thus the whole expression will have a negative sign only if the sum of the marginal propensities to spend on imports is less than one. If the sum is greater than one, a fall in the terms of trade produces a deficit. There is no *a priori* reason to assume that the sum is greater or less than one. Thus a statement like "a fall in the country's terms of trade will improve the trade balance" contains implicit assumptions about how that country and all other countries react to a change in relative goods prices. Furthermore, unless the supply and cross substitution effects are incorporated into the numerator of this expression, drawing any conclusions from this expression can be an empty exercise.

TRANSFERS, THE TERMS OF TRADE
AND INCOME

This section examines the question of whether a transfer can cause the transferor's terms of trade to improve sufficiently to raise the country's income more than the value of the initial transfer. The effect of a transfer on Country I's income is

$$\Delta Y = M\Delta P - \Delta T. \tag{7A-11}$$

The first term represents the terms of trade effect on Country I's income. The price P is the number of Country I imports per export. A rise in P means that Country I's exports now purchase more imports, or, in other words, Country I's income rises. Hence the first term has a positive sign. The second term is the actual transfer. Since it is assumed that income is transferred from Country I to Country II, this term has a negative sign.

Using either equation (7A-9) or (7A-10), an expression for the change in prices ΔP associated with a given transfer ΔT can be derived. Substituting this expression into (7A-11) yields

$$\Delta Y = \left[\left(\frac{1 - m_I - m_{II}}{1 - \eta_{II} - \eta_I}\right) - 1\right]\Delta T \tag{7A-12}$$

Equation (7A-12) shows the change in income ΔY associated with a given transfer ΔT. Under what conditions can this income change be positive? For a positive change to occur, the expression in the brackets in (7A-12) must be positive, or

$$\frac{m_I + m_{II} - 1}{\eta_I + \eta_{II} - 1} - 1 > 0.$$

This condition can be reexpressed as

$$\frac{m_I - \eta_I + m_{II} - \eta_{II} - 1 + 1}{\eta_I + \eta_{II} - 1} > 0. \tag{7A-13}$$

The term $m_I - \eta_I$ is the effect on demand for good A from a change in income minus the full or uncompensated change in demand for good A when the terms of trade change. Since the relationship between these two terms is $\eta_I = \eta_I' + m_I$, where η_I' is the compensated price elasticity of demand for good B,[2] equation (7A-13) becomes

$$\frac{-\eta_I' - \eta_{II}'}{\eta_I + \eta_{II} - 1} > 0. \tag{7A-14}$$

The numerator of this fraction is negative. Therefore, the fraction can be positive only if the denominator is also negative. But stability requires the denominator to be positive. Hence, real income can rise in Country I when it gives a transfer to Country II only if the two-country world is unstable. However, it is extremely unlikely that an unstable world could ever be observed.

Appendix Notes

1. For a more detailed analysis see Robert Mundell, *International Economics*, New York: Macmillan, 1968, Chapters 1-2.

2. See Mundell, op. cit., Chapter 2.

CHAPTER 8

A Wedge or Supply Side Model of Production, Tax Revenues, and the Trade Balance

Chapters 1–7 assume that all factors of production in an economy are actively engaged in market production. In terms of the Learner-Pearce diagram, the economy has a constant factor endowment point E, and the ratios and levels of factors employed in the two industries must add precisely to that overall combination. The factors are said to be fully employed. However, in recent years increased attention has been given to how the endowment of available market factors is likely to change, even if the overall population or capital stock of the country is constant. The variable supply of market factors in turn creates a variable supply of goods produced in the marketplace, and forms the basis of the current emphasis on *supply side* models of macroeconomics.

Variable labor and capital supplies occur because these factors are now considered to have alternatives to market employment. A painter, for example, can work for a contractor and receive an hourly wage. Alternatively, he can swap services with an automobile mechanic, painting the mechanic's house while the mechanic fixes his car, paint his own house, or even spend his time fixing his own car. Working for the contractor involves market payments which are readily observed and counted as part of the country's income. In none of the alternative employments, however, are any explicit payments made or recorded in the marketplace, so none are included in the country's measured income statistics. These alternative transactions are also likely to escape the view of the tax collector.

So, there are two ways in which an individual can use his time. One alternative is *market employment,* which pays explicit market wages and produces market goods; the wages can then be used to purchase market goods produced by others. The second alternative is *nonmarket employ-*

ment, which involves no wages and whose "goods" tend to be consumed directly by those who produce them. While both alternatives raise the economy's "output," only market-produced goods enter into conventional estimates of production.

The question for the individual (or owner of capital) then, is how to allocate his time between supplying *labor* for market production and supplying *leisure* or *nonmarket time* for his own consumption. Presumably, such an individual is a utility maximizer. The individual, therefore, equates the marginal value of his time in the two activities. He allocates his time so that on the margin a minute of additional time spent in market labor produces an income which provides as much satisfaction as a good produced with an additional minute of nonmarket activity. If the marginal values were not equal, the individual could increase his satisfaction by simply transferring more of his time to the activity with a higher marginal value.

While the individual may be initially equalizing the values of his time in the two activities, events beyond his control may make one activity suddenly more valuable. These events can include a rise in marginal tax rates, government regulations, a shift in the terms of trade, or other distortions in the economy. A rise in *marginal* income tax rates, for example, causes a bigger disparity or *wedge* between the gross income the worker earns in the market and the net purchasing power he takes home. For instance, if income tax rates rise from 20 percent to 25 percent of every dollar earned, the worker's "take home" pay would fall from 80 cents to only 75 cents. The relative marginal value of market time falls, and the individual wants to use more of his time in nonmarket production. The increasing wedge produces a substitution effect away from market production. Models which describe the reaction of market production to the changing size of these wedges have become known as *wedge models* of the economy.

This chapter develops a simple wedge model and incorporates it into the theory of international trade. The first section develops a wedge model for one country in isolation. A production possibilities curve involving market and nonmarket production is described, and it is shown how the individual or country moves along the curve in response to changing wedges. It is also shown how this production possibilities curve can be used to derive a *Laffer Curve* of government tax revenues. The second and third sections expand the model to the open economy case. The concept of time preference is introduced, and a graphical summary of the open economy is developed for describing the responses of the labor market, the level of market output, and the trade balance to exogenous shocks. The fourth section describes the response in a small country to two different government shocks. The fifth section elaborates on the trade balance model by describing the response in a large country to increased government expenditures and foreign transfers. The result is a general equilibrium macro model of a country's trade balance which incorporates many of the microeconomic relationships discussed in the previous chapters.

A WEDGE MODEL OF AN ECONOMY

A wedge model describes the effects on market production of changing incentives to capital, labor, or any other factors of production. As the rewards from market participation change relative to the rewards from alternative activities, the quantity of factors supplied to the market changes. A complete model should include the responses of all factors of production to changing rewards. However, in order to keep the present model as simple as possible, yet illustrate the basic point, only the substitution responses of labor are considered. There are still two factors of production, as before, but the quantity of capital available at a point in time can only be used for market production. Capital has no alternative to market employment, other than perhaps remaining idle.

Labor, on the other hand, has two possible uses for its time. Individuals can supply their labor to the market, for which they receive a real wage w. Alternatively, individuals can use some of their time together with goods produced in the marketplace to produce nonmarket "commodities." These commodities have a very general interpretation. For example, one possible nonmarket commodity is the painter using spark plugs, oil, grease, etc. in conjunction with some of his nonmarket time to keep his car running smoothly. Or an individual can combine food and nonmarket time to produce the commodity "meals." Or we can even think of parents as combining their nonmarket time with diapers, toys, clothes, food, etc. to produce "children."

As the incentives to the individual change, so does the way in which an individual allocates his time. If a painter suddenly finds his market wage rising, he may choose to pay an automobile mechanic to maintain his car so that he can spend more time painting for contractors. Or, as the wages available to members of the family rise, they may spend less time producing meals in the house. The released time can be used in the marketplace, and the home-cooked meals can be replaced by "eating out." Or, as a couple's alternatives in the market improve, they are likely to purchase paper diapers, baby-sitting services, more expensive toys, or anything else which reduces their nonmarket time requirements in raising children.*

Two conclusions can be drawn from this discussion. First, the relevant income for an economy is not just what is produced in the marketplace. Whether the painter maintains his own car, or the mechanic does it for him, the car continues to produce transportation services whenever the painter wants. Similarly, whether meals are produced at home or in a restaurant, people are being fed. So the relevant definition of income should include both market and nonmarket production. The sum of these two productions will be referred to as *full income*. Second, it makes a difference for government tax revenues which way the services are pro-

---

*There are also income effects, but we emphasize only the substitution effects in this discussion. If incomes rise, naturally more of any good or commodity with a positive income elasticity will be purchased.

duced. The tax collector does not tax the painter for maintaining his own car. But if the painter pays the mechanic for the service, the government may receive both sales tax and income tax revenue. Thus, an important aspect of nonmarket production is that it tends not to be taxed.

Given the individual's choice between allocating his labor to market or nonmarket production, what kinds of effects are wedges such as increased marginal tax rates likely to produce? Suppose that marginal income tax rates are raised. An individual may now keep a smaller percentage of each additional dollar of gross income he receives. An hour's pay now purchases fewer goods to combine with nonmarket time to produce satisfaction for the individual. The relative value of market participation falls. If the individual were initially equating the marginal value of time in market and nonmarket production, he would now want to spend less time supplying labor to the market and more time in non-market production. This substitution process ceases when the marginal values of time in the two activities are again equal.[1]

What is true for one individual facing higher marginal tax rates should be true for all. Less labor working with the same amount of capital in the marketplace means total market production must fall. Of course, non-market production rises as labor moves away from the market. Does full income therefore remain constant? Probably not, since the change in output composition occurs only after the government action. Prior to the tax rate rise, utility maximizing workers preferred more market production even though they could have had less. The lower market production is therefore a position of inferior income and satisfaction. Hence, the effect of higher marginal tax rates is to shift the composition of output towards nonmarket production and lower the value of full income. Also, since less economic activity occurs in the marketplace, the tax base of the government falls, and tax revenues may also decline.

How the tax revenue of the government is redistributed can also affect the market labor supply. If as marginal tax rates rise, the government spends each additional dollar of tax revenue on the person who is taxed, the individual experiences no additional tax burden. Increased taxes are just offset by increased benefits. There are no additional forces to encourage the individual to spend less time in the marketplace. However, a more common and realistic assumption is that the proceeds from taxation are disbursed back to individuals independently of how they are collected. In that case, the substitution effect remains for the individual, and less market output is observed.

Taxation can also create aggregate income effects. If the public services provided with the tax revenues are either more or less valuable than the consumption lost to the individual, an aggregate income effect results. It will be assumed in this model, however, that the public services are just valued at their cost, eliminating the income effect. There does still remain the loss of full income from distorting labor toward non-market production. It is usually assumed that a loss of income causes individuals to provide more labor to the market. To the extent that this income effect exists, it partially offsets the substitution effect described.

These relationships can all be summarized in a new production possibilities curve and set of community indifference curves which reflect the tradeoff between market and nonmarket opportunities for labor.[2] At any time, the total available capital to the market economy is a constant amount K. While the quantity of labor available to the market may vary, the labor employed in the two alternative uses must sum to total labor, or

$$L_M + L = T \qquad (8\text{--}1)$$

where L_M is labor supplied to the marketplace, L is nonmarket labor and T is the time constraint (24 hours/day, 365 days/year, etc.). Market output, with constant K, varies positively with market labor

$$Q = f(\overline{K}, L_M) \qquad (8\text{--}2)$$

where Q is market production. Naturally, the production function for market output exhibits diminishing returns when only the quantity of labor increases.

Nonmarket production involves combining nonmarket time L and market-produced goods Q to produce nonmarket commodities C.

$$C = g(L, Q) \qquad (8\text{--}3)$$

Nonmarket output increases as either input increases, but again at a decreasing rate. For ease of exposition, the nonmarket production functions are assumed identical across individuals.

Given technology and factor endowments, these two production functions together define a production possibilities curve for the economy, just as the production functions for goods A and B did in Chapter 2. This production frontier is shown in Figure 8–1. The horizontal axis describes the total quantity of market production Q. If available time T were utilized for market production, output would be Q_{max}. This extreme or cor-

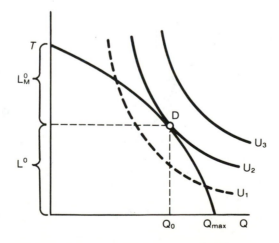

Figure 8–1   The "Full Income" Production Possibilities Frontier

ner solution would not normally be expected since individuals usually require some periods of time for rest. The vertical axis represents time spent in nonmarket activity. The difference between this time and T, of course, represents labor supplied to the marketplace. Notice that since the production possibilities curve represents the tradeoff between market and nonmarket production, the slope of the curve represents the trade-off between work and leisure, or the real market wage w.

The production possibilities curve represents only the supply oppor-tunities. Determination of the equilibrium quantities requires demand as well. Demand is again illustrated by a set of community indifference curves U_1 to U_3. Satisfaction is produced through consumption of the nonmarket commodity C. Market employment enters satisfaction only through its payment of market goods Q which can be combined with nonmarket time to produce C. Apples, per se, do not provide satisfaction. *Eating* apples provides satisfaction, an activity which combines market goods (apples) with nonmarket time. The curves U_1 to U_3 show three combinations of market goods and nonmarket time which produce a given level of nonmarket commodities. Satisfaction is maximized as be-fore where a community indifference curve is tangent to the production possibilities curve (point D). At that point, the community produces Q_o of market goods and splits its time between L^o nonmarket and L_M^o market time.

Figure 8–1 illustrates the equilibrium market-nonmarket output for an economy without any external distortions. But government policies can introduce a distortion and change the equilibrium quantities. For exam-ple, suppose the government raises the sales tax on market goods from zero to t percent. This case is illustrated in Figure 8–2, which assumes the

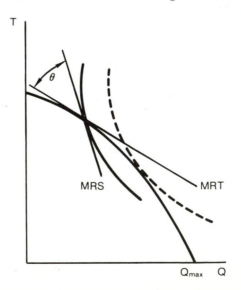

Figure 8–2   The Effect of a Sales Tax on Market and Nonmarket Production

tax revenues are redistributed to the economy in a neutral and costless fashion so that no income effects are generated. The effect of the sales tax in this case is to drive a wedge between the price of market output in terms of labor units paid by consumers (the MRS) and the relative price received by producers (MRT). The wedge is represented graphically by the angle θ.

The sales tax reduces the net-of-tax relative price received by producers as compared with the undistorted case in Figure 8–1. On the other hand, the gross-of-tax price faced by consumers rises. When workers buy market goods with their wages, they are taxed. Nonmarket time remains untaxed. Individuals shift more of their time to nonmarket production. The result is unambiguous: the equilibrium quantity of market production declines. The higher the tax rate (the greater θ), the lower the equilibrium level of output.

The effect of the reduced market tax base on total tax revenues is illustrated in Figure 8–3. Tax revenues are the product of both the tax rate and the tax base. As the tax rate rises, the tax base falls. The impact of a change in tax rates on tax revenues therefore depends on the magnitude of the elasticity of output with respect to the tax rate ϵ. As shown in Figure 8–3, this elasticity is expected to be at most zero, and in most cases,

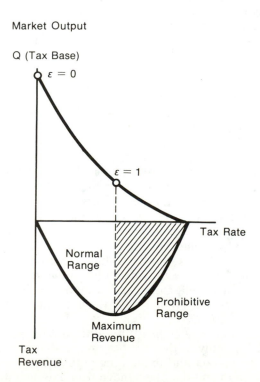

Figure 8–3   A Derivation of the Laffer Curve

negative. When its negative value exceeds minus one, tax revenues begin to fall as tax rates rise.

Tax rates, then, exert their influence on economic activity or the tax base through their impact on economic incentives. If individuals are concerned with after-tax income, then the imposition of a tax discourages production of the taxed commodity. At some levels of tax rates, the induced decline in production may more than offset any gain in tax revenues resulting from the tax rate increase alone.

The relationship between tax rates and tax revenues has become known as the *Laffer Curve*. The bottom half of Figure 8–3 illustrates the derivation of this curve from the behavior of market output. At a zero tax rate, production is maximized, but tax revenues are zero. At a tax rate of 100 percent, tax revenues are again zero since the tax base disappears when individuals are not allowed to keep any of their market production. Their net of tax wage falls to zero. As the tax rate varies from 0 to 100 percent, tax revenues at first rise in the normal range. But once the prohibitive range is reached, tax revenues peak and then fall with subsequent rises in the tax rate.

While the Laffer Curve is illustrated only for the effect of the labor market on the total quantity of output, the basic results are reinforced by including other effects which can change the size of the tax base without necessarily changing output. If capital has only market alternatives, but these alternatives are taxed differently, rising tax rates create distortions which lead to a loss of tax revenue. For example, as marginal income tax rates rise, capital moves from higher taxed traditional market activities, such as corporate bonds, to tax sheltered activities such as cattle feed lots and municipal bonds. Taxable income in the economy declines. Not only does this movement of capital reduce tax revenues, but by equating after-tax yields on the alternatives uses, it causes a discrepancy in gross yields across uses. Too much capital goes to cattle feed lots and not enough to other taxable uses. Such a discrepancy further reduces the level of output in an economy below its potential level.

In addition, the rate of marginal taxation directly influences the degree of tax avoidance in an economy. The higher the marginal tax rates, the higher the tax liabilities on the last dollars earned. The individual or businessman or businesswoman, therefore, has a greater incentive to avoid taxation on marginal earnings by hiring a team of accountants or lawyers to find ways to shelter earnings. Again, the amount of the economy's output which can be taxed falls. Cutting marginal tax rates reduces the tax liabilities and reduces the incentive to avoid the tax collector. Some individuals and businessmen and businesswomen find that it is now cheaper to pay the taxes than to pay the accountants and lawyers to avoid them.

So cutting marginal tax rates has three different expansionary effects on the tax base. Not only is the tax base expanded by more labor or capital entering the market and expanding output, but labor and capital currently working in the marketplace move from low-taxed to high-taxed activity, and some people in the marketplace decide to reduce their efforts to avoid taxes. These three effects together describe the simple logic of how a cut in marginal tax rates can actually increase tax revenues.

SOME BACKGROUND ASSUMPTIONS FOR A WEDGE MODEL OF THE TRADE BALANCE

The production possibilities curve in Figure 8-1 summarizes the aggregate choice between market and nonmarket output for a country in isolation. But assume now that there are a number of countries which have similar trade-offs between market and nonmarket production, and that these countries all trade. How does the opportunity for labor to choose between alternative types of employment influence the measured trade balance of a country? How do the actions of governments influence the choice of the allocation of labor between types of employment, and the measured trade balance?

To set the stage for answers to these questions, adjustments must be made to the barter model of trade from the previous chapters. For example, in this chapter, only the market-produced goods can be traded between countries. Yet, no attempt is made to partition market production into quantities of good A and good B as before. Rather, only the quantity of total market goods produced and traded is analyzed. This emphasis on aggregate production essentially assumes that the terms of trade between the individual goods is constant, so that the composition of output or trade does not affect the analysis. The emphasis on aggregate goods also corresponds to the treatment of the goods market in the second part of the book.

As in previous chapters, factor prices are assumed equalized across countries. Production functions for both market and nonmarket goods are therefore assumed to be similar across countries. However, with two factors of production, and only one aggregate market good traded, even similar production functions cannot guarantee factor price equalization. Recall that with two factors of production, two tradable quantities are required. Hence, capital must now also be assumed to be freely mobile among countries. Capital is assumed to move quickly and smoothly among countries to eliminate any potential difference in rental rates. This mobility of capital, together with the mobility of the traded good, assumes that capital, labor, and goods prices are the same in all countries. The mobility of capital also corresponds to the model of the second part of the book.

So, just as in the barter model, or the model of the second part, there are two sets of equilibrium one must keep track of. First, there is *world equilibrium*. World prices must adjust so that the excess demand for goods or factors in one part of the world just equals the corresponding excess supply in the rest of the world. When prices prevailing in the world market have completely adjusted, the world supply of goods and factors just equals world demand.

Second, there is *equilibrium within the specific countries.* Even though prices may have adjusted so that the world market as a whole is in equilibrium, excess demands and supplies may still remain within in-countries. The individual countries then achieve equilibrium as goods flow from countries where they are in excess supply to countries where they are in excess demand. This adjustment process, of course, is where the concept of the trade balance enters. The countries with an excess supply of goods export goods net to the countries with excess demand. The countries with excess supplies, therefore, are countries with trade balance surpluses, and those with excess demands have trade deficits. The trade balance is the mechanism which assures that total domestic supply and demand of goods are equal. More generally, the level of the trade balance adjusts so that

$$\begin{array}{c} \text{Total} \\ \text{domestic demand} \\ \text{for goods} \end{array} = \begin{array}{c} \text{Total goods} \\ \text{supplied} \\ \text{domestically} \end{array} - \text{Trade Balance.} \qquad (8\text{--}4)$$

When a country experiences a trade balance surplus and exports goods net to the rest of the world, the country is not assumed merely to give the goods away. The purpose of trade is still to get something of value in return. A country with a surplus is foregoing the consumption of some goods that it owned, and presumably the country voluntarily parts with the consumption only in return for promises of consumption of other goods. These promises take the form of financial claims on future consumption like money or bonds. In other words, a country with a trade surplus is accumulating money and bonds which can be redeemed in a later period for goods. The country is trading present consumption for future consumption.

The decision of whether or not to forego current consumption in exchange for future consumption should, in turn, depend on the incentives or rewards of such activities. If the country foregoes consumption this period in exchange for a bond, it can consume $(1+r)$ times that amount next period. The bond pays interest, and the interest provides the opportunity for larger future consumption. The higher the rate of interest, the greater the incentives or rewards from foregoing current consumption. So a country's trade balance is affected by the real rate of interest, or return to capital. The higher this return, the larger should be a country's trade surplus or the smaller its deficit. Another way to consider the world equilibrium rate of interest r, then, is as that level of rewards at which the total trade surplus (supply of investment resources) in one part of the world just equals the total trade deficit (demand for investment resources) in the remainder of the world.

Since a trade balance surplus or deficit implies that financial claims are entering or leaving the country, there must implicitly be some mechanisms through which the financial flows occur. These mechanisms, of course, are the balance of payments and the capital account. A balance of payments surplus represents the net inflow of money, while a capital account deficit represents a net inflow of bonds.

The next logical question is what proportion of the trade surplus (deficit) represents money inflows (outflows) or inflows (outflows) of bonds. That particular question is beyond the scope of the present chapter. Here, the existence of the balance of payments and capital account is explicitly acknowledged, but they are assumed to be operating somewhere in the background. However, in the second part of the book, these accounts are brought to the fore, and their behavior is explicitly analyzed. Following that analysis, it will be possible to show how a change in one account directly affects the levels of the other two.

A WEDGE MODEL OF THE TRADE BALANCE[3]

It is now possible to show the relationship between the existence of a variable market supply of labor and the trade balance of a country. At any one moment, the economy of this country is subject to two restrictions or constraints. One constraint is that the labor market be in equilibrium. At any moment, the total nonmarket and market demands for labor must sum precisely to the total supply of labor available:

$$L^D(\overset{+}{\Omega}, \overset{-}{w}, \overset{-}{r}) + L^D_M(\overset{+}{y}, \overset{-}{w/r}) = \overset{-}{T}. \qquad (8\text{--}5)$$

The nonmarket or leisure demand for time L^D depends on three factors. As total wealth Ω rises, the demand for nonmarket time increases. The greater the individual's wealth, the greater his command over market goods. The individual then does not have to spend as much time in the marketplace in order to obtain a given amount of market goods to combine with his leisure time. Some goods can just be purchased with income from his greater wealth. More of his time can be allocated to nonmarket production to produce the commodities which directly increase his level of satisfaction.

As real wage w rises, it is assumed that the individual substitutes towards market activity and away from nonmarket activity. The higher rewards from market participation provide incentives for the individual to provide more time in market production. These incentives toward greater market participation are assumed to outweigh the offsetting effects from higher real wages raising wealth and lowering market participation as in the previous effect.

Finally, the nonmarket demand for labor varies inversely with the real rate of interest r. As the interest rate rises, individuals receive more compensation from foregoing current consumption in exchange for future consumption. Since only market goods can be traded between individuals (as well as countries), the individual desires to produce more market goods to take advantage of the increased compensation. The individual's supply of market labor rises, and his demand for nonmarket time correspondingly declines.

The market demand for labor L_M^D is a derived demand by firms. As the level of market production y increases, firms desire more of both factors of production. Market demand for labor rises. The firms' desire for labor also varies inversely with the wage-rental ratio. As the wage-rental ratio rises, firms naturally desire to use more capital relative to labor. However, in the short-run model considered here, the quantity of capital (as well as total time) available to the economy is limited. Furthermore, capital is assumed to have no alternative to market production, while labor can be used in nonmarket production as well. Thus, the only way to increase the quantity of capital relative to labor employed is to hire less labor. The market demand for labor L_M^D, therefore, falls as w/r rises.

The interaction of the market and nonmarket demands for labor of a country can be summarized in a simple diagram. At all times the sum of these two demands must just equal the total quantity of time available to the economy. If supply and demand are not equal, relative prices adjust. From equation (8–5), the three relative prices which can adjust are w, r, and w/r. Notice that if the value of any two of the relative prices are known, the value of the third can also be determined. So the market clearing adjustment of relative prices in the labor market can be described in terms of any two of the three relative prices.

In Figure 8–4, labor market equilibrium is described in terms of the real interest rate r and the wage-rental ratio w/r. The $T^d = T^s$ curve shows those combinations of r and w/r at which the sum of market and nonmarket demand for labor just equals the amount of time available to the economy. The curve slopes downward and to the right. If the labor market of the economy is initially in equilibrium at point A on the $T^d = T^s$ curve, and w/r should rise, an excess supply of labor is created. A rising w/r means firms desire to hire less labor relative to capital. With a constant quantity of capital in the short-run, the absolute market demand for

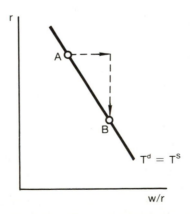

Figure 8–4   The Labor Market Equilibrium Curve

labor also falls. The real interest rate must now adjust to eliminate the excess supply of labor by increasing nonmarket demand. From equation (8–5), the real rate of interest must fall. A lower r reduces the rewards for foregoing current consumption in favor of future consumption. Individuals, therefore, have less incentive to produce market goods, which are the only goods that can be lent in return for interest. Less labor is supplied to the market, or alternatively, nonmarket labor demand rises. The excess supply of labor is eliminated, and the labor market of the economy is back in equilibrium at point B.

While total labor supply and demand are equal at any point along the $T^d = T^s$ curve, the composition between market and nonmarket production differs. As already described, the higher the wage-rental ratio, the smaller is the market demand for labor, and the more labor employed in nonmarket production. So, as the economy moves downward and to the right along the $T^d = T^s$ curve, less and less labor is employed in the marketplace. The quantity of labor employed in the market in turn directly affects the quantity of market goods produced. From equation (8–2) the quantity of goods produced is positively related to the quantity of factors employed. With a constant quantity of capital employed, output varies directly with the wage-rental ratio and the quantity of labor employed.

The inverse relationship between the wage-rental ratio and the level of output is summarized in Figure 8–5. As w/r becomes larger, the desired capital-labor ratio of firms becomes larger, lowering the equilibrium quantity of labor hired for market production. With fewer factors employed in the marketplace, market production falls. Conversely, as w/r falls, more labor is hired in the market, and market output increases. The concave shape of the curve in Figure 8–5 reflects diminishing returns. Both capital and labor are used for producing market goods. Since, however, only the quantity of labor employed varies, as successive amounts of labor are added, output rises by smaller and smaller amounts.

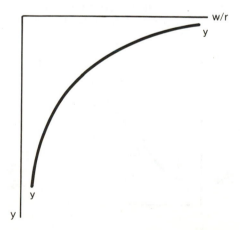

Figure 8–5   The Relationship between the Wage-Rental Ratio and Market Output

The relationship between market output and the wage-rental ratio leads directly into a description of the trade balance. From equation (8–4), the trade balance is simply the difference between the domestic supply of market goods and the domestic demand. Market supply, as just shown, varies inversely with w/r. Market demand also depends on relative prices and income, and hence, the trade balance can be summarized:

$$TB = S_Q(\overset{-}{w/r}) - D_Q(\overset{+}{\Omega}, \overset{-}{r})$$
(8–6)

where S_Q and D_Q are the domestic supply and demand for market goods.

The demand for market goods is positively related to wealth Ω. As wealth rises, more of all goods including market goods are demanded. is negatively related to the real interest ratio r. A higher interest rate means individuals are receiving greater rewards for giving up current consumption, which reduces the current demand for market goods.

This relationship between the supply and demand for market goods can be summarized in a diagram which is consistent with the two previous graphs. A curve can be drawn which describes those relative prices at which the supply of market goods just equals the demand. In other words, along this curve the trade balance of the country is precisely zero since domestic demand is just being satisfied by domestic production. This curve is the TB=0 line in Figure 8–6.

As with the labor market curve, the curve representing balanced trade depends on w/r and r. If the economy were to start from trade balance equilibrium at point C in Figure 8–6, and the wage-rental rate were to rise, an excess demand for market goods is created. A higher wage-rental ratio means less labor is employed in the market, and domestic production of market goods falls. In the absence of any further adjustment, the supply of market goods falls relative to demand, and the country experiences a trade balance deficit. Elimination of the deficit requires a fall in demand, which, from equation (8–6), requires the real interest rate to rise. Trade balance equilibrium is therefore consistent with a higher wage-rental rate and higher interest rate. The TB=0 curve has a positive slope.

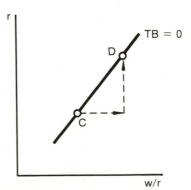

Figure 8–6   The Trade Balance Equilibrium Curve

The diagrams describing the trade balance, labor market equilibrium, and the level of market production are combined in Figure 8–7. Together these curves determine the level of market production and the trade balance for a country trading in a world market. Since capital is freely mobile among countries, this country faces the same value of r as every other country. In addition, with a traded good and similar production techniques, the country must also have the same equilibrium wage rate and wage-rental ratio as every other country. Prices are determined in world markets, but quantities such as production and the trade balance can vary from country to country.

The labor and goods markets within an individual country, of course, respond to the incentives created by the world equilibrium values of r and w/r. In the labor market, these values determine what proportion of the economy's time is spent in market production and what proportion in nonmarket activities. Since labor is assumed not to move from one country to another, the amount of time spent in the two activities in the country must sum to the total amount of time available. In other words, a country must always be somewhere along its $T^d = T^s$ curve. As will be

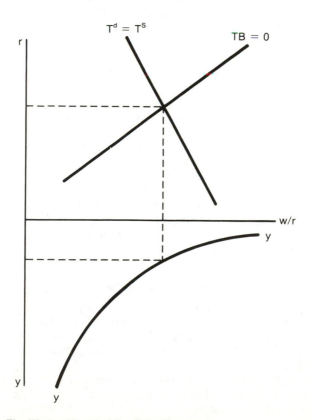

Figure 8–7   The Wedge Model of the Open Economy

seen, assuring that the world equilibrium values of w/r and r lie along all countries' $T^d = T^s$ curves probably requires a redistribution of capital (capital flows) among countries.

A country is not required, however, to remain along its TB=0 curve. The world equilibrium value of w/r (and the quantities of factors available to the economy) determine a country's level of market production. Demand for the goods is influenced by the equilibrium value of r. Given the equilibrium prices, those countries which find themselves to the right of their TB=0 curves experience trade balance deficits, and those to the left run trade surpluses.

With a basic framework for determining output and the trade balance, it is now possible to find the effects of various shocks to an economy. These shocks can take several possible forms. The government can decide to increase the level of its expenditure, the government can increase taxes, or purchasing power can be transferred to another country. Each of these possibilities is analyzed. First, the effects of taxes and government expenditures are analyzed in the context of a small country in isolation to show how the individual country adjusts. However, a second country is introduced in the following section in order to show how world equilibrium prices as well as quantity flows are determined. This expanded model also permits a further analysis of foreign transfers.

A WEDGE MODEL FOR A SMALL COUNTRY

A small country is a price taker. Hence, the small country cannot influence the world real rate of interest or the price of goods. Under the assumptions of factor price equalization, the small country also faces the same wage-rental ratio as every other country. So by examining the response of a small country to exogenous shocks, emphasis can be placed on the implicit substitution effects within the country and how quantities adjust in response to them. The additional complication of responses to adjusting world equilibrium prices can be ignored for the present. The responses and interactions of the labor market, level of market production, and the trade balance within such a small country are now analyzed for two different shocks.

i)   An Increase in Government Expenditure

One possible shock to a country is for the government suddenly to decide to raise its level of expenditure. Assume that this additional expenditure is financed by neutral taxes. Such a shock can have an effect on both the market for goods and the labor market. In the goods market there are three possible effects:

(1) Every additional dollar of government demand raises measured aggregate demand by one dollar. Conventional accounting techniques value government expenditure at factor cost, so a dollar more of government expenditure is counted as a dollar more of total demand. This effect raises the total demand for domestic goods by ΔG.

(2) However, to the extent that government purchases simply parallel anticipated private sector purchases, consumption in the private sector falls. If the government decides to provide free lunches for everyone, we will all stop buying our own lunches. Government expenditure on lunches goes up, but private lunch expenditure falls. The government simply replaces the private sector as the purchaser of lunches.

This offsetting effect, of course, depends on how much you like the government lunches. If the government buys everyone a lunch of spinach and spam, while it may have nutritional value, there is a good chance that many people will throw out the government lunches and still buy their own. If the lunches are steak, potatoes, and ice cream, however, individuals just replace their own lunches with the government ones. So the reduction in private expenditure is $-\gamma\Delta G$, where γ is the value to the private sector of a dollar of government expenditure. If the lunches are steak, potatoes, and ice cream, γ is very close, if not equal, to 1. If lunches are spinach and spam, γ is very close to zero.

(3) If the government is buying spinach and spam lunches, there is also a wealth effect. The government is using resources of the country to purchase spinach and spam. However, when these lunches are thrown away, the resources are being wasted. Wasted resources reduce the value of the economy's wealth. Since from equation (8-6) the private sector's demand for market goods is positively related to wealth, the wasting of resources further reduces the demand of the private sector by

$$- \frac{\Delta D_Q}{\Delta \Omega}(1 - \gamma)\Delta G$$

where $\Delta D_Q/\Delta\Omega$ is the change in private demand with a change in wealth, and $(1-\gamma)\Delta G$ is the "wastefulness" of government expenditure.

Putting these three effects together, the total change in aggregate demand for market goods caused by an increase in government expenditure is

$$\Delta AD = \left(1 - \frac{\Delta D_Q}{\Delta \Omega}\right)(1 - \gamma)\Delta G.$$

Notice that the value of γ plays a very important role in determining whether aggregate demand actually rises. If the private sector values government purchases at their cost, then $\gamma=1$, $(1-\gamma)=0$, and aggregate expenditure does not change. The government expenditures *crowd out* private expenditures. Only if government expenditures are "wasteful" is γ less than one, and does total aggregate demand increase.

The wastefulness of government expenditure also affects the labor market. From equation (8-5), a change in wealth affects the demand by the private market for nonmarket time. As wealth decreases, individuals can purchase fewer market goods, so they supply more of their time to the marketplace to increase their wages and purchasing power over market goods. The demand for nonmarket time, and the total demand for time, falls by

$$\Delta T^d = - \frac{\Delta L^d}{\Delta \Omega}(1 - \gamma)\Delta G,$$

where $\Delta L^d / \Delta \Omega$ is the effect of changes in wealth on the demand for non-market time.

Whether the increased government expenditure has an effect on output, employment or the trade balance therefore depends on the private market's appreciation of the government expenditure. For example, consider the small country Alpha in Figure 8–8. The $T^d - T^s$ and $TB = 0$ curves initially intersect at the prevailing world real interest rate r_0 and wage-rental rate $(w/r)_0$. The country therefore initially has a balanced trade balance and market output y_0. Assume that the government of Alpha increases its expenditure. If the government purchases lunches of steak, potatoes, and ice cream, $\gamma = 1$. Private sector expenditure falls by exactly the increase in government expenditure and there is no wealth effect. Neither aggregate demand for goods nor labor changes. Neither curve shifts, and the level of market employment, output and the trade balance are unaffected by the government action.

But what if the government of Alpha had bought spinach and spam

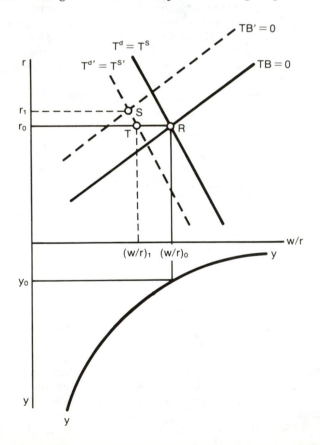

Figure 8–8   The Effect of Increased Government Expenditure on the Labor Market and Goods Market Equilibriums

lunches for the public? In this case, $\gamma < 1$, which would produce an excess demand for goods and an excess supply of labor at the prevailing world relative prices. Both the $TB = 0$ and $T^d = T^s$ are shifted to the left to $TB' = 0$ and $T^{d'} = T^{s'}$ respectively. The two new curves intersect at a higher rate of interest, r_1. If the country could not rely on other countries to relieve the excess demand for the inelastically supplied capital, which is caused by the additional aggregate demand, the return on capital would have been bid up. But the country is part of a well organized world capital market, and excess demands for capital can be supplied by importing more from abroad. The country continues to experience an interest rate equal to the world rate r_0.

Since labor is not mobile between countries, the country's labor market must be in equilibrium. At the prevailing world interest rate r_0, the labor market curve is at point T, to the right of the $TB' = 0$ curve. The increased government expenditure has caused the trade balance to deteriorate!

While point T is consistent with the world interest rate r_0, it is not consistent with factor price equalization. At point T the wage-rental ratio in country Alpha $(w/r)_1$ is less than the ratio in the rest of the world. Since returns to capital equal r_0 in all countries, the wage rate must be lower in Alpha than any other country. Under the assumption of similar production functions in all countries, the lower wage means that the cost of producing a unit of the traded good is less in Alpha. Profit maximizing entrepreneurs will want to take advantage of such an opportunity by expanding production in Alpha. But production can only be expanded by bidding capital away from other countries. Capital, therefore, flows out of other countries and into Alpha.

The increased quantity of capital in Alpha in turn affects the income and labor market curves. The inflow of capital increases the quantity of capital with which each unit of labor has to work. The increased capital per worker has two effects. First, the marginal productivity of each unit of labor rises, increasing the market demand for labor. This effect is reflected in a new rightward shift in the $T^d = T^s$ curve. Second, since at every wage-rental ratio more capital is employed per unit of labor, total output increases. The curve relating the wage-rental rate and output shifts down (expands outward).

The final effect of the increased level of government expenditure is shown in Figure 8–9. The inflow of capital continues until the $T^d = T^s$ curve shifts rightward back to its initial position. Only in that position is labor market equilibrium consistent with both prevailing world relative prices. The income curve has shifted from yy to y'y'. The trade balance curve is unaffected.* Since labor market equilibrium lies to the right of $TB' = 0$, the country is experiencing a trade balance deficit. The trade balance deteriorates from its initial equilibrium. Furthermore, the level of market income has risen from y_0 to y_1. The growth rate of income has

---

*With capital flows, however, the trade balance concept must be expanded to the balance of goods and services to account for the service flows on the imported capital.

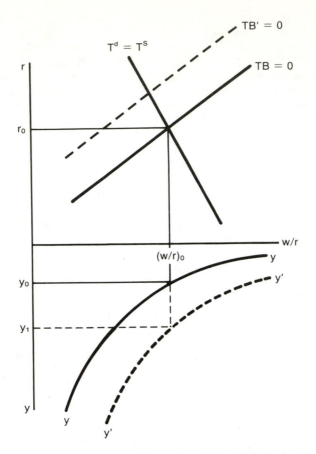

Figure 8–9   **The Small Country After Complete Adjustment to the Increased Government Expenditure**

increased. Thus, the expenditure shock has simultaneously increased the rate of income growth and caused the trade balance to deteriorate.

Remember, however, that these results follow only from the assumption that the government is wasting resources by spending more. Thus, the increased rate of growth in market output is misleading. Since the country's wealth as a whole is reduced, the faster rate of current market output growth must be more than offset by slower growth elsewhere. Lower wealth leads to less labor being supplied to nonmarket production, lowering the growth rate there. Also, the trade balance deficit indicates a loss of future income. The greater current demand is being satisfied in part by borrowing from the future. Hence, the faster growth in current measured output is achieved only at the expense of nonmarket and future consumption.

ii)   An Increase in Taxes

Next, consider what would happen if the government decided to finance its increased expenditure with nonneutral taxes. Assume that the government of Alpha increases its tax revenues by imposing a t percent sales tax. In order to emphasize the effects of taxes rather than expenditure, simultaneously assume that $\gamma = 1$, so that increased government expenditure does not separately shift the $T^d = T^s$ and $TB = 0$ curves. What effect do the higher taxes have on market output and the trade balance?

Changes in taxes change relative prices, thus distorting the choices in the economy and producing substitution effects. The sales tax does not directly affect the wage-rental ratio, so it does not directly alter the firm's input choice between capital and labor. But as previously pointed out, the sales tax does create a wedge between the gross wages received by labor in the marketplace and the net purchasing power of those wages. While nonmarket time can be directly consumed, market wages must first be converted into market goods. The sales tax reduces the number of market goods which can be purchased with a given amount of wages.

The sales tax, therefore, reduces the net rewards from working in the marketplace relative to working in the nonmarket sector. Workers, following their private incentives, now substitute towards more nonmarket production. Measured market output falls. If the net of tax wage rate $\hat{w}$ is defined as

$$\hat{w} = (1 - t)w$$

then the effect of the increased tax on the total demand for labor is

$$\Delta T^d = \overset{(-)}{\frac{\Delta L^d}{\Delta \hat{w}}} \cdot \overset{(-)}{\frac{\Delta \hat{w}}{\Delta t}} > 0.$$

$\Delta L^d / \Delta \hat{w}$ is the change in nonmarket labor demand when the net rewards from market participation increase. Clearly, the greater the rewards offered by the marketplace, the less nonmarket time desired. Hence, this effect has a negative sign. The effect of taxes on net market wages $\Delta \hat{w} / \Delta t$ is also negative. The product of these two effects then is positive. Higher taxes, by decreasing the net rewards in the marketplace, increase the individual's demand for leisure time, and thus the total demand for labor.

Higher taxes, on the other hand, reduce the total demand for goods. By reducing the net market wage, taxes reduce wealth and, therefore, demand for market goods, or

$$\Delta AD_M = \overset{(+)}{\frac{\Delta D_Q}{\Delta \hat{w}}} \cdot \overset{(-)}{\frac{\Delta \hat{w}}{\Delta t}} < 0.$$

The higher taxes create an excess supply of goods at previous equilibrium relative prices.

In terms of the graphical model, the excess demand for labor and excess supply of goods created by the higher taxes shifts both the $T^d = T^s$ and $TB = 0$ curves to the right. The shifted curves are shown at $T^{d''} = T^{s''}$ and $TB'' = 0$ in Figure 8–10. Again, the economy is assumed to be in equilibrium before the government action. After the shift in the curves, however, the labor market is no longer in equilibrium. The prevailing world real rate of interest r_0 is now consistent with a higher wage-rental ratio $[(w/r)_2]$ than exists in the rest of the world. The wage rate in country Alpha must, therefore, be higher than in the rest of the world. The costs of producing a unit of output are also higher, and entrepreneurs desire to reduce production there. Hence, capital now flows out of Alpha and into other countries. The declining stock of capital reduces the marginal product and real wage of labor, shifting the $T^d = T^s$ curve to the left again. The reduced amount of capital also reduces the quantity of factors of production available at any given wage-rental ratio, reducing output and shifting the income curve inward towards the origin.

The final equilibrium appears in Figure 8–11. At prevailing world relative prices r_0 and $(w/r)_0$, the level of domestic market output declines

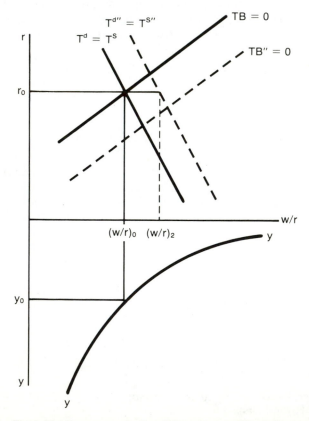

Figure 8–10　The Initial Response of a Small Country to a Rise in Tax Rates

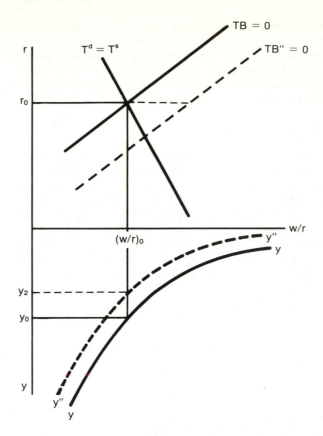

Figure 8–11   The Small Country after Complete Adjustment to a Rise in Tax Rates

from y_0 to y_2. The growth rate of market income has declined. Since the new trade balance curve lies to the right of the labor market equilibrium, there is now a trade balance surplus. The higher taxes have caused the trade balance to improve.

While the increased government expenditure with neutral taxes and the increased taxes with neutral expenditure cause opposite effects, the relationship between the trade balance and the rate of growth are the same. In both cases for this small country, changes in the trade balance are negatively related to changes in the rate of market income growth.

THE WEDGE MODEL
OF A LARGE COUNTRY

The analysis of the wedge model in the large country case is very similar to the analysis in the small country example. The major difference is that the large country is not a price taker. Changes in the supply or demand for goods or capital in the large country can now affect equilibrium world relative prices. There are now three different sets of adjustment to evaluate: the world as a whole, the country in which the government action occurred, and all other countries. The adjustment process in each of these areas is illustrated for the case where the government of one country increases the level of its demand.

i.)   The World as a Whole

Analyzing adjustment in the world as a whole is equivalent to analyzing adjustment in a closed economy, but where the closed economy is the entire globe. Assuming $\gamma < 1$, an increase in one government's expenditure increases the demand for goods and reduces the demand for labor, just as in the small country example. With no change in any other countries, total world demand for goods increases, and total world demand for labor declines. If a set of world labor market and world goods market equilibrium curves were drawn, the increased government expenditure shifts these curves to the left, just as in the small country case. These curves are shown in Figure 8–12. Notice, however, that the goods market equilibrium curve is labeled $AD_M = AS_M$ instead of TB=0. The change of label reflects the fact that in the world as a whole, all trade balances must sum to zero. Instead of having a potentially nonzero trade balance in the world market, aggregate demand for market goods (AD_M) must equal aggregate supply (AS_M).

How do world relative prices adjust to the increased demand? Since capital is inelastically supplied to the world in the short run, as demand for output increases, the return to capital should rise from r_0 to r_1 as in Figure 8–12. Further, the rise in the real interest rate r, together with the excess supply of labor, assure that the equilibrium world wage-rental ratio should fall, again as shown in Figure 8–12.

The decrease in the wage-rental ratio, in turn, implies an increase in the market employment of labor services, absorbing the labor released from nonmarket activities. The increase in total market employment unambiguously increases world market output to y_1. The increase in one country's government expenditure, where $\gamma < 1$, therefore raises the world real rate of interest r and the level of market production.

ii.)   Countries Where No Government
Expenditure Increase Occurs

Since government expenditure is unchanged in these countries, there is no reason for the $T^d = T^s$ or TB=0 curves to shift initially. Instead, the markets in the economies respond initially to the changing world relative prices by moving along their existing $T^d = T^s$ curves. Since labor is not traded, the domestic labor market must always be in equilibrium, which implies that the new equilibrium set of prices must lie along $T^d = T^s$. In Figure 8–13, the adjustment for one such country is shown. As the world equilibrium interest rate rises to r_1, the corresponding wage-rental ratio

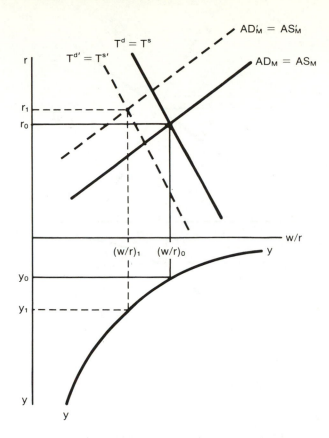

Figure 8–12   The Effect of an Increase in One Country's Government Expenditure on World Income and Relative Prices

falls, more labor is employed in the market, and market output rises from y_0^* to y_1^*. The country is also now to the left of the TB=0 curve, implying the trade balance has moved from equilibrium to a surplus.

For a country to be in complete equilibrium, however, the new point on the $T^d = T^s$ curve must be consistent not only with the new world interest rate r_1, but also, the new world wage-rental ratio $(w/r)_1$. With the assumption of similar labor market equilibrium curves in each country, and with the knowledge from Figure 8–12 that the world labor market curve has shifted to the left, it is clear that the wage-rental ratios associated with r_1 in these countries are initially above the world $(w/r)_1$. The cost of producing a unit of goods is higher than average in these countries. Entrepreneurs desire to reduce production here. A capital adjustment is required.

The capital adjustment is an outflow of capital from these countries. The outflow of capital shifts the $T^d = T^s$ curve to the left, making r_1 consistent with both labor market equilibrium and $(w/r)_1$. It also affects the

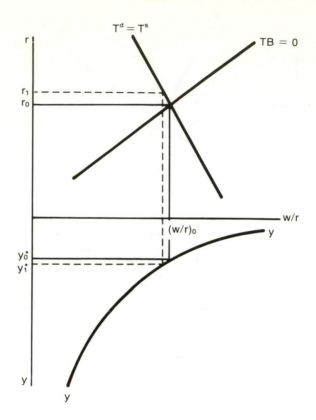

Figure 8-13   The Effect of Changing World Relative Prices on Nonexpenditure Shock Countries

level of production. Less capital shifts the yy curve inward towards the origin. The net effect is to reduce market output below what it would have been if capital had not departed. In Figure 8–14, output falls from y_1^*, which would have occurred in the absence of a capital outflow, to y_2^*.

iii.)   The Country Where the Government Expenditure Rose

The results in the country where the government expenditure increase took place is the same except for one additional effect. Since the expenditure increased here, and since $\gamma < 1$, both the $T^d = T^s$ and $TB = 0$ curves shifted to the left. As the world interest rate rises from r_0 to r_1, this country also moves up its $T^{d'} = T^{s'}$ curve, as shown in Figure 8–15. The movement along $T^{d'} = T^{s'}$ raises income as in the other countries. But the leftward shift of the labor market curve to $T^{d'} = T^{s'}$ also provides a boost to market income. So market income rises initially more (from y_0 to y_1) in the country where the expenditure increases, than in other countries.

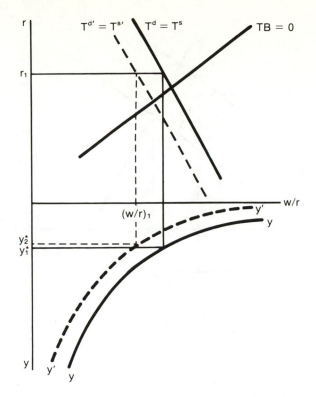

Figure 8–14   The Nonexpenditure Shock Country after Complete Adjustment

In addition, the wage-rental ratio which is consistent with r_1 along $T^{d'}$ $=T^{s'}$ lies to the left of world equilibrium $(w/r)_1$. Wages, and therefore unit production costs, are less in this country. Capital flows into the country as entrepreneurs expand production. The labor market curve shifts rightward in Figure 8–16 to $T^{d''}=T^{s''}$, and the income curve shifts outward to y'y'. Market income rises even further to y_2.

While income has been adjusting, so too, has the trade balance. The equilibrium position along the new labor market curve lies to the right of TB'=0. The increase in expenditure has caused the trade balance to move from equilibrium to a deficit.

The effects of the increase in government expenditure can now be summarized. First, the increased expenditure causes market income to grow relatively faster in the country in which it occurs. In all countries, the rise in the interest rate and fall in the wage-rental ratio causes market output to grow at a faster rate. But the redistribution of the world capital stock from all other countries to the country with the expenditure shock causes the income growth rates to finally diverge. Income grows faster in the expenditure shock country as capital flows in. Income grows slower in all other countries as the capital flows out. Thus, the expenditure

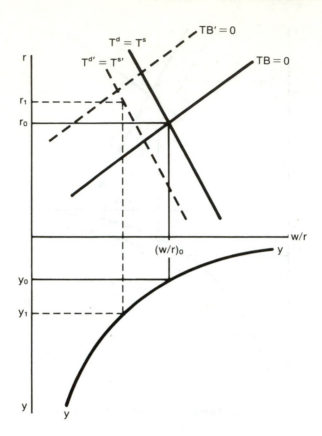

Figure 8–15   Initial Adjustment in the Expenditure Shock Country

shock causes the growth rate of income in the expenditure shock country to rise relative to the growth rate of income elsewhere.

Second, the increased government expenditure causes the trade balance of the expenditure shock country to deteriorate. All countries were assumed initially to have balanced trade accounts. Following adjustment, however, the rest of the world has a trade surplus and the expenditure shock country has a trade deficit, as described by Figures 8–14 and 8–16. The trade balance of the expenditure shock country has deteriorated.

This government expenditure example demonstrates the negative relationship between a country's relative growth rate and its trade balance, which should be associated with an expenditure shock. Following the expenditure shock, the rate of growth of the country's measured income should rise relative to the growth of income elsewhere, while its trade balance should deteriorate. As shown in Chapter 14, there is considerable evidence that this negative relationship accurately describes the real world.

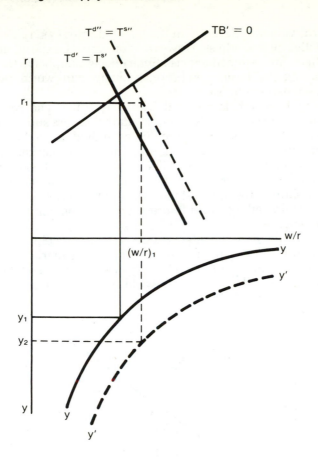

Figure 8–16   Complete Adjustment in the Expenditure Shock Country

A SUPPLY SIDE SHOCK IN A LARGE COUNTRY: THE EFFECT OF TRANSFERS AGAIN

An expenditure or demand shock is only one possible type of shock which a country can experience. The country can also have supply side shocks. One possible type of supply shock is a transfer of wealth from one country (the transferor) to another (the transferee). The traditional transfer problem was analyzed previously in Chapter 7. The concept of a transfer is used now, however, to evaluate the difference between demand and supply shocks within the wedge model of an open economy. As shown, where supply shocks exist, the relationship between changes in the relative growth rate and the trade balance becomes positive.

Assume that Country I transfers purchasing power to Country II. If tastes and preferences of current versus future consumption differ, or if the transfer is valued differently in the two countries ($\gamma < 1$), world equilibrium relative prices adjust. However, for ease of exposition, no distribution effects are assumed to exist. Such effects complicate the analysis without altering the basic conclusions. Changes in world prices are, therefore, assumed not to occur.

In Country I, wealth is reduced by the transfer. The reduction of wealth creates an excess supply of labor, and an excess supply of market goods. The excess labor supply is created as individuals reduce their demand for leisure time and supply more time to the marketplace in an attempt to rebuild their lost wealth. The excess supply of goods occurs as reduced wealth directly reduces the demand for market goods. The $T^d = T^s$ curve shifts to the left, and the $TB = 0$ curve shifts to the right as in Figure 8–17. At prevailing world interest rate r_0, income in the transferor country rises to y_1.

In Country II, the opposite effect occurs. With the receipt of wealth, an excess demand for labor and an excess demand for market goods arise. The $T^d = T^s$ curve shifts to the right and the $TB = 0$ curve shifts to the left as in Figure 8–18. At the prevailing world market interest rate, market income falls from y_0^* to y_1^*.

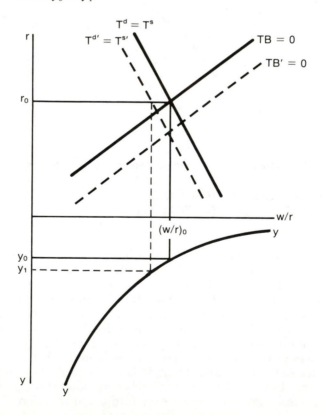

Figure 8–17   The Impact Effect in the Transferor Country

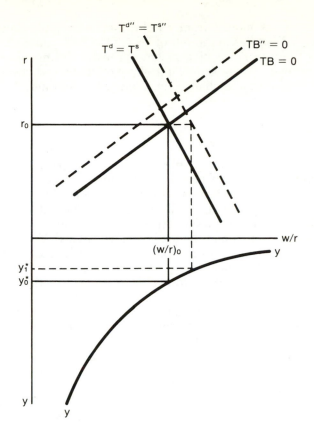

Figure 8–18   The Impact Effect in the Transferee Country

While the rental rate on capital is assumed not to change, the distribution of capital has to be rearranged. Before the transfer, both countries had the same equilibrium values of r and w/r. After the transfer and the shifts in the $T^d = T^s$ curves, however, the prevailing value r_0 is associated with different values of w/r in the two countries. In particular, w/r is lower in the transfer country, Country I. Capital, therefore, flows from Country II to Country I, shifting $T^d = T^s$ rightward and the yy curve outward in Country I, and $T^d = T^s$ leftward and yy inward in Country II.

The redistribution of capital reinforces the initial effect on income. As capital flows into Country I, income increases even more, beyond y_1. The outflow of capital in Country II further reduces income below y_1^*. The transfer, therefore, causes the growth rate of measured output in Country I to clearly rise relative to measured growth in Country II.

With an expenditure shock, as the relative growth rate of output increased, the country's trade balance deteriorated. However, with the transfer, the opposite result occurs. The TB'=0 curve lies to the right of the equilibrium point on the $T^{d'} = T^{s'}$ curve in Figure 8–17. Country I's trade balance has moved from equilibrium to surplus. Conversely, in Country II, $TB' = 0$ lies to the left of $T^{d'} = T^{s'}$ at r_0. Country II now has a deficit. As Country I's relative income growth rate increased, its trade balance improved. There is now a positive relationship between changes in the trade balance and changes in relative growth rates.

SUMMARY

An individual allocates his time between market participation and *leisure* or *nonmarket* participation so that the marginal values of time in the two activities are equal. *Wedges*, such as those produced by additional taxes on income, break that equality and cause the individual to reallocate his time away from market participation and towards nonmarket activity. Measured output and the tax base are reduced. Tax revenues may also decline. In addition to a smaller tax base, with greater incentives to avoid the tax collector, factors rely on accountants and lawyers to search for tax shelters or other ways to avoid taxes. The relationship between tax rates and tax revenues is embodied in the *Laffer Curve*.

The substitution of factor owners between market and nonmarket participation, as well as producers' substitution between capital and labor, are two basic forces underlying the *wedge model* of the trade balance. This wedge model is used to investigate the effect of government expenditure or taxation on the trade balance and measured output. A demand side policy which increases the domestic rate of income growth relative to abroad will be associated with a deterioration in the domestic trade balance. A supply side shock produces just the opposite relationship.

NOTES

1. For empirical evidence of how government taxes and subsidies significantly affect the supply of labor to the market, see, for example, Richard V. Burkhouser and John A. Turner, "A Time-Series Analysis on Social Security and Its Effect on the Market Work of Men at Younger Ages," *Journal of Political Economy*, Vol. 86, No. 4 (August 1978): pp. 701–15; Martin Feldstein, "The Effect of Unemployment Insurance on Temporary Layoff Unemployment," *American Economic Review*, Vol. 68, No. 5 (December 1978): pp. 834–46; Daniel K. Benjamin and Levis A. Kochin, "Searching for an Explanation of Unemployment in Interwar Britain," *Journal of Political Economy*, Vol. 87, No. 3 (June 1979): pp. 441–78; J. A. Hausman, "The Effect of Taxes on Labor Supply," paper prepared for Brookings Conference on Taxation, October 18–19, 1979.

2. Adapted from Victor A. Canto, Douglas H. Joines, and Robert I. Webb, "Empirical Evidence on the Effects of Tax Rates on Economic Activity," paper presented to the American Statistical Association, August 13, 1979.

3. Adapted from Victor A. Canto and Marc A. Miles, "Fiscal Policy, Wedges, and the Trade Balance: The Real Sector of an Open Economy in an Integrated World," University of Southern California, October 1979.

SECTION II

THE INTERNATIONAL FINANCIAL SYSTEM IN AN INTEGRATED WORLD

CHAPTER 9

The Basic Model of an Open Economy

The scope of the analysis of an open economy is now expanded to include the balance of payments. Until this point, our discussion has dealt exclusively with the demand and supply of goods. In economic jargon such a model is known as a *barter* model. In a barter model, goods are exchanged directly for other goods, that is, there is no intermediary asset such as money. The scope of the model is now broadened to consider the importance of the existence of other commodities besides physical goods. Specifically, two more markets are included in the economy, the *market for money* and the *market for bonds*. These two markets constitute the *financial sector* of the economy. The interaction of the financial markets with the goods market can therefore now be described. More specifically, it is now possible to determine under which assumptions or situations the financial and goods markets are independent of each other, and under which assumptions or situations the financial and goods markets interact.

The analysis of foreign trade of assets within either of the two financial markets proceeds in the same way as analysis of trade in the goods market. Recall that within any one country of the barter model, the decision to export or import a good is determined by the excess supply or demand for the good. If at prevailing relative prices the domestic supply of good A exceeds domestic demand, more of the good is produced than is required domestically, and the resulting excess supply leads to the exportation of A. Conversely, if the domestic demand for A exceeds the domestic level of production at prevailing relative prices, the domestic excess demand has to be satisfied from abroad, and A is imported.

For the world as a whole, however, when the demand for A exceeds the supply of A, the relative price or value must rise, since (excluding interstellar trade) there is no place for more A to come from. Thus there are two types of equilibria to keep track of. The first is *domestic equilibrium*, that is, that domestic demand for a good equals domestic supply. If the two do not initially equate within a country, then trade in that good occurs. The second is overall *world equilibrium*. If world demand for a good does not equal world supply, then the relative price of that good must adjust. Therefore, while there can be a redistribution of a good from an area of excess supply to an area of excess demand in order to satisfy a domestic equilibrium, for overall world equilibrium to occur, the total excess supplies of the good must precisely equal the overall excess demand.

The same type of analysis is now undertaken for the money and bond markets. Again the analysis of equilibrium is divided into equilibria within countries and equilibria within the world as a whole. Again adjustment to equilibrium within countries is accomplished by movements of quantities from areas of excess supply to areas of excess demand. Again equilibrium within the world as a whole is accomplished by changes in a relative price or value. But before this expanded model of trade in the world economy is presented, we first review briefly the relationship between money, goods, and bonds within the traditional closed economy, and then relate that traditional model to the present model of the open economy.

THE CLOSED ECONOMY MODEL

A) The Traditional IS–LM Framework— Only Money and Goods

How does the framework of goods and financial markets about to be developed differ from the kinds of models of economies you are probably already familiar with? For one thing, most of the macroeconomic models you have encountered until now have probably only dealt explicitly with the markets for money and goods. This approach is often summarized in the IS–LM framework which can be reviewed in the appendix. The IS and LM curves are shown in Figure 9–1. These curves describe how domestic supplies and demands for goods and money interact to determine equilibrium levels of income and interest rates.

For example, the IS curve represents equilibrium in the goods market. It shows combinations of real income y and the real interest rate r at which the domestic demand for goods just equals the domestic supply of goods. The two major components of aggregate demand for goods are consumption and investment demand. In a simple model, the demand for consumption goods depends upon income, while investment good demand depends upon the real interest rate. If the domestic goods market is initially in equilibrium, then domestic demand for goods equals supply. If income should now rise, while consumption demand also rises, since the marginal propensity to consume is less than one, consumption rises by less than supply. In order to again make supply equal to demand, an additional rise in demand is needed. Since the other major component is investment demand, which is inversely related to the real interest rate, a reduction in the real interest rate is needed. The IS curve therefore has a

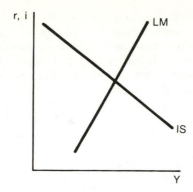

Figure 9–1   The IS–LM System

negative slope reflecting the fact that a reduction in the real interest rate must accompany a rise in real income in order to keep the goods market in equilibrium.*

Similarly, the LM curve represents equilibrium in the money market. It shows those combinations of real income and the nominal interest rate i at which the demand for *real cash balances* just equals supply. Real cash balances, as you perhaps recall, represent the real purchasing power of some level of nominal cash balances M. The nominal balances represent, say, the number of dollars individuals have in their wallets and checking accounts. If that quantity is divided by a measure of the national price level P, which says on average how many dollars it takes to purchase a given quantity of goods, a measure of the quantity of goods that can be purchased with M is obtained. The level of real balances is therefore defined as M/P.

The demand for real cash balances is assumed to vary positively with the level of real income and negatively with the nominal interest rate. The relationship with real income can represent a transactions demand for money. One of the uses of money is as a medium of exchange for making transactions, that is, for buying goods. Of course the number and size of such purchases are going to be positively related to the level of income. So the higher real income, the higher the real level of transactions and the higher the level of purchasing power in the form of money that is required to facilitate these transactions. Thus the demand for real cash balances increases as real income increases.

Since money is assumed not to earn an explicit rate of interest, the nominal rate of interest i represents the opportunity cost or what is foregone by holding these real balances. Following Irving Fisher[1] the nominal rate of interest is defined as $i = r + p^e$, where r is the real rate of interest and p^e is the expected rate of inflation. So there are two parts to

---

*As shown in the appendix, a particular IS curve is drawn for a given level of government expenditure and taxation.

the opportunity cost of holding money. The first part r represents the return that could have been obtained if instead the equivalent money value had been invested in real assets like machines. The second part p^e reflects the fact that when inflation occurs, the real value of any asset fixed in nominal or money terms is reduced. For example, a dollar bill is fixed in nominal terms, always precisely equal in value to one dollar. However, during a year of ten percent inflation, the real purchasing power of the dollar bill at the end of the year is only 90 percent of what it was at the beginning of the year. Thus, during the year, ten percent of the real purchasing power of the dollar bill has been eroded, representing an additional cost of holding money during periods of inflation. This additional cost also applies to holding any other nominally denominated assets such as a bond, whose face value is fixed in terms of dollars. Before an investor will accept such a bond, he will insist on receiving a return equal to what he could have received on a real investment such as a machine, plus compensation for the expected loss in real purchasing power of the face value over the period of investment. Thus investors in nominally denominated bonds will demand a total rate of return equal to the nominal interest rate. So another way of viewing the nominal interest rate is as the opportunity cost or interest foregone by holding noninterest-bearing real money balances, instead of an equivalent amount of interest earning bonds.

Returning to the LM curve, the preceding discussion implies that for retaining equilibrium in the money market, the nominal interest rate must rise with real income. For example, a rise in real income increases the demand for real cash balances. However, as described in the appendix, along an LM curve the supply of real balances is assumed constant. Thus the rise in real income creates an excess demand for money which must be eliminated. A rise in the nominal interest rate can eliminate this excess demand. The LM curve in Figure 9–1 therefore has a positive slope, reflecting the fact that with a constant supply of real balances, a rise in the nominal interest rate must accompany a rise in real income in order to keep the money market in equilibrium.

B)   Bonds—The Third Implicit Market

A second important difference between the framework that will be developed and traditional macro models you have already encountered is that the bond market will be explicitly considered. Basic macro models tend to concentrate exclusively on the money and goods markets. In a model with only money and goods there is explicitly only one relative price, the price of goods in terms of money $P_{G/M}$ or the price level. Yet in the IS–LM analysis, two additional relative prices, i and r, are used. The nominal interest rate i represents the relative price of money in terms of bonds or $P_{M/B}$. It shows how much it costs annually in terms of foregone earnings to hold money (a financial claim on current goods) instead of bonds (a financial claim on future goods). For example, if you hold $100 in cash for one year, at any time during the year, you can purchase $100 worth of goods. But at the end of the year you have only $100. However, if you forego the right to purchase goods during the year and hold $100 worth of bonds for one year, at the end of the year you receive $100 plus i • $100, where i is the nominal rate of interest. So giving up the right to purchase goods in the first year yields an additional i • $100 of financial claims over goods in the second year.

Similarly, the real interest rate r represents the relative price of goods in terms of bonds, or $P_{G/B}$. This rate shows how much it costs to hold nonincome-producing goods in the current year instead of only claims on future goods (bonds). Since goods are assumed to retain their real value (a tomato is always a tomato),* the dollar price of goods rises by the rate of inflation. Goods, just like bonds, produce an annual dollar return equal to the rate of inflation. Bonds, however, yield an additional return. This remaining portion of the return to bonds is equal to what the marginal investor is willing to pay the marginal bondholder for letting the investor have the use of the good (over which the bondholder initially had a claim) for one year. That return is what is foregone by holding or consuming goods during the year, instead of holding bonds, and represents $P_{G/B}$.

Notice that both of these additional relative prices involve a third commodity, bonds. Thus an analysis which discusses only the money and goods markets is incomplete. Such a discussion would have to exclude the real and nominal interest rates, and most economic models accept that these relative prices are important. The bond market therefore must be brought explicitly into the analysis. Essentially, incorporating the bond market would involve drawing a third curve in Figure 9–1 which represents those combinations of r (or i) and y for which a given bond supply just equals bond demand. Full equilibrium in the closed economy occurs then at the intersection of all three markets, that is, where all markets are simultaneously in equilibrium. Adjustment to equilibrium can now involve the change in all three relative prices.

C)   Goods, Money, and Bonds—The Closed Economy Walrasian Framework

A third important way the global model differs from the closed economy macro economic model is in the reliance on *quantity* as well as *price* adjustment for achieving domestic economic equilibrium. In closed economy models, all excess demands and supplies in a country are relieved by only relative prices adjusting. The precise changes in relative prices required are determined by a strict relationship between the excess demands and supplies in the three markets. That relationship, known as *Walras' Law*, states that at a given moment, the sum of the money values of excess demands in the three markets must be zero, that is,

$$EDM + EDG + EDB = 0. \qquad (9-1)$$

---

*And since the terms of trade are assumed constant in this part of the book, a tomato is always worth a constant amount of cucumbers, cars, wheat, etc. as well. Obviously, the problem of depreciation (rotting) is being ignored.

The relationship can also be expressed in terms of the excess supply in one market and the excess demands in the other two, that is,

$$ESG = EDM + EDB \tag{9-2}$$

$$ESB = EDM + EDG \tag{9-3}$$

$$ESM = EDG + EDB. \tag{9-4}$$

The value of excess supply in one market equals the sum of the excess demands in the other markets. This relationship does not mean that excess supply in one market must be accompanied by excess demand in each of the other two markets, only that the total excess demand in the other two markets must be positive and equal to the excess supply in the first.

As an example of how Walras' Law is used in the closed economy to describe the price adjustments necessary for a new equilibrium, assume that such a closed economy, initially at full employment equilibrium, suddenly finds that its money supply has increased. A popular theoretical vehicle for such a pure monetary operation is to have the monetary authorities drop money on the populace from a helicopter.[2] The people in the economy suddenly find that they have more money than previously. Since the price level is initially the same, the supply of real balances has also increased. However, since neither the level of real income nor the nominal interest rate have initially changed, the demand for real balances is the same as before. Thus the actions of the monetary authorities have increased the money supply relative to money demand. There is an excess supply of money. By Walras' Law, if there is an excess supply of money in the economy, the sum of the excess demands in the goods and bonds markets must be positive. For simplicity, it is assumed that there is positive excess demand in each market. Thus people in the economy now want to convert their excess real balances into both goods and bonds.

As we saw in the pure theory sections of this book, when demand shifts from one good to another, the relative price or value of the latter good in terms of the first should rise. For example, if demand shifts from good B to good A, the price of A in terms of B, $P_{A/B}$, should rise. In the present example there are shifts in demand from money to goods and to bonds. Relative values should adjust to reflect these shifts in demands. For example, the shift in demand from money to goods should cause the value of goods in terms of money $P_{G/M}$ to rise. This value, however, is precisely equal to the price level, which implies that the price level should rise. Such a price rise is expected when the supply of money increases relative to the supply of goods. The rise in prices also reduces the real value of the existing nominal money supply, bringing the supply of real balances back to the level of demand.*

---

*Of course, part of the excess demand for goods could be partially satisfied by an increase in the supply of goods if the economy were at less than full employment. But it is assumed in these models that the economy is always at full employment, though the results are similar for the less than full employment model.

Similarly it is expected that the shift in demand from money to bonds will be reflected in the rise in the value of bonds in terms of money, or the fall in the value of money in terms of bonds. Since the latter value is the nominal interest rate, the nominal interest rate is expected to fall when just the money supply increases. With additional supplies of current financial claims (real money balances) money holders do not require as much compensation to give up some of their claims for a year. Again this result is expected, because one way of helping to get the increased supply of real balances initially absorbed into the economy is for the opportunity cost of holding real balances to fall.

If the helicopter had dropped bonds rather than money, the analysis would proceed along the same lines. Given the demand for bonds, an increase in bond supply produces an excess supply. Associated with the excess supply of bonds is an excess demand for money and an excess demand for goods. The excess demand for money causes $P_{M/B}$ to rise, raising the nominal interest rate. The excess demand for goods is associated with a rise in the real interest rate r.

Notice that in each of these two examples, the change in only two of the three relative prices can be predicted. Where money has increased, only changes in the price of money relative to the other two commodities can be described. Nothing is said about the relative price of goods in terms of bonds, because to do that would require knowledge of whether the excess demand for goods or bonds increased by more. Similarly, where bonds have increased, only changes in the value of bonds relative to the other two goods can be described. Nothing is said about the price level $P_{G/M}$.

So in a closed economy, the mechanism for adjusting to an increase in one of the three commodities is an adjustment in relative prices. The price adjustment continues until the excess demands and supplies are eliminated from all markets. But at all times the relationship among the money, goods and bond markets remains

$$EDM + EDG + EDB = 0.$$

ADJUSTMENT IN THE SMALL, OPEN ECONOMY

The process of adjustment changes, however, when the model under discussion is converted from a closed economy to a small, open economy with a fixed exchange rate. As in the closed economy, Walras' Law can still be assumed to hold. But elimination of a country's excess supplies and demands is now shown to rely on quantity rather than price adjustments.

First, however, the meaning of a small open economy must be reviewed. As in the first part of the book, the concept of a small economy refers to a country which is a price taker in world markets. As in the barter models, the relative price of goods or terms of trade which this country faces is given or exogenous. No matter how much of the small country's resources are put into producing any particular good, or how much of the country's income is devoted to consuming a particular good, the small country is unable to affect the relative price of one good in terms of another. In the model where money and bonds also exist, the small country faces even more exogenous relative prices. For example, the relative price of goods in terms of money is also assumed fixed by world markets. The money in this case is foreign currency. The small country therefore faces goods prices fixed in terms of foreign currency. The domestic currency price of any good is proportional to the exchange rate according to

$$P = e \cdot P^*, \tag{9-5}$$

where P is the domestic currency price, P^* is the foreign currency price, and e is the exchange rate representing the number of units of domestic currency per unit of foreign currency. So if apples cost one dollar per pound on the world market, and the domestic currency, pesos, trades at five pesos per dollar, then the domestic price of apples is five pesos per pound. No matter how many apples this small country produces or consumes, it is unable to affect the world price of apples in terms of dollars. As long as the domestic exchange rate is unchanged, the small country is also unable to affect the domestic price of apples.

Just as the small country is unable to affect the world price of goods in terms of money, it is also unable to affect the world price of money in terms of bonds. The small country is therefore also a price taker for the nominal interest rate. The country can borrow or lend as much money in exchange for bonds as it wants (given unchanged riskiness) without affecting the nominal interest rate i. Of course if a country borrows too much on the world market it can affect its financial outlook for repaying its debt, which in turn affects the riskiness of its bonds and requires a risk premium. But the risk premiums are simply added onto the prevailing world interest i and do not affect it.

Using these assumptions about the small open economy, the experiment of dropping money from a helicopter can be repeated. Again, the increase in the money supply, with demand unchanged, causes an excess supply of money. Again, Walras' Law implies that the sum of the excess demands in the bonds and goods markets must be positive. Again, for simplicity, it is assumed that excess demand is positive in both of these markets. But while the initial effects of increasing the money supply are the same, the adjustment mechanism is quite different. In the closed economy case, the excess demand for goods causes the price level to rise. But in the small open economy with a fixed exchange rate, the price of goods in terms of money is given by the world price level. Thus the domestic price level cannot rise. There cannot be a *price response* to this excess demand for goods. Instead there is a *quantity response*. The excess demand for goods is satisfied by importing more goods net from abroad in exchange for money. Any attempt by the country to raise prices would be met by an infinite quantity response since the country is a price taker. If domestic prices rise only slightly, all foreign producers would want to supply goods to the country, since higher profits are possible there. This large increase in supply would cause prices to again drop to the world price level. Thus the excess demand for goods must be satisfied by a quantity response, which implies the trade balance worsens.

In the closed economy the excess demand for bonds and excess supply of money caused the relative price of money in terms of bonds, or the nominal interest rate, to fall. But again in the small, open economy this price is no longer free to adjust. If i falls even a small fraction, the cost of borrowing from the country would be less than anywhere else in the world and everyone would want to borrow (supply bonds) there. So again, instead of a price response, a quantity is needed. The quantity response is an inflow of bonds and an outflow of money or capital, which implies that the capital account deteriorates.

The obvious result of this experiment is that once the small, open economy is introduced, traditional price adjustment within an economy no longer brings an economy back to equilibrium. Instead, adjustment to equilibrium occurs through quantity responses. What is now needed is a mechanism through which these quantity responses can occur. This necessary mechanism is the three foreign accounts of the country, which correspond to the three commodity markets of the closed economy example.

The *trade balance* is the mechanism through which the goods market adjusts in the open economy and corresponds to the IS curve of the closed economy model. Whereas the IS curve shows those combinations of r and y at which the domestic demand for goods equals the domestic supply, the trade balance shows the net quantity of goods which have to be exported or imported in order for domestic demand to equal the sum of domestic supply minus that quantity supplied to foreigners. If domestic demand for goods increases relative to supply, less goods are supplied to foreigners or more goods have to be supplied from abroad, and the trade balance deteriorates.*

The *balance of payments* is the mechanism through which the money market adjusts in an open economy and corresponds to the LM curve of the closed economy model. Just as the LM curve shows those combinations of y and i at which the domestic demand for money equals the domestic supply, the balance of payments shows the net inflow of money necessary to make the domestic money demand equal the sum of the domestic supply plus the quantity of money supplied from abroad. A net inflow of money corresponds to a balance of payments surplus.

The *capital account* is the mechanism through which the bond market adjusts in the open economy. Again, it shows the net inflow of capital necessary to make the domestic demand of capital equal to the domestic supply plus foreign supplied capital. A capital account surplus corresponds to an inflow of capital or an outflow of bonds. An excess demand for bonds therefore causes an inflow of bonds, an outflow of capital, and thus a worsening of the capital account.

---

*In the open economy, the IS curve becomes the ISXM curve, reflecting the net outflow or inflow of goods through the trade balance. A description of the short-run Keynesian model of the open economy is presented in Chapter 16, and a derivation of the ISXM curve is presented in that chapter's appendix.

WALRAS' LAW IN THE SMALL, OPEN ECONOMY

In the open economy, just as in the closed economy, Walras' Law is assumed to hold. So for either an open or closed economy it is possible to write

$$EDM = ESG + ESB. \tag{9-6}$$

The only difference is that in the closed economy models these excess demands and supplies are expressed in terms of the IS, LM, and bond market curves and are eliminated by relative price changes, while in the open economy they are expressed in terms of the foreign accounts and are eliminated by quantity flows among countries. The excess demand for money in the open economy corresponds to a balance of payments surplus, because it means money is flowing net into the country. The excess supplies in the goods and bond markets correspond to surpluses in the trade and capital accounts, because they correspond to a net outflow of goods and inflow of capital (outflow of bonds) respectively. So for the open economy equation (9-6) can be written as

$$BOP = TB + KB. \tag{9-7}$$

The balance of payments is equal to the sum of the trade balance plus the capital balance.

To illustrate the Walrasian relationship with a second example, suppose that as in the closed economy case, the helicopter now flies over the small, open country and drops domestic government bonds. In Walrasian terms, this addition to bond supply produces an excess supply of bonds which is matched by excess demands for money and goods. In terms of the open economy, the excess supply of bonds causes a capital account surplus, while the excess demands for money and goods create a balance of payments surplus and a trade balance deficit respectively. In terms of equation (9-7), since the balance of payments moves from equilibrium into surplus and the trade balance moves into deficit, the improvement in the capital balance must be greater than the improvement in the balance of payments by an amount equal to the trade deficit.

For a numerical example, return to the case in which the money supply increases. Say a helicopter flies over the U.S., which is initially at equilibrium, and drops $1200. There is now an excess supply of money equal to $1200, and a corresponding excess demand for goods and bonds. Suppose, for simplicity, the actions of the monetary authorities create a $300 excess demand for goods and a $900 excess demand for bonds. A hypothetical adjustment process can now be examined.

First examine the trade balance. The excess demand of $300 implies that $300 more of goods are imported from abroad than would have been if the helicopter had not dropped the additional money. This excess demand implies that the trade balance must worsen by $300. Say that the $300 extra transaction consists of John Jones in the U.S. purchasing 60 six-packs of Worseburger beer at $5 per six-pack from Fritz Schmidt in

Germany. Jones gets the Worseburger and Schmidt gets the $300. Jones is happy with his Worseburger, but Fritz would prefer holding Deutschemarks rather than dollars. He therefore goes to the Bundesbank and says "You are fixing the value of the Deutschemark at 3 DM = $1 and I want to exchange my $300 for 900 DM." The Bundesbank of course must oblige, because it is committed to buy and sell Deutschemarks at the fixed value. So there is an inflow of $300 worth of goods into the U.S. and an outflow of money equal to $300.

Similarly, the $900 excess demand for bonds can be satisfied by an inflow of bonds equal to $900 and an outflow of money equal to the same amount. This time Schmidt sells Jones $900 worth of bonds and turns the $900 in at the Bundesbank for 2700 DM.

Using equation (9–7), we can determine the balance of payments or net change in the U.S. money supply. From that equation

$$\text{BOP} = (\$-300) + (\$-900) = \$-1200.$$

So the excess demand for goods, relieved by buying more goods from abroad, and the excess demand for bonds, relieved by buying more bonds from abroad, together just relieve the excess supply of money by causing a net balance of payments deficit of $1200. On the other hand, Germany runs a balance of payments surplus equal to 900 DM + 2700 DM = 3600 DM, and its money supply rises accordingly. Money has been redistributed from the U.S. to Germany. However, the total quantity of money in the world, whether expressed in Deutschemarks or dollars, remains constant.

Of course, there could have been more than just these two transactions. But regardless of the total number of transactions, the essential point is that after the helicopter increased the supply of money by $1200, the trade balance had to be $300 more in deficit, the capital account $900 more in deficit, and the balance of payments $1200 more in deficit than they would have been if the helicopter had not increased the money supply. Quantities of money, goods, and bonds have flowed between this and other countries.

SUMMARY

In a closed economy model, adjustment occurs through changes in relative prices. With integrated world markets, however, the world is the closed economy. Prices adjust to make total world supply equal total world demand. Given world market clearing prices, money, goods and bonds flow from areas of excess supply to areas of excess demand.

The money, goods, and bond markets in the open economy are interrelated. By *Walras' Law*, the sum of the excess demands in the three markets must be zero. In terms of the foreign accounts, this condition means that the country's balance of payments surplus will equal the sum of the trade balance and capital balance, which must sum to an equivalent surplus.

REFERENCES

BRANSON, WILLIAM H., *Macroeconomic Theory and Policy*, New York: Harper and Row, 1972.

FRIEDMAN, MILTON, *The Optimum Quantity of Money and Other Essays*, Chicago: Aldine, 1969.

MUNDELL, ROBERT A., *International Economics*, New York: Macmillan, 1968.

NOTES

1. Irving Fisher, *The Theory of Interest*, New York: Macmillan, 1930.

2. See Milton Friedman, *The Optimum Quantity of Money and Other Essays*, Chicago: Aldine, 1969.

APPENDIX 9
DERIVATION OF THE IS–LM FRAMEWORK
OF THE CLOSED ECONOMY

The IS and LM curves provide a framework for analyzing the comparative statics effects of policy actions within the closed economy Keynesian model. The curves summarize how changes in income or interest rates cause the goods and money markets to move towards or away from equilibrium, and thus indicate the changes in income and interest rates that would be required to bring both markets into simultaneous equilibrium. When both markets are in equilibrium, the economy is in full equilibrium.

The IS curve is derived first. This curve indicates those combinations of income and the interest rate at which the domestic demand for goods just equals the domestic supply. The derivation of the IS curve can begin with the 45° diagram of the very simple Keynesian model shown in Figure 9A–1. This diagram indicates the level of income at which

$$C + I + G = Y, \tag{9A-1}$$

or where the consumption demand C, investment demand I, and demand by the government G for goods just sum to the supply of goods produced Y. In the simple model investment and government demand are assumed exogenous or given, while consumption demand varies with the level of income. The higher income, the higher consumption demand, though demand always rises less than income (the marginal propensity to consume is less than one).

Adding the three sources of demand together yields the C + I + G curve in Figure 9A–1. This curve has a positive slope equal to the marginal propensity to consume. Equilibrium income in Figure 9A–1 occurs at Y_2 where the C + I + G curve crosses the 45° line, or where total goods demand in the economy equals total goods supply. If the level of income

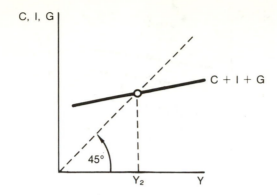

Figure 9A–1   Equilibrium Income

or goods supply were higher, supply would exceed demand, causing output to fall as inventories built up. Alternatively, if the level of income were lower, demand would exceed supply, providing an incentive for output to expand.

The effect of the interest rate* on the goods market is introduced by assuming that the level of investment is no longer exogenous or given. Instead, the level of investment is assumed to vary negatively with the interest rate. As the interest rate rises, it becomes more expensive to borrow money for investment. Fewer projects are now profitable enough to cover the higher interest costs. Hence, the level of investment falls as the interest rate rises. Conversely, with a fall in interest rates, the level of investment rises.

With investment now a function of the interest rate, changes in the interest rate affect the level of aggregate income. If interest rates rise, investment I falls, reducing the level of aggregate demand $C + I + G$, and thus the equilibrium level of income. So the level of aggregate income that is consistent with the demand for goods equaling the supply of goods is negatively related to the interest rate.

The relationship between investment and the interest rate requires altering the graph in Figure 9A–1 to include the interest rate effect. The interest rate effect is shown in Figure 9A–2. In that graph, consumption still varies positively with the level of income, and government expenditure is still assumed exogenous. Investment, however, varies inversely with the rate of interest. Thus as the interest rate rises from i_0 to i_1, the number of investment projects that are still profitable falls, the overall level of investment falls at each level of income and the $C + I + G$

---

*The discussion in the appendix refers only to "the" rate of interest. In the short-run Keynesian model, prices are assumed stable. Hence, there is no inflation and no divergence between real and nominal rates of interest. Once inflation is considered, however, real and nominal interest rates diverge, and the goods market behavior depends on the real rate of interest, while money supply and demand depend on the nominal rate. This distinction between the two rates is employed in the main text of this chapter.

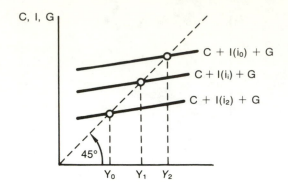

Figure 9A–2   Equilibrium Income with Investment a Function of Interest Rates

curve shifts downward. The new curve intersects the 45° at only Y_1, a lower level of income. Thus at a higher rate of interest i_1, equilibrium in the goods market is associated with a lower level of income Y_1. In Figure 9A–2, if the interest rate rose even higher to i_2, the equilibrium level of income would fall even lower to Y_0.

The IS curve is derived directly from the combinations of incomes and interest rates in Figure 9A–2 at which the demand for goods equals the supply. This curve is shown in Figure 9A–3. The three points graphed on the IS curve correspond to the three equilibrium combinations of the interest rate and income described in Figure 9A–2. The remaining points represent other combinations of the two variables at which the aggregate demand for goods just equals the aggregate supply, or in the Keynesian jargon, at which aggregate withdrawals just equal aggregate injections.

So each point on the IS curve is a potential point of equilibrium for the aggregate economy. At which point will the economy settle? The IS curve alone does not provide enough information to answer that question. However, with the additional information provided by the equilibrium points in the money market, the combination of interest rates and income

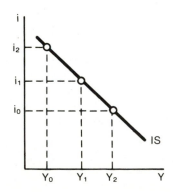

Figure 9A–3   The IS Curve

at which the economy will settle can be determined for the Keynesian model.

Equilibrium in the money market, not surprisingly, occurs where the aggregate demand for money equals the aggregate supply. The demand for money curve, like most other commodity demand curves, depends on income and its price. The price of money is i, the interest rate, because the interest rate represents what is foregone by holding money instead of an interest-earning asset. As shown in Figure 9A–4, the money curve slopes downward like other demand curves.

If the cost of holding money rises, the demand for money balances falls. Also, changes in the level of income shift the demand for money curve. Higher incomes imply higher levels of transactions, and thus larger demands for money. Alternatively, lower incomes would shift the money demand curve to the left.

The supply of money curve is assumed to slope upward as in Figure 9A–5. The positive slope reflects the fact that higher interest rates simultaneously make lending money more profitable for banks and holding excess reserves more costly. Both of the effects provide an incentive for banks to hold fewer excess reserves and expand loans, thus expanding the money supply.

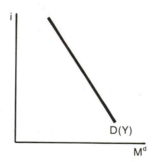

Figure 9A–4   Money Demand

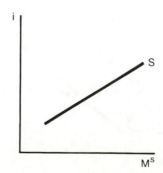

Figure 9A–5   Money Supply

Combining the money demand and supply curves into a single graph yields the combinations of income and the interest rate at which the money market is in equilibrium. These equilibrium points are shown in Figure 9A-6. As the level of income rises from Y_0 to Y_1 to Y_2, the demand for money at each interest rate rises, and the demand for money curve shifts to the right. Given the money supply curve (essentially given the supply of highpowered money), as the money demand curve shifts, the equilibrium level of the interest rate rises. Thus, equilibrium in the money market is consistent with a positive relationship between the interest rate and the level of income. Graphing the equilibrium values of income and the interest rate for the money market therefore yields an upward sloping curve known as the LM curve. This curve is shown in Figure 9A-7.

So there is one curve which describes those combinations of income and the interest rate that provide equilibrium in the goods market, and another curve which describes the same equilibrium combinations for

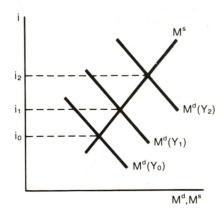

Figure 9A-6   Monetary Equilibrium

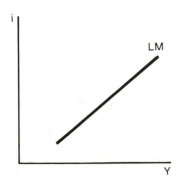

Figure 9A-7   The LM Curve

the money market. For there to be full equilibrium in the closed economy, there must be equilibrium in both markets simultaneously. Simultaneous equilibrium, of course, occurs only if there exists a given
combination of income and the interest rate at which both markets are in
equilibrium. Such a possible point can be found by graphing the IS and
LM curves in the same diagram, as in Figure 9A-8. The point of simultaneous or full equilibrium is where the two curves intersect.

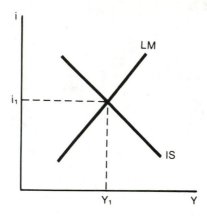

Figure 9A-8   Full Equilibrium—Closed Economy

CHAPTER 10

The Balance of Payments Accounts

Since international transactions involve the exchange of goods, bonds and money with other countries, governments like to keep track of the value and composition of such trade for their countries. For example, does the value of goods and services shipped to other countries exceed or fall short of the value of goods and services imported? An excess of exports over imports would imply that a country's wealth is increasing. Is the additional wealth being accumulated as short-term loans by the domestic private sector to the foreign private sector, or long-term loans? Or is the domestic central bank intervening in international money markets to transform some of the country's additional wealth into increased foreign exchange reserves or reduced liabilities to foreign governments?

The answer to questions like these are summarized in a country's *balance of payments statistics*. The meaning and measurement of these statistics is the subject of this chapter. The following section discusses the differences in the meaning of the balance of payments to an economist and an accountant. The next section presents what is estimated by some of the more prominent measures of the international accounts. Some recent developments concerning the measurement of these accounts are then described. The following sections discuss how the balance of payments can be interpreted as either a stock or a flow, and how, at least theoretically, there exists an overall global constraint on each account. Finally, the last section shows which balance of payments accounts correspond to the concepts analyzed by three popular theoretical approaches to balance of payments problems.

THE ACCOUNTANT VS. THE ECONOMIST

As an accountant would measure it, the balance of payments of a country is always zero. For example, for every item that is exported (a credit), there must be a corresponding import of goods or of financial claims on foreigners, both of which will be measured as a debit. So the accounting definition of the balance of payments simultaneously picks up both sides of the transaction. The accounting definition is therefore not of much interest to the economist, because it includes both the "regular" transactions (such as buying a good) and the "settling" transactions that settle the difference between the regular transactions (such as transferring money or other financial assets). The economist instead wants to separate the regular from the settling transactions. The economist wants to know how much will have to be paid other countries after all the private market transactions in regular goods and bonds have been added up. This remaining amount represents the quantity of reserves or other official financial assets that the country's central bank will have to send abroad or receive from other countries' governments.

This quantity of reserves transferred between countries in turn provides additional information. In the fixed exchange rate model that is developed in the beginning of this section of the book, the flow of official assets indicates what is happening to a country's level of reserves. An outflow represents a reduction in the quantity of reserves, which reduces the country's future ability to intervene in international financial markets to maintain its exchange rate. A continual outflow therefore means a country is probably headed towards an exchange rate crisis. In a floating exchange rate model, the size of the net outflow or inflow indicates the net extent to which the central bank has or must intervene in the private sector's foreign exchange market during the year. The intervention then indicates both the net degree to which the central bank has attempted to influence the exchange rate and the net degree to which it has transmitted monetary policy abroad.

In terms of the framework presented in Chapter 9, the accounting definition can be described as

$$TB + KB - BOP = 0, \qquad (10\text{--}1)$$

where TB is the trade balance, KB the capital account and BOP the balance of payments.* In each time period the three foreign accounts must sum to zero. But such a relationship is not of much interest since it does not postulate why the three accounts are changing, or what the value of any one account should be. Instead, the economic definition of the balance of payments is

$$BOP = TB + KB \qquad (10\text{--}2)$$

which is a behavioral relationship permitting the study of changes in the balance of payments and the underlying forces determining it. Also, given a theory about the trade balance or the capital balance, it permits an understanding of how the three accounts interact.

However, before commencing the discussion of the determinants of the foreign account behavior, it is first useful to describe some of the

---

*A more precise definition would be $CA + KB - BOP = 0$, where CA is the current account balance.

basic characteristics of the foreign accounts. The discussion begins with a description of the components of the three accounts.

BALANCE OF PAYMENTS STATISTICS

The U.S. balance of payments statistics are collected and published by the Department of Commerce. The objective of the data compilers is to measure every transaction between a U.S. resident and a "foreigner." Of course, with the enormous quantity of foreign transactions, many of which cannot be easily recognized, a complete accounting is very difficult. With enough resources devoted to the compilation, perhaps a complete accounting would be possible. However, such an aggressive gathering of statistics would not be socially desirable. Ideally, the data collection should not be pushed past the point where the marginal costs of data collection equal the marginal benefits, and so data gathering agencies often use data that are already collected and compiled for other purposes. Naturally this approach leads to less than complete coverage of all transactions and sizable errors in the final estimates.

One often hears the expression "above the line" or "below the line" when referring to foreign account balances. "The line" refers to the particular foreign balance being discussed. As can be seen in the Commerce Department's balance of payments statistics (Table 10–1), there are several different balances (see table headings) to which one can refer. Among these are the merchandise trade balance, the balance on goods and services, the current account, the net liquidity balance and the official settlements balance. If one refers to the current account balance, above the line simply refers to all the items in the foreign accounts that already have been measured. In fact, the sum of all items above the line is just equal to the current account balance. All items below the line are the items not yet counted, including the settling transactions. These items of course represent the transactions that finance the current account.

The Merchandise Trade Balance

The first line or account in the balance of payments statistics is the *merchandise trade balance*. This account records the net transactions of the domestic private sector in the exportation and importation of physical goods. A merchandise trade surplus represents an excess in the value of exports over imports, while a deficit implies that the value of physical goods imported exceeds those exported. For example, Table 10–1 shows that in 1974 the U.S. exported $5.3 million less in goods than it imported. In 1975, however, the U.S. had a merchandise trade surplus, exporting over $9 million more than it imported.

Trade balance statistics are among the oldest statistics gathered by governments, because revenues from tariffs have been traditionally an important source of revenue for national governments. For example, in the United States, prior to the imposition of the income tax in the begin-

Table 10–1   U.S. Balance of Payments Statistics (Millions of Dollars)

	1973	1974	1975
Exports	71,379	98,309	107,184
Imports	−70,424	−103,586	−98,139
Merchandise trade balance	955	−5,277	9,045
Military transactions, net	−2,317	−2,158	−819
Travel and transportation, net	−2,862	−2,692	−1,968
Investment Income, net	5,179	10,121	6,030
Other services, net	3,222	3,830	4,211
Balance on goods and services	4,177	3,825	16,500
Remittances, pensions and other transfers	−1,903	−1,721	−1,763
Balance on goods, services and remittances	2,274	2,104	14,736
U.S. government grants (excluding military grants of goods and services)	−1,938	−5,461	−2,820
Balance on current account	335	−3,357	11,916
U.S. government capital flows	−1,490	1,119	−1,726
Long-term private capital flows, net	177	−8,463	−8,789
Balance on current account and long-term capital (basic balance)	−977	−10,702	1,401
Nonliquid short-term private capital flow, net	−4,238	−12,936	−2,819
Allocation of SDRs	—	1,840	5
Errors and ommissions, net	−2,436	4,698	4,556
Net liquidity balance	−7,651	−18,940	−3,138
Liquid private capital flows, net	2,343	10,543	−5,601
Official reserve transactions balance	−5,308	−8,397	−2,463
Financed by changes in:			
Liabilities to foreign official agencies	5,099	9,831	3,070
U.S. official reserve assets, net	209	−1,434	−607

Source: U.S. Department of Commerce.

ning of this century, tariffs were a primary source of government revenue. So in the United States, the U.S. Treasury, which is in charge of administering the tariff laws, is the primary collector of trade balance data. Customs officials monitor all U.S. ports, land, sea, and air, to record the entry and exit of physical goods.

While such an extensive monitoring system probably observes the overwhelming majority of movements of goods across the borders, even the customs officials do not observe all movements. For example, packages mailed by private individuals to relatives in foreign countries are not recorded. Nor are goods which travelers may import or export unobserved in their suitcases. But these categories are probably insignificant compared with the total transactions. Another source of errors, however, is the valuation of goods actually recorded. The true market value of some items is known only when they are actually sold. For instance, the true value of imported tomatoes may be known only when they are auctioned off at the produce market. Yet U.S. customs officials must estimate the value of the tomatoes when they cross the border. An inaccurate estimate not only biases the import statistics, but also leads to an inequality of credits and debits when the value of what is imported is compared to what has actually been paid for it.

Because of the network of customs offices for measuring the movements of goods, these data can be rapidly collected and reported. In fact the merchandise trade balance is reported monthly by the Commerce Department. The preliminary trade figure for a given month is released to the news media by the end of the following month. Because of the frequency and speed with which these data are announced, the merchandise trade balance is one of the most popular and widely quoted of the foreign account balances. But the balance represents only the net valuation of imports and exports of physical goods, and as perhaps is already clear, such transactions represent only a fraction of all international transactions.

The Current Account

Moving down from the merchandise trade balance to the *current account balance* involves adding to the net flow of goods the net flows of services and gifts. Services include many categories, the most prominent of which are military transactions, air or sea transportation services, and the net repatriated income from investments abroad.

Prior to 1976 military transactions were a constant annual net inflow of services, representing the large purchases by military bases and personnel abroad. Repatriated income is income of foreign subsidiaries of U.S. firms which is returned to the parent company. Income which remains with the foreign subsidiary, in turn, is classified as U.S. direct investments abroad. Royalties and license fees, another important source of foreign income for firms, is included in the category of other services.

However, there are certainly many other forms of services which are sold to foreigners, such as the services rendered by college professors who lecture abroad for a fee, operators who provide hotel rooms for foreign tourists, or royalties on movies or books sold abroad. Naturally these various service transactions are much more difficult to count than physical goods crossing a border. For that reason, trade in services is often referred to as trade in *invisibles*. Estimates of these services are therefore obtained by sampling through questionnaires or surveys. Although the Commerce Department tries to pick a representative sample, the sampling technique produces an increased margin of error. So from time to time the Commerce Department attempts to adjust its estimates by making more in-depth studies of these trade categories.

The addition of the net flow of services to the merchandise trade account yields the *balance on goods and services*. This balance represents the net flow of goods and services from the country, and corresponds to the category of net exports included in the national income accounts that measure GNP. This balance also corresponds to many economists' concept of the trade balance.

Moving down to the current account involves the addition of unilateral transfers. These transfers include foreign aid given by the U.S. to other countries, social security and other pension payments sent to retirees who now live abroad, and other forms of private remittances. The outflow of transfers and private remittances is handled differently than the outflow of goods. Since any transaction which leads to foreigners receiving payments from the United States increases debits of (claims on) the U.S., a net outflow of transfers and remittances worsens the current account. So above the line of the current account balance is the sum of all the net goods and services and the net transfers and remittances received from foreigners. A positive current account balance means that the net quantity of goods and services sent abroad exceeds net transfers and remittances to foreigners. Items below the line therefore show the total addition to U.S. claims on foreigners, and how this addition is divided between various types of capital and official reserves. Hence, a current account surplus means that the U.S. is adding to its net foreign wealth (claims on foreigners), so the current account is very close to the concept of *net foreign investment* that appears in the national income accounts.* The surplus shows the net amount of current goods and services that the U.S. has given foreigners in exchange for rights to future goods and services.

The Capital Account and the Balance of Payments

People do not always agree on the precise definition of the balance of payments. Conceptually, the current account indicates the quantity of financial claims or assets that U.S. residents are accumulating from foreigners each year.** The capital balance should indicate the proportion of those claims which are claims on future goods. The balance of payments then should indicate the remaining claims or assets (on current goods) that must be transferred between central banks as money or official reserves. However, economists do not always agree on what are autonomous capital transactions undertaken voluntarily by the private sector in response to fundamental economic incentives and what are accommodating capital transactions undertaken or induced by the government. Because of that disagreement, several different definitions of the

---

*In fact the current account balance and net foreign investment differ by only the U.S. government's acquisition of SDR'S. An SDR is a form of international reserve asset created by the IMF.

**If this figure is negative, the U.S. has a current account deficit, and foreigners are accumulating net claims on U.S. residents.

balance of payments have been suggested, with different capital transactions remaining "below the line."

For example, Table 10–1 shows first a balance on current account and long-term capital (basic balance), then a net liquidity balance, and finally an official reserve transactions balance. The accounts become increasingly inclusive, drawing the line first between movements of long-term (more than one year to maturity) and short-term capital, then between the changes in short-term claims of U.S. residents and foreigners, and finally between changes in private and official asset holdings.

The definition corresponding to the concept of the balance of payments used in this book is the *official reserve transactions* or *official settlements balance*. This definition emphasizes the government's intervention with quantities of its own foreign exchange reserves or liabilities to foreign official agencies as the only direct measure of the government's net involvement in international markets, and hence, the only direct measure of the country's balance of payments. Examining the foreign accounts in Table 10–1 shows that the official reserve transactions definition is the sum of all the net foreign transactions in the goods and capital (bond) markets. The current account represents the balance of net private market transactions in goods. Similarly, the net private capital transactions are considered part of the "regular" transactions of the private sector. Were the governments never to intervene in international markets, these two accounts would always offset each other. If the private sector of a country imported a greater value of current goods and services than it exported, the imbalance would have to be "financed" by issuing claims on future goods and services (bonds) to foreigners. The balance of payments would always be zero.

In the real world, however, governments do intervene in private international markets, creating apparent imbalances in private market exchanges. For example, if General Computer, an American company, sells a computer system to some residents of France, it may receive as payment a deposit in a French bank. The balance of payments statistics of the U.S. would record a net export of goods and a capital account deficit (increased short-term liquid claims on foreigners) of equal magnitude. No payments imbalance arises. Even if General Computer transferred the account to an American bank in New York, no payments imbalance arises, because the increased claims on foreigners by the bank just offsets the reduced claims on foreigners by General Computer. However, if the government acts to transform the French franc deposit in Paris (whether held by General Computer or the U.S. bank) into dollars, an apparent payments imbalance appears.

The government may intervene either because it is fixing the dollar in terms of the franc or because it desires to influence a floating dollar/franc exchange rate. In the first case, General Computer or the U.S. bank may have desired to convert its franc balances into dollar balances, and the Federal Reserve was required to intervene. In the second case, the intervention may have been entirely at the Federal Reserve's discretion. In either case, however, the intervention reduces the claims of a private

U.S. transactor on foreigners, as the franc deposit is absorbed by the Fed, but does not simultaneously increase the claims of another private transactor. A private sector payments imbalance is created in the form of a capital account surplus. The capital account surplus, of course, is accompanied by a corresponding balance of payments surplus as the Fed's foreign reserves increase. This increase in official reserves is the settling transaction. It is the settlement required to make the international accounts balance after the government's intervention in the private international markets.

A desirable feature of this official reserve transaction definition is that it also corresponds most closely to the concept of the net flow of money into or out of a country. The net quantity of government intervention or the "settlement" transaction corresponds to net changes in the domestic supply of money. For example, as discussed in Chapter 9, as long as under a fixed exchange rate system the private sector converts foreign money into domestic money, any net private money flow is reflected in changes in the central bank's reserves. The change in reserves can be a rise in either the quantity of official reserve holdings or the quantity of interest-bearing claims on foreign governments in one country, and a corresponding reduction of reserves or increased official liabilities to foreign governments in the other country. In the present example, when General Computer sells the system to France, if the Federal Reserve intervenes to convert the francs to dollars, the dollar money supply rises by an amount equal to the increase in U.S. foreign reserves. This definition therefore indicates the degree to which the Fed transmits monetary policies among countries.

RECENT DEVELOPMENTS

In mid-1976, the Commerce Department began reporting the balance of payments statistics in a slightly different form from Table 10-1. The change in the presentation of the numbers coincided with the release of the official report of the advisory committee on the presentation of balance of payments statistics. The primary reason for convening the committee was the belief that "because of major changes in the world economy and in the international monetary system in the past few years—notably the widespread abandonment of par values—the form in which the balance of payments is presented has been subjected to recent question and scrutiny."[1] The major concern of the committee was how the presentation of the U.S. balance of payments statistics should be changed to permit the continued use of the data by interested persons, but not to encourage "preconceived and perhaps misleading conclusions as to their significance for the United States and other countries."[2] The committee concluded that "a meaningful picture of U.S. international transactions can be obtained only from an analysis of information on several if not all of the categories of transactions, rather than by concentration on one or even several overall balances."[3]

Table 10–2 U.S. International Transactions [Millions of Dollars]

(Credits +; debits —)	1970	1971	1972	1973	1974	1975	1976	1977	1978	1979
Exports of goods and services	65,673	68,837	77,495	110,241	146,666	155,729	171,630	184,705	221,036	286,508
Merchandise, adjusted, excluding military	42,469	43,319	49,381	71,410	98,306	107,088	114,745	120,186	142,054	182,055
Transfers under U.S. military agency sales contracts	1,501	1,926	1,384	2,559	3,379	4,049	5,454	7,451	8,240	7,194
Travel	2,331	2,534	2,817	3,412	4,032	4,697	5,742	6,150	7,186	8,335
Passenger fares	544	615	699	975	1,104	1,039	1,229	1,366	1,603	2,156
Other transportation	3,125	3,299	3,579	4,465	5,697	5,840	6,747	7,264	8,306	9,793
Fees and royalties from affiliated foreigners	1,758	1,927	2,115	2,513	3,070	3,543	3,531	3,793	4,775	5,042
Fees and royalties from unaffiliated foreigners	573	618	655	712	751	757	822	920	1,065	1,150
Other private services	1,294	1,546	1,764	1,985	2,321	2,920	3,584	3,802	4,217	4,291
U.S. Government miscellaneous services	332	347	357	401	419	446	489	557	620	522
Receipts of income on U.S. assets abroad:										
Direct investment	8,168	9,159	10,949	16,542	19,157	16,595	18,999	20,081	25,165	37,815
Interest, dividends, and earnings of unincorporated affiliates	4,992	5,983	6,416	8,384	11,379	8,547	11,303	12,795	13,696	19,401
Reinvested earnings of incorporated affiliates	3,176	3,176	4,532	8,158	7,777	8,048	7,696	7,286	11,469	18,414
Other private receipts	2,671	2,641	2,949	4,330	7,356	7,644	8,955	10,881	15,964	25,861
U.S. Government receipts	907	906	868	938	1,074	1,112	1,332	1,625	1,843	2,294
Transfers of goods and services under U.S. military grant programs, net	2,713	3,546	4,492	2,810	1,818	2,207	373	204	236	305
Imports of goods and services	−60,050	−66,569	−79,435	−99,219	−137,357	−132,836	−162,248	−194,169	−230,240	−281,630
Merchandise adjusted, excluding military	−39,866	−45,579	−55,797	−70,499	−103,649	−98,041	−124,051	−151,689	−175,813	−211,524
Direct defense expenditures	−4,855	−4,819	−4,784	−4,629	−5,032	−4,795	−4,895	−5,823	−7,354	−8,469
Travel	−3,980	−4,373	−5,042	−5,526	−5,980	−6,417	−6,856	−7,451	−8,475	−9,413
Passenger fares	−1,215	−1,290	−1,596	−1,790	−2,095	−2,263	−2,568	−2,748	−2,896	−3,100
Other transportation	−2,843	−3,130	−3,520	−4,694	−5,942	−5,688	−6,852	−7,874	−8,912	−10,466
Fees and royalties to affiliated foreigners	−111	−118	−155	−209	−160	−287	−293	−243	−393	−471
Fees and royalties to unaffiliated foreigners	−114	−123	−139	−176	−186	−186	−189	−191	−214	−235
Private payments for other services	−827	−956	−1,043	−1,180	−1,262	−1,551	−2,006	−2,194	−2,566	−2,779
U.S. Government payments for miscellaneous services	−725	−746	−788	−862	−967	−1,044	−1,227	−1,358	−1,545	−1,714
Payments of income on foreign assets in the United States:										
Direct investment	−875	−1,164	−1,284	−1,610	−1,331	−2,234	−3,110	−2,834	−4,211	−6,033
Interest, dividends, and earnings of unincorporated affiliates	−441	−621	−715	−699	−266	−1,046	−1,451	−1,248	−1,628	−2,303
Reinvested earnings of incorporated affiliates	−434	−542	−569	−910	−1,065	−1,189	−1,659	−1,586	−2,583	−3,730
Other private payments	−3,617	−2,428	−2,604	−4,209	−6,491	−5,788	−5,681	−6,224	−9,188	−16,361
U.S. Government payments	−1,024	−1,844	−2,684	−3,836	−4,262	−4,542	−4,520	−5,540	−8,674	−11,066
U.S. military grants of goods and services, net	−2,713	−3,546	−4,492	−2,810	−1,818	−2,207	−373	−204	−236	−305
Unilateral transfers (excluding military grants of goods and services), net	−3,294	−3,701	−3,854	−3,881	−7,187	−4,613	−4,998	−4,605	−5,055	−5,666
U.S. Government grants (excluding military grants of goods and services)	−1,736	−2,043	−2,173	−1,938	−5,475	−2,894	−3,146	−2,775	−3,171	−3,524
U.S. Government pensions and other transfers	−462	−542	−572	−693	−694	−813	−934	−971	−1,086	−1,187
Private remittances and other transfers	−1,096	−1,117	−1,109	−1,250	−1,017	−906	−917	−859	−798	−955
U.S. assets abroad, net (increase / capital outflow (—))	−9,336	−12,474	−14,497	−22,874	−34,745	−39,703	−51,269	−35,793	−61,191	−61,748
U.S. official reserve assets, net	2,481	2,349	−4	158	−1,467	−849	−2,558	−375	732	−1,107
Gold	787	866	547	9		−66	−78	−118	−65	−65
Special drawing rights	−851	−249	−703	−33	−172	−466	−2,212	−121	1,249	−1,136
Reserve position in the International Monetary Fund	389	1,350	153	182	−1,265	−317	−268	−294	4,231	−189
Foreign currencies	2,156	382	−1		−30			158	−4,683	283

Item										
U.S. Government assets, other than official reserve assets, net	-1,589	-1,844	-1,568	-2,644	366	-3,474	-4,214	-3,693	-4,644	-3,783
U.S. loans and other long-term assets	-3,293	-4,181	-3,819	-4,638	-5,001	-5,941	-6,943	-6,445	-7,470	-7,651
Repayments on U.S. loans	1,721	2,115	2,086	2,596	4,826	2,475	2,596	2,719	2,942	3,852
U.S. foreign currency holdings and U.S. short-term assets, net	-16	182	165	-602	541	-9	133	33	-115	16
U.S. private assets, net	-10,228	-12,939	-12,925	-20,388	-33,643	-35,380	-44,498	-31,725	-57,279	-56,858
Direct investment	-7,589	-7,617	-7,747	-11,353	-9,052	-14,244	-11,949	-12,898	-16,345	-24,319
Equity and intercompany accounts	-4,413	-4,441	-3,214	-3,195	-1,275	-6,196	-4,253	-5,612	-4,877	-5,904
Reinvested earnings of incorporated affiliates	-3,176	-3,176	-4,532	-8,158	-7,777	-8,048	-7,696	-7,286	-11,469	-18,414
Foreign securities	-1,076	-1,113	-618	-671	-1,854	-6,247	-8,885	-5,460	-3,450	-4,643
U.S. claims on unaffiliated foreigners reported by U.S. nonbanking concerns: Long-term	-586	-168	-243	-396	-474	-366	-42	-99	-53	-2,029
Short-term	-10	-1,061	-811	-1,987	-2,747	-991	-2,254	-1,841	-3,800	
U.S. claims reported by U.S. banks, not included elsewhere: Long-term	155	-612	-1,307	-933	-1,183	-2,357	-2,362	-751	-33,631	-25,868
Short-term	-1,122	-2,368	-2,199	-5,047	-18,333	-11,175	-19,006	-10,676		
Foreign assets in the United States, net (increase/capital inflow (+))	6,359	22,970	21,461	18,388	34,241	15,670	36,518	50,741	64,096	37,575
Foreign official assets in the United States, net	6,908	26,879	10,475	6,026	10,546	7,027	17,693	36,575	33,293	-14,271
U.S. Government securities	9,439	26,570	8,470	641	4,172	5,563	9,892	32,538	24,189	-21,891
U.S. Treasury securities	9,411	26,578	8,213	59	3,270	4,658	9,319	30,230	23,523	-22,356
Other	28	-8	257	582	902	905	573	2,308	666	465
Other U.S. Government liabilities	-456	-510	182	936	301	1,517	4,627	1,159	2,220	-714
U.S. liabilities reported by U.S. banks, not included elsewhere	-2,075	819	1,638	4,126	5,818	-2,158	969	773	5,488	7,219
Other foreign official assets			185	323	254	2,104	2,205	2,105	1,395	1,116
Other foreign assets in the United States, net	-550	-3,909	10,986	12,362	23,696	8,643	18,826	14,167	30,804	51,845
Direct investment	1,464	367	949	2,800	4,760	2,603	4,347	3,728	7,897	9,713
Equity and intercompany accounts	1,030	-175	380	1,890	3,695	1,414	2,687	2,142	5,313	5,984
Reinvested earnings of incorporated affiliates	434	542	569	910	1,065	1,189	1,659	1,586	2,583	3,730
U.S. Treasury securities	81	-24	-39	-216	697	2,590	2,783	534	2,197	4,830
U.S. securities other than U.S. Treasury securities	2,189	2,289	4,507	4,041	378	2,503	1,284	2,713	2,811	2,942
U.S. liabilities to unaffiliated foreigners reported by U.S. nonbanking concerns: Long-term	1,112	384	594	298	-90	406	-1,000	-520	-194	1,692
Short-term	902	-15	221	737	1,934	-87	422	993	1,834	
U.S. liabilities reported by U.S. banks, not included elsewhere: Long-term	23	-250	149	227	9	-280	231	373	16,259	32,668
Short-term	-6,321	-6,661	4,605	4,475	16,008	908	10,759	6,346		
Allocations of special drawing rights	867	717	710							1,139
Statistical discrepancy (sum of above items with sign reversed)	-219	-9,779	-1,879	-2,654	-1,620	5,753	10,367	-880	11,354	23,822

Memoranda:

Item										
Balance on merchandise trade (lines 2 and 18)	2,603	-2,260	-6,416	911	-5,343	9,047	-9,306	-30,873	-33,759	-29,469
Balance on goods and services (lines 1 and 17)	5,624	2,268	-1,941	11,021	9,309	22,883	9,382	-9,464	-9,204	4,878
Balance on goods, services, and remittances (lines 77, 35, and 36)	4,066	609	-3,622	9,078	7,599	21,175	7,531	-11,293	-11,088	2,736
Balance on current account (lines 77 and 33)	2,330	-1,434	-5,795	7,140	2,124	18,280	4,384	-14,068	-14,259	-788

Transactions in U.S. official reserve assets and in foreign official assets in the United States:

Item										
Increase (−) in U.S. official reserve assets, net (line 38)	2,481	2,349	-4	158	-1,467	-849	-2,558	-375	732	-1,107
Increase (+) in foreign official assets in the United States (line 57 less line 61)	7,364	27,389	10,293	5,090	10,244	5,509	13,066	35,416	31,072	-13,558

Source: Commerce Department, Survey of Current Business, June 1980.

To make the balance of payments reflect the conclusions and findings of the committee, several changes were recommended. Among the recommendations were moving official reserve transactions above the line in the capital account, eliminating the distinction between liquid and nonliquid assets, and discontinuing publication of the traditional balances. The relocation of the official reserve transactions was to make the international accounts consistent with the belief that, under floating exchange rates, "changes in reserve assets are no longer the passive consequence of all other international transactions." So the official reserve transactions must no longer appear to be the residual after all other accounts have been summed. Removing the distinction between liquid and nonliquid assets resulted from the blurring of the distinction of the two on international capital markets. An asset may appear on its face to be nonliquid, yet conversion of the asset into liquid assets may be quite easy. The decision not to publish any of the traditional individual account balances resulted from the committee's feeling that no one account continues to accurately reflect the international position of the U.S. So rather than risk an individual zeroing in on any particular balance, no balances would be presented.

However, as shown in Table 10–2, all current international transactions continue to be reported so that interested persons can still complete individual accounts for themselves. In fact some of the previously reported accounts even appear below the international transactions tables as "memoranda" items. For example, the net change in U.S. official reserve assets and the net change in U.S. liabilities to foreign official agencies each appear as memoranda items. The sum of these two accounts, the official settlements balance, however, does not. In other words, while there continues to be an official settlements account, the Commerce Department no longer directly computes it, in order to discourage people from focusing on it. However, this figure continues to reflect the net intervention of the government in international financial markets, even under the current regime of floating rates.

Another interesting development concerns the line labeled *errors and omissions* in Table 10–1. When the other changes were made, this line was euphemistically renamed *statistical discrepancy*. Essentially this number represents transactions that were missed by the government due to causes ranging from error to deception. Whatever the name attached, however, this number has been growing by leaps and bounds in recent years. As shown in Figure 10–1, the discrepancy was only minus $219 million in 1970. By 1976 the discrepancy had expanded to over $10 billion. In 1979 the errors totaled $23.8 billion, over 100 times the absolute size of the 1970 discrepancy. The size of the error is projected to jump by about another one-third in 1980, to almost $33 billion.

There are several theories concerning the sources of these discrepancies. One source is human error. With increasing quantities and complexity of forms that must be filled out to comply with federal laws, clerks in banks and other businesses may not concentrate as much on accuracy as in the past. Further, with the volume of international cur-

Billions of
U.S. Dollars

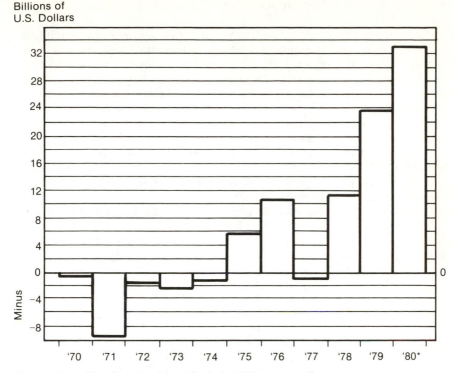

Figure 10–1   The Growth of the "Statistical Discrepancy"

*First quarter 1980 projected at annual rate

Source: U.S. Department of Commerce.

rency trading running close to $60 trillion a year, the possibility of large errors in reported figures is greatly increased.

A second important source of errors is transactions which are deliberately unreported. With rising instability in the Middle East, individuals of substantial wealth began searching for safer places to store their assets. The United States was one recipient of these mobile assets. However, some assets presumably were sneaked into the U.S. Others were placed in the U.S. under the name of a U.S. trust, a U.S. lawyer, or even a U.S. relative or friend of the foreigner. The movement of the assets then becomes difficult, if not impossible, to identify for international transactions purposes.

A third important source stems from payments for traded goods. A foreign purchaser may, for example, pre-pay for U.S. goods or greatly delay payment. These actions may be designed to take advantage of swings in currencies. They also create discrepancies in credits and debits. Or a foreign importer may desire to circumvent his country's exchange controls by building up account balances in the United States. A common procedure is to arrange with the U.S. exporter to pad the import bill and transfer part of the excess to a U.S. account. Like the other gimmicks, this one also causes the international payments data to suffer.[4]

STOCK VS. FLOW DEFINITION

If the official settlements definition is used, the balance of payments at any point in time represents the rate at which the supply of money is flowing into or out of a country. For example, at a given point in time money may be flowing into the country at $500 per month, or equivalently $1500 per quarter or $6000 per year. However, the balance of payments as recorded in the official settlements definition shows the net change in the stock or quantity of reserves over a specific interval of time. For example, if the balance of payments in the third quarter is $2400, between July 1 and September 30 the total quantity of reserves has increased by $2400. The stock and flow concepts can be related to each other by stating that the stock change equals the average flow per period times the number of periods. If reserves have been entering the country at the average flow rate of $800 per month, then the stock change over three months (one quarter) will be $2400.

The distinction between the rate at which reserves are flowing and the total quantity of reserves that has changed hands is very important. For example, returning to the helicopter example, if $2000 is dropped on the public, the excess supply of money equals $2000. In order to restore the economy to full equilibrium, $2000 will have to flow out of the country. The $2000 is therefore the stock of money that has to change hands. But precisely how fast this necessary adjustment will be achieved is not known. The length of time required for the adjustment will be determined by the rate at which money flows out of the country. For instance, if money flows out at the rate of $400 per month, the adjustment will take five months. Alternatively, if the flow rate is $1000 per month, the adjustment will take only two months.

THE GLOBAL BALANCE OF PAYMENTS

The balance of payments, or any sub-balance such as the merchandise trade balance, of an individual country is not independent of the corresponding balances in other countries. For example, if the quantity of world reserve assets is constant, then the balance of payments of the individual country must be the negative equivalent of the total balance of payments of the rest of the world. With a fixed quantity of reserves, when a reserve asset enters one country, it must have originated in and therefore left another country. So for every balance of payments surplus, there must be a corresponding deficit. Algebraically, this relationship can be expressed

$$\sum_{i=1}^{n} BOP_i = 0. \qquad (10-3)$$

In other words, the balance of payments of all countries must sum to zero. Hence, while most countries would simultaneously like to improve their balances of payments, for every country with an improvement, another country must experience a simultaneous deterioration.

Expression (10–3) would change if the quantity of world reserves were not constant. For instance, where there exists an international body such as the International Monetary Fund which annually increases the quantity of an international monetary asset such as the SDR from nowhere, the sum of the individual countries' balances of payments would no longer equal zero. Instead each year countries will receive reserves which do not originate in other countries. Hence, while the balances of payments of the recipient countries improve, the balance of payments of no other country worsens. The total world balance of payments therefore improves by an amount equal to the quantity of reserves created and (10–3) becomes

$$\sum_{i=1}^{n} \text{BOP}_i = \Delta\text{SDR}. \qquad (10\text{–}4)$$

A similar argument can be made for any other account. The sum of these accounts for all countries should also be zero. After all, one country's import of goods or bonds is another country's export. However, in recent years the OECD has warned about how the sum of the current account for all countries is moving further and further from zero.[5] Obviously such an imbalance is theoretically impossible unless trade is occurring with another planet. But the size of the world's current account deficit can hardly be explained by the few moon rocks that have been brought back to earth. The estimated deficit in 1978 was about $50 billion, which dwarfs the $9 billion surplus of Germany, or even the $13.5 billion deficit of such a large country as the United States. The OECD suggests that the apparent growing deficit in the world may be the result of tax evasion, payoffs, secret arms deals, and other measures which attempt to prevent one side of a transaction from being recorded.

THEORETICAL APPROACHES TO UNDERSTANDING THE BALANCE OF PAYMENTS

The particular approach one uses to analyze the behavior of the balance of payments can strongly influence the definition of the balance of payments one chooses to use. For example, our analysis focuses upon problems primarily through the *monetary approach to the balance of payments*. This approach can be represented by

$$\text{BOP} = \Delta M^d - \Delta M^s, \qquad (10\text{–}5)$$

where ΔM^d is the change in the money demand of a particular country and ΔM^s is the change in the money supply. The monetary approach is primarily interested in changes in the excess demand for money in the economy that will affect the inflows of money into the country from abroad. This approach therefore emphasizes the official settlements definition of the balance of payments since it most closely approximates the net inflows and outflows of money.

A second, perhaps more conventional approach is the *elasticities approach*. This approach can be expressed as

$$\text{BOP} = X - M, \tag{10-6}$$

where X and M are the country's levels of exports and imports respectively. This approach equates the balance of payments to the trade balance. Exports and imports in turn each depend independently on the level of income and prices, and hence the balance of payments is assumed to depend on these variables. As already discussed, such an approach is deficient because it completely ignores the inflows and outflows of capital in the country, which can greatly influence the balance of payments. However, there are other problems with this approach on both empirical and theoretical levels. These other problems will be dealt with in Chapter 17 in the discussion of traditional approaches to devaluation.

A third approach is the *absorption approach* that can be represented

$$\text{BOP} = Y - E, \tag{10-7}$$

where Y is the level of domestic money income and E is the level of domestic money expenditure or absorption. This expression implies that if absorption rises relative to income, the balance of payments will worsen. For example, if the rate of growth of a country rises this year, then permanent income will rise by more than this year's income. Expenditure, which depends on permanent income, may then rise more than this year's income rises, producing a deterioration in the balance of payments.

Because the absorption approach emphasizes the behavior of income relative to expenditure, it concentrates on policies which reduce or switch the demand for goods, or which augment factor supplies or otherwise increase output. In many ways this approach incorporates the analysis used for the barter model. But again, the absorption approach as a theory of the balance of payments has the drawback of concentrating on only the goods market, ignoring the bonds market, and equating the balance of trade with the balance of payments. However, much of the analysis of the goods market in this approach is basically sound, and, as we shall see, parts of the basic absorption approach have been incorporated into some monetary approach models to explain the behavior of the goods market or trade balance.

SUMMARY

Transactions of a country with other countries are summarized in its *balance of payments statistics*. The *merchandise trade balance* summarizes only a part of all international transactions, the trade in physical goods.

The *current account* adds net trade in services and remittances and transfers. It represents the change in net claims on foreigners, and thus changes in a country's wealth. The *capital balance* measures the proportion of these additional claims held as short-term or long-term private assets. The *official reserve transactions* definition of the balance of payments measures the changes in official assets held. This definition of the balance of payments also corresponds to both the net intervention of the government in foreign exchange markets and the net transmission of money supplies across countries.

The balance of payments or any sub-balance can be interpreted as either a stock or flow change in the corresponding commodity. However, there is a global constraint which requires a given balance over a particular time period to sum to zero across all countries. Actual measurements of the global sums have differed markedly from zero in recent years.

The *monetary approach* to the balance of payments focuses on the net flow of money between countries. It therefore concentrates on the behavior of the official reserve transactions definition of the balance of payments. The *elasticities* and *absorption* approaches, however, are primarily theories of the goods markets. They therefore are theories of the trade balance and not of the balance of payments.

REFERENCES

COOPER, RICHARD N., "The Balance of Payments in Review," *Journal of Political Economy* 74, No. 4 (August 1966):379–95.

KEMP, DONALD S., "Balance of Payments Concepts—What Do They Really Mean?" Federal Reserve Bank of St. Louis, *Review* (July 1975).

KINDLEBERGER, CHARLES P., "Measuring Equilibrium in the Balance of Payments." *Journal of Political Economy* 77, No. 6 (Nov–Dec, 1969):873–91.

MUNDELL, ROBERT A., "The Balance of Payments," Chapter 10 in his *International Economics* , New York: Macmillan, 1968.

"Report of the Advisory Committee on the Presentation of Balance of Payments Statistics," *Survey of Current Business* 56 (June 1976):18–27.

NOTES

1. United States Dept. of Commerce, *Survey of Current Business*, June 1976, p. 18.

2. *Ibid.*

3. *Ibid.*

4. These examples are taken from " 'Discrepancy' in the Balance of Payments Grows and Grows, but Remains a Puzzle," *Wall Street Journal*, July 29, 1980, p. 48.

5. See "Gap in World Current Account Indicates Seriously Distorted Statistics, OECD Says," *Wall Street Journal*, August 14, 1978, p. 6.

CHAPTER 11

The World as an Integrated Market

THE CONCEPT OF INTEGRATED WORLD MARKETS

Chapter 9 points out two implications of opening up a closed economy:

a. the nominal money supply is no longer exogenous, and
b. the price level is no longer endogenous.

Recall that in the example where the helicopter increased the money supply in the closed economy, the additional money had no place to go. Everyone had an excess supply of money, but there were no additional goods or bonds to spend money on. Thus the only possible equilibrium adjustment was for the price level to rise. In the open economy, however, there are other possibilities. When the domestic money supply increases, even though there are no additional domestic bonds or goods to purchase, there are foreign goods and bonds that domestic residents can try to purchase. There is now a new channel through which equilibrium can be restored. The excess supply of money creates excess demands for goods and bonds, and rather than eliminating the excess demands by price changes, they can now be eliminated by quantity changes. Bonds and goods can be imported from abroad in exchange for money, and the excess supply of money can then be exported through the balance of payments. Conversely, if the monetary authorities do not increase the money supply fast enough to satisfy an increasing demand, additional money can be imported through the balance of payments. The money supply is therefore no longer exogenously controlled by the monetary authorities.

An assumption underlying this open economy model, however, is that prices are determined on world rather than domestic markets, while all commodities are free to move from areas of excess supply to areas of

218

excess demand. In such a model prices within a country with a fixed exchange rate do not change relative to prices in other countries. For example, the price of goods in terms of money behaves according to

$$P = e \cdot P^*. \qquad (11\text{-}1)$$

According to this expression, known as *purchasing power parity*, domestic prices are directly tied to foreign prices through the exchange rate. Thus if the exchange rate is fixed, domestic prices change only if foreign prices also change. The price level in just one country does not change by itself. Instead, prices in all countries move together. So in this model, inflation is not described as U.S. inflation or French inflation, but rather as worldwide inflation. There is a common inflation rate in all countries, and countries can deviate from that rate only if their exchange rates depreciate or appreciate.

The concept that prices are the same in all countries is very similar to the assumptions that are made in the barter model. Recall that in that model, it is assumed that goods and factor markets are arbitraged, resulting in relative goods prices and relative factor rewards that are the same between countries. If these relative prices differed between countries by more than tariffs or transportation costs, incentives would exist for goods and/or factors to move until the relative prices were again equated.

In the present model, money and bonds have been added to the barter framework. Now there are not only relative prices of goods, but also relative prices of money and bonds. Thus, the concept of arbitrage is extended to include not only the relative price of goods (the terms of trade), but also the relative price of goods in terms of money (the price level) and the relative price of money in terms of bonds (the nominal interest rate). If the dollar price of wheat in the U.S. is less than the equivalent dollar price of wheat in the U.K., there is an incentive for wheat traders to buy wheat in the U.S. and to sell it in the U.K. The decreasing supply in the U.S. raises the price there. The increasing supply in the U.K. lowers the price there. This process continues until the dollar prices in the two countries are precisely equal. Similarly, if in the absence of barriers to capital flows, the nominal interest rate on equivalent risk bonds is higher in the U.K. than in the U.S., investors desire to withdraw their money from the U.S. bonds and place the funds in the U.K. The reduction of available capital in the U.S. raises nominal interest rates there, while the increase in available capital lowers rates in the U.K. This process continues until the rates of return are precisely equal.

The type of world being considered is a highly integrated one, in which commodities can quickly and easily flow from areas of excess supply to areas of excess demand, eliminating the need for relative price changes.

This concept of a highly integrated market is quite different from the assumptions of the simple Keynesian or Monetarist models. In those models, what happens to economic variables such as y, i, or P is usually assumed to be a direct function of what occurs in that country alone. The outside world is assumed either not to exist or to be constant. Unemployment again is a domestic phenomenon, related only to factors such as the domestic business cycle.

But that is not the type of world currently being considered. Domestic y and P, for example, are now assumed related not only to demand at home, but also demand abroad. The domestic nominal interest rate is not assumed independent of the world nominal interest rate, but rather depends on the total world bond supply relative to bond demand. Thus, what is experienced in one country is highly related to what is experienced elsewhere.

However, the concept of integrated economies is not unfamiliar. An analogy to a familiar economic system can help to demonstrate how plausible and relevant the integrated model is. The familiar analogy is the relationship between the United States as a whole and the individual states. In traditional economic models, the United States is viewed as a closed economy composed of fifty states engaged in various forms of trade among themselves. This framework is directly analogous to a global economy with fifty countries of varying sizes.*

Each of the fifty states has an autonomous government which collects taxes and spends revenues and even issues bonds. The state governments are therefore capable of running budget deficits or surpluses, just like individual countries. Yet in the traditional model, little emphasis is placed on what is occurring in the individual states and almost all emphasis is placed on the economic conditions of the country as a whole. For example, although Texas is equivalent to a "large country" in this framework, little emphasis is placed on the economic conditions of Texas. Few argue, for example, that Texas should solve an unemployment problem through economic policies that are independent of the rest of the country. The swings in unemployment in Texas are recognized to be closely related to the unemployment swings in the country as a whole. Thus there is little that Texas by itself can do to solve its unemployment problem. In an analogous manner, in an integrated world unemployment rates should be highly correlated, and there is little that individual countries can do to cause their unemployment rates to differ from the global trend.**

Similarly, there is little discussion of controlling the "price level in Texas." Prices in Texas are not seen as something distinct from prices in say, Missouri. Apples, oranges, and most other goods tend to be priced approximately the same in all regions of the United States. If prices differed between regions by more than transportation costs, then suppliers

*Since the Constitution prohibits trade barriers between states, a more precise analogy is fifty countries engaged in free trade and unencumbered factor mobility.

**This statement is not precisely true. As discussed in Chapter 8, cutting payroll taxes reduces the gross amount employers have to pay and increases the net amount employees receive, thus causing total employment demand and supply to increase, and possibly changing the unemployment rate compared to a similar economic unit. For example, the higher taxes in the Northeastern U.S., compared with the Southern and Southwestern parts of the country, is one factor explaining the simultaneous contraction of employment in the "frostbelt" states and the employment boom in the "sunbelt" states.

would ship the goods from areas where they are lower priced to the high price areas. There is "one market" for apples and oranges, and these goods must therefore have the same price everywhere. Therefore the rates of inflation in various states should be highly related. Analogously, in an integrated world, goods flow to equilibrate prices among countries, and inflation rates should be closely related.

In the bond market, people do not talk of the rate of return or interest rate on bonds in Texas as being distinct from the return on bonds in Missouri (other than for risk factors such as in the case of New York City). Or, to take a more concrete example, the price of a given stock will not differ at a given moment on the New York Stock Exchange and the Pacific Stock Exchange. If the prices differed, the stock would be arbitraged by buying on the cheaper market and selling on the more expensive until the prices are the same. Similarly, in an integrated world, rates of interest and values of equities cannot differ among countries.

This analogy points out that in an integrated economy, whether a union of states or a global union of countries, there should be a correlation of experiences among countries or economic bodies, and there should be evidence among these bodies that economic variables move together. The existence of such evidence is now investigated.

MEASURING WORLD INTEGRATION[1]

There are at least three avenues through which market integration may appear. One avenue can be called *internal quantity integration*. This type of integration is represented by the degree to which quantities internal to countries, such as GNP, unemployment, or money supply move in a similar or harmonic pattern among countries of an integrated world. A second avenue can be called *external quantity integration*. This type of integration is represented by the degree to which quantities of goods, money, or bonds flow from areas of excess supply to areas of excess demand to offset demand and supply imbalances among countries. A third type of integration is the *integration of prices*. Evidence of this type of integration would be a similarity of movement among prices and price indices in various countries.

Measurements of each of these types of market integration can now be presented. While it is clearly possible for markets to be simultaneously integrated or not integrated in all three ways, it is by no means a necessity. For example, markets in different countries could exhibit large quantity flows between them or even harmonic movements in GNP and unemployment, yet display little tendency for similar movements in measured prices. Likewise, it is also possible for countries to show little in the way of similar internal or external quantity movements and yet display markedly similar patterns in price movements. But while divergences in the difference measurements are possible, one would expect on average that the results for one type of measurement would be closely related to the results for another.

In the remaining sections of this chapter, a sampling of data and research of each type of integration is surveyed in order to develop some
sense of the degree to which markets are integrated. The overall results
strongly support the integration hypothesis. In quantity as well as price
measures, markets in the developed world are about as integrated as the
data permit measuring. Likewise integration appears to be about as complete and as fast as the quality of the data permit measuring.

INTERNAL QUANTITY INTEGRATION

Early studies on the intercountry relationships between aggregate output
and employment tend to find weak, yet noticeable, harmonic movements. In the case of major swings in GNP, in unemployment, or in other
measures of aggregate economic activity, the association among almost
all of the developed countries was pronounced and clear. Yet there was a
great deal more dispersion among smaller movements.

The association among countries' fluctuations in aggregate output or
employment could, of course, result from either the fact that virtually all
the countries experienced the same external stimulus such as a world
war, or from the fact that the initial shock was distributed throughout the
various countries by a closely integrated system of economic relationships. To the extent that world markets were fully integrated, of course,
both common stimuli and international diffusion would lead to the obser-
vation of similar movements among countries' output, employment, and
other measures of economic activity.

One of the early studies was undertaken by Abramovitz.[2] Using
Thorp's description of business conditions in seventeen developed countries from 1890 to 1932,[3] Abramovitz attempted to measure the similarity
of business cycles. Each country in the study was classified for each year
according to whether it was in the expansion, contraction, peak, or trough
phase of its business cycle. The parts of the cycle were assigned weights.
Peaks were given a weight of ten, expansions and contractions five, and
troughs zero. An annual summary number for the world business cycle
was then calculated by averaging across countries the numerical designa-
tion for that year. The war years of 1915–1920 were not included in the
sample. The trough and peak years and the corresponding average value
are reported in Table 11–1. If the business cycles among the countries
were independent, the expected value of the index would be about 5.0
with some countries in peaks, some in troughs, and the rest in expansions
or contractions. If the cycles were perfectly correlated, the average index
would be ten in peak years and zero in the trough. From Table 11–1 it is
quite clear that the values of the index reported are significantly different
from what they would be if the cycles were independent.

Abramovitz next examined the relationships between countries. In
these comparisons, two countries were designated as being in the same,
adjacent, or opposite phases of the business cycle. The number of times
the two countries were in opposite phases was subtracted from the num-

Table 11-1   Index of the World Business Cycle, 1893-1932

Year	Designation	Index	Year	Designation	Index
1893	Trough	1.4	1912	Peak	8.3
1899	Peak	8.3	1914	Trough	1.6
1901	Trough	2.4	1921	Trough	0.5
1906	Peak	8.2	1925	Peak	6.5
1908	Trough	1.0	1932	Trough	0.0

Source: Moses Abramovitz, Class Lecture Notes, Economics 212, Stanford University (Spring 1964)

ber of times they were in the same phase. This difference was then divided by the total number of times the countries were in the same or opposite phase. If the cycles were independent, one would expect the above ratio to be roughly equal to zero. The higher the ratio, the more dependent the countries appear. In Table 11-2, the United States and the United Kingdom are compared with a number of other countries. The table shows that during the period 1890-1932, the United Kingdom was far more highly integrated with other European countries than was the United States.

In a paper written several years ago, Laffer updated the Abramovitz study for the period 1949-1960.[4] Using the same weighting scheme used by Abramovitz it again became clear that countries had highly synchronized cycles. It was also evident that the United States, while clearly sharing harmonic movements, was not nearly as synchronized as other developed countries. Using one measure of the degree to which a country is synchronized with the world cycle, the United States appears to be less synchronized than any other developed country except Denmark.

In a study of the United States, Canada, and Rest-of-Developed-World, Laffer and Ranson compared real GNP growth rates over the period 1950-1971.[5] Consistent with the earlier data, Canadian and the United States growth rates were closely associated (correlation coefficient of .73), while both Canadian and the U.S. growth rates were only weakly associated with the average of some thirteen other developed countries.

Another measure of the relation of economic activity is unemployment

Table 11-2   Bilateral Cycle Comparison, 1890-1932

Countries	Ratio
United Kingdom/France	.62
United Kingdom/Germany	.78
United Kingdom/Austria	.42
United Kingdom/United States	.37
United States/France	.27
United States/Germany	.08
United States/Austria	.00

Source: Abramovitz, Class Lecture Notes, Stanford University

rates. Laffer and Ranson also analyzed the unemployment rates for the United States, Canada, and Rest-of-Developed-World over the period 1959–1971. Here again the Canadian and U.S. series are closely related (a correlation coefficient of .83), while both Canada and the United States appear to be only slightly correlated with the sum of the rest of the developed countries.

Comparable international unemployment rate data described in Sorrentino, and updated by Sorrentino and Moy, allow a broader comparison of these rates.[6] The unemployment data cover the period 1959 through 1973. As shown in Table 11–3, the United States appears to be closely related to Canada and imperceptibly related to the other countries, while Canada appears only weakly related to the other countries. The other countries, France, Germany, the United Kingdom, Italy, and Japan, appear moderately closely related. These relationships are shown in the correlation matrices of both the unemployment rates and changes in unemployment rates.

A final indicator of overall business conditions in a country is the stock market. This measure provides a proxy for following short-term fluctuations in the market value of a country's aggregate capital stock.

Agmon found that stock prices in the United States, the United Kingdom, Germany, and Japan behave as if there were one multinational stock market.[7] Using the U.S. stock market index as a proxy for the world market, Agmon regressed foreign stock price changes on the world market price change. While he found a less than one-for-one correspondence in each case, the relationships were highly statistically significant and essentially contemporaneous.

The behavior of stock market indices for the seven major developed countries is shown in Figure 11–1. A modest degree of congruence is visible, with the U.S. and Canadian indices tracking each other quite closely. This picture is confirmed by the correlation matrix of percentage changes

Table 11–3   Unemployment: Correlation Matrices, 1959–1973

	U.S.	Canada	France	Germany	U.K.	Italy
Unemployment Rates						
Canada	.83	—	—	—	—	—
France	.01	.33	—	—	—	—
Germany	−.13	.18	.65	—	—	—
U.K.	.05	.21	.76	.32	—	—
Italy	−.11	.04	.26	.67	−.14	—
Japan	.37	.40	.13	.60	−.18	.81
Changes in Unemployment Rates						
Canada	.73	—	—	—	—	—
France	.07	.28	—	—	—	—
Germany	−.19	−.20	.65	—	—	—
U.K.	.27	.23	.45	.40	—	—
Italy	−.33	−.41	.25	.42	.00	—
Japan	−.02	−.19	.39	.61	.42	.77

Indexes

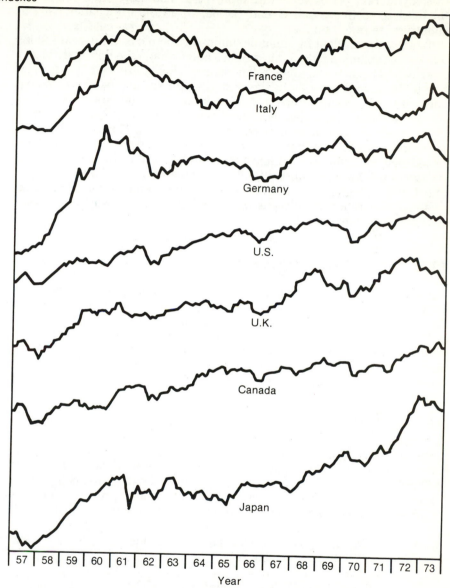

Figure 11–1   Stock Market Indexes of Seven Major Countries, Monthly, 1957–1973
Note: The graph is scaled so that the distance between the plot of each country at
the right-hand side is 1.0—that is, one factor of 10.
Source: IMF, *International Financial Statistics*, line 62.

in stock market prices shown in Table 11–4. The correlation coefficient for the United States and Canada is .82, while those for other pairs of countries are much smaller.

In all, whether data for unemployment, economic activity, or the stock market are examined, the United States and Canada are definitely highly intertwined in their economic relationships. This inference appears to be roughly the same now as in the past. To a lesser extent, the principal countries of Western Europe are also economically integrated. Whether there is substantial independence between the regions of North America, and Western Europe, and perhaps Japan is not clear. However, the careful reader should note that while dependence appears quite well established between, say, the United States and Canada, the failure of the measures used to find substantial dependence between Western Europe and North America does not necessarily imply independence. Internal quantity integration is only one of several possible measures; a second measure is now explored.

EXTERNAL QUANTITY INTEGRATION

Another indicator of the degree of economic integration is the extent to which relative divergences in markets are accommodated by external or intercountry commodity flows. Thus, as discussed before, within integrated markets, commodities should move from areas of excess supply to areas of excess demand. These potential commodity flows can be divided into two categories, the flow of goods and financial flows. Evidence of each type of flow is discussed in turn.

The Flow of Goods

The net flow of goods in a country, or net absorption, is nothing more than the difference between the country's income and its total expenditure. Thus to the extent that a country increases its demand for goods without a corresponding income increase, the country is likely to import or absorb goods net from the Rest-of-World. One major drawback to this approach to integration is that one must specify the factor or factors that

Table 11–4   Percentage Changes in Stock Market Indices: Correlation Matrix, 1957–73 (based on monthly data)

	U.S.	Canada	France	Germany	U.K.	Italy
Canada	.82	—	—	—	—	—
France	.27	.25	—	—	—	—
Germany	.36	.31	.33	—	—	—
U.K.	.45	.44	.19	.29	—	—
Italy	.17	.16	.25	.34	.18	—
Japan	.23	.32	.14	.13	.20	.14

Source: IMF, International Financial Statistics, line 62 of the respective country pages.

affect net absorption. The measures, therefore, become as much a test of the specific formulation of the absorption relationship as they are of integration.

The principal measure of a country's short-run incipient excess demand for goods has generally been postulated to be its growth rate of real income. This corresponds closely to the traditional view that expenditures on imported goods depend upon a country's income, while a country's exports depend upon total foreign income. It also closely corresponds to the general equilibrium approach to the trade balance described in Chapters 8 and 14. In a test of this latter formulation, Laffer introduced growth rates into the relationship and tested the proposition that the world goods market is integrated.[8] During much of the postwar period for fifteen countries, good flows were found to be moderately sensitive to incipient excess demands as determined by changes in relative rates of growth. The specific cross-section test was to look at five-year changes in a country's ratio of trade balance to GNP in relation to the change in that country's growth rate.

In a later paper, Laffer and Ranson attempted to include other factors along with growth in their measures of economic integration of the United States, Canada and Rest-of-World.[9] Although the additional factors of fiscal policy measures and exchange rates did not prove very helpful, the overall results were successful. The relationship between the United States and Rest-of-World was exceedingly close and displayed a close degree of economic integration. This relationship is shown in Figure 11–2. As is quite apparent, the measure of excess demand is very closely correlated with actual trade flows. In Figure 11–3, the relationship of net goods flows to excess demands is also shown to be close between Canada and Rest-of-World. While the results were unimpressive for the U.S./Canada relationship, the apparent lack of relationship in this case arises because, as already discussed, there is so little difference in the two countries' growth rates.

In subsequent studies these same relationships were found to also hold for the U.K./Rest-of-World, EEC/Rest-of-World, and a number of other individual countries.[10] While the level of integration is striking, so is the rapidity with which these responses occur. Figures 11–2 and 11–3 show the rapidity with which the trade balance responds and the amount of variation explained by the relative growth rates. Another surprise is just how little variation is left for exchange rate changes to explain; this point will be expanded in Chapter 17.

In all, this examination of flows of goods between countries fills in several of the gaps left in the previous section. In that section Canada and the United States were found to be very closely integrated, while there was little evidence of the North American region being closely integrated with, say, Europe or Japan. In this section the bulk of evidence points to a very close degree of integration between Canada and Rest-of-World as well as the United States and Rest-of-World. Using net absorption measures, these areas are closely integrated and over very short periods. Goods move as if there were only one market.

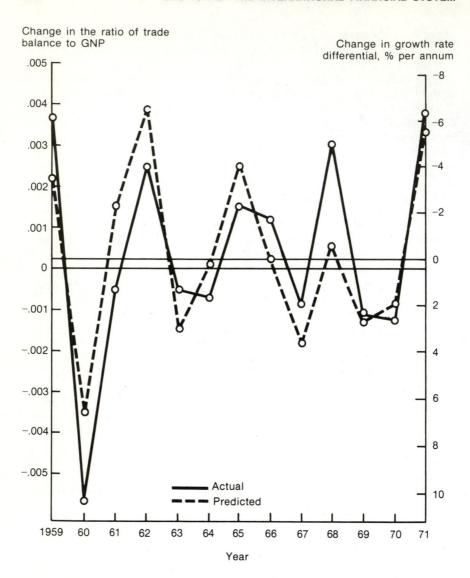

Change in the ratio of trade balance to GNP

Change in growth rate differential, % per annum

Figure 11–2   United States Bilateral Trade Balance with the Rest-of-World
Note: The vertical scales have been so arranged that the dashed line represents either the explanatory variable (right scale) or the prediction of the dependent variable derived from the regression (left scale).
Source: Arthur B. Laffer and David Ranson, "Canada, the United States and the Rest of the Developed World: A Study in the Integration of Markets," in *Policy Formation in an Open Economy*, edited by R. Mundell and E. Van Snellenberg, University of Waterloo, 1974.

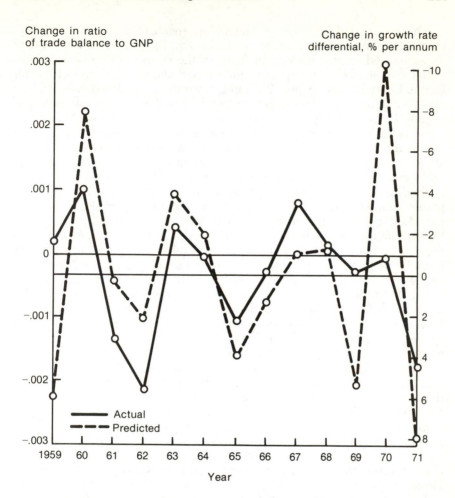

Figure 11–3   Canadian Bilateral Trade Balance with the Rest-of-World
Note: The vertical scales have been so arranged that the dashed line represents
either the explanatory variable (right scale) or the prediction of the dependent variable derived from the regression (left scale).
Source: Arthur B. Laffer and David Ranson, "Canada, the United States and the Rest
of the Developed World: A Study in the Integration of Markets," in *Policy Formation
in an Open Economy*, edited by R. Mundell and E. Van Snellenberg, University of
Waterloo, 1974.

The Flow of Financial Assets

The flow of financial assets encompasses the flow of money and bonds
and the equilibration of nominal returns in all countries. Money and
bonds again are assumed to flow in an integrated world from areas of
excess supply to areas of excess demand, and the flows assure that the
cost of holding these assets (the nominal interest rate) is the same in all
countries.

The recent revival of the monetary approach to the balance of payments has stimulated a number of studies that have rejected the concept of segmented money markets in favor of the concept of market integration. For example, covering the historical periods, McCloskey and Zecher for the United Kingdom and Williamson for the United States found that money markets were highly integrated during the nineteenth century.[11] Money flowed quickly, via the balance of payments, to areas where income (and hence money demand) was growing and away from areas where income was falling. Gold discoveries resulted in overall deficits (or lower surpluses) for the gold-discovering (money-creating) nations and led to balance-of-payments surpluses elsewhere.

Studies of more recent periods also tend to corroborate the view that money markets are highly integrated across countries. In a series of papers, Laffer looks at the monetary approach with special reference to the United States.[12] Here the extent to which the results are consistent with the theory is quite striking. Using quarterly data for the later postwar period, the balance of payments was found to be quite closely related to changes in U.S. income, in U.S. velocity, and in the U.S. money supply. The United States, as the world producer of reserves, tends to run balance-of-payments deficits in order that these reserves can be exported. However, these deficits tended to be larger when U.S. income rose more slowly, when velocity rose more slowly, and when increases in the domestic stock of money were great.

Guitian with regard to Spain, Zecher for Australia, Porter for Germany and Genberg for Sweden have all found similar results.[13] In each of these studies, the monetary integration appears to have held up well. Money flows moved swiftly to neutralize potential imbalances in the demands for and supplies of money. Lags were not found to be appropriate and the proportion of variance explained was quite great in each case. Laffer and Ranson, however, were not successful in recreating a model that corroborated the monetary approach between Canada and the United States.[14]

One interesting implication of these studies is the effect of devaluation on the overall balance of payments. In an integrated world a devaluation leads to a sufficiently large increase in domestic prices which brings them back into line with foreign prices. This rise in the domestic price level has the effect of reducing real money balances relative to real income and therefore leaving the country short of money. One implication of an integrated world is that a devaluation leads to a once-and-for-all surplus in the overall balance of payments, while the country in question reaquires the requisite money balances. Guitian found evidence of such a temporary improvement in the balance of payments of Spain.[15] Miles also found evidence that on average, the balance of payments improves temporarily in the case of sixteen devaluations of fourteen countries.[16]

The literature on the movement of bonds and the equality of nominal interest rates also appears to support the concept of integrated markets. Two papers in particular have interesting results. Frenkel and Levich found that once forward exchange rate discounts and premiums are accounted for, capital markets among countries appear well arbitraged.[17] A forward premium (discount) on a country's currency represents an additional gain (loss) from investing in that country. Including these forward gains or losses for weekly data from January 1962 through October 1967, the overwhelming proportion of nominal interest rate differentials fell within narrow bands representing the transactions costs of covered interest arbitrage. Capital flows then from areas of excess supply to areas of excess demand to eliminate any unexploited profit opportunities. Interest rate parity, or the equalizing of capital costs, holds across countries.

A paper by Agmon and Bronfeld comes to much the same conclusion, except that it attributes the failure of earlier writers to find exact parity in interest rates to the methods used in measuring the data and not to the data themselves.[18] Using daily data for the period February 1973 through May 1973, this paper concludes that "the Interest Rate Parity Theory holds in the short-term international money market."

The closeness of the interest rates is summarized in the correlation matrix in Table 11–5, which covers treasury bill yields in Canada, the United States, and the United Kingdom, as well as the yield on Eurodollars. The correlations are close and do not in any way support the idea that the world financial market is segmented.

In all, the market for money and bonds appears to be much the same as the goods market. Integration among numerous countries appears to be the rule rather than the exception. Thus economic integration appears to be a rather old pheomenon and to be descriptive not just in the limiting case of "the long run" but also of short-term effects.

PRICES AND ECONOMIC INTEGRATION

From the standpoint of economic theory, no evidence can be as convincing of integration as adherence to the law of one market price. In the literature of the barter model, complete economic integration implies equalization of factor prices and relative good prices. Incorporating money markets into the analysis, economic integration also implies some forms of the purchasing power parity doctrine that has been discussed previously.

From a theoretical standpoint, the concept of a fully integrated world market, assuming utility maximization, leads one directly to the view that

Table 11–5   Interest Rates: Correlation Matrix January 1964–February 1974 (based on monthly data)

	United States	Canada	United Kingdom
Canada	.89	—	—
United Kingdom	.80	.67	—
Eurodollars	.94	.84	.73

Source: See Table 11–3

only one market price should hold. All commodities' prices should be fully arbitraged in each and every numeraire at each and every moment in time. If this were not true, then exceptional profit opportunities would arise for anyone who wished to arbitrage the discrepancies. Thus, if one market price does not hold, either profit maximization does not hold or markets are segmented, via natural or artificial barriers. One of the earliest of the modern versions of purchasing power parity is found in Cassel.[19]

Formally, efficient integrated markets, along with profit maximization, imply that the price of any one commodity in any one country's numeraire will equal that same commodity's price in any other numeraire times the exchange rate between the two numeraires, that is,

$$P_{i/A} = P_{i/B} \cdot e_{B/A} \qquad (11\text{--}2)$$

where $P_{i/A}$ and $P_{i/B}$ are the prices of good i in currencies A and B, and $e_{B/A}$ is the exchange rate in country A. This concept for an individual good can be extended to the overall price indexes of two countries by taking a weighted average of the prices of goods consumed in both countries. If the weights in the indexes are not systematically associated with relative price changes, the following propositions hold for an integrated efficient market:

1. Individual good prices measured in a common numeraire move together across countries.
2. Positive percentage changes in the price of foreign exchange will result in correspondingly greater domestic percentage price index increases than abroad.
3. Inflation rates will tend toward equality during periods when exchange rate changes do not occur.

While the conceptual issues are, at least on the surface, relatively straightforward, there are numerous empirical complications. In the first place, many of the available data consist of prices from price lists and not prices at which transactions actually take place. Price lists, of course, take longer to change and will not reflect any discounts or premiums paid. Second, many of the data are imputed and not measured directly. Third, there are obvious problems in standardization of products across time and among countries. Fourth, individual prices are often measured with considerable error and not at the same moments in time. Fifth, weights used on a particular good in various countries can differ. Sixth, there are differences among countries in taxes, price controls, and transport costs. Yet it is still worthwhile to survey the data while recognizing their shortcomings.

Genberg has made several tests of the first proposition.[20] Using specific internationally traded commodities, Genberg established beyond any reasonable doubt that these commodities at least move very closely together. Genberg looked at quarterly rates of change for cacao, copra, jute, rubber, tin, and copper in several specific markets. In attempting to look for leads or lags, his results were not encouraging because even when such possibilities were considered, the concurrent effect was virtually everything. The coefficients also approximated unity. Other studies on specific prices have been carried on in several other contexts. Usually the results have not deviated substantially from these.*

Evidence of the relationship between changes in the exchange rate and inflation has been investigated by Laffer, Genberg, Laffer and Ranson, Gaillot, and Lee.[21] Laffer's two papers are concerned primarily with the postwar experiences of a limited number of highly developed countries. Using wholesale prices, he found in general that countries which devalued tended to experience more rapid inflation than the countries they devalued against. In his other study, he examined the price performances of a few of the largest industrial countries during the period 1961–1971. Converting all the indexes to a dollar base, there was little if any evidence of systematic loss of competitive position by any one country. Different indexes, however, displayed notably different behavior. In Table 11–6, the percentage changes in the dollar-converted price levels are displayed for the consumer price indexes, wholesale price indexes, and export prices indexes. Notice that within any one type of index, once the change in the country's currency vis-à-vis the dollar is accounted for, the change in the index across countries is similar.

Genberg compared the overall rate of inflation in Sweden with a proxy for the world's rate of inflation.[22] Quarterly data were used for the

Table 11–6   Percentage Price Increases in Dollar Indexes, 1961–1971

Country	Consumer Prices	Wholesale Prices	Export Prices
United States	53	21	24
Japan	88	18	15
Germany	55	31	40
Italy	53	35	20
France	38	23	23
Canada	35	26	25
United Kingdom	37	24	29

Source: Arthur B. Laffer, "Stylized Fallacies of International Trade," mimeo. (University of Chicago, 1972)

*There have been studies which have challenged the validity of the law of one price. (See for example Peter Isard, "How Far Can We Push the 'Law of One Price'?", *AER*, Vol. 67, No. 5 (December 1977):942–48, or J. D. Richardson, "Some Empirical Evidence on Commodity Arbitrage and the Law of One Price," *Journal of International Economics* Vol. 8, No. 2 (May 1978):341–51). These studies have emphasized that measured prices can deviate for sustained periods. The apparent deviations may be due to price index measurement problems discussed above. Alternatively, some argue that the deviations are due to non-traded factors or goods specific to individual countries. We obviously feel that the law of one price is a good first-order approximation of the way international goods markets adjust. It appears to be consistent with other observed results, such as the behavior of trade balances following devaluation. Our faith in the ability of prices to adjust quickly, however, is not yet universally accepted.

period 1950–1970. Genberg found that Sweden's rate of inflation was closely related to the world's and that the coefficient was not significantly different from unity. Laffer and Ranson found similar results in their study of the United States, Canada, and Rest-of-World.[23] They, too, used quarterly data that covered the period from the second quarter of 1948 to the fourth quarter of 1970. Using both ordinary least squares and generalized least squares, they found, as did Genberg, little evidence for systematic lags or leads, a very significant association among countries, and finally, the relationships for the percentages that were insignificantly different from unity.

The Lee results are very impressive evidence on the issue of purchasing power parity.[24] Lee collected annual data for wholesale prices from 1900 to 1972. The countries covered included the United States, the United Kingdom, Canada, France, Germany, Italy, Japan, the Netherlands, and Switzerland. He basically viewed the data in three ways. First, he related each non-U.S. country's rate of inflation to both the U.S. rate of inflation and to the rate of change of the exchange rate. Second, he related what he called excess inflation (a country's rate of inflation less the U.S. inflation rate) to the rate of change of the exchange rate. The third and final set related the rate of change of the exchange rate to the country's excess inflation. These tests were carried out using both annual data and three-year averages. The tests also included two years' worth of lags and leads, in addition to the concurrent relationships. Finally, the tests reported the results using both ordinary least squares and generalized least squares.

Table 11–7 shows the numbers used for relating excess inflation to exchange rate changes using tests on means. The first column shows the country's average annual excess inflation and average annual rate of change of the exchange rate. If purchasing power parity holds, the average excess domestic inflation over U.S. inflation should equal the average change in the exchange rate. The second column reports the "means," the third, the "standard deviations," and the fourth, the size of the sample. Even without performing the actual means test, the results quite evidently support purchasing power parity.

Lee also regressed the rate of inflation in each country by year on the rate of inflation in the United States and the percentage change in the country's exchange rate (the inverse of our measure e, that is, the dollar price of a unit of the country's currency). The results for both the concurrent and the lag-lead data for the pooled cross-section of countries are reported in Table 11–8. The first reported equation shows only the average relationship between inflation of the countries and concurrent exchange rate changes on U.S. inflation. The second reported equation shows how the relationship changes when leads and lags in the data are included.

Both results are consistent with an integrated world economy. In the first equation, where no lags were assumed, there is a close relationship between the inflation rates in non-U.S. regions and the rate of inflation in the United States. The higher the U.S. rate, the higher the non-U.S.

Table 11-7   Means of the Inflation Rate and Exchange Rate Change Data, 1900–1972 (annual rates)

Country	Mean	Standard Deviation	Sample Size
Canada			
Excess Inflation	−.001	0.04	72
Exchange Rate Change	.0001	0.03	72
France			
Excess Inflation	−.063	0.12	72
Exchange Rate Change	−.064	0.20	72
Germany			
Excess Inflation	−.044	0.21	61
Exchange Rate Change	−.044	0.23	61
Italy			
Excess Inflation	−.066	0.22	72
Exchange Rate Change	−.064	0.22	72
Japan			
Excess Inflation	−.073	0.23	72
Exchange Rate Change	−.070	0.25	72
Netherlands			
Excess Inflation	−.001	0.09	66
Exchange Rate Change	.001	0.07	66
Switzerland			
Excess Inflation	.002	0.08	58
Exchange Rate Change	.005	0.07	58
United Kingdom			
Excess Inflation	−.009	0.07	72
Exchange Rate Change	−.009	0.07	72

Source: Moon Hoe Lee, *Excess Inflation and Currency Depreciation* (New York: Marcel Dekker, 1976).

Table 11-8   Regression Analysis with Foreign Inflation Dependent Variable, 1900–1972 (annual data)

Constant	U.S. Inflation					Change in Exchange Rate					R^2	D-W
	t−2	t−1	t	t+1	t+2	t−2	t−1	t	t+1	t+2		
(1) .015	—	—	.75	—	—	—	.71	—	—	—	.70	1.79
(3.54)	—	—	(17.4)	—	—	—	(29.6)	—	—	—	—	—
(2) .002	−.05	.05	.72	.18	.21	.08	−.23	−.53	−.13	−.09	.79	1.62
(0.5)	(1.3)	(1.1)	(17.7)	(4.5)	(5.3)	(3.3)	(8.3)	(19.9)	(5.0)	(3.8)	—	—

Source: Lee, *Excess Inflation*
t-statistics in parentheses

rate, and vice versa. Likewise, Lee's results show a close association between changes in a country's exchange rate and in its inflation rate. A country's inflation rate relative to the U.S. is found to rise when the country devalues and to fall when it revalues. In this very simple form, some 70 percent of a country's inflation rate in a given year can be "explained" by the U.S. rate of inflation and changes in the country's exchange rate with the dollar in the same year.

When leads and lags are included, the concurrent variables still maintain their significance. While some leads and some lags turn out to be statistically significant, by far the majority of the variance explained is due to the concurrent variables. Given the numerous numerical problems as well as the gross nature of the relationship postulated, these results are strong evidence for an integrated world economy.

If one sums the estimated coefficients across each variable, there is little evidence that the coefficients differ from unity in the case of U.S. inflation or minus unity in the case of changes in the exchange rates, precisely the values predicted from purchasing power parity. The actual sums are 1.11 and $-.90$, respectively. It is also worthy of note that the

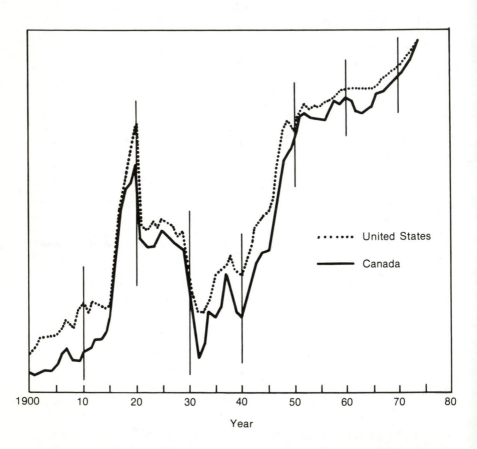

Figure 11–4   Canada: Wholesale Price Index Converted to U.S. Dollars, Annual, 1900–1972
Source: Moon Hoe Lee, *Excess Inflation and Currency Depreciation* (New York: Marcel Dekker, 1976)

constant term, while significant in the simple equation, turns out to be statistically insignificant in the lags and lead equation.

To date, the Lee results appear to be the single most definitive work on the subject of international economic integration. To see visually how close the relationships are (Figures 11–4 through 11–8), Lee's data are plotted for direct comparison of the U.S. wholesale price index with the dollar-converted wholesale price indexes for Canada, the United Kingdom, Japan, France and Italy respectively.

In all, there appears to be little, if any, reason to presume independence among countries' rates of inflation or other price data. Adjustments appear to be quick and complete to the extent that data exist. Inflation is a one-market world phenomenon and will differ among countries to the extent, and to the full extent, of changes in their exchange rates.

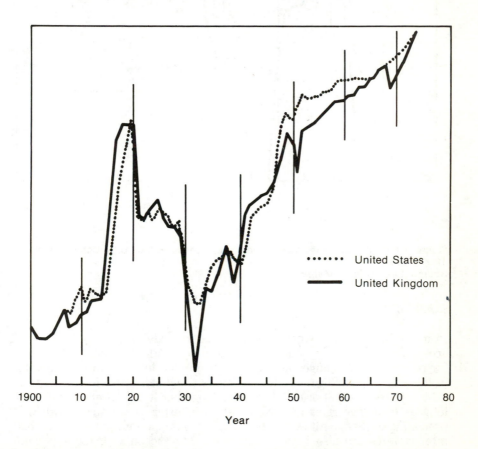

Figure 11–5   United Kingdom: Wholesale Price Index Converted to U.S. Dollars, Annual, 1900–1972
Source: Lee, *Excess Inflation.*

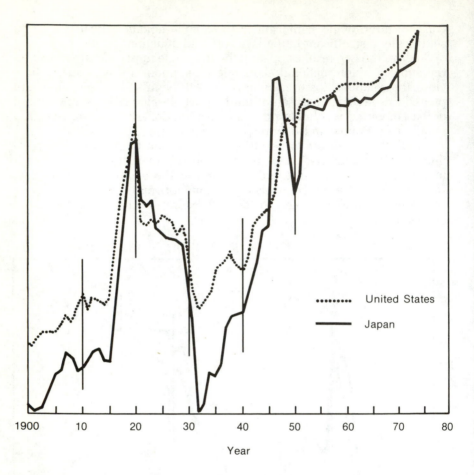

Figure 11–6 Japan: Wholesale Price Index Converted to U.S. Dollars, Annual, 1900–1972
Source: Lee, *Excess Inflation.*

SUMMARY

In a highly integrated world, commodities quickly and easily flow from areas of excess supply to areas of excess demand, eliminating the need for relative price changes among countries. The integration of countries in the world is analogous to the relationship of states in the U.S. Goods arbitrage assures that price levels move together in different countries as long as exchange rates are fixed, but rise faster in countries with depreciating exchange rates. Arbitrage in the financial markets assures that interest rates are also highly correlated after accounting for expected changes in exchange rates. With demand and other shocks dispersed throughout the world, GNP and unemployment exhibit similar swings across countries. The empirical studies reported in this chapter provide substantial evidence of such an integrated world.

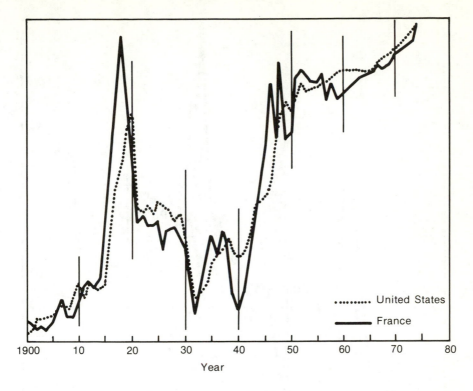

Figure 11–7   France: Wholesale Price Index Converted to U.S. Dollars, Annual, 1900–1972
Source: Lee, *Excess Inflation*.

REFERENCES

AGMON, TAMIR. "The Relations among Equity Markets: A Study of Stock Price Co-movements in the United States, United Kingdom, Germany and Japan." *Journal of Finance* 27 (September 1972):839–56.

CASSEL, GUSTAV. "Abnormal Deviations in International Exchanges." *Economic Journal* (September 1918):413–15.

FRENKEL, JACOB and JOHNSON, HARRY G., EDS., *The Monetary Approach to the Balance of Payments*, Toronto: University of Toronto Press, 1976.

FRENKEL, JACOB and LEVICH, RICHARD. "Covered Interest Arbitrage: Unexploited Profits?" *Journal of Political Economy* 83, No. 2 (April 1975):325–38.

LAFFER, ARTHUR B. and RANSON, R. DAVID "Canada, United States, and the Rest of the Developed World: A Study in the Integration of Markets" in *Policy Formation in an Open Economy*, R. Mundell and E. Van Snellenberg, eds., University of Waterloo, 1974.

LEE, MOON HOE. *Excess Inflation and Currency Depreciation*. New York: Marcel Dekker, 1976.

MILES, MARC A. *Devaluation, The Trade Balance, and The Balance of Payments*. New York: Marcel Dekker, 1978.

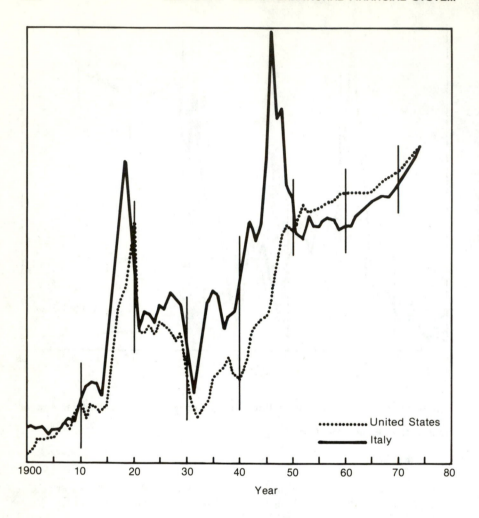

Figure 11–8   Italy: Wholesale Price Index Converted to U.S. Dollars, Annual, 1900–1972
Source: Lee, *Excess Inflation*.

NOTES

1. Adapted from A. B. Laffer, "The Phenomenon of Worldwide Inflation: A Study in Market Integration," in *The Phenomenon of Worldwide Inflation*, edited by D. Meiselman and A. Laffer, Washington, D.C.: American Enterprise Institute, 1975.

2. Moses Abramovitz, Class Lecture notes, Economics 212, Stanford University (Spring 1964).

3. Willard Thorp, *Business Annals*. (New York: National Bureau of Economic Research, 1929).

4. Arthur B. Laffer, "International Business Cycles," mimeo. (Stanford Business School, 1964–65).

5. Arthur B. Laffer and R. David Ranson, "Canada, United States, and the Rest of the Developed World: A Study in the Integration of Markets," in *Policy Formation in an Open Economy*, edited by R. Mundell and E. Van Snellenberg, University of Waterloo, 1974.

6. Constance Sorrentino, "Unemployment in Nine Industrialized Countries," U.S. Bureau of Labor Statistics, *Monthly Labor Review*, June 1972, pp. 29–33; and Constance Sorrentino and Joyanna Moy, "Unemployment in the United States and Eight Foreign Countries," *Monthly Labor Review*, January 1974, pp. 47–52.

7. Tamir Agmon, "The Relations among Equity Markets: A Study of Stock Price Co-movements in the United States, United Kingdom, Germany and Japan," *Journal of Finance*, Vol. 27 (Sept. 1972), pp. 839–56.

8. Arthur B. Laffer, "An Anti-Traditional Theory of the Balance of Payments Under Fixed Exchange Rates," mimeo, University of Chicago, February 1969.

9. Laffer and Ranson, "Canada, U.S., and Rest of Developed World."

10. Arthur B. Laffer, "Do Devaluations Really Help Trade?" *Wall Street Journal*, February 5, 1973; Marc A. Miles, *An Absorption Model of the Trade Balance*, Report for U.S. Treasury Department, December 1974; Marc A. Miles, *Devaluation, the Trade Balance and the Balance of Payments*, New York: Marcel Dekker, 1978.

11. Donald McCloskey and Richard Zecher, "How the Gold Standard Worked, 1820–1914," in Jacob Frenkel and Harry Johnson, eds., *The Monetary Approach to the Balance of Payments*, Toronto: University of Toronto Press, 1976, and Jeffery G. Williamson, *American Growth and the Balance of Payments 1820–1913: A Study of the Long Swing*, Chapel Hill: University of North Carolina Press, 1964.

12. Laffer, "An Anti-Traditional Theory"; Laffer, "Monetary Policy and the Balance of Payments," *Journal of Money, Credit and Banking*, Vol. 4 (February 1972), pp. 13–22; and Laffer, "International Financial Intermediation: Interpretation and Empirical Analysis," in *International Mobility and Movement of Capital*, edited by Fritz Machlup, Walter S. Salant, and Lorie Torshis, Universities-National Bureau Conference Series 24, New York: National Bureau of Economic Research, 1972.

13. Manuel Guitian, "Devaluation, Monetary Policy and the Balance of Payments," Ph.D. diss., Department of Economics, University of Chicago, 1973; Richard Zecher, "Monetary Equilibrium and International Reserve Flows," mimeo, University of Chicago, January 1973; Michael Porter, "Capital Flows as an Offset to Monetary Policy: The German Experience," *IMF Staff Papers*, Vol. 19 (July 1972), pp. 395–424; and Hans Genberg, "Aspects of the Monetary Approach to Balance of Payments Theory: An Empirical Study of Sweden," Ph.D. diss., Department of Economics, University of Chicago, 1974.

14. Laffer and Ranson, "Canada, U.S. and Rest of Developed World."

15. Guitian, "Devaluation, Monetary Policy and the Balance of Payments."

16. Marc A. Miles, *Devaluation, the Trade Balance and the Balance of Payments*, and "The Effects of Devaluation on the Trade Balance and the Balance of

Payments: Some New Results," *Journal of Political Economy* Vol. 87, No. 3 (June 1979): pp. 600–620.

17. Jacob Frenkel and Richard Levich, "Covered Interest Arbitrage: Unexploited Profits?" *Journal of Political Economy*, Vol. 83 (April 1975), pp. 325–38.

18. Tamir Agmon and Saul Bronfeld, "The International Mobility of Short Term Covered Arbitrage Capital," Solomon Brothers and Center for the Study of Financial Institutions, Graduate School of Business Administration, New York University, December 1973.

19. Gustav Cassel, "Abnormal Deviations in International Exchanges," *Economic Journal*, September 1918, pp. 413–15.

20. Genberg, "Aspects of the Monetary Approach."

21. Laffer, "The Bitter Fruits of Devaluation," *Wall Street Journal*, January 10, 1974; Laffer, "Stylized Fallacies of International Trade," mimeo. (University of Chicago, 1972); Genberg, *ibid*; Laffer and Ranson, "Canada, U.S., and Rest of Developed World"; Henry Gaillor, "Purchasing Power Parity as an Explanation of Long-Term Changes in Exchange Rates," *Journal of Money, Credit and Banking*, Vol. 2 (August 1970), pp. 348–54; and Moon Hoe Lee, *Excess Inflation and Currency Depreciation* (New York: Marcel Dekker, 1976).

22. Genberg, "Aspects of Monetary Approach."

23. Laffer and Ranson, "Canada, U.S., and Rest of Developed World."

24. Lee, *Excess Inflation*.

CHAPTER 12

The Monetary Approach to the Balance of Payments: The Adjustment of Money Markets in an Integrated World I

The previous chapter has shown that there is substantial evidence that the world consists of highly integrated markets for money, goods, and bonds. With integrated markets, these commodities should flow from areas of excess supply to areas of excess demand. What is now needed is a description of the mechanism which identifies the areas of excess supply and demand and generates the requisite flows of commodities. Such a mechanism is now discussed for the money market.[1]

THE BALANCE OF PAYMENTS OF A SMALL COUNTRY

The determinants of the *balance of payments* are first developed for a small country. In developing this model, several specific assumptions are made. First, each country is always at full employment equilibrium. Second, the overall money supply of each country is affected by the accumulation or decumulation of reserves. Third, each country was previously not growing and was at full equilibrium, that is, the demand for money precisely equals the supply, implying the balance of payments is initially zero. Fourth, there are no monetary authorities, which means any changes in the money supply must occur through the balance of payments.* The last two assumptions are very important, and they will subsequently be relaxed to show how the analysis is affected.

---

*The assumption of no monetary authorities is only partly possible. This is a fixed exchange rate model, and obviously a monetary authority is needed to stand by to fix the rate. What we are attempting to eliminate by the current assumption are any unilateral increases or decreases in the money supply in an attempt to influence the domestic economy. The total quantity of money in the world is constant.

Recall from Chapter 9 that the demand for money in any country is a demand for *real cash balances*. This demand depends upon the level of real income and the nominal interest rate, or

$$\frac{M}{P} = f(y, i). \qquad (12\text{--}1)$$

To make the demand for money consistent with the balance of payments, the demand should be expressed in nominal terms, or

$$M^d = P \cdot f(y, i) = M^s. \qquad (12\text{--}2)$$

Since the country is initially in full equilibrium, nominal money demand must also precisely equal nominal money supply. What is now examined is how money demand changes, relative to supply, and how the balance of payments is affected by these changes.

As described in previous chapters, the small country is a *price taker*. For a small country with a fixed exchange rate, domestic values of relative prices such as P and i are the same as abroad and are unaffected by changes in demand in the country. The simplest assumption is that demand and supply are constant in the rest of the world, and thus that these relative prices are also constant. Changes in money demand in the small country therefore do not occur because of changes in these relative prices. Instead the changes can only occur because of changes in domestic real income. Hence, the change in nominal money demand can be written

$$\Delta M^d = k\Delta y \qquad (12\text{--}3)$$

where k is a factor of proportionality. Changes in demand are directly proportional to changes in real income.

If, for example, income rises, expression (12–3) indicates that the demand for money in the small country will rise. The increase in demand moves the country away from the initial full equilibrium. For the country to return to equilibrium, the supply of money must increase sufficiently to eliminate the excess demand. Since no domestic monetary authorities are assumed to exist, the excess demand cannot be satisfied domestically. The only remaining source of additional money is abroad, which means money must be imported through the balance of payments. Thus a rise in real income should be associated with an inflow of money and thus an improvement in the balance of payments. In terms of the algebraic relationships, for the small country initially at full equilibrium, the change in money supply from abroad (BOP) must equal the change in domestic money demand minus the change in the money supply from domestic sources

$$BOP = \Delta M^d - \Delta M^s. \qquad (12\text{--}4)$$

In the model under consideration, the domestic change in the money supply is zero, and the change in money demand is $k\Delta y$. The expression for the balance of payments reduces to

$$BOP = k\Delta y. \qquad (12\text{--}5)$$

Equivalently, equation (12–5) can be written in terms of growth rates of income

$$\frac{BOP}{y} = kg \qquad (12\text{–}6)$$

where $g = \Delta y/y$, or the percentage change in real income.

Notice that equation (12–6) holds only for a small country initially in full equilibrium. For instance, if the country were running a balance of payments deficit, there is no reason to believe that a small rise in the country's growth rate would suddenly cause the balance of payments to be in surplus. Rather, the more general relationship is between changes in the variables in the above expression, that is

$$\Delta\!\left(\frac{BOP}{y}\right) = k\Delta g. \qquad (12\text{–}7)$$

Increases in the small country's growth rate tend to improve the ratio of the balance of payments to income, while decreases in the growth rate should be associated with a reduction in that ratio.*

THE BALANCE OF PAYMENTS OF A LARGE COUNTRY

While the basic analysis is the same for a large or a small country, there are some obvious differences. The primary difference is that relative prices like P can no longer be assumed exogenous to the country. Changes in the demand for money relative to goods in the large country can be expected to affect the world level of P. How P will vary with demand is first determined.

In each country i in the world, it is assumed that the nominal demand for money is proportional to the level of nominal income, that is,

$$M_i^d = k_i P y_i. \qquad (12\text{–}8)$$

The price variable P does not have a subscript i because, consistent with the theory of integrated markets, it is assumed to be the same in all countries. The demand for money therefore changes when either the price level or level of real income changes. A rise in the price level means more nominal dollars must be held in order to keep the real value of one's cash balances constant. A rise in real income increases the demand for real balances, which means that at a constant price level, the nominal demand for money rises. The change in the demand for money within a large country can therefore be partitioned into the two effects

$$\Delta M_i^d = k_i(\Delta y_i P + y_i \Delta P). \qquad (12\text{–}9)$$

*Notice that this result is in conflict with the popular notion that income growth induces a balance of payments deficit. This popular notion probably stems from the confusion of the trade balance and the balance of payments. The effect of growth on the trade balance is discussed in Chapter 14.

Again, in order to maintain full equilibrium within the money market for the country, the country's nominal money supply must increase by this amount.

For the world money market as a whole to be in equilibrium, the world supply of money must equal the world demand. If the world market is initially at equilibrium, then to maintain equilibrium, the change in total world demand must equal the change in total world supply. The total change in demand is simply the sum of changes within all the countries. The change in total world demand is therefore derived by summing equation (12–9) across all n countries of the world. Similarly, the change in total world supply is equal to the sum of the domestically produced changes in all n individual countries. Equating the change in total world demand and supply yields

$$\sum_{i}^{n} \Delta M_i^d = P\sum_{i}^{n} k_i \Delta y_i + \Delta P \sum_{i}^{n} k_i y_i = \sum_{i}^{n} \Delta M_i^s = 0. \qquad (12\text{--}10)$$

Since it is assumed that there are no monetary authorities to create more money, it is implicitly assumed that the total change in the world money supply is zero. Thus the maintenance of world money market equilibrium requires that equation (12–10) sum to zero. With this additional piece of information, equation (12–10) can be rearranged to describe the behavior of the world price level

$$\frac{\Delta P}{P} = -\frac{\sum k_i \Delta y_i}{\sum k_i y_i}. \qquad (12\text{--}11)$$

The left hand side of (12–11) is the *world rate of inflation*. The numerator on the right hand side is the sum of all changes in the demand for money in all countries. The denominator is the sum of all initial demands for money. The right hand side therefore represents the percentage change in the demand for money in the world. So equation (12–11) says that the world rate of inflation is negatively related to the percentage change in the total world demand for money.

What is the mechanism behind this expression? Increases in the level of real income in the world increase the world demand for real balances. There are two ways in which real balances can be increased. One way is for the nominal level of the money supply to increase with constant prices. The second way is for the price level to fall with a constant nominal money supply. Since the world money supply is assumed constant, the adjustment in the level of real balances must occur through the second channel. So if world income and money demand are rising, prices must fall, while prices would rise to eliminate world excess real balances if money demand were falling. The change in the price level is the mechanism for world money markets to maintain equilibrium.

But in order to show the complete adjustment of world money markets, we need not only an expression for world market equilibrium, but also an expression for the adjustment to equilibrium in the money markets of each individual country. In other words, given the change in the world price level needed to equilibrate the world money market, what flow of money is needed to equilibrate the money market within a particular country? That expression is now developed.

The first step for obtaining such an expression for each country is to simplify equation (12–11) even further. The simplification is achieved by assuming that the factor of proportionality k_i is the same in all countries, that is, $k_i = k_j = k$. The k's in the numerator and denominator then cancel and (12–11) can be rewritten

$$\Delta P = -P\bar{g}_w \qquad (12\text{–}12)$$

where $\bar{g}_w$ is the average growth rate of real income among all n countries.

Substituting (12–12) into (12–9), the expression for the change in demand for money within a country can be rewritten

$$\Delta M_i^d = k(\Delta y_i P - y_i P\bar{g}_w). \qquad (12\text{–}13)$$

The balance of payments of a large country then equals this change in money demand minus any change in the quantity of money supplied domestically. However, since there still is not a domestic monetary authority, all additional money must again be supplied from abroad. Hence, for a large country that is initially at full equilibrium, the balance of payments must precisely equal the domestic change in money demand, or

$$\text{BOP}_i = kPy_i(g_i - \bar{g}_w) \qquad (12\text{–}14)$$

where g_i is the domestic growth rate of real income. Putting (12–14) into a form equivalent to (12–6) yields

$$\frac{\text{BOP}_i}{Y_i} = k(g_i - \bar{g}_w) \qquad (12\text{–}15)$$

where $Y_i = Py_i$ is nominal income.

In the large country case, the ratio of the balance of payments to income is not a function of only the domestic growth rate. Rather it depends on the domestic growth rate relative to the rate of foreign growth. As has been discussed, in an integrated world with a constant world money supply, it is expected that money will be redistributed from areas of excess supply to areas of excess demand. Which will be the areas of excess supply and demand? If only one country's income is growing, money demand in that country will be growing relative to money supply, creating excess demand. But what if the incomes of all countries are growing? Not all of these excess demands can be fulfilled with a constant world money supply. Money will therefore on average tend to flow to countries where money demand is growing fastest and away from all other countries. The fastest growing countries are those which are growing faster than the average rate of growth in the world. Equation (12–15) says that those countries which are growing faster than average will have a relatively large excess demand for money and will therefore run a balance of payments surplus.

Again, as for equation (12–6), equation (12–15) holds only for a large country in full equilibrium. The more general expression for the large country is

$$\Delta\left(\frac{BOP}{y}\right)_i = k\Delta(g_i - \bar{g}_w), \tag{12-16}$$

that is, changes in a country's ratio of the balance of payments to nominal income is positively related to changes in the country's growth rate relative to the average world growth rate.

This discussion has illustrated the way in which the money markets in the world maintain equilibrium. In the world market, equilibrium is maintained by the relative value of money in terms of other commodities (here goods) changing to ensure that the total world demand for money precisely equals the total world supply. This price adjustment is shown in equation (12–11). However, on the country level, equilibrium is maintained by quantities of money flowing from areas of excess supply to areas of excess demand. In the absence of monetary authorities the primary determinant of excess demand and supply is postulated to be the growth rate of income. Those countries which grow fastest will have the largest increase in excess demand, and thus, the improvements in the balance of payments. This adjustment in the quantities of money is shown in equations (12–15) and (12–16).

While the present framework has illustrated many of the basic concepts involved in determining the behavior of the balance of payments, one important determinant is missing—the monetary authorities. This additional force is now integrated into the framework.

THE EFFECTS OF CHANGES IN THE MONEY SUPPLY

As discussed above, when the demand for money increases, the additional demand for money can be satisfied either through importing money or by receiving it from the domestic monetary authorities. The monetary authorities therefore represent a potential alternative channel for eliminating the excess demand or supply of money. For example, if a rise in income causes nominal money demand to rise by $2000, one possible way of satisfying this extra demand is for the country to run a $2000 balance of payments surplus. But to the extent that some of the extra demand is satisfied by the domestic monetary authorities, the required surplus is reduced. If the monetary authorities fly a helicopter over the country and drop 1200 one-dollar bills, the excess demand for money is reduced to only $800. The balance of payments surplus required to eliminate the excess demand is then also reduced to only $800. Similarly, if income fell in the country, any excess supply of money which developed could be offset by the monetary authorities reducing the money supply. In this case, the balance of payments deficit that the country must run is reduced or eliminated.

The main point of these examples is that the balance of payments surplus (deficit) will be negatively related to the easiness (tightness) of monetary policy. In fact, one of the primary causes of balance of payments deficits is the creation of money at too fast a rate.[2]

For a small country, the one-to-one negative relationship between the amount of money creation and the level of the balance of payments surplus is probably a good approximation. However, as was found for growth rates, a large country cannot be analyzed in isolation. For example, for one country alone, an increase in the domestic money supply is expected to worsen the balance of payments. But given that the sum of the deficits and surpluses of all countries must be zero, if all countries increase their money supplies, they cannot all run deficits. Again a relative concept is needed. The concept this time is excess money supply. Money is expected to flow out of those countries with the largest excess supplies. So not all countries that increase their money supplies experience deficits, but only those which increase their money supplies at above average rates. Just as relative growth rates are used for choosing those countries which are expected to run surpluses, a variable such as relative changes in the ratios of the money supply to income can be used for choosing countries which are expected to run deficits.

The precise relationship between relative changes in the money supply and the balance of payments can be easily derived in terms of the present framework. The only required change in the initial assumption is that changes in the total world money supply are no longer zero. Equation (12–9) described the change in money demand in any country i

$$\Delta M_i^d = k_i(\Delta y_i P + y_i \Delta P). \tag{12–9}$$

Again, the country's nominal money supply must increase by this amount in order to maintain money market equilibrium. Summing this equation across all n countries yields

$$\sum_{i}^{n}\Delta M_i^d = (P\sum_{i}^{n}k\Delta y_i + \Delta P\sum_{i}^{n}ky_i) = \sum_{i}^{n}\Delta M_i^s \neq 0. \tag{12–10'}$$

Notice that the one changed assumption is reflected in the fact that $\sum_{i}^{n}\Delta M_i^s \neq 0$, that is, monetary authorities now print money. With this additional assumption, equation (12–10') can be rearranged into a new expression for world inflation

$$\frac{\Delta P}{P} = \frac{\sum\Delta M_i^s}{k\sum Py_i} - \frac{\sum\Delta y_i}{\sum y_i} = \bar{g}_w^M - \bar{g}_w \tag{12–11'}$$

where $\bar{g}_w^M$ is the average growth rate of the money supplies of all n countries. The right hand side of (12–11') reflects the fact that world inflation now depends upon the average rate at which the world's money supply is increasing, as well as upon the average rate of income growth. While a higher world income growth rate still implies lower inflation (greater deflation), a larger increase in the nominal world money supply relative to nominal income implies higher inflation.

Equation (12–11′) in turn can be rearranged into an expression for the change in the price level

$$\Delta P = \frac{P \sum \Delta M_i^s}{k \sum P y_i} - \frac{P \cdot \sum \Delta y_i}{\sum y_i}. \tag{12–12′}$$

Substituting (12–12′) into (12–9), the expression for the balance of payments of a country becomes

$$BOP_i = \Delta M_i^d - \Delta M_i^s$$

$$= k \cdot P \Delta y_i + P y_i \frac{\sum \Delta M_i^s}{\sum P y_i} - k P y_i \frac{\sum \Delta y_i}{\sum y_i} - \Delta M_i^s. \tag{12–14′}$$

Rearranging the terms and putting them into a form equivalent to (12–15) yields:

$$\frac{BOP_i}{Y_i} = k(g_i - \bar{g}_w) - \left(\frac{\Delta M_i^s}{Y_i} - \frac{\Delta M_w^s}{Y_w} \right) \tag{12–15′}$$

where $Y = Py$ is again nominal income. This expression is precisely the relationship described in the discussion above.

Again, as was true for equation (12–15), equation (12–15′) holds only for a large country which initially is in full equilibrium. The more general expression for the large country is again in terms of changes, or

$$\Delta \left(\frac{BOP}{Y} \right)_i = k\Delta(g_i - \bar{g}_w) - \Delta \left(\frac{\Delta M_i^s}{Y_i} - \overline{\frac{\Delta M_w^s}{Y_w}} \right). \tag{12–16′}$$

So, given the relative rates of income growth, the largest deteriorations in the balance of payments relative to income occur in those countries which on average are increasing their changes in the money supply relative to income by the largest amount.

The usefulness of equation (12–16′) for describing the behavior of the balance of payments is shown in Figures 12–1 to 12–4. These figures compare estimated annual changes in the ratio of the balance of payments to income to actual changes for four countries over the period 1956–73. The estimated changes were derived from an equation very similar to (12–16′).* Notice that the growth rate and money supply variables tend to capture not only the direction, but also the magnitude of the changes. Very little change is left to be explained by other variables.

---

*These equations are taken from M.A. Miles, *Devaluation, the Trade Balance, and the Balance of Payments,* op.cit., Table 3, p. 74. One important difference is that in each equation only the effects of changes in the money supply due to changes in the monetary base by the government are measured. The equations attempt to measure the effect of government policies on the balance of payments. The effects of changes in the money supply due to the actions of banks and the private sector through the money multiplier are not measured.

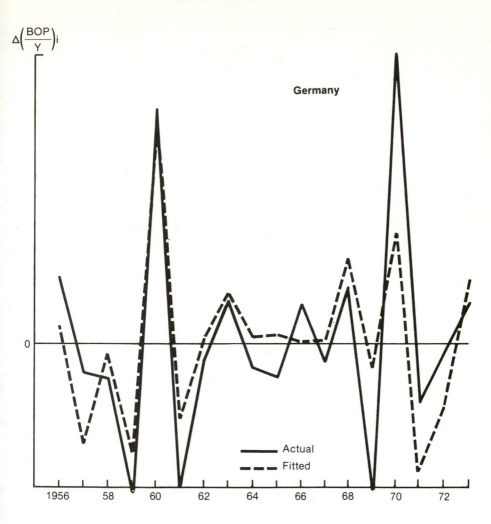

Figure 12–1   Changes in the Ratio of the Balance of Payments to Income
Germany

BURDEN OF ADJUSTMENT AND RELATIVE SIZE

Equations (12–15) and (12–15′) both describe the balance of payments as a ratio to income. In other words, both equations describe the behavior of the balance of payments, standardizing for the size of the country. However, the relative size of the balance of payments is also of interest. This relative variable shows, for any given adjustment, which country experiences the largest change in the ratio of the balance of payments to in-

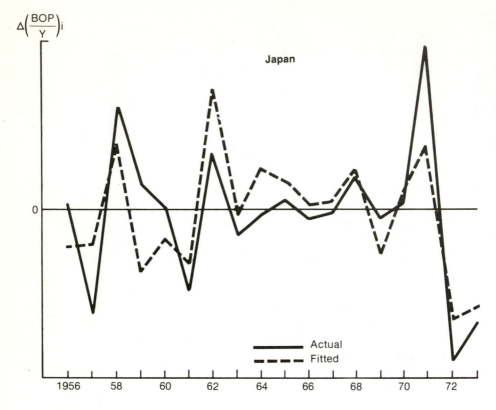

Figure 12–2   Changes in the Ratio of the Balance of Payments to Income
Japan

come, or in other words, which country will experience the largest *burden of adjustment.* As will be shown, the larger the relative size of a country, the smaller the relative burden of adjustment experienced.

The relationship between size and burden can be developed directly from equation (12–15')

$$\frac{BOP_i}{Y_i} = k(g_i - \bar{g}_w) - \left(\frac{\Delta M_i^s}{Y_i} - \frac{\overline{\Delta M_w^s}}{Y_w}\right). \qquad (12\text{--}15')$$

By definition it is known

$$\bar{g}_w = S_i g_i + (1 - S_i)g_{Row}$$

$$\frac{\overline{\Delta M_w^s}}{Y_w} = S_i \frac{\Delta M_i^s}{Y_i} + (1 - S_i)\frac{\Delta M_{Row}^s}{Y_{Row}}$$

where $S_i = y_i/\Sigma y_i$ is the proportion of a country's income in total world income, and where the subscript "Row" refers to all other countries in the rest of the world. Using these two relationships, equation (12–15') becomes

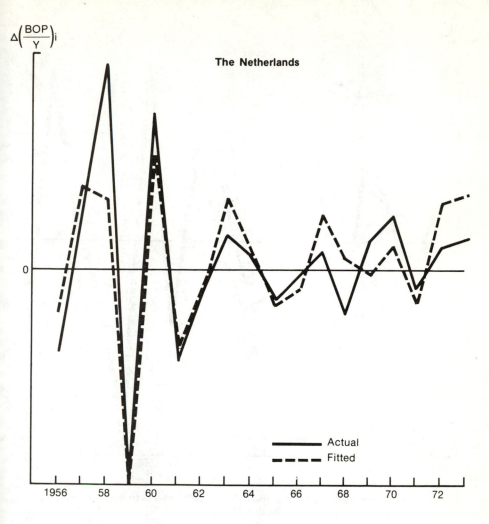

$\Delta\!\left(\dfrac{BOP}{Y}\right)_i$

The Netherlands

——— Actual
- - - - Fitted

1956   58   60   62   64   66   68   70   72

Figure 12–3   Changes in the Ratio of the Balance of Payments to Income
The Netherlands

$$\frac{BOP_i}{Y_i} = k(g_i - S_i g_i - (1 - S_i)g_{Row})$$

$$- \left(\frac{\Delta M_i^s}{Y_i} - S_i \frac{\Delta M_i^s}{Y_i} - (1 - S_i)\frac{\Delta M_{Row}^s}{Y_{Row}}\right)$$

or

$$\frac{BOP_i}{Y_i} = (1 - S_i)\left[k(g_i - g_{Row}) - \left(\frac{\Delta M_i^s}{Y_i} - \frac{\Delta M_{Row}^s}{Y_{Row}}\right)\right].$$

Given the adjustment that must occur in the world money market, the
term $(1-S_i)$ implies that the greatest relative burden of adjustment falls

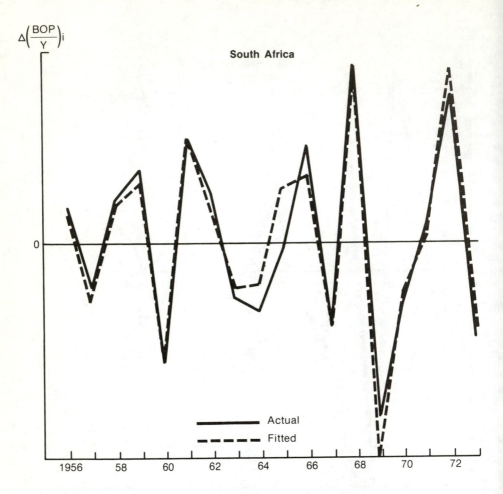

Figure 12–4   Changes in the Ratio of the Balance of Payments to Income
South Africa

on the smallest countries. The inflows and outflows of money for these small countries are a larger proportion of the country's total resources. The partitioning of the burden inversely to a country's relative size is a result often attributed to Mundell.[3]

SUMMARY

The balance of payments represents the net flow of money between countries. In an integrated world, the equilibrium world price level is the one which equates total world money supply and money demand. Given this equilibrium price, money then tends to flow from countries with relative excess supplies to countries with relative excess demands. The relative growth rates of income and money are the key determinants of excess demands and supplies. A country which grows faster than the world average rate of growth tends to be an area of relative excess demand. A country whose monetary authorities are increasing the supply of money faster than the world average rate tends to be an area of relative excess supply. Hence, a country which finds its rate of income growth increasing relative to the world average should find its balance of payments improving. Conversely, a country whose rate of money expansion increases relative to the world average should experience a deteriorating balance of payments.

The burden of adjustment is the size of the balance of payments adjustment as a proportion of the country's total resources. This burden tends to be inversely related to the relative size of the country.

REFERENCES

FRENKEL, JACOB and HARRY G. JOHNSON, EDS., The Monetary Approach to the Balance of Payments. Toronto: University of Toronto Press, 1976.

LAFFER, ARTHUR B. "Monetary Policy and the Balance of Payments," Journal of Money, Credit and Banking 4 (February 1972): 13–22.

MILES, MARC A. Devaluation, The Trade Balance, and The Balance of Payments. New York: Marcel Dekker, 1978.

MUNDELL, ROBERT A. "Growth and the Balance of Payments," International Economics, Chapter 9, New York: Macmillan, 1968.

PUTNAM, BLUFORD H. and D. SYKES WILFORD, The Monetary Approach to International Adjustment. New York: Praeger, 1978.

WHITMAN, MARINA V.N. "Global Monetarism and the Monetary Approach to the Balance of Payments," Brookings Papers on Economic Activity No. 3 (1975):491–536.

NOTES

1. Adapted from Arthur B. Laffer, "An Anti-traditional Theory of the Balance of Payments under Fixed Exchange Rates," mimeo. University of Chicago, February 1969.

2. For empirical evidence of this negative relationship between the balance of payments and the growth rate of domestically created money, see for example, A.B. Laffer, "Monetary Policy and the Balance of Payments," Journal of Money, Credit and Banking, Vol. 4 (February 1972): 13–22, M.A. Miles, Devaluation, the Trade Balance and the Balance of Payments, New York: Marcel Dekker, 1978, or the studies of Australia, Sweden and Spain in The Monetary Approach to the Balance of Payments, edited by J.A. Frenkel and H.G. Johnson, Toronto: University of Toronto Press, 1976; or Bluford H. Putnam and D. Sykes Wilford, "International Reserve Flows; Seemingly Unrelated Regressions," in The Monetary Approach to International Adjustment edited by B.H. Putnam and D.S. Wilford, New York; Praeger, 1978.

3. Robert A. Mundell, "The Burden of Adjustment," Chapter 13 in his *International Economics.*

APPENDIX 12
A GRAPHICAL TECHNIQUE FOR DETERMINING EQUILIBRIUM DISTRIBUTIONS IN THE WORLD

In an integrated world, the world price level is determined by the price level at which world money demand precisely equals world money supply. Given this price level, money then flows from countries with excess supplies of money to countries with excess demand to obtain individual country equilibrium. The adjustment process to the country equilibrium is summarized in Figure 12A–1. Two countries (domestic and foreign) are represented in the diagram. The horizontal axis shows P, the price level in the domestic country. The vertical axis shows the domestic currency price level in the foreign country, where P* is the foreign currency price and e is the exchange rate. In an integrated world, the equilibrium price level expressed in terms of a given currency must be the same in both countries. This locus of world equilibrium prices is illustrated by the line $P = eP^*$, which has a slope of 45°.

The remaining two lines in Figure 12A–1 show the price level for which the existing money supply just equals money demand (excess demand is zero) in a given country. For example, $EDM_d = 0$ shows the domestic country price level at which the excess demand for money is zero. To the right of this line the price level is too high, causing nominal money demand to exceed the nominal money supply and a positive excess demand for money. Similarly, $EDM_f = 0$ shows the price level at which the existing foreign nominal money supply just equals money demand. Above this curve there is an excess demand for money in the foreign country, and below the curve there is an excess supply.

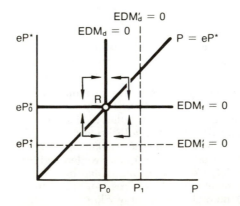

Figure 12A–1   Determining the Equilibrium Distributions of World Money

The equilibrium point along $P = eP^*$ is determined by world demand and supply of money. Given the supplies and demands for money in the two countries, a unique equilibrium world price can be determined. Suppose the equilibrium price is equivalent to point R in Figure 12A–1. At point R, the domestic price level must be P_0 and the foreign price level expressed in domestic currency must be eP_0^*.

However, the initial distributions of the world money supply may not be consistent with both world and country money market equilibrium. For example, suppose that given the domestic country's money supply, the domestic money market would be in equilibrium only at price level P_1. This case is represented by the dotted line EDM'_d. At world price P_0, there is a domestic excess supply of money, illustrated by the fact that the point R is to the left of $EDM'_d = 0$. In the absence of an integrated world money market, the domestic price level would have to rise to P_1.

Conversely, in the foreign country the share of the world money supply is too small for the money market to be in equilibrium at world price level eP^*_0. Hence, at the equilibrium world price there is an excess demand for money in the foreign country, and the zero excess demand curve lies below point R at $EDM'_f = 0$. Notice that since there are only two countries, and the world money market is in equilibrium at price level $P_0 = eP^*_0$, if one country has an excess demand for money at P_0, the other country must have an equivalent excess supply.

An adjustment is now required to bring the two countries' money markets into equilibrium. Since individual domestic prices are not free to adjust, quantities must adjust. Hence, money flows from the domestic country which has an excess supply of money to the foreign country which has an excess demand. The shifting of the money supplies in turn shifts the two EDM = 0 curves in Figure 12A–1. As money flows out of the domestic country, the reduction in the excess supply of money means the domestic country's money market can be in equilibrium at a lower price. The $EDM'_d = 0$ curve shifts to the left. Simultaneously the inflow of money into the foreign country permits a higher equilibrium price level there. The $EDM'_f = 0$ curve shifts up. The shifting of the curves continues until they intersect at point R as $EDM_d = 0$ and $EDM_f = 0$. Only then are both the world money markets and domestic money markets in equilibrium.

More generally, if the foreign and domestic zero excess demand curves intersect at any point other than R, a redistribution of money among countries will be necessary. The redistribution of money in turn shifts the position of the curves. The arrows in Figure 12A–1 show the market response that will be necessary for each type of disequilibrium.

CHAPTER 13

Inflation: The Adjustment of Money Markets in an Integrated World II

INTRODUCTION

The previous chapter shows how quantity adjustments of money occur in a highly integrated world. Money flows from areas of excess supply to areas of excess demand in order to even out the levels of excess demand among countries. This chapter discusses the dual of that adjustment process, that is, how price adjustments occur in an integrated world. While this adjustment process has been briefly described previously, the present discussion concentrates on the link between the world price adjustment and the price adjustment or inflation within individual countries. It concludes that domestic inflation is primarily a phenomenon of the international monetary market, and that individual countries under fixed exchange rates are unable to control the domestic rate.*

An important starting point is a precise definition of inflation. *Inflation* is an increase in the price of goods in terms of money. Inflation therefore implies that the excess supply of money is increasing relative to the excess supply of goods. In other words, the supply of money is growing faster relative to money demand than is the supply of goods relative to goods demand. Such a definition is not new to those familiar with the standard domestic monetary approach to inflation. Usually the excess supply of money is assumed positive, while the excess supply of goods is assumed negative (excess demand). The monetary approach also holds that the origins of inflation are primarily a change in the relative excess supplies of goods and money. Where the two approaches differ is in the discussion of *which supply of money* and *which supply of goods*. The domestic monetary approach would cite as the cause of domestic inflation the increase in the domestic excess supply of money relative to the

---

*Why domestic inflation continues to be influenced heavily by the international money market even under floating rates is expanded upon in Chapter 17 on Devaluation and Chapter 19 on Currency Substitution.

domestic excess supply of goods. The international monetary approach would respond that in an integrated world one cannot speak of one country's excess supply of money or excess supply of goods affecting relative prices. Such excess supplies may be eliminated merely by flows of money and goods between countries. Instead the relative price of goods in terms of money is affected only when the sum across all countries of the excess supplies in the money market or in the goods market is not zero. Inflation only occurs when the world excess supply of money is greater than the world excess supply of goods. Inflation, then, is a *worldwide phenomenon*, not a domestic one. The relevant money supply to follow is the supply of money to the whole world, not just domestic residents. And since inflation is determined by the adjustment necessary to clear the world money market relative to the world goods market, the rate of inflation experienced by all countries participating in the world market should be the same, and not directly affected by domestic policy actions.

The international monetary view therefore holds that international prices will be stable unless a shock affects the supply of money relative to the supply of goods. There are historical examples which support the international monetary view. For example, a great inflation followed the Black Death in the mid-fourteenth century. Given the supply of money in the world, and the fall in world output due to a decreased labor force, the level of money balances greatly increased relative to the level of production following the Black Death, and worldwide inflation became the mechanism for returning real balances to their desired level. In the sixteenth century, the influx of gold and silver from the New World produced a period of inflation in Europe, as money supplies increased relative to the supply of goods. Similarly, discoveries of gold in California and Australia in the nineteenth century led to two decades of moderate world inflation.[1] The international view is also useful for explaining recent episodes of inflation, such as in the early 1970s. The explanation of this recent inflation is the topic of the next section.

THE BREAKDOWN OF THE BRETTON WOODS SYSTEM AND THE EMERGENCE OF INFLATION

In the late 1950s the countries of the world complained that their level of "liquidity" was not increasing at a rate sufficiently fast to facilitate the level of world commerce. During this period the world operated under an international financial arrangement called the *Bretton Woods System.* Under the Bretton Woods System, all governments except the United States fixed the value of their currencies to the U.S. dollar. The dollar in turn was fixed in value at the rate of $35 per ounce of gold. The fixing of parities limited the quantity of money that foreign countries could create. Foreign countries could not increase their money supplies at a rate faster than the growth in demand for their currencies at that parity or they would experience a loss of reserves. Assuming similar growth rates of money demand in the U.S. and abroad, the promise to maintain parity essentially limited countries to increasing their money supplies at the same rate the U.S. was increasing its money supply (see Chapter 18). The rate of increase in the U.S. money supply in turn was limited by the relationship between the dollar and gold. The fixed price of the dollar in terms of gold meant that the rate of growth of the supply of dollars could exceed the growth rate of the gold supply by only the amount by which dollar demand growth exceeded gold demand growth. As the world's liquidity demand grew, more dollars could be issued. But to the extent that dollar demand and gold demand grew at similar rates, this dollar-gold price restriction closely tied the rate at which the U.S. could create dollars to the rate at which gold reserves were being increased. So under the Bretton Woods System, the rate of gold mining still had a restrictive force on the growth of liquidity in the world. In the rapidly expanding post-World War II world, however, it was felt that gold was becoming increasingly scarce.

Several steps were taken by world governments in an attempt to relieve the liquidity shortage, yet maintain the $35 value of gold. First, the U.S. dollar was permitted to serve as a foreign reserve asset in addition to gold. The use of the dollar as a reserve asset meant that the potential supply of reserves to individual countries was greatly increased, which in turn meant countries could now support a greater quantity of their foreign currencies. Second, a *two-tier* market for gold was created in 1968, in which the price of gold was supported at $35 per ounce on only the official or central bank gold market. The price of gold on private markets was allowed to seek its own level. This move meant that since the United States was agreeing to support only the demands of central banks at $35 per ounce, the entire gold reserves of the United States could now be used to support the value of a larger quantity of dollars on world central bank markets. It also represented the first formal step of cutting loose the value of the dollar from gold internationally. Third, the IMF agreed to create an additional source of reserves, an "artificial gold." This new reserve, called a *Special Drawing Right* (SDR), was first issued in 1970 and could be used for settling international debts just like gold.

While none of the above steps alone caused the breakdown of the Bretton Woods System or the rise of international inflation, when viewed in perspective of other events of this period, the beginning of worldwide excess liquidity and thus worldwide inflation can be seen. The important characteristic of the Bretton Woods System was that as long as the rules of the system were being followed, the supplies of all currencies were constricted to a strict price relationship among one another and to gold. Thus, as long as the supply of gold was not increasing at too fast a rate, the world supply of money could not increase too fast relative to the supply of goods, and inflation would not be a problem. Indeed, during most of the Bretton Woods period, inflation remained at less than 3 percent. Average inflation in the U.S. between 1947 and 1972 was less than 2 per cent per annum. But the restrictions on the money supply worked largely because countries expected each other to honor the basic Bretton Woods Agreements. Unfortunately, the events of the late 1960s and early 1970s undermined this confidence and led eventually to the breakdown of the system:[2]

1. The United States financed much of the Vietnam war by printing money. Two alternative methods of financing the war would have been to raise taxes or float bonds. But the war was not politically popular, which hindered the practicality of increased taxation, and the issuance of long-term bonds was limited by the fact that interest rates had exceeded the congressional limit of 4½ percent. Instead the rate of monetary expansion in the United States was increased. If the United States had maintained the strict relationship between the quantity of dollars and gold required to maintain the value of $35 per ounce of gold, such a dollar increase would not have been possible. But the relationship was not maintained. In addition, in 1965 the United States abolished the 25 percent gold reserve requirements behind Federal deposits, and in 1968, abolished the reserve requirements behind Federal Reserve notes. These actions eliminated any national gold standard and further eroded the confidence in the international system. People knew that the United States no longer was "playing by the rules" of maintaining a relationship between the dollar and gold.

2. Additional dollars were being created by the international short-term capital, or Eurodollar, market. These dollars were not within the control of the United States government. As described below, these Eurodollars further expanded the number of dollars that could be created from existing dollars because deposits at U.S. banks were used as reserves by Eurobanks. The rise of Eurodollars therefore represented a further pyramiding on the monetary base.

3. As gold began to rise in price on private world markets, central banks naturally became reluctant to use gold for settling transactions at the official value of $35 per ounce. But if they did not use gold, another medium was needed as reserves. So dollars replaced gold as the reserve medium for actually settling transactions. This shift to dollars increased the amount of reserves held by foreign governments. Rather than just holding gold as reserves, they now held gold (inactive) and dollars (actively used). The inflationary potential of these augmented foreign exchange holdings, supplemented by an enormously high shadow (market vs. official) price of gold, created an enormous potential reserve backing for monetary expansions outside the United States. Table 13–1 shows the explosions of world reserves held. Between 1968 and 1973 the total level of world reserves increased almost two and one-half times. Over 85 percent of that increase was due to increased holdings of foreign exchange, largely dollars. And by the early 1970s, monetary expansion rates were double those of the 1960s.

4. In August 1971 President Nixon slammed the gold window shut and the dollar was devalued relative to gold. An ounce of gold became officially valued at $38 per ounce. This action made it obvious that the United States had no intention of restricting its monetary policy in order

Table 13-1   The Explosion of Foreign Exhange Resources (billions of U.S. dollars)

	1968	1969	1970	1971	1972	1973
Foreign Exchange	32.0	32.3	44.6	78.2	103.6	123.1
Gold	38.9	39.1	37.2	39.2	38.8	43.1
SDRs			3.1	6.4	9.4	10.3
IMF Reserve Position	6.5	6.7	7.7	6.9	6.9	7.4
Total	77.4	78.1	92.6	130.6	158.7	184.3

Source: Robert A. Mundell, "Inflation From an International Viewpoint."

to maintain the dollar price of gold. The Bretton Woods System was replaced in December 1971 by the Smithsonian System, under which the dollar was no longer convertible into gold.

5. In February 1973 the last vestige of the Bretton Woods System finally disappeared. The dollar was further devalued as its official value fell to $42.20 per ounce of gold. In addition, other central banks agreed to allow their currencies to "float" against the dollar. The gold reserves of the central bank could now be officially valued at the free market price, which reached as high as $180 per ounce.

Thus there was a general breakdown of the system that had been controlling the creation of money in the world, combined with several actions that created additional international reserves. What had worked as the international monetary system during the relatively stable period of the 1950s and early 1960s was dismantled piece by piece. As long as people felt that the United States would maintain the value of gold at $35 per ounce and that other countries would maintain the value of their currencies in terms of the dollar, the system worked well, and average inflation remained below two percent. But the two-tier system was created, then the dollar was devalued relative to gold, and finally the dollar was cut completely loose from gold. Once the relation between the dollar and gold was completely severed, there was no longer even the semblance of a constraint on the creation of dollars. The United States was now free to create dollars at an even faster rate. And even if other countries had desired to maintain the dollar value of their currencies, a faster rate of dollar creation meant a faster possible rate of, say, franc creation. It is therefore not at all surprising that the period of the collapse of the Bretton Woods System corresponded to a period of tremendous world inflation.

WORLD INFLATION AND THE
WORLD MONEY SUPPLY

If markets are highly integrated, there should be a strong link between the growth of the world supply of money and the average world rate of inflation as the Bretton Woods System was disintegrating. Direct evidence of this relationship is now presented. Essentially a measure of both the money supply and the price level of the world must be created in order to determine at what rate each is changing. One of the first problems of such a task, however, is to properly define what precisely the world money supply should consist of. In each country there are different types of monetary assets which perform monetary services. In some countries the commonly used concept of currency plus demand (checking) deposits is a good estimate for what is used for providing monetary services. In other countries, however, other types of deposits or near monies also serve this purpose. For example, in the United States, the rapidly expanding money market funds provide many services formerly provided by only demand deposits. Only in 1980 did the Federal Reserve in the U.S., for example, begin tracking the growth of some near monies. It is difficult therefore to get a definition of money which is consistent across all countries. So, for ease of exposition in this discussion, the money supply within any one country is defined as simply currency plus demand deposits.

While currency and demand deposits may represent the monetary assets which originate in each country, they do not necessarily represent the only monetary assets available to the residents of a particular country. There may exist other forms of money which originate outside of individual countries. A good example of such a type of money is *Eurodollars*. Thus before continuing the discussion of the sources of world inflation, an understanding of the nature and implications of these alternative monetary assets is essential.

EURODOLLARS[3]

A *Eurobank* is a financial intermediary which simultaneously bids for deposits and makes loans, just like a savings and loan association in the U.S. The important distinction, however, is in the location of the banks and the types of currencies they deal with on both the asset and liability sides. A Eurobank always deals in currencies other than the legal currency of the country in which it exists. Hence, Eurocurrency banking is not subject to domestic banking regulations,* such as reserve requirements and interest rate restrictions. Furthermore, since Eurobanks are engaged exclusively in foreign currency banking activities, Eurobanking activity is quite mobile from country to country. Eurobanks therefore tend to be established in countries with traditional hands off policies with respect to foreign currency deposits. For this reason Eurobanking centers have become places like London, the Bahamas, the Grand Cayman Islands, and Luxembourg, while no Eurobanking occurs in a highly regulated country such as the United States. Because Eurobanks are not restricted like domestic banks in the quantity or terms of their deposits or reserves, Eurobanks are more efficient from a banking point of view, and banks have an incentive to engage in Euromarket activity.

*The countries which house Eurobanking activity are, of course, free to impose any regulations they choose. But the response to such restrictions would be the movement of Eurobanking to a country without restrictions.

A better understanding of Eurobanking activity can perhaps be achieved by contrasting Eurobanking activity with other forms of banking performed by U.S. commercial banks. Table 13–2[4] shows the various types of banking activities performed by the mythical Manhattan City Bank, as well as the currency denomination of the bank's assets and liabilities associated with each type of banking. For example, traditional domestic commercial banking in the U.S. involves dollar-denominated demand deposits backed by dollar-denominated reserves and loans. People in Manhattan have checking accounts with Manhattan City. Similarly, domestic financial intermediation involves dollar time deposits backed again by dollar reserves and loans. These are the savings accounts and CDs (certificates of deposit) that residents have with Manhattan City. The foreign department of the bank, however, mixes the currency denomination of loans and deposits. Dollar deposits may be partially backed by foreign currency denominated loans or investments, or foreign currency denominated deposits may be backed by dollar re-

Table 13–2   Categories of Banking Business—Manhattan City Bank

Assets	Liabilities	Type of Banking
1. Dollar cash and reserves Dollar loans and investments	Dollar Demand deposits and similar liabilities	Traditional domestic commercial banking
2. Dollar reserves Dollar loans and investments	Dollar time deposits and similar liabilities	Domestic financial intermediation
3. Dollar reserves Foreign loans and investments in dollars on other currencies	Dollar time deposits and similar liabilities	Foreign department
4. Dollar reserves Dollar loans	Foreign currency deposits (currently not permitted in U.S.)	Foreign department
5. Sterling reserves Sterling loans and investments	Sterling time deposits	London branch
6. Loans and investments in dollars, German marks, Swiss francs, etc.	Time deposits in dollars, German marks, Swiss francs, etc.	Eurocurrency business

Source: Dufey/Giddy, *The International Money Market,* © 1978, p. 11. Reprinted by permission of Prentice-Hall, Inc., Englewood Cliffs, New Jersey.

serves. This foreign department banking may be done partly by the Manhattan office of the bank, and partly by the foreign branch. While it may
in part involve Eurocurrency deposits, it is not Eurocurrency banking.

Manhattan City, of course, has several foreign branches in various
countries. The banking activities of the London branch are presented in
sections 5 and 6 of Table 13–2. Traditional foreign branch banking is
analogous to domestic financial intermediation. Time deposits are issued
in the currency of the country in which the foreign banking occurs, and
these deposits are backed by reserves in the same currency. Thus, the
London branch deals in sterling time deposits and sterling reserves, just
like other British financial intermediaries. The London branch banking
of Manhattan City therefore is subject to the banking regulations of Britain, just like the British institutions. However, the Eurocurrency business
of the London branch is not subject to such regulation. The Eurocurrency
operations involve deposits, reserves, and loans in major currencies other
than sterling. The Eurocurrency activities are therefore viewed as foreign
banking activities by the British officials and are not subjected to British
banking regulations.

Of course, not all Eurocurrency or even Eurodollar operations are undertaken by U.S. banks. British banks (and those of other countries) are
also engaged in Eurocurrency activities. They can undertake Eurodollar
operations in London by forming a separate unit to handle the dollar
operations, but since their sterling operations are regulated by the Bank
of England, they (and Manhattan City as well) have to conduct all Euro-
sterling business in another Eurocurrency center, such as Paris.

While Eurocurrency banking could conceivably occur in all currencies, in fact the overwhelming proportion is in only a few currencies,
such as dollars, Deutschemarks, sterling, and Swiss francs. The reason is
that the currencies in which Eurobanking is conducted must be relatively
freely convertible into other currencies. This requirement is probably
one reason that the overwhelming majority of Eurobanking activity was
initially in U.S. dollars. In the late 1960s and early 1970s when the Euromarket began to grow rapidly, the dollar was still the primary international medium of exchange. However, with the decline in the role of the
dollar, the proportion of total Eurocurrency activity in dollars has declined, and the proportion in currencies such as Deutschemarks has increased.

How do Eurodollar deposits differ as assets from conventional dollar
deposits? As Friedman[5] describes Eurodollars, there really is no difference between Eurodollars and dollar-denominated claims on U.S. institutions. He compares Eurodollars to dollars held in deposit at U.S.
banks. Either can be owned by anyone, that is, either residents or non-
residents of the geographical area. So while dollar deposits of a New
York bank can be held by a resident of New York, they do not have to be.
A resident of Chicago or Los Angeles may also hold such a deposit. Similarly, a Eurodollar deposit can be held by a resident of the country in
which the Eurobank exists, but it can just as easily be held by General
Motors Corporation in the United States. So the main difference between

the United States dollar deposits and Eurodollar deposits is that the latter are under little or no regulation by a monetary authority. This distinction means that Eurobanks have neither required reserves nor maximum ceilings on the rates of interest that they are permitted to pay on deposits.

To Friedman, Eurodollars work on the same fractional reserve system as regular bank deposits. Recall how the fractional reserve system works for U.S. banks. Assume that Mr. Jones deposits $1000 cash in a demand deposit in a Manhattan City bank office in New York. If the Federal Reserve requires Manhattan City to hold 20 percent reserves against any demand deposit, then $200 of the cash must be held as reserves. The remaining $800 in cash may then be used as reserves against additional deposits which Manhattan City may now create in the form of loans. After the loans have been made, the balance sheet for this transaction will be as follows.

Assets	Liabilities
$1000 cash	$1000 DD to Mr. Jones
$4000 IOUs	$4000 DD to others

So while the example started with $1000 in money in the form of cash, through the use of the fractional banking system the amount of money has been multiplied to $5000 in demand deposits.* The $1000 in cash is now used as reserves against deposits by Manhattan City, and with a 20 percent reserve requirement, the $1000 cash can support up to $5000 in deposits.

The balance sheet for a Eurobank would be very similar. The main difference, however, would be that while U.S. banks use currency (or equivalently, deposits at the Fed) as reserves against their deposits, Eurobanks would simply use dollar deposits at other banks, say the home office in New York, as reserves. For example, the Grand Cayman branch of Manhattan City could use deposits at the home office of Manhattan City in New York as reserves. If a person withdraws money from a Eurodollar account, the Grand Cayman branch can just give that person a check drawn on the New York office of Manhattan City.

Continuing with this example, assume Mr. Jones instead deposited his $1000 cash in a Eurodollar account in the Grand Cayman branch of Manhattan City. The Eurobank would now have a $1000 liability to Mr. Jones and $1000 in cash assets. The Eurobank now does two things. First, since it is not required to hold reserves in the form of cash, it transfers the cash to the main office in exchange for a $1000 deposit. This deposit in New York is now used as reserves against the Eurodollar deposits. Second, since the bank will only want to hold a fraction of reserves against deposits, more deposits can be created in the form of loans. In the

*In this simplified example, all multiplication occurs in Manhattan City Bank. In reality, as Manhattan City makes loans, some reserves may leak to other banks, and some of the multiplication of deposits occurs in other banks. A more correct statement, then, is that a $1000 increase in reserves to the banking system will lead to a multiple increase in deposits to the system.

U.S. bank example, with the Federal Reserve requiring 20 percent reserves against deposits, $4000 in loans could be created. But the Eu-
robank has no such required level of reserves. Usually the level of
reserves held will be much below 20 percent. Assume for simplicity that
10 percent reserves are held. The $1000 in reserve deposits can therefore
support up to $10,000 in Eurodollar deposits. In other words $9,000 in
loans can now be created.

This example can be summarized in the balance sheets of the Eurobank and the home office. The Grand Cayman branch has $10,000 in
deposits against which it holds a $1000 deposit at the home office in New
York. The $1000 cash that Mr. Jones deposited in the Eurobank now ap-
pears as reserves for the New York office. Notice that the existence of
Eurodollars means that the total amount of money in the world is larger
than it would be without it. Recall that in the example where the $1000
cash was deposited directly into Manhattan City in New York, the $1000
turned into $5000 through the creation of deposits. Each dollar of cash
reserves could support up to five dollars in deposits. But now the $1000
cash creates many more deposits. For the Eurobank which holds fewer
reserves, $1000 can support up to $10,000 in deposits. But since the Eurobank does not have to hold its reserves in cash, the cash is transferred to
New York where it can be used as reserves for making additional deposits. Thus the balance sheets above show that the $1000 cash deposited in
the Eurobanks can create up to $15,000 in deposits (actually $14,000 when
the interbank deposit is subtracted).

Manhattan City Grand Cayman		Manhattan City New York	
Assets	Liabilities	Assets	Liabilities
$1000 deposit in N.Y.	$1000 DD to Mr. Jones	$1000 cash	$1000 DD to Manhattan City Grand Cayman
$9000 IOUs	$9000 DD to others	$4000 IOUs	$4000 DD to others

This example, of course, is making certain specific assumptions, such
as that any loan made by the Eurobank remains in the Eurobank (or at
least the Eurobank system) as a deposit and that the home office is required to hold reserves against its liabilities to the foreign branch. However, the analysis could be easily adjusted to become consistent with
other assumptions. For example, the numerical example assumes that
there is a money multiplier greater than one for Eurodollar deposits, just
like for domestic dollar deposits. However, this assumption has come under strong attack by Klopstock and other writers in recent years. These
economists feel that the fractional reserve banking analogy is inappropriate and that the Eurodollar multiplier is close to one. When Eurobanks
receive a Eurodollar deposit, they simultaneously match it with a Eurodollar loan, just like other financial intermediaries such as savings and
loan associations in the U.S.

But whether one prefers a fractional reserve or savings and loan analogy, one point can be agreed on: the existence of Eurobanks increases the quantity of monetary assets that can be created from a given quantity of monetary base. Whether the Eurobank multiplier is fifty or one, channeling the dollar monetary base through the Euromarket creates additional dollar deposits that would not have been created if the Euromarket did not exist.

The only remaining question is whether these additional dollar deposits should be considered part of the dollar "money supply." The question of whether to include Eurodollars closely parallels the unresolved argument over whether time deposits, savings and loan deposits, CDs, etc., should also be included in the definition of money. No clear answer exists. However, a number of facts imply that Eurodollars are as close to money as other monetary assets. For example, on the one hand, Eurodollars are a type of time deposit. They are therefore close substitutes for other sorts of time deposits such as time deposits at commercial banks, savings and loan accounts, and CDs. This fact would seem to argue that all or part of Eurodollars should be included in the broader definitions of money (such as the new M2 and M3). But on the other hand, about 30 percent of Eurodollar deposits are of very short maturity (less than thirty days), and many of these are overnight deposits. So, even if Eurodollar deposits do not appear to satisfy a transactions demand for money (you cannot write a check on a Eurodollar account), there are substantial Eurodollar deposits which closely resemble demand deposits, except that the short-term Eurodollar deposits pay interest. Hence, at least part of the Eurodollar market provides an alternative to domestic M1.

Furthermore, in the last few years with the growth of NOW accounts, money market funds, etc., there has been an increased awareness that M1 no longer accurately reflects (if it ever did) the conditions in the nation's money markets. There have been increasing calls to broaden the standard definition of money,[6] and in February 1980 the Federal Reserve began reporting a reformulated M1(M1–B), which includes some of these domestic near monies, and a reformulated M2, which includes some overnight Eurodollar deposits. Hence, one can safely argue that recognition of the importance of Eurodollars as an alternative source of money is increasing rather than decreasing.

The existence of this alternative source of money provides one additional avenue for offsetting the efforts of Federal Reserve monetary policy. The Eurodollar market can provide a cushion for the private market against the Fed's policy. For example, as the Federal Reserve attempts to tighten monetary policy, Euromarket activity can expand. Domestic corporations find that at prevailing interest rates they cannot find as much financing as they desire, so they turn to the Eurodollar market to borrow more for their projects. With higher loan demand, Eurobanks offer slightly higher interest rates to attract more deposits to finance the loans. Eurodeposits expand. But since Eurobanks hold deposits at home offices in the U.S. as reserves against Eurodollar deposits, no monetary base must leave the U.S. Total reserves available to the U.S. banking system are the same as if the Euromarket did not exist. So while the Fed might be able to reduce the quantity of domestic deposits that can be created, by creating increased quantities of Eurodollar deposits, the total quantity of dollar deposits in existence can remain unchanged. Alternatively, if the Federal Reserve increases the quantity of monetary base in an attempt to increase the dollar money supply, the better terms on which loans and deposits can be made in the U.S. will expand the quantity of domestically created monetary assets, and reduce the need for Euromarket activity. Corporations simply reduce the quantity of their Eurodollar borrowings. Eurodollar deposits decline by a corresponding amount. Thus the Eurodollar market acts as a buffer for counteracting and easing the effects of domestic monetary policy.

The offsetting nature of the Eurodollar market is portrayed vividly by Figure 13–1. The figure shows the growth rate of Eurodollars and the growth rate of the U.S. monetary base (currency in circulation and commercial bank reserves). The two time series move in opposite directions. When the growth in the monetary base slows (contractionary) the Eurodollar market expands more quickly. And, when the monetary base grows rapidly (expansionary) the growth in the Eurodollar market slows. It is as if the FED were attempting to control the quantity of air in a long balloon. As it squeezes the domestic end of the balloon the Eurodollar end simply expands. And, as it relieves constraints on the domestic end, the Eurodollar end contracts.

Another interesting way in which the Eurodollar market permits the private market to avoid government restrictions is the circumvention of Regulation Q. *Regulation Q* is a restriction by the Federal Reserve which limits the interest which can be paid on time deposits. Regulation Q is the reason all the commercial banks in your neighborhood pay 5¼ percent and all the savings and loan associations pay 5½ percent on simple passbook accounts. Prior to May 1973 Regulation Q also controlled the maximum interest rate payable on large CDs. No such restriction existed in the Eurocurrency market, however. A major problem with the enforcement of Regulation Q on these large deposits is that if U.S. banks are already paying the maximum interest rates allowed, but interest rates in the world continue to rise, U.S. bank deposits become relatively less attractive investments. Investors, particularly large ones, have an incentive to place their money in alternative investments.*

For example, suppose an Arab sheik notices that interest rates in the world have risen relative to the return he is receiving on a million dollar certificate of deposit he holds at Manhattan City, New York. He therefore notifies the bank that although he would like to keep his money there, economic considerations force him to move it elsewhere. Manhattan City replies that they understand what the sheik must do, and while the Federal Reserve will not allow them to pay a higher rate of interest, their

---

*In the late 1970s, as interest rates rose dramatically, smaller investors also began searching for alternatives to savings deposits. The growth of the unregulated (until 1980) money market funds can be explained as a response to that need.

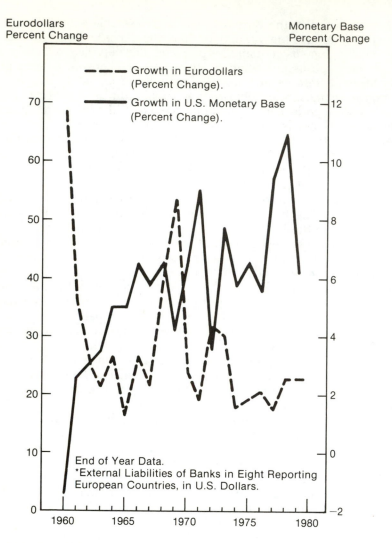

Figure 13-1   Eurodollars* and the U.S. Monetary Base 1960–1979

branch in the Grand Cayman Islands stands ready to pay a competitive rate. So the sheik's million dollar deposit is transferred to the Grand Cayman branch and the branch is credited with a million dollar deposit at the home office. Manhattan City has been able to circumvent the Federal Reserve's restriction on the payment of interest. By this circumvention Manhattan City has also been able to avoid the loss of a million dollars in reserves, which would have required a multimillion dollar contraction in the loan portfolio. Thus, as interest rates rose in the early 1970s, and rates on CDs elsewhere in the world surpassed the Regulation Q ceiling, banks in the U.S. experienced increasing difficulty in attracting funds in the domestic market, and they switched much of their borrowing to the Eurodollar market. A realization by the Federal Reserve that the Regulation Q ceiling was simply driving business to the Euromarkets was largely responsible for the removal of interest rate ceilings on CDs over $100,000 in May 1973.*

A more recent example of how the Euromarkets are used to circumvent Federal Reserve policy is the reaction of banks to President Carter's November 1, 1978 proposal. Part of that proposal was a directive by the Federal Reserve doubling the reserve requirements on large CDs from 2 to 4 percent. The reserve requirement change was intended to slow the rate of growth of the U.S. money supply. The major effect of the change, however, was simply to switch part of the CD market from the U.S. to the Eurodollar market. Creating dollar CDs now became relatively more expensive for home offices in the U.S., and relatively cheaper for the Euromarket branches. The change therefore probably had only a minor effect on the total supply of dollars, as Eurodollar CDs replaced domestic CDs, and any monetary base that found its way to the Eurodollar market was transferred back to home offices to serve as reserves against other outstanding deposits.

One may wonder why, if the Euromarkets permit the private sector to avoid government restrictions, the government does not simply try to restrict Eurodollar activity. The simple answer is that since Euromarkets are beyond the control of any government, no government can regulate them by itself. All that any one government can do is restrict the activity of its banks in the Euromarkets, worsening the competitive position of its banks, but doing little to stop the circumvention of government policies.

For example, in October 1969 the Federal Reserve instituted *Regulation M*, which established reserve requirements on deposits of the Eurobank branches at the home office (liabilities to foreign branches). Initially the reserve requirements were set at 10 percent, and in January 1971 they were raised to 20 percent. The idea behind these restrictions was to reduce the attractiveness and therefore the incentive for U.S. banks to transfer part of their activities to the Euromarket. There was now an additional cost to Eurobanking in the form of the noninterest-bearing reserves the home office had to hold.

Regulation M probably did retard the Euromarket activity of domestic banks. But the primary effect of the restriction on U.S. banks was to affect the competition between U.S. and foreign banks. The foreign banks, of course, were not subject to such a reserve requirement on their Eurodollar activities. Hence, Regulation M made Eurodollar activity relatively more expensive for U.S. banks. The foreign banks then used the change in competitive advantage to gain a foothold in the domestic U.S. market. The realization of the negative effect on the business of U.S.

---

*On March 31, 1980 the Monetary Control Act of 1980 was passed which, among other things, phases out remaining Regulation Q ceilings over a six-year period. This legislation was prompted by the movement of deposits from banks to other financial assets, such as money market funds, as interest rates rose sharply.

banks probably played a large part in the decision to lower the Regulation M reserve requirements. Marginal reserves were lowered to 8 percent in June 1973, later to 4 percent, and then to zero in August 1978.

Regulation M reappeared in October 1979 in the form of an 8 percent reserve requirement against any additional deposits to foreign branches above a prescribed base level. As in November 1978, the Fed was again trying to reduce the dollar money supply by raising reserve requirements against CDs. An additional reserve requirement of 8 percent was applied against the CDs of domestic banks above a certain base level. Perhaps with the November 1978 experience in mind, the Fed applied higher reserve requirements simultaneously to both domestic CDs and liabilities to foreign branches. The Fed wanted to discourage the use of the Eurodollar market to circumvent its policy.

To the extent that the deposits of U.S. banks exceeded the base levels, the Federal Reserve's new restrictions did impose new taxes on U.S. banks and made U.S. banks less competitive in world money markets. Deposits of U.S. banks would contract. But in the highly mobile world money market, the actions of the Fed did not necessarily reduce total dollar deposits significantly. Within the month, descriptions of how banks were now circumventing Fed policy began to surface.[7] Since attracting deposits for creating funds for loans was now more expensive in the U.S., banks simply began both to borrow and lend outside the U.S. Funds were borrowed through Eurodollar deposits, and then lent directly to U.S. companies (or their foreign subsidiaries) by the foreign bank or foreign branch of a U.S. bank. Since no U.S. deposit was necessary, the Fed's new restrictions were ineffective.*

This experience of the U.S. emphasizes an important fact: the U.S. is incapable of eliminating the Eurodollar market by itself. The Eurodollar market operates outside the jurisdiction of the U.S. monetary authorities. Hence, all the Fed can potentially do by flexing its powers is reduce or eliminate the U.S. banks' share of the Eurodollar market.

The fact that the Eurodollar market is outside the jurisdiction of the U.S. government underlies one conventional theory of the origin of the market. It is argued that during the height of the Cold War, the Russians, holding significant dollar deposits in the U.S., were fearful of expropriation. They therefore transferred their dollar accounts to European money markets to lessen this risk. The lack of U.S. control also makes the Euromarkets attractive to the Arabs for recycling "petrodollars." The seizure of Iranian assets in the U.S. in 1980 emphasizes the additional risk to foreigners of holding their dollar deposits in domestic U.S. banks.

---

*Under the Monetary Control Act of 1980, not only is Regulation M set equal to the reserve requirement against CDs, but the same reserve requirement is also applied to loans by foreign branches of U.S. banks to U.S. residents. Obviously the Fed wants to close the latest loophole. To the extent that the new restriction is effective, it only hurts the competitive position of foreign branches of U.S. banks relative to foreign branches of foreign banks. Quite likely, however, the restriction will not be effective, as the banking system finds new ways to circumvent Fed controls.

There are now some discussions in the U.S. of taking steps in the opposite direction from Euromarket controls through the establishment of a *free zone* for international banking in New York City. Within that zone the Fed would not regulate dollar deposits, and would permit banks to issue foreign currency deposits, which they are currently forbidden to do. The primary effect of such a decision would be to move much of the Eurodollar market to New York. The U.S. would then be able to reap some of the advantages from the Eurocurrency market that other countries have been experiencing. It is estimated that several thousand jobs would be created in New York. In addition, while banks operating in the zone would not pay New York state or city taxes, Uncle Sam would now be the recipient of income taxes that the banks now pay other countries. Opposition to this proposal is currently coming from banks in other parts of the U.S. who claim the plan gives New York banks an unfair edge in competition. An alternative suggestion has therefore been to establish free zones in cities such as San Francisco and Chicago, as well as New York.

In summary, the Eurodollar market seems as though it is likely to remain an important part of the domestic money market for years to come. The Eurodollar market provides important channels for banks and the rest of the private sector to circumvent price and quantity restrictions of the domestic monetary authorities. In the process of circumvention, monetary assets are created which can serve as substitutes for assets created by the domestic banking system. The behavior of the Eurodollar market therefore provides important information about what is happening to the world supply of money.

WORLD INFLATION AND THE WORLD MONEY SUPPLY (continued)

In this analysis of world inflation, therefore, the total world money supply is defined to consist of two parts, the sum of currency and demand deposits for eleven major industrial countries of the world and the level of Eurodollars. When dealing with various foreign currencies, however, a third source of change arises due to changes in the relative values of currencies. Just as apples and oranges cannot be added because they are entirely different entities, neither can guilders, francs, and pounds sterling. To get the total value of all money supplies, the currencies must first be converted into a common unit of account or numeraire. This discussion uses the U.S. dollar as the common unit.

If the relative values of currencies are constant, as under fixed exchange rates, then changes in the world money supply measured in dollars occur only when the quantities of domestic monies or Eurodollars change. But if the dollar values of currencies change, a new source of changes in the world money supply is created. For example, if there are 6000 Deutschemarks in Germany and the dollar value of the Deutschemark is $0.25, then the dollar value of the German money supply is

$1500. Now assume that the quantity of Deutschemarks remains constant, but the dollar value rises to $0.333. The dollar value of the German money supply rises to $2000. Holding all other quantities and relative values constant, the dollar value of the world money supply rises without an increase in the quantity of any country's money.* So changes in relative currency values or exchange rates is the third source of changes in the world money supply.

Taking the U.S. money supply (the numeraire currency) separately, four sources of world money growth can be considered; U.S. money, foreign monies, exchange rates, and Eurodollars. The relative importance of each of these sources in explaining changes in the world money supply has changed over time. This partitioning of effects is shown in Figure 13–2. Notice that prior to the late 1960s almost all of the growth in the world money supply was due to changes in the quantity of domestic money supplies, U.S. and foreign. During this period, of course, the world operated under the Bretton Woods System and there were relatively few changes in exchange rates. In the late 1960s Eurodollars became increasingly important. The late 1960s, as you perhaps recall, was a period in which various governments, including the United States, tried to reduce the domestic money supply, creating a situation referred to as a "credit crunch". Eurodollars served as one channel for circumventing the governments' policies. Then, starting in the early 1970s, exchange rate changes became increasingly important as the Bretton Woods Agreements started to break down and the world moved to "floating" rates. In 1971, for example, exchange rate changes caused a growth in the world's dollar money supply of 4 percent. During the 1970s, foreign monies, Eurodollars, and exchange rate changes each contributed substantially to world money growth, while the effect of U.S. money was minimal by comparison.

The rate of increase in the world money supply is measured by the annual percentage change in the dollar value of the money supply. In order to compare the relationship between this number and the world rate of inflation, a measure of the dollar rate of inflation must also be calculated. This inflation measure is computed in a three-step process. First, the price index of each country is multiplied by the relevant dollar exchange rate. The resulting price index may be called the dollar price index of that country. Second, the percentage change in each of these indexes is calculated, yielding the dollar inflation rate in each country. Third, these dollar inflation rates in turn are combined into an average world inflation rate by taking a weighted average of the individual rates. A country's GNP as a proportion of the total GNP of all countries in the sample is used as the weight for the country's dollar inflation rate.

The percentage changes in the world money supply and prices are graphed in Figure 13–3. The relationship between the two series is quite

---

*The value of the world money supply in Deutschemarks, however, falls. As shown in Chapter 17 on devaluation, a depreciation of the dollar should lead to higher dollar inflation, but lower Deutschemark inflation.

Percent

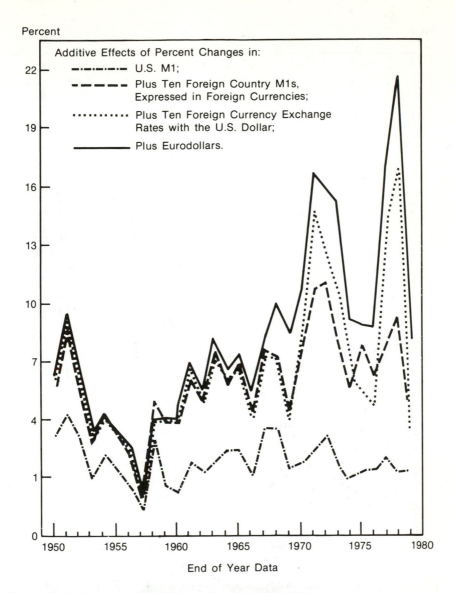

Figure 13-2   Sources of World Money Growth 1950-1979
Sources: *BIS Annual Report, International Financial Statistics*

close, especially for the post-1968 period when the world money supply and prices began increasing at faster and faster rates. On the basis of this relationship, one cannot reject the hypothesis that the world is an integrated economy with one world money market and one world goods market, and where the relationship between money and income is worldwide in scope.

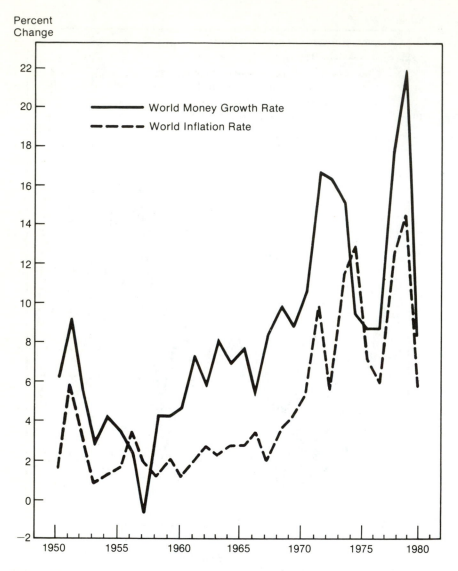

Figure 13-3   World Monetary Growth Rate and the World Inflation Rate 1950–1979

SUMMARY

In an integrated world, inflation is a *worldwide phenomenon*, not a domestic phenomenon. The world rate of inflation is the one which makes
the total world demand for money equal to the total world supply. With
fixed exchange rates, the rate of inflation experienced by countries participating in world markets will be the same and equal to the world rate.

Attempts to lower the domestic rate of inflation should therefore concentrate on the world supply of money, not just the domestic supply.

The *Bretton Woods System* limited the growth of the world money supply and kept inflation low by maintaining the value of other currencies in terms of the dollar, and maintaining the value of the dollar in terms of gold. The dismemberment of the system in the late 1960s and early 1970s, however, removed the constraints on world money growth and led directly into a period of tremendous world inflation.

An increasingly important source of dollars in the world is the *Eurodollar* market. The Eurodollar market not only represents deposits beyond the control of the Federal Reserve, but provides domestic banks with an avenue for circumventing restrictions of the domestic monetary authorities. The highly mobile nature of Eurodollars makes controlling that market extremely difficult, if not impossible.

REFERENCES

DUFEY, GUNTER and IAN GIDDY, *The International Money Market.* Englewood Cliffs, N.J.: Prentice Hall, 1978.

FRIEDMAN, MILTON, "The Euro-Dollar Market: Some First Principles," *Morgan Guarantee Survey* (October 1969):4–14.

KLOPSTOCK, FRED K., "Money-Creation in the Eurodollar Market—A Note on Professor Friedman's Views." Federal Reserve Bank of New York, *Monthly Review* (January 1970):12–15.

MUNDELL, ROBERT A., "Inflation From an International Viewpoint." D. Meiselman and A. Laffer, eds., *The Phenomenon of Worldwide Inflation.* Washington, D.C.: American Enterprise Institute, 1975.

NOTES

1. For these and other examples see Robert Mundell, "Inflation From an International Viewpoint," in *The Phenomenon of Worldwide Inflation,* edited by D. Meiselman and A. Laffer, Washington: American Enterprise Institute, 1975.

2. Robert A. Mundell, "Inflation From an International Viewpoint."

3. Perhaps the analysis of the Eurodollar market which has been most influential in forming impressions about how the Euromarkets function is Friedman's "The Euro-Dollar Market: Some First Principles," *Morgan Guarantee Survey,* (October 1969): pp. 4–14. An alternative to Friedman's view was presented by Fred K. Klopstock, "Money Creation in the Eurodollar Market—A Note on Professor Friedman's Views," Federal Reserve Bank of New York, *Monthly Review,* (January 1970): pp. 12–15. A recent book by Gunter Dufey and Ian Giddy (*The International Money Market,* Prentice Hall, 1978) has provided an in-depth overview of the market which contrasts various views of the market, including Friedman's and Klopstock's. Dufey and Giddy conclude that the market behaves quite differently than Friedman has postulated. While we do not agree with all of Dufey and Giddy's conclusions, the book is quite informative and has provided us with food for thought.

4. Dufey and Giddy, *The International Money Market*, p. 11.

5. Milton Friedman, "The Euro-Dollar Market: Some First Principles."

6. See for example, the Wall Street Journal editorial "Avoiding the Monetary Shoals," May 9, 1979.

7. "Loophole Is Found in Federal Reserve's Tight-Credit Policy," *Wall Street Journal*, October 26, 1979.

CHAPTER 14

Determinants of the Trade Balance: The Adjustment of the Goods Market in an Integrated World

The previous two chapters have shown how the money market adjusts in a highly integrated world. Quantities of money flow from areas of excess supply to areas of excess demand, while prices adjust to assure that the total world demand equals the total world supply. The same type of adjustment mechanism must now be shown to exist for the goods market as well. In this chapter a model of the goods market is developed which describes the factors that affect the flow of goods between countries, and thus a country's trade balance. While the model used here is somewhat different, the final implications are the same as those developed in Chapter 8. Changes in a country's ratio of its trade balance to its GNP are found to be negatively related to changes in the country's growth rate relative to growth in the rest of the world.

THE BASIS OF THE TRADE BALANCE MODEL

The *trade balance* model developed in this chapter is complementary to the model used in Chapter 12 for describing how a country's balance of payments is determined. First, each country is always at full employment. Second, each country is assumed not to have been growing initially and to have been at full equilibrium, that is, the domestic demand for goods precisely equals the domestic supply, which means that the balance of trade is initially zero. Furthermore, it is assumed that the relative price of one good in terms of another (the terms of trade) does not change. As discussed in Chapter 7, changes in relative good prices can be incorporated into the analysis. However, by assuming for the present that the relative prices of all goods are constant, the various goods can be treated as just one good. This simplification allows a clearer exposition of the basic points of the analysis.

The real value of the trade balance of some country i may be expressed in two equivalent ways. The most familiar of course is

$$x_i - m_i, \tag{14-1}$$

where x_i is country i's real exports and m_i the real level of imports. However, recall from Chapter 9 that an alternative way to express the trade balance is in terms of the absorption approach framework

$$y_i - e_i, \tag{14-2}$$

where y_i is country i's level of real income and e_i is the real level of expenditure. This approach simply says that a country will not have a trade balance surplus unless it produces more than it expends. Given that these two methods of expression are equivalent, at any point in time it is true that

$$y_i - e_i = x_i - m_i. \tag{14-3}$$

These four variables are therefore interrelated, and by making assumptions about how any three behave, the behavior of the fourth is also determined. Describing the behavior of the trade balance therefore depends upon how these variables are assumed to behave.

The procedure in this chapter is as follows. The level of real income y is assumed in each period of time to be given and equal to the level of full employment income. Assumptions are then made about how expenditure e and exports x depend upon other variables such as income, changes in income, and the real interest rate. These assumptions are summarized in the expenditure and export functions of the economy. Given the assumptions about income, expenditure and exports, equation (14-3) then dictates what the import function must also look like. An expression for the trade balance can then be derived in either of two identical ways. Either equation (14-1) may be used along with the expressions for exports and imports, or equation (14-2) may be used along with the expressions for income and expenditure. Both equations produce the same final expression for the trade balance.

THE TRADE BALANCE OF A
SMALL COUNTRY

The small country is a price taker. Therefore relative prices such as the real interest rate, which might be expected to affect the overall level of current expenditure, can be taken as constant or given. For that reason the interest rate can be excluded from the expenditure function of the small country. Instead, expenditure is assumed to depend upon the level of income and changes in the level of income. The expenditures function for small country i can be written

$$e_i = a_i + b_i y_i + c_i \Delta y_i, \tag{14-4}$$

where a, b, and c are constants. As the level of income rises, expenditure is also assumed to rise, so the constant b is assumed to have a positive value. The relationship between expenditure and changes in income, however, is slightly more complicated, reflecting the relationship between expenditure and permanent income. If the current increase in the level of income Δy is expected to continue in the future, then the larger Δy, the higher income is expected to be in the future. The *Permanent Income Hypothesis* states that an economic unit (whether a person or country) will base its expenditure decisions upon what it expects its average or permanent income to be, not just upon its present income. For example, two individuals, one a recent college graduate and one 55 years old, but each earning $15,000 per year, are not expected to have the same level of current expenditure. The college graduate earns $15,000 this year, but expects his income to rise substantially in the future. On the other hand, the 55-year-old has probably reached the peak of his earnings. The college graduate therefore has a higher average expected income, and his expenditure level should be higher than for the older person. Similarly, the higher a country's average expected income in the future, the higher should be the current level of expenditure. So expenditure should be positively related to changes in income, and the constant c should also have a positive value.

The level of exports is assumed to be positively related to income as

$$x_i = d_i + s_i y_i. \tag{14-5}$$

A more common assumption in many models of international trade is that the level of exports is exogenous, that is, determined solely by forces in other countries. Equation (14-5) can be made consistent with that assumption by removing the sy term. But, especially for a small country that is facing a perfectly elastic demand for exports curve, it is quite reasonable to assume that the total quantity of goods exported depends upon the total quantity of goods produced in the country. Furthermore, since under either assumption the final expression for the trade balance is the same, the assumption about exports is not crucial to the analysis.

With the assumed expenditure and export functions and exogenous real income, the import function can now be determined from equation (14-3). Real imports are

$$m_i = x_i - y_i + e_i$$
$$= d_i + s_i y_i - y_i + a_i + b_i y_i + c_i \Delta y_i$$
$$m_i = (a + d)_i + (s + b - 1)_i y_i + c_i \Delta y_i. \tag{14-6}$$

The decision to use equation (14-3) to determine the import function is quite arbitrary. For example, instead of the export function, the form of the import function could have been assumed. Equation (14-3) would then have been used to determine the export function.

The behavior of each of the four variables has been specified. The behavior of the trade balance can now be determined. The trade balance can be derived from either equation (14–1) or equation (14–2). Substituting equations (14–5) and (14–6) into equation (14–1) yields

$$\begin{aligned} TB_i &= x_i - m_i \\ &= d_i + s_i y_i - (a_i + d_i) - (s_i + b_i - 1)y_i - c_i \Delta y_i \\ &= -a_i + (1 - b_i)y_i - c_i \Delta y_i \end{aligned} \tag{14–7}$$

or by dividing both sides by income

$$\frac{TB_i}{y_i} = a_i' - c_i g_i \tag{14–8}$$

where $a_i' = -a_i/y_i + (1 - b_i)$, and g_i is country i's growth rate of real income. So for the small country, the trade balance is negatively related to the growth rate of the country. Just as growth was assumed to increase the demand for money in Chapter 12, growth increases the demand for goods here. The increased demand for goods causes more to be imported, or less to be exported, or both, and the trade balance to deteriorate.

Notice that as was pointed out in the chapter on the balance of payments, equation (14–8) holds only for a small country initially in full equilibrium. Again, if the country were initially running a trade surplus, there is no reason to believe that a small rise in the country's growth rate to a positive number will suddenly cause the trade balance to be in deficit. Rather the more general relationship is between changes in the above variables, that is,

$$\Delta\left(\frac{TB_i}{y_i}\right) = a_i' - c_i \Delta g_i . \tag{14–9}$$

Increases in the small country's growth rate tend to reduce the ratio of the trade balance to income, while decreases in growth should be associated with an improvement in that ratio.

THE TRADE BALANCE OF A LARGE COUNTRY

As with the balance of payments, the trade balance model is now adapted to explain the more general case where the country is not small. There are two adjustments made to the model. First, the expenditure function is adapted to reflect the fact that the country is no longer a price taker with respect to the real interest rate. Second, the export function now reflects the fact that the level of exports may depend upon the size of the country relative to other countries. Each of these changes is dealt with in turn.

With the small country assumption the level of expenditure in a country is incapable of significantly affecting the world demand for current consumption relative to future consumption, or goods relative to bonds. The level of current expenditure in a large country, however, can affect this relative world demand. A rise in current expenditures in the large country raises world demand for current goods relative to the demand for future goods. World stability conditions then require the price of goods in terms of bonds, or the real interest rate, to rise. The rise in the real interest rate r in turn affects the level of expenditure. A rise in r means more future goods have to be foregone in order to consume a good now. Such a relative price rise makes current goods now less attractive and causes a drop in current expenditure. The expenditure function must therefore be adapted to reflect this last effect.

The adaptation of the expenditure function is accomplished by adding a term which reflects the negative relation between expenditures and the real interest rate. Equation (14–4) now becomes

$$e_i = b_i y_i + c_i \Delta y_i + h_i r,* \qquad (14–10)$$

where h_i is a constant with a negative sign.

The real interest rate r is a relative price that adjusts to ensure that the world goods market is in equilibrium. When this equilibrium occurs, the sum of the current demands for goods in each country, or total world demand, equals the sum of the current goods supplies in each country, or total world income. Algebraically

$$\Sigma e_i - \Sigma y_i = 0. \qquad (14–11)$$

Equation (14–11) can be further expanded by substituting equation (14–10) into it, yielding

$$\Sigma b_i y_i + \Sigma c_i \Delta y_i + \Sigma h_i r - \Sigma y_i = 0. \qquad (14–12)$$

This expression may now be solved for r,

$$r = \frac{\Sigma y_i}{\Sigma h_i} - \frac{\Sigma b_i y_i}{\Sigma h_i} - \frac{\Sigma c_i \Delta y_i}{\Sigma h_i}. \qquad (14–13)$$

At this point a simplifying assumption must be made in order to obtain a simple final result. The assumption is that all countries have symmetrical reactions to each of the variables in the expenditure function. More precisely, symmetrical reactions mean that the value of, say, the constant c is the same in each country so that $c_i = c_j = c$. The same is true for the constant b_i and the ratio y_i/h_i. Similar ratios y/h indicate that the reactions of expenditure to changes in the interest rate are in the same proportion to income in each country. However, the larger the absolute size of the country, the larger the absolute reactions. Employing this assumption and redefining the ratio $y/h = Z$, equation (14–13) can be written

$$r = Z - bZ - c\frac{\Sigma \Delta y_i}{\Sigma h_i}$$

$$= Z - bZ - c\bar{g}_w Z \qquad (14–14)$$

where $\bar{g}_w$ is the average world growth rate of real income that was introduced in Chapter 12.

---

*The constant term has been dropped to simplify the algebra.

Having solved in equation (14–14) for the value of r that clears the world goods market, this value of r can now be substituted back into the original expenditure function in equation (14–10) to show how expenditure varies in a large country, given equilibrium in the world market. The expenditure function for country i becomes

$$e_i = by_i + c\Delta y_i + y_i - by_i - cy_i\bar{g}_w$$

which can be simplified to

$$e_i = y_i + c(\Delta y_i - y_i\bar{g}_w). \tag{14–15}$$

Equation (14–15) is the adapted expenditure function for a large country.

Similarly, the export function of the large country is adapted to account for the fact that the relative size of a country can influence the level of exports. The relationship between relative size and exports should be negative. The larger a fraction of the total world economy that a country is, if all other variables are held constant, the smaller should be the level of exports. As a country becomes a larger fraction of the world, the ability of the rest of the world to absorb its exports decreases simply because there is less of the rest of the world. Also, the larger a country, the more diversified its production tends to be, so that the fewer the types of goods that must be supplied from abroad. For example, the gross national product of the United States in 1910 was not very different from the gross national product of Great Britain or Germany in 1965. But the United States accounted for a much larger part of the total world economy in 1910 than did Britain or Germany in 1965. As predicted, the level of U.S. exports in 1910 was much less than for Germany or Britain in 1965. The limiting case of course is where a country becomes the entire world. In that case the level of exports falls to zero regardless of the size of GNP.

The relative size argument is included by adding a term to the small country export function (equation (14–5). The term contains the relative size ratio, $v_i = y_i/\Sigma y_i$. Equation (14–5) becomes

$$x_i = d_i + s_i y_i + p_i v_i \tag{14–16}$$

where p_i is a constant with a value of less than zero.

Equation (14–16) can be simplified by considering the extreme case where a country is the entire world. In that case $v_i = 1$, and the level of exports x_i must be zero. Using this information p_i may be solved for

$$0 = d_i + s_i y_i + p_i^{(1)}$$

$$p_i = -d_i - s_i y_i. \tag{14–17}$$

Substituting (14–17) into (14–16) provides a new expression for exports

$$x_i = d_i + s_i y_i - d_i v_i - s_i y_i v_i$$

which can be rearranged to yield the final expression

$$x_i = (1 - v_i)d_i + (1 - v_i)s_i y_i. \tag{14–18}$$

Equation (14–18) is a very general equation for exports. Not only does it explain the behavior for large countries, but also for small countries. A small country is an insignificant part of the world, which implies $v_i = 0$. Substituting that value of v_i into equation (14–18) yields equation (14–5), the small country export function.

As in the case of the small country, once the expenditure and export functions have been determined, the import function can also be expressed. Substituting equation (14–15) and equation (14–18) into equation (14–3) yields

$$y_i - y_i - c(\Delta y_i - y_i \bar{g}_w) = (1 - v_i)d_i + (1 - v_i)s_i y_i - m_i$$

$$m_i = (1 - v_i)d_i + (1 - v_i)s_i y_i + c(\Delta y_i - y_i \bar{g}_w) \qquad (14\text{–}19)$$

the import function for a large country.

The trade balance equation for a large country can now be determined. For a small country the trade equation was derived from equation (14–1) which expressed the trade balance in terms of exports and imports. This time the trade equation is derived from the absorption relationship between income and expenditure. Assuming the level of real income at any point in time to be given, and using the information about expenditure in equation (14–15), equation (14–2) yields

$$TB_i = y_i - y_i - c(\Delta y_i - y_i \bar{g}_w).$$

$$= - c(\Delta y_i - y_i \bar{g}_w), \qquad (14\text{–}20)$$

or dividing both sides by y_i

$$\frac{TB_i}{y_i} = -c(g_i - \bar{g}_w). \qquad (14\text{–}21)$$

For a large country the ratio of the trade balance to income is negatively related to the difference between domestic and average world income growth.

As with the money market of the large country, the inflow of goods depends not only on domestic demand but also foreign demand. In an integrated world, goods tend to be redistributed from areas of excess supply to areas of excess demand. With relative prices adjusting to assure that current total world goods demand equals current total world supply, the areas of excess demand are those which are growing fastest on average, that is, those countries that are growing faster than the world average growth rate. In these countries, the excess demand causes an inflow of goods, which causes a trade balance deficit and hence the negative sign on the constant c in equation (14–21).*

Again, as with the balance of payments and the trade balance for the small country, equation (14–21) holds only for a country initially at full

---

*As shown in the next chapter, increased growth deteriorating the trade balance is consistent with the simultaneous improvement in the balance of payments shown in the previous chapter. The key to the reconciliation of the two balances is the capital account.

equilibrium. The more general trade balance expression for the large country is

$$\Delta\left(\frac{TB_i}{y_i}\right) = -c'\Delta(g_i - \bar{g}_w), \qquad (14\text{–}22)$$

that is, changes in a country's ratio of the trade balance to income is negatively related to changes in the country's growth rate relative to the average world growth rate.

Equation (14–22) is precisely the relationship already developed in Chapter 8 using a slightly different approach. The usefulness of equation (14–22) for explaining the trade balance of a country is shown in Figures 14–1 to 14–3. These figures report actual and estimated values of the trade balance for the U.S., Japan, and the European Economic Community.* These figures are derived from precisely equation (14–22), by comparing changes in the country's income growth rate relative to the growth rate in other OECD countries.

There are many factors which potentially can complicate or reverse the relationship being tested. Institutional factors which proscribe a country's trade balance, such as quotas on imports and exports, could make the trade balance insensitive to demand shifts. Accounting conventions which lead to misrepresentations of actual trade balances could also weaken the association. Or shifts in the aggregate supply of output, rather than demand, could, if sufficiently large, reverse the association completely.

In each of the three figures, there is considerable positive correlation between the two series. While modest differences in the strength of the association are apparent, the results conform quite closely to the hypothesized behavior. The model developed in this chapter (or Chapter 8) may therefore be taken as a good approximation of the basic forces behind the flow of goods between countries.

THE OPEC TRANSFER AND THE TRADE BALANCE

The trade balance model developed in equation (14–22) presumes that the dominant force determining the trade balance is changes in relative excess demands associated with changes in relative income growth rates. In modeling the trade balance, then, one would want to include income growth rates for major trading partners in the $\bar{g}_w$ term. As outlined in

---

*These results are taken from Marc A. Miles, "An Absorption Model of the Balance of Trade," a report prepared for the U.S. Treasury Department, August, 1975. The growth rate for an individual country in year t was computed by taking the logarithm of the ratio of real income (constant dollar gross domestic product) in year t to real income in year t-1. The average world growth rate was computed as a weighted average of individual growth rates of 22 OECD countries, excluding country i. The nominal gross domestic products of year t, converted to U.S. dollars at current rates of exchange, were used as weights.

Change in Ratio of
Trade Balance To GNP

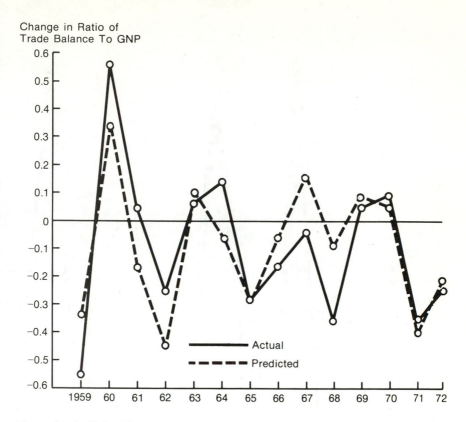

Figure 14–1   United States

Chapter 8, however, forces other than demand shocks can occur, which means that equation (14–22) may not always accurately reflect the behavior of the trade balance.

A good example of such a shock was the OPEC price rise of 1973. This oil price rise represented a change in the terms of trade in favor of the OPEC countries. Oil-consuming countries now paid more real goods for a barrel of oil than previously. Given a relatively inelastic demand for oil, the real value of the payments to oil-producing countries rose significantly. The change in the terms of trade, in effect, resulted in a transfer of wealth or purchasing power from oil-consuming countries to oil-producing nations.

Such a transfer of wealth, of course, is completed through the trade account. Equation (14–22) assumes that the trade balance behavior is dominated by relative demands among traditional industrialized trading partners. Income in the industrialized countries receives the greatest weight and dominates the $\bar{g}_w$ term. The U.S. trade balance is assumed determined by demand in the U.S. relative to demand in Germany, Japan, France, the U.K., etc. If the trade balance in the U.S. deteriorates,

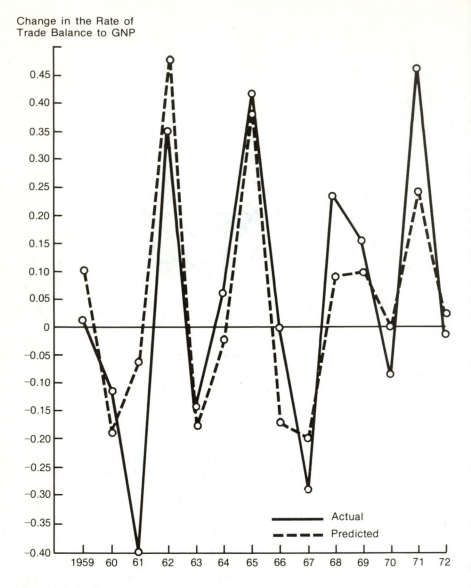

Figure 14–2   Japan

the trade balance in some of these other countries must be improving. However, as the transfer occurs following the oil price rise, the dominant movement in the trade balance should be between oil consumers and oil producers. If all industrialized countries are net oil consumers, their trade balances are not expected to move relative to each other, but rather relative to OPEC. The growth rate differential term does not capture the most important forces.

Change in Rate of
Trade Balance to GNP

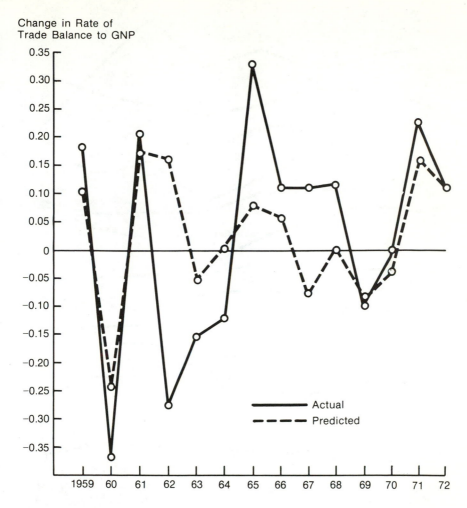

Figure 14-3   EEC Countries

The behavior of the trade balances during this period for twelve major industrialized countries is shown in Figure 14-4. As expected, prior to 1974, the trade balances of the countries move relative to one another. During 1974 and 1975, however, as the transfer was accomplished, the trade balances of these countries (except for Germany) move remarkably in unison. Trade balances tend to deteriorate in 1974 and improve in 1975. By 1976, however, the trade balances of these countries again were moving relative to each other.

The importance of the transfer on the trade balance is reinforced by Figure 14-5 which plots the sum of the trade balances of the twenty-five countries of the OECD against the trade account of OPEC countries. Notice that following the 1973 oil price rise, the trade balances of oil

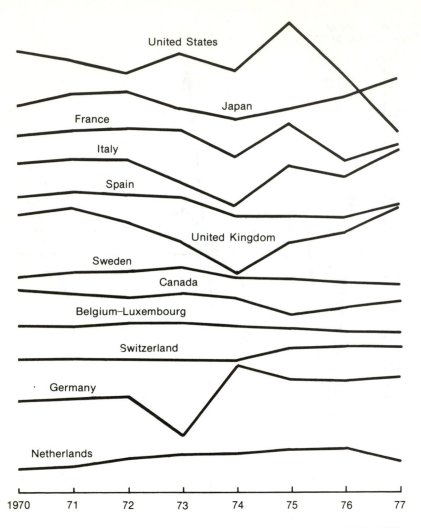

Figure 14–4   The Trade Balances of Twelve Industrialized Countries 1970–1977
Source: National Accounts of OECD Countries 1952–77, Vol. 1

consumers and producers move sharply in opposite directions in 1974
and 1975. The sharp deterioration of the trade balances of consumers,
and improvement for oil producers, in 1974 can be described as the initial transfer. The huge deficits of oil consumers involved transferring
financial assets or purchasing power to oil producers. The sudden movement in the opposite directions in 1975 comprised the effectuation of the
transfer. Possessing increased purchasing power, the OPEC countries increased their rate of absorption of goods manufactured by oil consuming
nations. The trade balance of oil consumers improved, while the trade
balance of OPEC deteriorated.

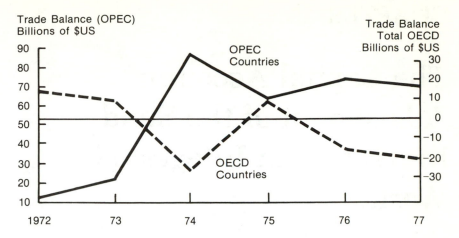

Figure 14–5   The Response of the Trade Balances of OPEC and OECD Countries to the Oil Price-Induced Transfer

SUMMARY

The *trade balance* represents the net exportation of goods from a country. In an integrated world, the real interest rate adjusts to assure that the total current demand for goods equals the total quantity of goods currently supplied. Given equilibrium in world markets, goods then tend to flow from countries of relative excess supply to countries of relative excess demand. Countries of excess demand tend to be those countries growing faster than average, while those growing more slowly than average tend to be the areas of excess supply. Hence, a country which finds its rate of income growth increasing relative to the world average should also find its trade balance deteriorating.

Forces other than demand shocks, such as transfers, can also influence the behavior of the trade balance. The transfer associated with the oil price rise of 1973, for example, caused most trade accounts of OECD countries to move relative to the OPEC trade account, and not relative to each other.

REFERENCES

LAFFER, ARTHUR B. and R. DAVID RANSON, "Canada, United States, and the Rest of the Developed World: A Study in the Integration of Markets," *Policy Formation in an Open Economy,* R. Mundell and E. Van Snellenberg, eds. University of Waterloo, 1974.

MILES, MARC A., *Devaluation, The Trade Balance, and The Balance of Payments.* New York: Marcel Dekker, 1978.

CHAPTER 15

The Capital Account: Adjustment of the Bond Market in an Integrated World

As outlined in Chapter 9, there are three foreign accounts corresponding to the money, goods, and bond markets. It was also pointed out that these three markets are interrelated through Walras' Law, so that only two of the three markets can really be independent. Chapter 12 described the behavior of the balance of payments, and Chapter 14 developed a model of the trade balance. The discussion of the behavior of the two accounts in those chapters also implicitly described the behavior of the capital account. This chapter shows the behavior of the *capital account*, along with its implied role. The description of the capital account completes the basic model of the international accounts. The chapter concludes with a discussion of the implication of the model for capital controls, and some related empirical evidence.

THE CAPITAL ACCOUNT

Chapter 9 showed that the relationship between the capital account, the balance of payments and the trade balance is

$$KB = BOP - TB. \tag{15-1}$$

Using expressions already derived in previous chapters for the balance of payments and the trade balance, equation (15-1) provides an expression for the capital account in both the small and large country cases.

The expression for the balance of payments of a small country is given by equation (12-7) of Chapter 12. The expression for the small country's trade balance is equation (14-9) of Chapter 14. Substituting these two expressions into (15-1) yields

$$\Delta\left(\frac{KB_i}{Y_i}\right) = k\Delta g_i + c\Delta g_i = (k + c)\Delta g_i. \tag{15-2}$$

The important feature of this equation is that since k and c are both positive, the size of the capital balance coefficient on the growth rate (k+c) is larger than the coefficient for either the balance of payments or the trade balance. This fact implies that the capital balance is more sensitive to changes in the growth rate than either of the other two accounts. The reason for the greater sensitivity is the role of the capital account in this model.

The behavior of the balance of payments and the trade balance have been explicitly defined. The role of the capital account is to assure that the behavior of the two accounts is compatible. Thus, when the growth rate of the country increases, the demand for money and goods both rise, improving the balance of payments and causing the trade balance to deteriorate. The improvement in the balance of payments defines how many additional reserves must flow into the country. Yet the deterioration in the trade balance represents a net outflow of reserves. The two accounts are acting in opposite directions. The capital account adjusts to assure that the changes in the other two accounts are not inconsistent. So the capital account improves by the amount required by the balance of payments (kΔg), plus by an amount to offset the loss due to the deterioration of the trade balance (cΔg). The capital account therefore adjusts by more than either of the other two accounts individually adjusts.

The adjustment of the capital account for a large country is similarly derived. Using the behavior described for the balance of payments and the trade balance in equations (12–16) and (14–22) respectively, equation (15–1) above yields

$$\Delta\left(\frac{KB_i}{Y_i}\right) = k\Delta(g_i - \bar{g}_w) + c'\Delta(g_i - \bar{g}_w) = (k + c') \Delta (g_i - \bar{g}_w).$$

$$(15\text{--}3)$$

Again the capital account responds more to growth than either of the other two accounts. As with the other two accounts, in the large country model, the changes in the ratio of the capital account to income depend upon changes in the country's growth rate relative to the average growth of the world.

The large country model can be expanded further to bring in the effects of domestic monetary policy. Using the relationship between monetary policy and the balance of payments described in equation (12–16'), the capital account equation becomes

$$\Delta\left(\frac{KB_i}{Y_i}\right) = (k + c')\Delta(g_i - \bar{g}_w) - \Delta\left(\frac{\Delta M_i^s}{Y_i} - \frac{\overline{\Delta M_w^s}}{Y_w}\right). \quad (15\text{--}3')$$

While the changes in the ratio of the capital account to income still depend positively upon changes in the country's growth rate relative to the average growth in world income, the capital balance ratio depends negatively upon changes in the country's ratio of money supply changes to income compared to the corresponding average ratio in the world.

With the description of the behavior of the capital account, the model of the international accounts is complete. A framework has been developed for analyzing the effects of shocks to the economy and policy decisions of the government. As an illustration, consider the effects of one possible policy tool, capital controls.

CAPITAL CONTROLS

Capital controls are a tool often employed by governments to stem the flow of reserves out of a country. Essentially they are an attempt by a government to affect the balance of payments by attempting to control one part of the account. While such a policy might work if all other parts of the account remained constant, as has been described in the preceding chapters, the various parts of the balance of payments are highly interrelated, and typically a change in one part causes a change in another. A policy that attempts to control the total balance of payments by controlling only one subaccount must therefore be immediately suspect.

Not only do capital control programs usually attempt to control the level of just the one account, typically they affect only a fraction of the total account transactions. A common policy is to restrict only the capital outflows by domestic residents. But the capital account balance is defined as the difference between capital *inflows* and capital *outflows* of both domestic and foreign residents. Controls on outflows therefore still allow inflows to readjust so as to affect the overall capital balance. Similarly, controls on only domestic residents mean that the net inflows or outflows of foreigners can still adjust to affect the overall balance.

An example makes this point even clearer. Suppose that Country A is initially at full equilibrium with all three foreign accounts in balance, and the country growing at a rate relative to other countries that just maintains these balances. The country now imposes controls that reduce the permitted outflow of capital by its residents. Ignoring any second order effects such as a reduction in income due to a restriction in freedom of where an individual may invest, nothing else is assumed to change in the economy. With no other changes, the balance of payments, trade balance and capital account balances should all remain zero. But the capital account balance is defined as the net difference between capital inflows and capital outflows. If capital outflows alone were reduced, the capital account would improve to a positive number, which in turn implies that the balance of payments must also have a surplus or the trade balance must go into deficit to offset the capital account improvement. However, neither of these alternatives is consistent with the stated equilibrium condition for the country that all accounts remain in balance.

Probably what would occur instead is that other capital flows would adjust in order to maintain the capital balance equilibrium. During a particular time period, given wealth, interest rates, etc., individuals in a country have a given amount of net capital assets or liabilities they wish to hold in their portfolios. The capital controls attempt to make them hold fewer net capital assets or bonds (or more net liabilities) by reducing the rate of lending abroad. Were the controls successful, private portfolios would be out of equilibrium at prevailing world interest rates. Desiring to remain in portfolio equilibrium, the private market will use whatever avenues are available to circumvent the government's restrictions.

Since the capital balance is the net difference between capital inflows and outflows, one possibility is for domestic residents to simply reduce their inflows of capital by the amount of the capital restrictions. As capital accumulates at a faster than desired rate, domestic interest rates implicitly fall relative to foreign rates. Foreigners, finding the return to domestic investment falling, would lend less to domestic residents. With the inflows and outflows of capital reduced by the same amount, the overall capital balance and domestic interest rates are unchanged, and the capital balance can remain in balance. Alternatively, the net capital flows of foreigners may adjust to maintain equilibrium. For example, if the capital outflows of domestic residents are reduced, but they do not simultaneously reduce their capital inflows by the same amount, domestic residents find themselves accumulating (decumulating) capital at a faster (slower) rate than before. Capital holdings are therefore rising above the desired level, creating excess supplies of capital. Again, domestic interest rates implicitly fall. One way of reducing the excess capital is to transfer the domestic ownership of capital to foreigners. So the amount of domestic capital made available to foreigners increases. But if foreigners can now obtain more of the capital that they would like to hold within Country A from the residents of that country, at perhaps more favorable rates, less of their capital will be supplied from the foreign countries. In other words, foreigners now reduce their inflows of capital into Country A.

The point above is that if only *part* of the flows of capital are controlled, the *remaining flows can adjust to offset* the net effect of the controls. Capital controls on the outflow of capital by residents can certainly reduce the amount of capital that residents can export abroad. However, whether the controls can affect the net capital balance, much less the balance of payments, is highly questionable. While the outflows of capital are reduced, the above example shows how the capital inflows of either residents or foreigners may be reduced correspondingly, resulting in no net change in the balance. Thus the ability of the government to control some of the components of the capital account does not guarantee them control over the entire account.

VOLUNTARY FOREIGN CREDIT RESTRAINT PROGRAM

In February 1965, the President of the United States enacted the *Voluntary Foreign Credit Restraint Program* (VFCRP). The stated purpose of this program was to limit the amount of U.S. private short-term capital outflows, especially to developed countries. By limiting the amount of capital that was sent abroad by Americans, it was hoped to retard the massive outflow of dollars which was occurring at that time.

Economic arguments for the VFCRP were based on the concept of segregated, rather than integrated, capital markets. The assumption had to be made that U.S. private short-term capital flows could, in general, be separated from other capital flows as well as from goods movements. A reduction in the outflow of U.S. private short-term capital, therefore, would not adversely affect other balance-of-payments accounts, but would have the bulk of its impact on reserve flows. The success of the program was therefore to be measured solely by changes in the U.S. short-term capital outflow category in isolation.

As outlined in the previous section, however, concentrating on the one account in isolation may lead to a misleading interpretation of the success of the program. For example, it is quite possible for short-term capital outflows of U.S. citizens to be reduced as the program desires, but simultaneously for this improvement to be offset by reduced domestic capital inflows by foreigners. A study by Laffer[1] has shown that such an offsetting adjustment is precisely what occurred. Using an econometric estimating technique, Laffer was able to estimate what the net short-term capital flows of U.S. residents and of foreigners would have been in the absence of the VFCRP. Comparing these estimated values to the actual net outflows of these two groups, he was then able to determine the effect of VFCRP on the capital flows. Laffer's results are graphed in Figure 15–1.

The upper part of Figure 15–1 shows the cumulative effect of the VFCRP on the private short-term capital flows of U.S. residents starting in January 1965. The cumulative effect is obtained by adding the effects in each month to the effects of all previous months. Notice that after about three months the cumulative effect on the capital flows of U.S. residents is positive. These capital flows are less negative or more positive than they would have been in the absence of the VFCRP.

Were the analysis to stop there we might conclude that the VFCRP improved the capital account and the balance of payments of the U.S. But in the lower part of Figure 15–1 the cumulative net effect of the VFCRP on the capital flows of foreigners is graphed. Notice that the VFCRP had just the opposite effect on foreign capital flows than on the flows of domestic residents. In all months the cumulative capital flows are more negative or less positive than they would have been in the absence of VFCRP.

With the VFCRP having opposite effects on the two sets of capital flows, the important question is whether the two effects are offsetting. In Figure 15–1 the sum of the two cumulative effects is graphed as a dotted line. The graph shows that the net effect lies within a range of only a $100 million improvement and a net deterioration of $1.5 billion. In most periods the apparent success of the VFCRP with respect to U.S. short-term capital flows appears to have been negated by private foreign short-term capital flows. These results are consistent with the theory that capital controls are unable to affect the overall capital balance, much less the balance of payments.

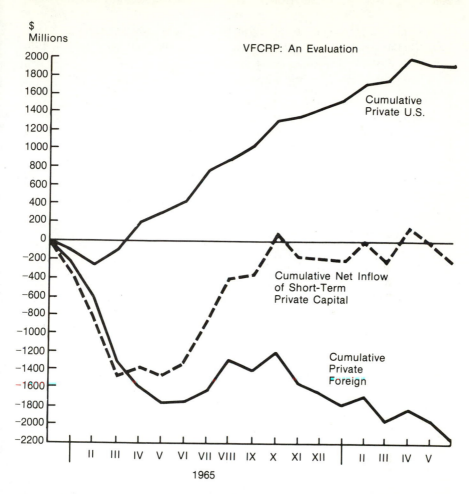

Figure 15–1   Accumulated Effect of the VFCRP on Short-Term Capital Flows

Source: Arthur B. Laffer, *Private Short-Term Capital Flows.* New York: Marcel Dekker, 1975.

SUMMARY

The *capital account* of a country represents the net inflow of capital or outflow of bonds. In an integrated world, capital tends to flow from countries of relative excess supply to countries of relative excess demand. The countries of excess supply and excess demand are implicitly determined by the previous specifications of balance of payments and trade balance behavior, along with Walras' Law. Faster than average growth of income creates excess demand, while faster than average growth of the money supply caused by the monetary authorities creates excess supply. Given its role of assuring that the behavior of the other two accounts is consistent, the capital account is more sensitive to changes in growth rates than the other two accounts.

Capital controls are a policy often employed by countries to try to improve the balance of payments. They are an attempt to influence the overall balance of payments by controlling *one* account or subaccount. However, even if the controls achieve their immediate target, the private market is likely to find ways to circumvent the government's restrictions, and prevent the overall capital account and balance of payments from improving. Evidence from the effects of the U.S.'s Voluntary Foreign Credit Restraint Program in the mid-1960s provides evidence of such private market behavior.

REFERENCES

KOURI, PENTTI and PORTER, MICHAEL. "International Capital Flows and Portfolio Equilibrium." *Journal of Political Economy* 82, No. 3 (May/June 1974): 443–67.

LAFFER, ARTHUR B. *Private Short-Term Capital Flows.* New York: Marcel Dekker, 1975.

MUNDELL, ROBERT A. *International Economics.* New York: Macmillan 1968.

NOTE

1. Arthur B. Laffer, *Private Short-Term Capital Flows,* New York: Marcel Dekker, 1975.

CHAPTER 16

The IS-LM-FF Model: A Keynesian Model of Internal-External Balance

The preceding four chapters present a classic model of how economies adjust in an integrated world. The focus of the discussion now shifts to present an alternative, Keynesian model of macroeconomic adjustment. Recall that Chapter 9 and its appendix present a basic Keynesian IS-LM model of adjustment in a closed economy. The present chapter amends the IS-LM framework to include the effects of the possibility of trade in money, goods, and bonds. The adaptation requires the grafting on of a Keynesian trade balance model and a Keynesian capital account model, resulting in the inclusion of a third curve, the Keynesian balance of payments or foreign exchange market. As shown, some of the assumptions of this model, such as that an excess supply of money causes a balance-of-payments deficit, are consistent with the model of the integrated world. However, other assumptions, such as how the capital account adjusts to changes in the rate of interest or how the trade balance adjusts to exchange rate changes, are inconsistent with the integrated world model. The model presented in this chapter therefore introduces some alternative hypotheses which are the basis of the discussion and tests in the next chapter. Furthermore, since this *internal-external balance* model has served as the framework for formulating international policy decisions for most countries during the postwar period, an understanding of this model helps to emphasize how the policy implications of the integrated world model differ from the policies currently followed by most countries.

THE BASIC IS-LM-FF MODEL

The IS-LM-FF model analyzes the implications of using certain policies to achieve certain goals or targets. In particular the government is assumed to desire both to keep the economy at the full employment level of income and to keep the balance of payments balanced. The government is assumed to have fiscal policy, monetary policy, and the exchange rate as the policy tools with which to try to achieve these targets.

The IS-LM-FF model is shown in Figure 16-1. As in the closed economy case, the *IS curve* represents those combinations of the interest rate and income at which the demand for goods equals the supply in the domestic country. However, as described in the appendix, the concept of demand has been expanded to include net exports of goods. Hence, if domestic supply exceeds domestic demand, in order for equilibrium to exist there must be a net foreign demand for domestic goods, or trade balance surplus, equal to the difference. As shown in the appendix, the IS curve has a negative slope in the i, y space. At low rates of interest, demand is high in the economy, and supply must expand to satisfy the excess demand. Furthermore, the IS curve shifts with changes in either government expenditure or the exchange rate. An increase in government expenditure shifts the curve upward and to the right because the increased government expenditure is assumed to represent excess demand that can be eliminated only by an increase in supply Y and/or by a rise in i that reduces demand. Similarly, a rise in the exchange rate e (a devaluation) also shifts the IS curve to the right. A devaluation is assumed in this model to increase the demand for exports and reduce import demand, thus increasing the net demand for goods.

The *LM curve* again represents those combinations of income and the interest rate at which the current domestic supply of money equals the domestic demand. The LM curve has a positive slope because money demand reacts in the opposite direction to increases in income and the interest rate. For example, an increase in income increases the transactions demand for money. Given the current domestic money supply, the increased demand produces an excess (or an increased) demand for money. The excess demand must then be eliminated by a rise in the rate of interest which reduces money demand. The LM curve is also assumed to shift with changes in the exchange rate or changes in the money supply. An increase in the exchange rate e shifts the LM curve upward and to the left because it increases the demand for money. The devaluation is associated with a rise in the domestic price level, which means that a

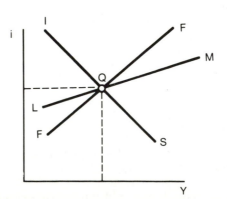

Figure 16-1   The IS-LM-FF Model

given level of transactions has a higher dollar value and therefore requires a higher quantity of money. Given the supply of money, the higher
demand has to be offset by a reduction in income or a rise in the rate of
interest. Hence the shift in the LM curve.

An increase in the money supply causes the opposite, downward and
to the right shift in the LM curve. This shift implies that the only way the
additional money balances can be absorbed is for the level of income to
rise and for the interest rate to fall. The difference between the LM
curves in the open and closed economies, however, is the source of these
money supply increases. In the closed economy, only the monetary authorities were assumed able to increase the money supply. But in the
open economy, money may also flow in through a balance-of-payments
surplus. A balance-of-payments surplus therefore shifts the LM curve to
the right.

The FF curve reflects those combinations of income and the interest
rate at which the balance of payments is zero, that is, where the trade
balance surplus or deficit is just offset by a balance of opposite sign on
the capital account. The curve has a positive slope because under the
Keynesian assumptions the level of imports increases with domestic income, increasing the trade balance deficit, while the net inflow of short-
term capital varies positively with the interest rate. Therefore, if the level
of income rises, causing the trade balance to deteriorate, in order for the
balance of payments to remain balanced, the interest rate must rise to
produce an offsetting increase in the inflow of capital. As with the other
two curves, the FF curve shifts with a change in the exchange rate. For
example, under the assumptions of the model, an increase in e causes a
reduction in the trade deficit or an increase in the trade surplus. Hence,
balance-of-payments equilibrium can be achieved with a smaller capital
inflow or larger outflow, and thus a lower interest rate. A devaluation
therefore causes the FF curve to shift downward and to the right.

As the FF and LM curves are drawn in Figure 16-1, the FF curve has
a steeper slope. However, the precise slope of the FF curve depends on
the interest elasticity of capital flows. The more capital flows respond to
the interest rate, the less steep the FF curve. The extreme case, of course,
is the small country which faces an infinitely elastic supply of capital. At
the prevailing world interest rate, the country can import as little or as
much capital as it needs. Hence, the FF curve in this case is horizontal
(zero slope) at the prevailing interest rate, because at that interest rate
whatever capital flows are necessary to offset the trade balance and
make the balance of payments zero can be achieved. The other extreme
case is where capital flows are completely insensitive to the interest rate.
In that case the FF curve is vertical at the level of income associated with
the trade balance that is just offset by the existing capital balance. Regardless of the rate of interest, the capital account balance will remain
the same, and thus no other level of income can be associated with balance-of-payments equilibrium. Only by changing the relationships between income and the trade balance (in this model by devaluation) can
another level of income become consistent with balance-of-payments
equilibrium.

SOME FUNDAMENTAL DIFFERENCES BETWEEN THE INTERNAL-EXTERNAL BALANCE MODEL AND THE MODEL OF THE INTEGRATED WORLD

While this internal-external balance model appears to summarize the effects of government economic policies, there are at least two important ways in which this basic model differs from the conclusions of the integrated world model. One way the two models differ is in the response of capital flows to changes in interest rates. In the Keynesian model it is assumed that if the domestic interest rate rises (of course, holding foreign interest rates constant), then capital flows into the country at a faster rate now and in the future. In other words, higher interest rates imply continuously higher flows of capital. Yet such a reaction to changing interest rates can occur only in the short run for at least two reasons. First of all, if more and more capital is flowing into the domestic country, foreigners must have less and less capital. Presumably, the value of each marginal unit of capital must therefore be rising abroad and falling in the domestic country. Hence, interest rates must be rising abroad and falling in the domestic country, thus reversing the flows. The continuous, increased capital flows are unsustainable in the long run.

Second, if the increased rate of capital flow were sustained beyond the short run, it would eventually drive the country to bankruptcy. Remember that in a final equilibrium in this model, such as at point Q in Figure 16–1, there is no growth, and hence no increasing income to borrow against. Instead income remains at Y_0 each period. But as more and more capital is imported each period, larger and larger interest payments must be made each period to foreigners. As the interest payments grow, they approach the income level Y_0. When payments reach Y_0, all of the country's income goes to just debt servicing. No income is left for residents to consume. If capital is still flowing in at this point, interest payments then rise above Y_0. In other words, the country has to pay foreigners each period more than the country's entire income. The country will be unable to meet its debt payments. Obviously, at some point the continued higher capital inflows must stop.*

The internal-external balance model, then, emphasizes only the short-run behavior of capital market. The integrated world model, in contrast, emphasizes both the short and long-run effects. The higher interest rate is a signal that the value of capital has increased relative to abroad, and capital should flow into the domestic country until the value of capital across countries is equated. In other words, the higher interest rate should induce a short-run stock adjustment—a finite increase in the stock

---

*One might argue that capital inflows should lead to investments whose returns should finance the debt service. However, this argument points out another short-run assumption of the model. According to the Rybczynski Theorem, increases in capital increase output. Yet in the internal-external balance model, continued capital inflows or outflows are associated with a constant level of income.

of capital that equates returns across countries. The higher interest rate therefore produces a temporary improvement in the capital account that disappears when returns are again equated. Such an adjustment process will be described in the next chapter under the discussion of the portfolio balance model.

The importance of this point for the current internal-external balance model is that unless an intersection of the three curves such as point Q represents a zero trade balance, the intersection represents only a flow equilibrium, not a stock equilibrium. A flow equilibrium can be, at most, a short-run equilibrium. A final, sustainable equilibrium can occur only at a stock equilibrium. So, unless by chance point Q represents a stock equilibrium, the internal-external balance model can describe only short-run behavior.*

A second underlying difference concerns the way that the trade balance is assumed to respond to changes in the exchange rate. Both the IS and FF curves are assumed to shift to the right when the country devalues, because devaluation is assumed to reduce the level of imports, increase the level of exports, and thus improve the trade balance associated with each level of income. So many of the conclusions and implications of this model require the trade balance surplus to increase following devaluation. However, as discussed in detail in the next chapter, the integrated market model questions the assumption that devaluation improves the trade balance on both theoretical and empirical levels. The conclusions and implications of the two models with respect to the goods markets are therefore likely to differ substantially.**

THE ROLE OF MONETARY AND FISCAL POLICY IN THE IS-LM-FF MODEL

Given the assumptions of the internal-external balance framework described above, the implications of the model for the proper use of fiscal and monetary policy can be outlined. The model assumes that there are a number of domestic goals or targets which the domestic government would like to achieve. Two obvious goals from Figure 16–1 are full employment and balance-of-payments equilibrium. A third possible goal might be a certain rate of economic growth, though such a goal is difficult to illustrate in the comparative statics diagram being used. In turn there are three possible policy tools for achieving the goals, fiscal policy, mone-

---

*The short-run nature of the internal-external balance model is consistent with the basic Keynesian model, which also addresses short-run phenomena. The internal-external balance model appears to run into additional difficulties since, given the speed with which international capital markets apparently adjust, the short-run may not be very long.

**A substantial number of economists probably disagree currently with our contention that there is little, if any, relationship between the exchange rate and the trade balance. However, as detailed in Chapter 17, the empirical evidence involving the trade balance (versus only exports or only imports) strongly supports our view.

tary policy and the exchange rate. The remaining question is how to employ these policies.

An important principle of the theory of economic policy used in finding equilibrium in the internal-external balance model is that in order to achieve a given set of policy objectives it is necessary that the number of policy instruments equal the number of policy objects. This principle, first developed by Nobel Prize laureate Jan Tinbergen, is a direct corollary of the mathematical principle that a unique solution to a system of equations does not exist unless there are an equal number of independent equations and unknowns. The application of this principle to the model under both fixed and flexible exchange rates is now shown.

In the fixed exchange rate case, the central bank fixes the value of the domestic currency in terms of either a foreign currency or some commodity such as gold. Thus the exchange rate is not free to vary and cannot be used as a policy tool. The remaining two policies, fiscal and monetary policy, must be used to achieve the desired goals of full employment and balance-of-payments equilibrium. For example, consider the country initially at equilibrium at point R in Figure 16–2. All three curves initially pass through point R, indicating that the country has a balance-of-payments equilibrium. However, the level of income Y_1 associated with point R represents less than full employment. The government would therefore like to maintain balance-of-payments equilibrium, yet increase the economy's income to the full employment level Y_2.

Attaining these dual goals requires two policies, a restrictive monetary policy and an expansionary fiscal policy to shift the IS and LM curves to make them pass through point S. At point S, not only the money and goods markets, but also the balance of payments are in equilibrium, shown by the fact that the FF curve also intersects point S. This point also corresponds to the full employment level of income.

But suppose that the government attempted to achieve these goals by using only one policy, say monetary policy. For instance, suppose the government undertakes only the restrictive monetary policy required to

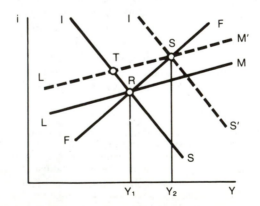

Figure 16–2   Monetary and Fiscal Policy in the IS-LM-FF Model

move the economy to point S. In that case the LM curve shifts upward to LM', but the IS curve does not shift. Internal equilibrium occurs at point T. But at point T the balance of payments is not in equilibrium. In particular the interest rate is higher or the level of income is lower than required for external equilibrium, or both. The balance of payments is in surplus. An external surplus in turn implies that the country's money supply is increasing, shifting the LM curve back to the right. Equilibrium is again achieved at point R.

This example illustrates two points. First, attainment of the desired two goals requires two policies. Second, under fixed exchange rates monetary policy is of only temporary use, if any, for influencing domestic economic variables. This second point is one shown earlier in the model of the integrated world.

In the flexible exchange rate case, the central bank allows the exchange rate to vary in response to market forces. Thus the government now has three variables at its disposal. Achieving the two goals of full employment and external balance requires the use of only two policies. Thus the government can achieve the goals by allowing the exchange rate to adjust and using either monetary or fiscal policy, but not both. For example, in Figure 16–3, the government could choose to use monetary policy in conjunction with flexible rates. The monetary authorities first shift the LM curve out to LM'. Internal equilibrium occurs at point W. But at point W the interest rate is lower or income is higher than required for external equilibrium, or both. Hence, the exchange rate depreciates. The depreciation in turn shifts each of the three curves. On the assumption that currency depreciation improves the trade balance and the balance of payments, the FF and IS curves shift to the right to FF' and IS' respectively. The depreciation also reduces the value of real money balances, and, the LM curve on the other hand shifts to the left to LM''. The

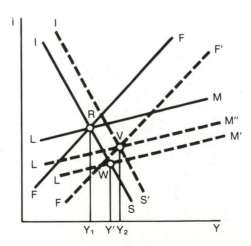

Figure 16–3   Using Monetary Policy and the Exchange Rate to Attain Internal and External Equilibrium

three curves now intersect at point V, where not only external equilibrium, but also full employment income Y, are attained.

Alternatively, fiscal policy could be used in conjunction with the exchange rate to achieve internal and external equilibrium. This case is illustrated in Figure 16–4. Again the economy is initially in equilibrium at point R. Now the government uses expansionary fiscal policy to shift the IS curve to the right to IS′. Internal equilibrium occurs at point X where IS′ intersects the initial LM curve. As in the previous case, the point of internal equilibrium is below the FF curve and therefore is associated with pressure for the exchange rate to depreciate. Again the depreciation shifts the three curves. The IS curve shifts further to the right to IS″. The FF curve also shifts to the right, while the LM curve shifts to the left. Final equilibrium occurs at point Z, again a point of both internal and external balance.

Notice that while both approaches yield the same equilibrium full employment level of income, the equilibrium interest rate differs in the two cases. Where monetary policy is used, the equilibrium interest rate at point V is below the initial rate at point R. Conversely, where fiscal policy is used, the equilibrium interest rate at point Z is above the initial rate at point R. The reason for the differing results is quite straightforward. In mathematical terms, when there are three policies to achieve two targets, the system is *overdetermined*. Hence there is not one unique solution or equilibrium. The desired income and foreign balance targets are consistent with a multiple number of interest rates.

While there is an extra policy variable in each of these two cases, the additional variable would become important if the government chose an additional target. For example, if the government decides that a specific rate of economic growth is desirable, the additional policy variable could

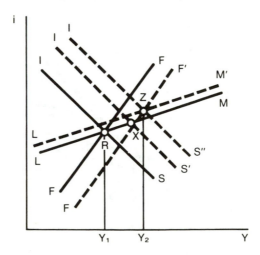

Figure 16–4   Using Fiscal Policy and the Exchange Rate to Attain Internal and External Equilibrium

be used for that target. Then the government could use, say, the exchange rate for achieving external balance, monetary policy for achieving internal balance, and fiscal policy for achieving the desired rate of growth.

THE SMALL COUNTRY CASE WITHIN THE IS-LM-FF MODEL

Just as the basic implications of the model of the integrated world were analyzed from examining the adjustment of a small country, the small country case can also be used to illustrate some implications of the IS-LM-FF model. This small country case has been analyzed by Mundell.[1] As before, the small country is assumed to be a price taker in the financial markets. In other words, the country faces a given interest rate which it is powerless to affect. Thus the country is free to borrow or lend as much as it would like on world markets without causing a change in the interest rate. However, the current model differs in its assumption about prices in the goods market. The small country is not considered a price taker in the goods market. Specifically, a depreciation of the exchange rate is still assumed to improve the trade balance, probably reflecting an assumption that domestic prices do not rise by the percentage of depreciation. Such an assumption is of course not consistent with the concept of a small country in the integrated world model.*

The importance of the small country assumption for the internal-external balance model is the assumed shape of the FF curve. Since the country can borrow or lend as much as desired at the prevailing world interest rate, capital flows in the country can be whatever are needed to attain external balance. In other words, the infinite interest elasticity of capital flows makes the FF curve horizontal. The implications of the horizontal FF curve for monetary and fiscal policy under both fixed and flexible rates are now shown.

The fixed exchange rate case is illustrated in Figure 16–5. As before, the LM curve is upward sloping, the IS curve is downward sloping, but the FF curve is horizontal reflecting the infinite interest elasticity of capital flows. Consider first the effects of monetary policy on this small country. For example, suppose the monetary authorities conduct an expansionary monetary policy. The increase in the money supply shifts the LM curve to the right to LM'. The internal equilibrium attempts to move from point A to point B. However, the interest rate that is consistent with internal equilibrium at point B is below the prevailing world interest rate. But since the interest elasticity of capital flows is infinite, the domestic interest rate cannot fall. Instead, the downward pressure on the interest rate causes a quantity adjustment in the form of capital outflows.

---

*As will be discussed in the next chapter, a temporary improvement in the trade balance is theoretically possible, even if prices rise to fully reflect depreciation, if a real balance effect is assumed. However, the real balance effect does not appear to have much empirical importance for the trade balance.

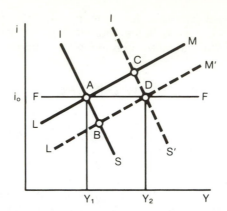

Figure 16–5   Monetary and Fiscal Policy in a Small Country Facing Perfect Capital Mobility and Fixing Its Exchange Rate

The capital outflows in turn reduce the domestic supply of money. The LM curve therefore moves back to the left, and the economy returns to equilibrium when the LM curve returns to its position. Thus the small country cannot run an independent monetary policy under fixed rates and a high degree of capital mobility, just as was shown in previous chapters.

Fiscal policy, however, is more successful for the small country in this model. Assume the government undertakes an expansionary fiscal policy that shifts the IS curve to the right to IS'. With an unchanged monetary policy, internal equilibrium tries to move from point A to point C. However, the interest rate consistent with internal equilibrium differs from the prevailing world rate. Again the policy change changes capital flows. But since this time the interest rate at point C is above the prevailing world rate, a capital inflow is induced. Hence the LM curve shifts to the right this time as additional money or capital flows in, permitting a new equilibrium to occur at point D. At point D both full employment income Y_2 and external balance have been achieved. The conclusion is that within this model a small country facing a perfectly elastic supply and demand for capital and fixing its exchange rate can only influence its level of income through fiscal policy.

This conclusion changes, however, when the country is assumed to allow the exchange rate to fluctuate. For example, again consider the effects of an expansionary monetary policy. This case is shown in Figure 16–6. Again, the economy is initially in equilibrium at point A associated with a less than full employment level of income. Again, the LM curve shifts to the right, moving the implicit internal equilibrium to point B. Again, point B is consistent with a rate of interest below the prevailing world rate. But in this flexible rate case, the pressure of a potential capital outflow causes a price adjustment instead of a quantity adjustment. The exchange rate depreciates, shifting the IS curve rightward to IS' and

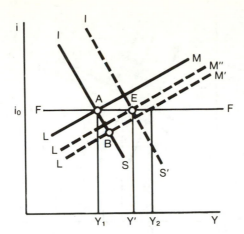

Figure 16–6   Monetary Policy in a Small Country Facing Perfect Capital Mobility and a Flexible Exchange Rate

the LM curve leftward to LM''. The new point of full equilibrium is at point E associated with a higher level of income Y'. A repetition of the expansionary monetary policy could therefore move the economy to full employment income Y_2. Thus, under flexible rates, monetary policy is useful for reaching full employment.

Under flexible rates, however, fiscal policy is less useful than under fixed rates. This case is illustrated in Figure 16–7. Again, an expansionary fiscal policy shifts the IS curve to the right. Again, internal equilibrium would occur at point C if possible. However, the interest rate at point C is above the prevailing world rate. The resulting pressure for an improved capital inflow causes the exchange rate to appreciate. The appreciating exchange rate in turn causes the IS curve to shift leftward to IS'', and the LM curve to shift rightward to LM'. The new full equilibrium occurs at point G.

While the level of income associated with point G is higher than at the initial point A, the increase in income is less than under the fixed exchange rate case. Recall from Figure 16–5 that the shift in the IS curve to IS'' caused a money inflow that allowed the LM curve to shift out to intersect IS' and FF at the full employment level of income Y_2. But with flexible rates, the same shift in the IS curve in this model causes an appreciation of the exchange rate that reduces aggregate demand, shifting the IS curve back to IS''. Thus income rises to only Y''', less than full employment income Y_2.

With these conclusions, the basics of the Keynesian model of international adjustment with money and capital mobility have been shown. Remember, however, that the model relies on two important underlying short-run assumptions. Depreciation of the currency is assumed to improve the trade balance, and an increase in the level of the rate of inter-

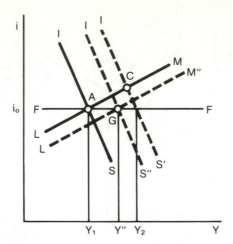

Figure 16–7   Fiscal Policy in a Small Country Facing Perfect Capital Mobility and a Flexible Exchange Rate

est is assumed to improve the level of capital flows. These basic assumptions can be contrasted in the next chapter with the behavior of economic markets under an integrated market assumption. The conclusions of that chapter will show why the usefulness of the IS-LM-FF framework for analyzing market responses and formulating policy has come increasingly into question.[2]

SUMMARY

The short-run Keynesian model becomes the IS-LM-FF model in an open economy. The model differs from the integrated world model primarily in its assumptions of how capital flows respond to interest rate changes, and how the trade balance responds to changes in the exchange rate.

The Keynesian model emphasizes the use of three policies, monetary policy, fiscal policy, and the exchange rate to achieve *internal-external* balance in the economy. Where only the two goals of full employment and external account balance are targeted, only two policies are required. If a third goal, such as a desired rate of growth, is also targeted, all three policies must be used.

A small country in the IS-LM-FF model faces an infinitely elastic supply of capital, and so the FF curve is horizontal. In a small economy with fixed exchange rates, monetary policy is useless. Only fiscal policy can influence the level of income. Under flexible rates, however, the usefulness of monetary policy for reaching full employment increases, and that of fiscal policy decreases.

REFERENCES

FLEMING, MARCUS J. "Domestic Financial Policies Under Fixed and Under Floating Exchange Rates," *IMF Staff Papers*, 9 (November 1962).

JOHNSON, HARRY G. "Towards a General Theory of the Balance of Payments." In
his *International Trade and Economic Growth: Studies in Pure Theory*.
Cambridge, Mass: Harvard University Press, 1961; reprinted in R. Caves and
H. G. Johnson, eds. *Readings in International Economics*, Homewood, Ill.: Irwin, 1968.

KUSKA, EDWARD. "On the Almost Total Inadequacy of Keynesian Balance-of-Payments Theory," *American Economic Review* 68, No. 4 (September 1978): 659–
70.

MEADE, JAMES E. *Theory of International Economic Policy*, Vol. 1, *The Balance of
Payments*. New York: Oxford University Press, 1951.

MUNDELL, ROBERT A. "The Appropriate Use of Monetary and Fiscal Policy Under
Fixed Exchange Rates," *IMF Staff Papers* 9, No. 1 (March 1962): 70–79; reprinted in his *International Economics*. New York: Macmillan, 1968, Chapter
16.

WHITMAN, MARINA V. N. *Policies for Internal and External Balance*. Special Papers in International Economics, No. 9. Princeton, N.J.: International Finance
Section, Princeton University, 1970.

NOTES

1. R. A. Mundell, *International Economics*, Chapter 18, New York: Macmillan
   1968.

2. See for example, Herbert C. Grubel, *International Economics*, Homewood, Ill.:
   Irwin, 1977, Chapter 18, or Edward A. Kuska, "On the Almost Total Inadequacy
   of Keynesian Balance-of-Payments Theory," *American Economic Review* 68,
   No. 4 (September 1978): 459–670.

APPENDIX 16
EXPANDING THE IS-LM FRAMEWORK TO
AN OPEN ECONOMY MODEL

The Appendix to Chapter 9 derives the basic IS-LM framework for analyzing the behavior of income and the interest rate in the Keynesian
closed economy. That framework is now expanded to demonstrate the
effects of opening the economy to the possibility of trade in money, goods
and bonds. The expansion requires including the effects of a trade balance on equilibrium in the goods market, and the effects of exchange rate
changes on equilibrium in the money market, as well as the effects of a
completely new market, the market for foreign exchange. With the inclusion of these effects, the model becomes a Keynesian IS-LM-FF model of
the open economy. This model is used in the text of this chapter to de-

scribe the internal-external balance approach to macroeconomic policy. As discussed in the text, the model describes only short-run phenomena, and its usefulness for formulating policy decisions has come increasingly into question.

ADJUSTING THE IS CURVE TO THE OPEN ECONOMY

The appendix to Chapter 9 describes the derivation of the traditional closed economy IS curve from the forty-five degree diagram of the simple Keynesian model. The IS curve in that case represents those combinations of the interest rate and income at which the domestic demand for goods just equals the domestic supply. With the opening of the economy, however, it now becomes probable that some of the domestically produced goods are consumed abroad and some of the domestically consumed goods originate in foreign countries. The concept of goods market equilibrium must therefore be expanded to include the effects of trade in goods. These effects are incorporated by adding the net foreign demand for goods, or the trade balance $X-M$, to the other demands for goods. The demand curve for domestic goods therefore now represents $C+I+G+X-M$, as shown in Figure 16A-1.

The level of net foreign demand is assumed in the Keynesian model to depend on two variables, income and the exchange rate. The level of imports M is assumed to vary positively with the domestic level of income and negatively with the exchange rate. An increase in domestic income increases the demand for all goods, including imports. The precise increase in import demand will be $m\Delta Y$, where m is the marginal propensity to import. Since import demand is a demand for foreign goods instead of domestic goods, including imports increases the number of demand leakages. The demand curve in Figure 16A-1 therefore has a flat-

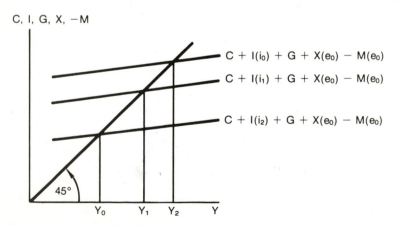

C, I, G, X, $-$M

$C + I(i_0) + G + X(e_0) - M(e_0)$

$C + I(i_1) + G + X(e_0) - M(e_0)$

$C + I(i_2) + G + X(e_0) - M(e_0)$

45°

Y_0 Y_1 Y_2 Y

Figure 16A-1   The Forty-five Degree Diagram in the Open Economy

ter slope than the closed economy counterpart in Chapter 9, since an increase in domestic income now results in a smaller increase in the demand for domestic goods.

A change in the exchange rate is assumed to affect the demand for both exports and imports. An increase in the exchange rate e (a depreciation) is assumed to increase the price of imports relative to exports and thus switch demand from imports to exports. As shown in the next chapter, this assumption can be questioned both theoretically and empirically. However, with this assumption, the net foreign demand for domestic goods varies positively with the exchange rate e. A depreciation shifts the domestic expenditure curve upward at each level of income.

The IS curve again is derived by varying the rate of interest, causing changes in investment demand and therefore the level of income at which demand for domestic goods equals domestic supply. In Figure 16A–1, as the interest rate falls from i_2 to i_1 to i_0, investment demand continues to rise, causing equilibrium income to rise from Y_0 to Y_1 to Y_2. These combinations of income and the interest rate are drawn as the IS curve in Figure 16A–2. However, that IS curve is drawn for a given level of exports, a given relationship between imports and income, and hence for a given exchange rate. If the exchange rate changes, these variables change, and the IS curve shifts.

For example, suppose the exchange rate depreciates. As the exchange rate rises from e_0 to e_1, the level of exports rises and the level of imports falls. At each level of income, the level of aggregate demand rises. This effect is shown in Figure 16A–3 for a given interest rate i_2. When e rises to e_1, the level of aggregate demand rises, raising equilibrium income to Y_1. Hence the interest rate i_2 is now associated with equilibrium in the goods market when income is Y_1 instead of the previous Y_0. As shown in Figure 16A–2, the IS curve reacts to the depreciation by shifting to the right at each interest rate to I'S'. Similarly, an increase in government expenditure G, which is also assumed to increase aggregate demand, shifts the IS curve to the right.

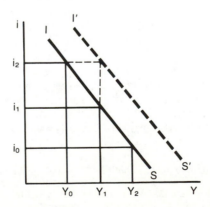

Figure 16A–2   The IS Curve in the Open Economy

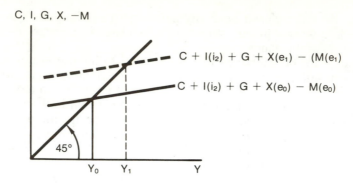

Figure 16A–3   The Effect of an Exchange Rate Depreciation on the Aggregate Demand Curve

ADJUSTING THE LM CURVE TO THE OPEN ECONOMY

The LM curve of the closed economy is transformed into an LM curve of the open economy by incorporating two possible effects on money market equilibrium. First, a nonzero balance-of-payments affects the country's supply of money. A balance-of-payments surplus implies that money is flowing into the country, increasing the money supply. Conversely a balance of payments deficit implies the country's money supply is decreasing. Second, a change in the exchange rate affects the demand for money. A depreciation of the exchange rate is assumed to increase the domestic price level, increasing the quantity of money required to facilitate a given level of transactions. Hence, the demand for money rises. Conversely, an appreciation of the exchange rate increases the real purchasing power of each dollar, reducing the number of dollars demanded. While this assumption appears similar to the assumption about prices in the integrated world, the actual size of the domestic price change differs in the two cases. In the integrated market model, a 10 percent depreciation is assumed to cause domestic prices to rise 10 percent more than foreign prices. However, in this Keynesian model, the price rise is usually assumed to be proportionate to the percentage of goods actually traded. So if the exchange rate depreciates 10 percent and the value of goods traded with other economies is 30 percent of domestic GNP, domestic prices are expected to rise only 3 percent.* The fact that domestic prices are assumed not to rise completely to affect the depreciation in part explains why the trade balance is assumed to improve in this model.

*An alternative interpretation might be that the integrated market model assumes no non-traded goods, and the Keynesian model assumes a substantial nontraded sector with zero substitution in demand between the two. But as Komiya (1967) has shown, in a model with three goods (two traded and one nontraded) and two factors of production, competitive factor markets assure that the relative price of traded and nontraded goods is constant, and hence the money prices of both goods can be assumed to rise by the same percentage.

The derivation of the open economy LM curve is shown in Figure 16A–4. As in the appendix of Chapter 9, the supply of money is assumed positively related to the interest rate, while the demand for money is negatively related. An increase in the level of income from Y_0 to Y_1 is also assumed as before to increase the demand for money and therefore to shift the money demand curve upwards. As income increases, the interest rate that equates the domestic demand and supply of money rises from i_0 to i_1. Repeating this type of experiment, the LM curve is derived in Figure 16A–5.

A change in the exchange rate will shift the LM curve. In Figure 16A–4, as the exchange rate rises from e_0 to e_1 (a depreciation), holding income at Y_0, the demand for money curve shifts up because more units of money are needed to facilitate current transactions. Given the money supply, the rate of interest that equates domestic supply and demand for money rises from i_0 to i'. Thus the depreciation causes the equilibrium interest rate to rise at each level of income. In terms of Figure 16A–5, the depreciation causes the LM curve to shift upwards and to the left to LM'. Conversely, a currency appreciation would shift the LM curve downwards and to the right.

A balance-of-payments deficit or surplus also causes the LM curve to shift. For example, a balance-of-payments deficit means some of the

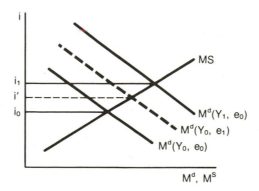

Figure 16A–4   Derivation of the LM Curve of the Open Economy

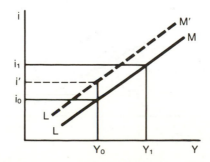

Figure 16A–5   The LM Curve of the Open Economy

monetary base is removed from the economy. At each level of interest rate, the money supply is smaller. Hence the money supply curve in Figure 16A–4 shifts to the left (not shown). The equilibrium interest rate associated with each level of income rises. So the balance-of-payments deficit also causes the LM curve to shift upwards and to the left to LM'. Conversely, a balance-of-payments surplus, by increasing the money supply, causes the LM curve to shift downwards and to the right.

THE NEW CURVE—THE FF CURVE

The FF curve represents those combinations of income and the interest rate at which the balance of payments is zero. So at any point on the FF curve, the current account deficit or surplus is just matched by an offsetting capital account surplus or deficit. Thus at any point along the FF curve, there is no net inflow of foreign exchange or money into the country. The derivation of the FF curve is shown in Figure 16A–6. The horizontal axis measures trade balance surpluses and the equivalent capital account deficits. Thus from left to right along the horizontal axis the trade balance moves from deficit to surplus, while the capital account moves from surplus to deficit. The vertical axis measures the level of income in the economy.

The trade balance is assumed to be a function of the level of domestic income and the exchange rate. The trade balance is negatively related to income. As the level of domestic income rises, the level of imports increases, worsening the trade balance. The trade balance curve TB in Figure 16A–6 therefore slopes downward from left to right. Changes in the exchange rate shift the trade balance curve. A depreciation of the exchange rate from e_0 to e_1 increases the trade balance surplus (reduces the deficit) at each level of income, shifting the trade balance curve upward and to the right to TB'.

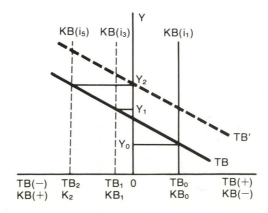

Figure 16A–6   The Derivation of the FF Curve

The capital balance is assumed to depend only on the rate of interest in this short-run Keynesian model. The higher the domestic rate of interest, the more capital attracted to the country, and the higher the capital account surplus (lower the deficit).* Thus in Figure 16A–6 the capital account curve is vertical, reflecting the insensitivity of capital flows to income. However, as the interest rate rises from i_1 to i_3 to i_5, the capital account moves from a deficit into a surplus and then a larger surplus.

As stated in the text, this formulation can describe only short-run capital account behavior. If the domestic interest rate rises, there is little reason to expect a perpetual improvement in the capital account. Instead, only a temporary improvement in the capital account is expected until the stocks of assets in domestic portfolios have adjusted to their new desired levels. Furthermore, in an integrated world, the domestic rate of interest on assets of a given risk is not expected to deviate from the prevailing world rate of interest.

The FF curve is derived by finding those combinations of income and the interest rate at which the trade balance surplus is just offset by the capital account deficit. For example, in Figure 16A–6 at domestic income level Y_0, the trade balance surplus is TB_0. To offset the surplus, the level of interest associated with a capital account deficit of KB_0 must be found. In the graph, that interest rate is i_1. Similarly, as the domestic level of income rises to Y_1, the trade balance deteriorates to a deficit of TB_1. To offset that deficit, the domestic interest rate must rise to i_3, producing a capital account surplus KB_1. Repeating the exercise, income level Y_2 and interest rate i_5 are also found to be a combination where the balance of payments is zero. Plotting these points of balance-of-payments equilibrium yields the FF curve in Figure 16A–7.

A depreciation of the exchange rate shifts the FF curve to the right. As the exchange rate depreciates from e_0 to e_1 the trade balance curve shifts upward and to the right, indicating a smaller trade deficit at each level of domestic income. At each level of income, a smaller capital account surplus and hence lower interest rate is required to attain balance-of-pay-

*The model implicitly assumes that foreign interest rates and incomes are constant.

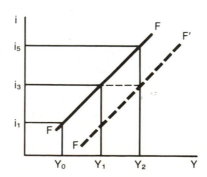

Figure 16A–7   The FF Curve

ments equilibrium. In Figure 16A–7, therefore, the FF curve shifts downward and to the right to FF', reflecting a lower equilibrium interest rate associated with each level of income. Conversely, an exchange rate appreciation shifts the FF curve upward and to the left.

AN ALGEBRAIC SUMMARY

To summarize the above discussion, there are equations for three markets (goods, money, and foreign exchange) that are used to solve for three unknowns in the economy (the level of income, the interest rate and the exchange rate). Equilibrium in the goods market can be described by

$$Y = \overset{+}{c(y)} + \overset{-}{I(i)} + G + \overset{+}{X(e)} - \overset{+\ -}{M(y,\ e)} \quad \text{(16A–1)}$$

where the plus and minus signs indicate whether the particular variable varies positively or negatively with the variable in the parenthesis. This equation says that the supply of goods in the economy should equal total demand. Similarly, equilibrium in the money market can be described by

$$\overset{+\ \ +}{M^S(i,\ BOP)} = \overset{-\ \ ++}{M^d(i,\ Y,\ e)} \quad \text{(16A–2)}$$

The supply of money varies positively with the interest rate and balance-of-payments surplus, while money demand varies negatively with the interest rate and positively with income and the exchange rate. Finally, the third equation describing external balance is

$$\overset{+}{KB(i)} = \overset{-\ +}{TB(Y,\ e)}. \quad \text{(16A–3)}$$

The capital account surplus varies positively with the rate of interest, while the trade surplus varies negatively with income and positively with the exchange rate. Given the value of government expenditure G, the equilibrium values of Y, i and e could be determined. Those values would then indicate at which point the IS, LM, and FF curves all intersect.

These equations also show which curves the different government policies affect. For example, since government expenditure G only enters the goods market equation, fiscal policy only shifts the IS curve. Similarly, since monetary policy affects the money supply, which only enters the money market equation, monetary policy shifts only the LM curve. However, the exchange rate enters all three equations. Thus any policy that affects the exchange rate causes all three curves to shift.

CHAPTER 17

Devaluation

Devaluation is one of the most misunderstood of all policies. Many claims are made as to what devaluation will or will not do to a country's foreign accounts. In this chapter a number of the claims are examined both theoretically and empirically. In the first section the implications of the integrated market framework for devaluation are examined. The second section explores the origins of currently popular beliefs about devaluation. Additional models of devaluation are then developed and evaluated. Finally, data from actual devaluation episodes are presented in order to evaluate the relevancy and usefulness of these theories for formulating policy decisions.

DEVALUATION IN AN INTEGRATED WORLD

In Chapter 8 and in Chapters 9–15 a model of a fully integrated global economy is developed. In such a model, arbitrage guarantees that in the absence of trade barriers and transportation costs, the price of any product, as measured in one country's currency, equals the price of that same product in any other country's currency times the exchange rate between the two currencies. As long as this condition does not exist, arbitrage profits are possible.

For example, imagine that coffee sells for £2 per pound of coffee in the U.K., and for $4 in the United States. If a U.K. pound sterling exchanges for $2.25 U.S. in the international money markets, then by purchasing coffee in the U.S. for dollars, selling that coffee in the U.K. for pounds sterling, and using the proceeds to repurchase dollars, for every $4 of initial capital, one would end up with $4.50. Likewise, if the pound exchanges for less than $2.00, U.S. dollar profits can be made by reversing the transactions flow. Only if the pound exchanges for $2.00 is there no arbitrage potential. In the limit there is only one exchange rate where arbitrage profits do not exist, that is, where each and every price converted at the exchange rate equals the world price.

This arbitrage relationship is presented in Chapter 9 as

$$P_I = e \cdot P_{II}, \qquad (17\text{-}1)$$

where e is the number of units of currency II per unit of currency I and P_I and P_{II} are the respective price levels in Countries I and II. (Country II can be thought of as the rest of the world.)

Barriers to trade or transportation costs can cause discrete differences in prices between countries. But if prices diverge by more than these discrete differences, again opportunities for arbitrage appear. With trade barriers, equation (17-1) simply becomes

$$P_I = e \cdot P_{II} + t \qquad (17\text{-}1')$$

where t is the absolute size of the barrier.

Since the equality in either form holds both before and after devaluation, it follows that a change in exchange rates simply leads to a fully offsetting change in the domestic price level. In terms of discrete changes

$$\Delta P_I = e \cdot \Delta P_{II} + \Delta e \cdot P_{II}, \quad \Delta t = 0 \qquad (17\text{-}2)$$

or in terms of percentage changes

$$\% \Delta P_I = \% \Delta P_{II} + \% \Delta e, \% \quad \Delta t = 0. \qquad (17\text{-}3)$$

Remember an increase in e ($\Delta e > 0$) is a devaluation of Country I's currency.

In other words, a devaluation of Country I's currency leads to higher inflation in Country I relative to Country II by the exact amount of the exchange rate change. The higher inflation in Country I implies that money demand is increasing faster there than in other countries. Recall from Chapter 12 that the change in money demand in Country I can be written

$$\Delta M_i^d = k_i(\Delta y_i P + y_i \Delta P). \qquad (17\text{-}4)$$

The higher inflation implies that ΔP is larger in Country I than any other country. Ignoring differences in the level or changes in the level of income for the moment, the larger rise in prices implies that money demand increases by more in Country I than in any other country. In the absence of offsetting money creation by Country I's monetary authority, Country I therefore becomes an area of increased relative excess demand for money. Since money flows in an integrated world from areas of excess supply to areas of excess demand, the devaluing country should experience an improvement in its balance of payments.

The excess inflation caused by the devaluation therefore has four important implications for the effect of devaluation. First, since the higher inflation fully offsets devaluation in order to eliminate the possibility of profits through the arbitrage of goods, the relative (dollar) price of goods between countries will not change. Hence there is no incentive for the real flow of goods to change, and therefore no reason for the trade balance to improve. Second, the excess inflation means that the country's predevaluation money supply will not suffice for the new higher level of nominal income. The improvement in the balance of payments reflects the importation of nominal money balances to satisfy this new demand. Third, the improvement in the balance of payments will be only temporary. Once the excess demand for money created by the excess inflation is satisfied by improved balance-of-payments surpluses, there is no longer an incentive for continued importation of money, and the balance of payments should return to the predevaluation level. Fourth, since the trade balance does not improve, the balance-of-payments surplus is accompanied by a capital account surplus. Therefore, in an integrated world, devaluation affects only nominal variables such as prices and the nominal money supply, not real variables such as the trade balance. Adjustment occurs through only financial markets.

While the arbitrage condition (17-3) shows that prices must rise by relatively more in the devaluing country, from that relationship alone it is impossible to determine whether the relative price change is satisfied by prices in Country I rising by the full additional amount, or prices in Country II falling by the full amount, or some combination of the two. In order to obtain a more precise description of the behavior of prices it is necessary to formulate how the burden of price adjustment is divided among countries. The division of the adjustment is similar to the division in Chapter 12 where it is shown that the division of balances-of-payments adjustment is inversely proportional to a country's relative income size. Again, it is shown that the burden of inflation/deflation adjustment is inversely proportional to a country's relative size in the world economy, but size is now measured in terms of relative money supplies, not incomes.

In order to see why relative money supplies are important, consider the world price level in terms of currency I. Using the concept of a world quantity theory of money introduced in Chapter 13, the relationship between money and prices in terms of currency I can be written

$$(M_I^s + e \cdot M_{II}^s) \cdot V = P_I(y_I + y_{II}),\qquad(17\text{-}5)$$

where

$$M_I^s = \text{supply of currency I}$$

$$e \cdot M_{II}^s = \text{supply of currency II expressed in terms of currency I}$$

$$V = \text{world velocity of circulation of money}$$

$$P_I = \text{world price level in terms of currency I*}$$

$$y_I, y_{II} = \text{real incomes in Countries I and II.}$$

While this relationship between money and prices is expressed in terms of currency I, it could just as easily be expressed in terms of the quantity of currency II and the currency II price level. This alternative relationship would be

---

*The symbol for world price level in terms of currency I, P_I, is the same as the symbol used for the currency I price level of Country I in equation (17-1). In an integrated world with no trade barriers, the two will be identical.

$$\left(\frac{M_I}{e} + M_{II}\right)V = P_{II}(y_i + y_{II}) \tag{17-6}$$

Both (17–5) and (17–6) can in turn be rearranged to describe the price level in terms of the other variables. For the price level in terms of currency I the expression is

$$P_I = (M_I^s + e \cdot M_{II}^s) \cdot \frac{V}{(y_I + y_{II})}. \tag{17-7}$$

A relationship between the percentage change in the price level following devaluation and the relative money supply sizes can now be derived. In performing this derivation it is assumed that real incomes and the velocity of circulation are unaffected by a once-for-all devaluation. Furthermore, the percentage change in the world's money supply as measured in the devalued currency is assumed due solely to the exchange rate change. In deriving this relationship between price changes and relative money supplies, equation (17–7) is first expressed in terms of logarithms.

$$\log P_I = \log (M_I^s + e \cdot M_{II}^s) + \log V - \log(y_I + y_{II}). \tag{17-8}$$

Next, the derivative of (17–8) is calculated. Since velocity and real income are assumed unaffected by devaluation, their derivatives are zero. Equation (17–9) becomes

$$\% \Delta P_I = \frac{M_I^s}{M_I^s + eM_{II}^s} \% \Delta M_I^s + \frac{eM_{II}^s}{M_I^s + eM_{II}^s} (\% \Delta M_{II}^s + \% \Delta e). \tag{17-9}$$

Since at present changes in the money supply by the domestic monetary authorities are not being considered, $\% \Delta M_I^s = \% \Delta M_{II}^s = 0$ and (17–9) reduces to

$$\% \Delta P_I = \frac{eM_{II}^s}{M_I^s + eM_{II}^s} \cdot \% \Delta e. \tag{17-10}$$

Using the same procedure equation (17–6) yields

$$\% \Delta P_{II} = \frac{-M_I^s}{M_I^s + eM_{II}^s} \cdot \% \Delta e. \tag{17-11}$$

The preceding two equations describe the effects of percentage change in the currency I and currency II price levels when Country I devalues. The positive sign in equation (17–10) indicates that with constant quantities of world money, prices rise in Country I, while the negative sign in (17–11) indicates that with constant quantities, prices in Country II fall. The precise magnitude of the price change is inversely proportional to the share of the country's money supply in the total world money supply. For example, in equation (17–10), for every 1 percent of devaluation, prices rise in Country I by $(eM_{II}^s/M_I^s + eM_{II}^s)$ percent. The term $(eM_{II}^s/M_I^s + eM_{II}^s)$ is of course the share of Country II's money supply in the total world money supply. The larger this share (and hence the smaller the share of Country I's money supply) the larger the percentage change in prices in Country I. Similarly, equation (17–11) shows that the smaller the share of Country II's money supply in the total world money supply, the larger is the percentage fall in Country II's prices.

Again the fundamental lesson is that the burden of adjustment is inversely proportional to a country's relative size.[1] Here the burden of inflation/deflation due to devaluation is inversely related to the relative size of the country's money supply.

To summarize, if S_I^M is used to represent the share of Country I's money supply in the total world money supply, under the assumptions made, a devaluation by Country I produces the following price changes

$$\% \Delta P_I = (1 - S_I^M) \% \Delta e \qquad (17\text{--}12)$$

$$\% \Delta P_{II} = -S_I^M \% \Delta e \qquad (17\text{--}13)$$

$$\% \Delta P_I - \% \Delta P_{II} = \% \Delta e. \qquad (17\text{--}14)$$

As an example, imagine there are only two countries in the world, the U.S. and Germany. If the money supply in Germany is 1,000,000 Deutsche marks, the U.S. money supply is $400,000, and the exchange rate equals 40 cents per Deutsche mark, then each country initially has 50 percent of the total world's money supply. If the U.S. devalues by 20 percent, the dollar price of the Deutsche mark rises to 48 cents. The price level in the U.S. will increase by $\% \Delta P_{US} = \% \Delta e(1 - S_{US}^M)$ or [(20%) · (.5)] = 10%, while simultaneously the price level in Germany will fall by 10% = [(−20%) · (.5)].* If the U.S. money supply were greater than 50 percent of the world money supply, the U.S. price level would rise by less than 10 percent and the German price level would fall by more than 10 percent.

As already described, with a constant quantity of money, the rise in the price level in Country I following devaluation produces an excess demand for money. Conversely, with constant money supplies, the falling price level in Country II produces an excess supply of money. Country I satisfies its excess demand by importing money, while Country II satisfies its excess supply by exporting money. Since these are the only two countries in the world, for world monetary equilibrium, the balance-of-payments surplus of the devaluing country must precisely equal the excessive money balances of the revaluing country. Hence, the division of the price adjustment between the two countries must produce these equal and opposite excess demands. This additional constraint provides a convenient check for the relationships that have been just derived.

*Notice that a 20 percent devaluation of the dollar in this simple numerical example is a 16⅔ percent revaluation of the Deutsche mark. So while the German price level falls by 10 percent in terms of dollars, as measured in Deutsche marks, the price level would be expected to fall only [(16⅔%) · (.5)] = 8⅓%. The U.S. price level would be expected to rise by a similar amount. The discrepancy arises from the reliance on simple arithmetic percentage changes, which are not symmetrical by numeraire. If instead percentage changes were calculated using changes in the logarithms of exchange rates, a rise to $.48 per DM would equal 18.2 percent in either numeraire, approximately the geometric mean between 20 percent and 16⅔ percent.

In algebraic terms the balance-of-payments constraint implies

$$BOP_I = -BOP_{II} \cdot e. \tag{17-15}$$

Since the balance of payments in either country equals the excess demand for money, which in this case equals the initial money supply times the percentage change in prices, equation (17-15) can be rewritten

$$BOP_I = M_I^S \cdot \%\Delta P_I = -M_{II}^S \cdot e \cdot \%\Delta P_{II} = -BOP_{II} \cdot e. \tag{17-16}$$

Substituting equations (17-12) and (17-13) into equation (17-16) yields

$$BOP_I = M_I^S \cdot \%\Delta e \cdot (1 - S_I^M) = M_{II}^S \cdot e \cdot \%\Delta e \cdot S_I^M$$

$$= -BOP_{II} \cdot e \tag{17-17}$$

or

$$\frac{M_I^S}{S_I^M} = \frac{M_{II}^S \cdot e}{1 - S_I^M}$$

or

$$\frac{1 - S_I^M}{S_I^M} = \frac{M_{II}^S \cdot e}{M_I^S} \tag{17-18}$$

Equation (17-18) is of course an identity, which implies that the balance-of-payments constraint is consistent with the required behavior of prices.

Putting the results of this section in more intuitive terms, if a country devalues, it experiences inflation inversely proportional to its relative size in the world economy. It runs a one-period balance-of-payments surplus proportional to its inflation rate, which is inversely proportional to its relative size. The larger a country is, the less its price level rises, and the smaller is its payments surplus (as a proportion of its initial money supply).

In terms of our U.S. and Germany example, the devaluation of the dollar relative to the Deutsche mark leads to a 10 percent price rise in the U.S., and a 10 percent fall in the German price level. Concomitantly, the U.S. has a one-period $40,000 surplus in its balance of payments and Germany the equivalent deficit of 83,333 DM (83,333 DM @48 cents per DM = $40,000).

As previously stated, within the framework of the integrated world, devaluation will not cause the country's trade balance to change. The inflation which occurs to eliminate arbitrage profits means that the relative price of Country I's goods in terms of any currency does not change, and neither does the real flow of goods.

A devaluation therefore causes the following phenomena:

1. An increase in the price level in the devaluing country by the percentage devaluation, times one minus that country's share of money in the world economy (equation (17-12)).

2. A fall in other countries' price levels equal to the percentage devaluation, times one minus their share in the world economy (equation (17-13)).

3. A one-period balance-of-payments surplus in the devaluing country equal to its price rise times its money supply (equation (17–16)).

4. A one-period balance-of-payments deficit in all other countries equal to their percentage price fall times their money supplies. In terms of the devaluing country's currency, this is precisely equal to the devaluing country's surplus (equation (17–16)).

5. No change in either country's trade balance when measured in physical units.

6. A one-period capital account surplus (deficit) in the devaluing (revaluing) country, equal to the balance-of-payments surplus (deficit).

The model of devaluation in an integrated world is now completed. The implications of this integrated market model can now be contrasted with the implications of other popular models of devaluation. In particular, in sharp contrast to the integrated world model, the notion that devaluation improves a country's trade balance remains widespread. Where does this notion come from, and what are some of the reasons for rejecting it? These two questions are examined in the following two sections.

THE EARLY KEYNESIAN MODELS

One source of the notion that trade balances respond positively to devaluation was the early simple Keynesian models of devaluation[2] which portrayed trade in a two-country context. Each country specializes by producing only one good. Country I is the sole producer and exporter of good A, and Country II the sole producer and exporter of good B. The monetary authority in Country I is assumed to maintain a constant price of good A in terms of the domestic currency. Symmetrically, Country II's monetary authority maintains a constant price of good B in terms of Country II's domestic currency. Under these assumptions, if Country I devalues its currency, good A becomes cheaper relative to good B. As a result of good A becoming cheaper, Country II imports more of it. Therefore, Country I's exports of A increase. If good A is cheaper relative to good B, then obviously good B is dearer relative to good A. With a more expensive good B, Country I imports less of it. According to this reasoning, Country I's imports decrease. As a consequence of these two effects, Country I's trade balance improves in terms of physical units.

This simple model of devaluation contains a number of theoretical problems. One problem is that the model is essentially a barter model. As you will recall from the first section of this book, a barter model is a model of only the goods market. There is no explicit money market. Devaluation, however, refers solely to a change in exchange rates. An exchange rate is the price of a single unit of one currency as measured in terms of another currency. In a barter model the money price of goods is never mentioned. How, then, can devaluation be analyzed in a model where there is no money, only goods?

Monetary policy, to the extent that it exists, is assumed to be simply whatever is necessary to maintain a constant domestic currency price of the exported good. There is no well-defined demand for money, or supply of money, or price level. Rather, the workings of monetary policy and the money market exist in the background and are never made explicit. In fact, if one were to eliminate completely the monetary authorities or any reference of money or money prices, the model would be unchanged. The money market simply does not play an important role in this type of model.

A model which does not contain an explicit monetary sector cannot contain exchange rates. And without exchange rates, devaluation cannot exist. Instead, what these models refer to as devaluation is actually a change in the price of good A relative to good B. In barter models, the only prices that can change are these relative values of goods, $P_{A/B}$, which we are already familiar with as the terms of trade. So this early Keynesian model analyzes the effects of changes in the terms of trade, not the exchange rate.

Exchange rates and terms of trade are two separate and distinct concepts, and there is no reason to expect that a change in the one will lead to a predictable change in the other. Likewise, there is no reason to expect that the effects of a change in the one will be even remotely similar to the effects of a change in the other. For example, it is intuitively difficult to see why a decision to devalue the dollar against the mark should cause the price of eggs in terms of shoes to change. This early Keynesian model is therefore not really analyzing devaluations at all. Rather, it is providing one interpretation of what happens in a barter model to the flow of goods when the terms of trade change.

Furthermore, in order to improve the trade balance in real terms, not only must a devaluation lead to an expansion of exports and a contraction of imports, but these changes must be sufficiently large to overcome the pure relative price effects of a devaluation. Imagine a situation in which devaluation does lead to a change in the terms of trade, but exports and imports in physical units for whatever reason do not change. If the home country exports the same amount as before and imports the same amount as before, a worsening of its terms of trade will worsen its balance of trade in real terms. If Country I exports 15 computers per year to Country II, imports 800 bicycles, and the terms of trade are initially 50 bicycles per computer, then Country I's deficit is equivalent to 50 bicycles, or 1 computer. If Country I's terms of trade worsen by 10 percent, so that 45 bicycles now exchange for 1 computer, and if Country I's exports and imports do not change, then Country I's deficit expands to 123 bicycles, or 2.8 computers. This worsening of the trade balance is due solely to the pure price effect. In order for a devaluation to improve the measured trade balance (in either computers or bicycles), the devaluation has to elicit a sufficient expansion of exports and contraction of imports to more than offset this pure price effect.

A condition often employed for determining whether devaluation will improve the trade balance in real terms is called the *Marshall-Lerner* *condition.* In its simplest form it states that if the elasticities of import demand in the domestic and foreign countries sum to more than one, then devaluation will improve the trade balance. Historically, discussions of the efficiency of a devaluation have focused on whether or not the Marshall-Lerner condition is satisfied. The condition is derived from the simple Keynesian model just described. However, since this Keynesian model is purely a barter model, the Marshall-Lerner condition must refer to the flow of goods when the terms of trade (not the exchange rate) change. In fact, the Marshall-Lerner condition was previously developed in Chapter 7, which describes the relationship between the trade balance and the terms of trade. In that chapter, it was shown that for the Marshall-Lerner condition to have any meaning, it must be interpreted simply as a stability condition of the barter model. When the terms of trade of a country improve, stability requires this relative price change to cause an excess supply of the country's export good. All the Marshall-Lerner condition tells us is the demand conditions necessary for such an excess supply to occur.*

A FURTHER COMPLICATION

For the moment, accept the hypothesis that a change in the exchange rate can be considered equivalent to a change in the terms of trade. However, the question still remains as to whether such a change in the terms of trade results in a predictable change in the trade balance. A traditionally popular view portrays a scenario where the devaluation raises the domestic price of imports relative to exports. The relative rise in import prices both decreases the domestic demand for importables and, simultaneously, increases the domestic production of importables. Together these effects unambiguously reduce domestic net imports. Similarly, the foreign country finds that the relative price of its imports (the devaluing country's exports), has fallen. This price change both increases the demand for the foreign country's imported goods and reduces the foreign country's production of import-competing goods. Thus the domestic country, it is reasoned, finds its net imports decreasing while its net exports increase. The domestic country's trade balance, if measured in constant prices, must therefore improve.**

---

*In the simplest form, the Marshall-Lerner condition assumes supply elasticities are infinite and cross elasticities are zero. More complex forms relax these assumptions. Yet, even in the more complex forms, the Marshall-Lerner condition still only refers to the stability condition of the barter model.

**Another currently popular view is that devaluation raises the price of traded goods relative to nontraded goods, and, by similar analysis, improves the trade balance. Such an analysis is subject to the same types of criticisms as the analysis above. Furthermore, as pointed out by Ryutaro Komiya ("Nontraded Goods and the Pure Theory of International Trade," *International Economic Review*, Vol. 8 (June 1967):132–52), in a model with two factors of production, two traded goods, and one nontraded good, with competitive factor markets the relative price of traded to nontraded goods cannot vary.

This argument on logical grounds alone is deficient. In order to show such a trade balance improvement, the scenario must focus exclusively on each country's demand for and supply of imports. The scenario completely neglects the corresponding changes in the demand for and supply of exports. For the analysis to be complete, the effects of the change in the terms of trade on both exports and imports in both countries must be considered and be consistent. When all effects are taken into account, an improvement in the devaluing country's trade balance can no longer be illustrated.

For example, if the relative price of the good imported domestically rises, not only consumers in the domestic country, but also consumers in the foreign country want less of that good. Similarly, the fall in the relative price of the good imported in the foreign country increases the demand for that good in the domestic as well as the foreign country. Supply responses to either good in both countries should also be similar. Hence, with all reactions to the relative price change considered, there is no clear-cut movement in either country's trade balance. Worldwide, an excess demand is created for domestic exportables, since demand for that good rises in both countries and supply falls, while an excess supply for domestic imports is created, since demand falls but supply rises in both countries. Relative prices must therefore move back towards their pre-devaluation levels.

To see the entire analysis and precisely the difference consideration of exports makes, examine Table 17-1. This table shows the effect on the demand for (D) and supply of (S) exports and imports in both the home (h) and foreign (f) countries when the relative price of the home country's imports $P_{M/X}$ rises. X and M refer to the home country's (domestic) exports and imports, respectively.

Notice that there are a total of eight effects. For example, the rise in $P_{M/X}$ causes the foreign demand for imports (domestic exports and therefore X) to rise. Notice also that only four of the eight possible effects will work to improve the devaluing country's trade balance. These are the four effects described in the initial example above. The rise in $P_{M/X}$ is assumed to raise the foreign demand for domestic exports and the domestic supply of import-competing goods, while reducing the domestic

Table 17-1   A Rise in the Home Country's Price of Imports Relative to Its Exports ($P_{M/X}$)

Good	Source of Change			
	D^h	D^f	S^h	S^f
X	↑	↑*	↓	↓*
M	↓*	↓	↑*	↑

X, M = export and import good of the home country
D^h, D^f = demand in the domestic and foreign countries
S^h, S^f = supply in the domestic and foreign countries

demand for imports and the foreign supply of import-competing goods. These four effects are marked with an "*" in Table 17-1.

But as was discussed in the first section of the book, when relative prices change, they affect the demand for and the supply of both goods in both countries. So the remaining effects must also be considered. These are the effects on the demand for and supply of exportables. Not only does the rise in $P_{M/X}$ increase the demand for domestic exportables in the foreign country, but it increases the demand for domestic exportables in the domestic country as well. In addition, it causes the domestic supply of exportables to be reduced as producers switch production into the now relatively more profitable import-competing good. The increased demand and reduced supply mean that fewer exportables are available for export, which works to worsen the domestic trade balance. Furthermore, in the foreign country the rise in $P_{M/X}$ increases the supply and reduces demand for the foreign exported (domestic imported) good. Thus, foreigners now have more goods free for exportation to (importation by) the domestic country. This shift in demand and supply again works to worsen the domestic trade balance.

Obviously, all of these described effects cannot happen simultaneously, since the trade balance cannot simultaneously worsen and improve. Instead, the important point of this discussion is to emphasize that the traditional description of the effects of a rise in $P_{M/X}$ is strictly a *partial equilibrium* description. Only one-half of all possible demands and supplies changes are permitted to occur in their logical direction following the price change. The only changes which are permitted to occur are those which imply an improvement in the trade balance. However, the other half of the changes in demand and supply is just as likely to occur. When the effects of these other four changes are included, any pretense at a definitive answer is precluded. As shown below, the conclusions of the traditional description are no longer automatic, and probably do not occur.

Table 17-1 shows that when $P_{M/X}$ increases, in both countries demand shifts from M to X. Thus we find both D^h and D^f rising for X and falling for M. Similarly, Table 17-1 shows that in both countries producers want to shift supply to the now relatively more profitable good M. S^h and S^f therefore are shown to rise for M and fall for X. Taking the net result of these changes, in both countries there is an increase in demand for X but a reduction in its supply. Conversely, in both countries the demand for M falls while the supply rises. The rise in $P_{M/X}$ produces an excess demand for good X and an excess supply of M. These excess demands in turn cause $P_{M/X}$ to fall right back to its initial level to eliminate the excess demands. In other words, even if the initial effect of a devaluation were to increase $P_{M/X}$, the price change would immediately unleash market forces which would return $P_{M/X}$ to its original level.

To summarize, in order for a change in the exchange rate to affect the trade balance, it must be assumed that a change in the exchange rate also changes the terms of trade. Then to produce an improvement in the trade balance, it must also be assumed that only the import market reacts in the correct direction to the relative price change. The export markets must behave perversely or at a minimum be insensitive to relative price changes. Somehow the effects in the import market dominate the effects in the export market. Such assumptions, however, are not consistent with a general equilibrium economic theory.[3]

BRINGING MONEY INTO THE ANALYSIS

In order to have a complete model of devaluation, it is important not only to analyze the effects on the goods market, but also on the money market. Including the money market introduces an exchange rate as well as the terms of trade into the model.

The analysis of models with money starts with a very simple monetary approach model which contains only the money and goods markets. The purpose of this model is to show how the real balance effect may integrate the money and goods markets. In subsequent sections, the inclusion of bonds as well as money and goods are considered. While the model containing only money and goods is useful for explaining some basic concepts, the empirical tests will show that a realistic model can only be constructed when a bonds market is also included. The framework of a pure money market and goods market model requires such restrictive assumptions that it is useful only for pedagogic purposes and not as a guide to the affairs of real countries.

A SIMPLE MODEL WITH MONEY

For describing the simple monetary model, the small country case is considered. Under the small country assumption, the domestic price of goods equals the world-determined foreign currency price of goods times the exchange rate. If P is the domestic currency price, e the exchange rate and P* the foreign currency price, then $P = eP^*$. Since P* is fixed from the small country's viewpoint, if the country devalues, the domestic price level will rise by the percentage of the devaluation. The rise in the price level immediately has an effect on the real value or purchasing power equivalence of all nominally denominated assets and liabilities. A unit of domestic currency simply does not purchase as many goods as it did before the price rise. Since the only nominally denominated asset in this model is money, the rise in the price level has the effect of reducing the real purchasing power of domestic currency money balances. Another way of stating this effect is that the value of real cash balances M/P has fallen because P has risen.

The devaluation-induced fall in the value of real balances has an effect on market equilibrium. In the money market the demand for real cash balances is postulated to be

$$\left(\frac{M}{P}\right)^d = f(y, i), \tag{17-9}$$

where y is the level of real income, and i is the nominal rate of interest. Since the country is small, the terms of trade are given to it. A change in the relative price of currencies therefore does not affect the relative price of goods or their production. Real income is unchanged. Also, since the country is a price taker, the nominal interest rate is unaffected.* The determinants of the demand for real balances are unaffected, and demand therefore remains unchanged. But the rise in the price level does have an effect on the real supply of money. Given the nominal quantity of money M^s, the real quantity of money $(M/P)^s$ is reduced by the percentage of devaluation. Thus, in the absence of the government creating more money internally, additional money balances must be imported through the balance of payments in order to make $(M/P)^s = (M/P)^d$ again.

Hence, by reducing the supply of real balances, through an increase in domestic prices, devaluation causes an excess demand for money that must be satisfied by an improvement in the balance of payments. An improvement in the balance of payments, in turn, means that more reserves are flowing in or fewer are flowing out. So the primary effect of devaluation is to help a country's reserve position.

Presumably a country is forced to devalue in the first place only because it is running out of reserves and is unwilling to alter the rate at which it creates money internally. As often as not, the underlying cause of the reserve losses and deficits is that the domestic money supply has been increased to the point where people are returning the domestic money to the central bank in exchange for other currencies. For example, if the monetary authorities of the Netherlands have been increasing the domestic money supply too greatly, there will be an incipient increase in the supply of guilders relative to the demand for guilders, producing an incipient excess supply. In terms of the current model with a fixed exchange rate, an incipient excess supply of guilders leads the Dutch public to send guilders abroad. In exchange for their guilders, they can acquire either foreign bonds or foreign goods. Because we are assuming a world without bonds, in this model, the Dutch public must import goods. The foreigners, in turn, return the guilders to the Dutch central bank in order to exchange them for their own local currencies. Thus there is an outflow of reserves from the Netherlands. Since the Dutch supply of foreign reserves is finite, were this process to continue, the supply would eventually begin to run low. At that point, the Netherlands finds that it can no longer simultaneously support both the present fixed value of its exchange rate and its monetary policy. One possibility is for the Netherlands to devalue the guilder. A devaluation of the guilder reduces the supply of real balances in the Netherlands relative to the demand, causing a reduction in the outflow of guilders (and thus foreign reserves), and possibly may even reverse the direction of the flow.

---

*Devaluations may change the perceived risk of holding the domestic currency, which can be reflected in a risk differential that is added to the prevailing nominal interest rate. However, the significance of such a potential change in the nominal interest rate will be saved for the chapter on currency substitution.

Notice, however, that a once-and-for-all devaluation provides only a temporary solution to the Netherlands' reserve problem. If the country continues to maintain its expansive monetary policy, it will eventually have to devalue again. An expansive monetary policy does not enable the Dutch Government to change directly the permanent real value of the quantity of guilders in the Netherlands. Initially, the expansive monetary policy causes an excess supply of guilders shown in the quantity adjustment of an outflow of guilders from Holland. After devaluation, the real value of the quantity of guilders returns to the desired level through a simultaneous rise in the guilder price level and a flow of reserves back into the country. However, if the increase in the supply of guilders continues, the process will be repeated, again leading to further deficits and eventually necessitating another fall in the value of the guilder.

Since internal monetary expansion by the central bank and the inflow of money from abroad are two alternative sources of money, to the extent that the government satisfies the devaluation-induced excess money demands by creating money internally, the balance-of-payments surpluses will be reduced. Thus, a continued expansion of the supply of guilders means that the balance of payments will not improve by as much as predicted by the devaluation alone. Not as many foreign reserves flow back into the country. In fact, if the increase in the domestic money supply brought about by internal money creation is larger than the excess demand for money created by the devaluation, the balance of payments will not even improve at all. Thus, while devaluation alone may provide for a temporary improvement in the balance of payments, if monetary policy remains expansive, the balance of payments will return to its previous deficits.

This discussion illustrates another case where a distinction must be drawn between cause and symptom. Just as in the discussion of production versus consumption versus trade policies in Chapter 6, the optimal policy must be determined for dealing with balance-of-payments deficits. And just as in these cases, before the optimal policy can be chosen, it is first necessary to determine the actual cause of the initial problem.

In the example above, the problem of a continued outflow of Dutch reserves is not that the guilder is priced "too high." Rather, the basic source of Dutch reserve losses comes from an excessively expansionary monetary policy. Thus, devaluation at most can provide a once-for-all reflow of reserves that allows the balance-of-payments deficits to continue for an extended period of time. It does not eliminate the deficits. If the symptom to be rectified is balance-of-payments deficits, then the only permanent cure is to reduce the rate of money creation. Only then will reserves not continually flow out of the Netherlands, causing a drain on the stock of reserves. In fact, devaluation is actually entirely unnecessary for dealing with this symptom. For example, if the monetary authority reversed its policy and decreased (or sufficiently slowed the growth rate of) the money supply, the result would be to create an excess demand for money and reverse the flow of reserves. Devaluation is thus never necessary to solve the problem of a balance-of-payments deficit. In fact, it is a highly indirect method of solution and is accompanied by some undesirable side effects.

Except in very special instances, devaluation occurs in countries which have been increasing their money supplies at too fast a rate. As just discussed, the most direct method of counteracting this problem is for the country to cut the rate of increase, or even decrease, the money supply. Of course, reducing the rate of growth of the money supply may not be feasible on political grounds. In such cases, devaluation may be the only alternative. Devaluation can quickly move a country from a position of incipient excess money supply to incipient excess demand. However, devaluations do involve adjustment costs. The question is whether these costs may be less than the benefits.

STOCK VS. FLOW ADJUSTMENT

The traditional elasticities approach of the simple Keynesian variety described above predicted that devaluation would cause a *flow* or *permanent adjustment* to the trade balance. Devaluation affects relative prices, and permanently alters trade flows. On the other hand, the monetary model just described predicts a *stock* or *temporary adjustment* in the balance of payments. This temporary improvement is called a stock adjustment because it lasts only until the stock of money has grown from its postdevaluation level back to its predevaluation level. In this section, the simple monetary model is used to show that even if the trade balance were to improve in addition to the balance of payments, the adjustment to devaluation should be at most temporary.

The twist used to resurrect the simple Keynesian model within the simple monetary model is that the trade balance adjusts in response to changes in relative prices of tradables and nontradables. Assume that there are two types of goods, one produced and consumed in all countries (tradables), and a second which is produced and consumed solely within the individual countries (nontradables). The price of the traded good is assumed to behave according to $P = eP^*$. Thus, devaluation will immediately raise the price of the traded good by the percentage of devaluation. The price of the nontraded good, however, is assumed not to adjust immediately to the devaluation.*

The difference in the price adjustments to devaluation means that the relative price of traded goods rises following devaluation. This relative price change in turn produces demand and supply changes. On the demand side, demand switches away from tradables and toward the now relatively cheaper nontradable goods. On the supply side, production

*As previously noted, however, Komiya has pointed out that where there are at least as many traded goods and factors as there are factors of production, factor costs of all goods will rise by the same percentage. The relative price of traded to nontraded goods is not expected to change. The trade balance adjustment of this section should therefore be interpreted as pedagogical, rather than necessarily realistic.

switches in the opposite direction to traded goods. Both of these effects appear to improve the trade balance. The increased domestic production of tradables means that, given supply, less importables must be imported and more exportables are freed for exportation.

If the analysis were to stop at this point, it would appear that the trade balance is permanently improved with fewer goods being imported and more being exported. However, we already know that such a result is impossible for two reasons. First, the balance of payments improves only temporarily and the trade balance must do the same. Second, as was shown previously for the change in the terms of trade, there are automatic corrective forces which are activated by the relative price change. While demand moves away from tradables and towards nontradables, supply shifts in just the opposite direction. In other words, if the demand and supply of nontradables were equal before devaluation, the shifts in demand and supply following the relative price change create an excess demand for nontradables. Since, by definition, more nontradables cannot be obtained from abroad, the excess demand must be alleviated by a relative price change. The required price change is a rise in the relative price of nontradables. This price rise offsets the initial relative price change caused by the devaluation. In fact, if the nontraded goods market was in equilibrium before devaluation, the market will return to equilibrium only when the relative price of nontraded goods has returned to its predevaluation level. Thus, the return to goods market equilibrium requires the relative price change caused by devaluation to be completely offset. So even if the trade balance were to improve following devaluation, the improvement would be, at most, temporary.

The model of devaluation that has just been described has shown both the balance of payments and the trade balance to improve following devaluation. The reason for the joint improvement in this model is quite clear. In a model containing only money and goods, if money must be imported to relieve the resultant excess demand for money, the only remaining asset to trade for the money is goods. However, if a bonds market is now introduced into the analysis, a second conduit for the procurement of money is opened. The public can now exchange bonds directly for money. As shown in the next section, the introduction of bonds means that it is no longer theoretically necessary for the trade balance to improve following devaluation.

INCLUDING THE BONDS MARKET

A major point of emphasis in the second part of this book has been that a properly specified model requires simultaneous analysis of all three commodity markets. For that reason, the model of devaluation is now expanded to include explicitly the bonds market. In addition to a nominal asset, money, there is now an alternative, nominal, interest-paying asset, bonds. An investor now may own two different nominal financial assets. Presumably, an investor who wants to minimize the amount of risk, yet obtain a positive return, wants to hold some of each asset. The precise ratio in which he divides his assets depends on the investor's tastes for risk versus return and the prevailing rate of interest.

The inclusion of the bond market also means that there is now a capital account in addition to the trade balance and balance of payments. Hence, the trade balance no longer must move in the same direction as the balance of payments. In fact, as shown in this section, since the capital account now represents an alternative avenue for money to flow into the country to satisfy an excess money demand, it is no longer necessary for the trade balance to improve at all following devaluation.

A second, less traditional alteration of the model is now also presented. The public is now assumed not to view their real cash balances as representing net wealth.* In most traditional monetary models, these balances are assumed to be net wealth, as the public is aware of only the asset portion of each dollar bill. But now the public is also assumed to recognize that a liability is associated with each dollar asset. For bank-created money, the asset and liability are obvious. The public holds an asset (the bank deposit) while the bank holds an off-setting liability (a promise to repay the deposit on demand). Hence, bank-created money does not represent net wealth for the private sector as a whole. The only remaining question is whether fiat money produced by the government represents net wealth.

Many economists would agree that in an efficient market, bonds issued by the government are not net wealth. When the government issues bonds, on the one hand, the public holds an asset (a bond). On the other hand, however, it simultaneously holds a liability in the form of future taxes to pay for the interest on, and retirement of, the bonds. In an efficient market, the discounted value of the tax liabilities should just equal the market value of the bond, producing no change in wealth.[4]

These same economists might argue that governments do not directly retire fiat money, and thus the public does not regard the potential retirement of money as a liability to them. However, incidents of direct monetized debt retirement have been observed, such as the reduction of "greenbacks" in the U.S. in the post-Civil War period. Yet, even if monetized debt is never retired, there is still a future cost to the private sector of the economy. In modern economies, money supplies are not normally increased by directing helicopters to fly over and drop money. Instead, the government issues the money assets to the private sector in exchange for an equivalent dollar value of resources.** Until the monetized debt is retired, these resources are never returned to the private sector. Hence, until the debt is retired, the private sector foregoes the services from the resources that have been relinquished.

*The more traditional portfolio model in which money is still considered net wealth, is described in the appendix of this chapter.

**A more precise description of the process might be that the U.S. Treasury issues bonds in exchange for resources, and the Federal Reserve then monetizes the debt through an open market purchase of bonds. The net effect is the same as if the Treasury directly issued money in exchange for the resources.

So on the one hand, the private sector has a dollar's worth of money assets which provides money services. The present or capitalized value of these services is an asset to the private sector of the economy. On the other hand, the private sector is foregoing a stream of services from a dollar's worth of resources. The present or capitalized value of this stream of services is a negative asset to the private sector. It is just like a liability. Alternatively, the capitalized value of the lost stream can be described as a negative bond. A normal (positive) bond provides a stream of yearly services (interest). This capitalized value of lost services represents a stream of yearly losses. It has exactly the opposite (negative) characteristics of a bond.

In an efficient market, the private sector should be willing to give up only a (capitalized) dollar's worth of services from resources for the last dollar's worth of money assets. In other words, the dollar value of the money assets should equal the dollar value of the negative bonds. The two sides of the private sector's balance sheet are increased by the same amount, and no wealth is created.

What implications does the assumption that money does not represent net wealth have for monetary policy? Suppose the government increases the money supply. Two things now happen. First the supply of money assets increases, just as in any monetary model. Second, the quantity of liabilities or negative bonds increases, reducing net bond holdings. At the prevailing world interest rate, the country has a desired ratio of real money balances to real bond holdings that it wishes to hold. The effect of the increase in real money balances and decrease in real bond holdings means that the ratio of money to bonds is greater than desired. The inhabitants of the country will desire to exchange money for bonds. The result is likely to be a deterioration in the balance of payments and the capital account.

The change in the assumption about money also means that devaluation affects both the money and bond markets. Not only the money asset, but also the corresponding negative bond is now nominally denominated. Devaluation will therefore reduce the real value of each. A given quantity of dollar services foregone now represents less real services foregone. But a reduction in the real value of negative bonds is equivalent to an increase in the real value of (positive) bonds. Devaluation must therefore reduce the existing ratio of money to bonds, both reducing real money balances and increasing real (positive) bond holdings. With the interest rate unchanged, the resultant ratio is now below the desired level. The public therefore exchanges bonds for money on the international financial market in order to bring the portfolio back into equilibrium. There are balance-of-payments and capital account surpluses as this adjustment occurs.

Notice that the above scenario makes no mention of the trade balance. The reason is that there is no longer a mechanism through which the trade balance is to be affected. Since money no longer represents net wealth, devaluation no longer reduces real wealth by reducing real balances.* The real value of money assets does decrease, but there is now a corresponding decrease in the bond liabilities. Aggregate net wealth remains unchanged. Expenditure therefore has no reason to fall, and the trade balance does not improve.

While there is no aggregate change in wealth, there still may be distribution effects. A reduction in the real value of a liability benefits the debtor to the detriment of the creditor. The reduction reduces the real value of what the debtor pays back and what the creditor receives. So, for example, in the case of bank-created money, the real value of the deposit is reduced, but the real value of the bank's liabilities to its customers is also reduced. The bank's wealth rises, and the depositor's wealth falls. In the aggregate, these effects cancel. However, if these two types of individuals were to have different marginal propensities to expend out of their wealth, then the trade balance could be affected. But, such possible distribution effects are ignored in the analysis.

The effect of a devaluation where money is not perceived as net wealth is therefore equivalent to an open market sale of bonds by the central bank. Both reduce the real quantity of money assets and increase the quantity of (positive) bonds, one by price changes, the other by quantity changes. Either an open market sale or devaluation, then, elicits only a portfolio response by the public, improving both the balance of payments and the capital account. No adjustment in the trade balance is needed.

SUMMARY

Each of the models discussed above has implications about the behavior of the trade balance and balance of payments following devaluation. All the models imply that the balance of payments should improve. The simple Keynesian elasticities model predicts a permanent improvement, while the monetary models predict only temporary changes. The models do differ, however, on whether the trade balance should improve. Models which focus on changes in the relative price of tradables or the relative price of tradable to nontradable goods, indicate that the trade balance will likely improve at least temporarily. Monetary models which focus on the real balance effect also predict an improvement in the trade balance. The integrated world model, in contrast, argues that devaluation is likely to affect only the balance of payments and capital accounts, causing little, if any change in the trade balance.

Of course, in even the integrated market model, devaluation can produce phenomena such as distribution effects which transfer wealth from creditors to debtors. If propensities to spend in the two groups differed significantly, then even the integrated market model would predict a

---

*The reduction in real wealth through the reduced value of real balances is often assumed to reduce expenditure relative to income, and thus improve the trade balance. See the portfolio model in the appendix for details.

trade balance adjustment. Obviously, which models or phenomena are most consistent with the behavior of the foreign accounts is an empirical issue. The focus of the remaining sections of this chapter is therefore on the investigations of several researchers who have studied devaluation. These studies are reported in order to show which theoretical models are most consistent with the actual data.*

WHAT TESTS OF THE RAW DATA TELL US

In recent years, several empirical studies have appeared which have tried to estimate the effect of devaluation on the trade balance and the balance of payments. The procedure in most of these studies has been simply to compare the levels of the trade balance or the balance of payments from a few years prior to devaluation until a few years after. Such a procedure ascribes all changes in the levels of the accounts following devaluation to the devaluation itself. However, the levels of the foreign accounts can also be affected by other government policies as well as by nongovernment factors. Thus, in order to measure properly the effects of devaluation alone, the effects of these other factors should be accounted for. A more inclusive test is described in the next section; this section summarizes only the earlier attempts to analyze the effects of devaluation. As will become apparent, regardless of the comprehensiveness of the test, there is considerably more evidence of improvement in the balance of payments following devaluation than in the trade balance.

One widely quoted study by Richard Cooper[5] analyzes the effects of twenty-four devaluations carried out by nineteen countries during the period 1959–1966. Cooper emphasizes the impact effect of devaluation by examining the change in the level of the foreign accounts from the year of devaluation to the following year. In fifteen of the twenty-four cases, the balance of goods and services improves in the year following devaluation as compared to the year of devaluation. In seventeen cases, the balance of payments improves. These results are interpreted as evidence that devaluation improves the accounts.

Two shortcomings in the Cooper study are immediately apparent. First, levels of the foreign accounts for earlier and later years are not reported. Thus, there is no basis for comparing the "improved" level of the account with predevaluation levels. There is no way to tell if the improvement is simply compensating for an initial deterioration that would appear in the year of devaluation. Furthermore, by omitting re-

---

*This summary of studies excludes some well-known articles that attempt to explain the effect of devaluation on the percentage change in exports, imports, market shares, or some other related variables. While these articles purport to explain the effect on the trade balance (a general equilibrium concept), their technique is to examine changes in exports or imports in isolation (a partial equilibrium concept). Given the emphasis in this book on the simultaneous net change in exports and imports, the discussion has been restricted to studies which have also dealt explicitly with this concept.

sults for additional years after devaluation, it is impossible to determine whether the reported improvement is temporary or permanent.

A second problem with Cooper's approach is that policy variables are not taken into account. For example, the monetary approach to the balance of payments predicts that, all other things held constant, devaluation should cause only a temporary surplus in the balance of payments. But typically all other things are not held constant. Specifically, changes in government policies such as increases in the rate of domestic credit creation often accompany devaluations. The monetary approach predicts these policies also have sizable effects on the balance of payments. In order to measure accurately solely the effects of devaluation, the effects of the additional policies should be incorporated into the analysis. Omission of these other effects could well result in mistakenly ascribing all changes in the accounts to devaluation.

Another study by Michael Connolly and Dean Taylor[6] overcomes some of the omissions of the Cooper paper. Using sixteen of the devaluations included in the Cooper sample, they relate improvements in the balance of payments and rates of domestic credit creation. For the sample as a whole they find that the rate of domestic credit expansion is, on average, 14 percent in the year prior to devaluation. In that year, the average foreign reserve loss is 31 percent. In the year following devaluation, the rate of credit expansion is approximately the same as before, but the countries have an average gain of 42 percent in reserves. So, holding the average rate of domestic credit expansion approximately constant, devaluation increases the rate of foreign reserve accumulation. However, within four to eight quarters following devaluation, the average rate of domestic credit expansion rises to 29 percent, and the rate of reserve accumulation falls to 19 percent. So most of the improvement in reserve holdings occurs within the first year following devaluation, with the rate of domestic credit expansion possibly accounting for the fall-off in the second year.

Regressions are run across all sixteen countries relating the percentage change in the net foreign reserves of the central bank in the year after devaluation to the rate of devaluation and the rate of domestic credit expansion in the year following devaluation. Connolly and Taylor find that (1) the higher the rate of devaluation, the greater the improvement in the reserve position, and (2) the higher the rate of domestic credit expansion following devaluation, the smaller the improvement. But while this study uses one method to account for monetary policy, it still concentrates only on the impact effect of devaluation and makes no attempt to account for other exogenous variables. The analysis implicitly assumes that the balance of payments of a country would remain unchanged in the absence of devaluation.

Other studies of devaluation have concentrated less on the impact effects and more on whether a devaluation improves the foreign accounts over a period of several years. Arthur Laffer[7] performs one such test for fifteen postwar devaluations. Laffer examines the time path of the trade balance over seven years, from three years before devaluation until three years after. The trade balance is defined in these tests as the level of f.o.b. exports minus the level of c.i.f. imports, both measured in domestic currency. The purpose of the tests is to determine if trade balances are, on average, more or less negative in the years following devaluation as compared to preceding years.

Examining all fifteen countries in the sample, Laffer finds that the trade balance on average tends to worsen. Ten of the fifteen countries have the largest deficit of the seven-year period in the three years following devaluation. Two more have the largest deficit in the year of devaluation. Eleven out of the fourteen countries with data for the third year following devaluation have a larger deficit in that year than in the year before devaluation. Eight of the fourteen have larger deficits two years after than one year before devaluation. There is little evidence of devaluation causing significant or sustained improvement in the trade balance. However, Laffer still does not account for any domestic policy variables other than devaluation, nor does he present a formal statistical test of the significance of devaluation. In addition, Laffer's data all relate to balances measured in domestic currencies, while much of the theory relates to balances measured in physical units.

The Laffer results, however, do emphasize possibly misleading implications of Cooper's analysis. While Cooper finds that in fifteen of the twenty-four cases the balance of goods and services improves, in ten of the fifteen cases the account is still negative. So Cooper's improvements do not imply surplus, and, as Laffer shows, the improvements may merely represent an offset of the initial deterioration in the year of devaluation. In contrast, Cooper finds that the balance of payments improves in seventeen of the twenty-four cases, and that for fourteen of the seventeen improvements the account is actually a surplus.

A more comprehensive analysis of pre- and postdevaluation balance of payments is contained in a study by Michael Salant.[8] Defining the balance of payments as the change in international reserves minus allocations of SDRs, he compares the average level of the account in the three years following devaluation to the average level in the three years prior to devaluation.

Salant appropriately measures the data in a common numeraire—the dollar. The results are shown in Table 17-2. Salant examines seventy-eight devaluations by less developed countries and twenty-three by de-

Table 17-2   Results of Salant's Analysis

Countries	Trade Balance			Balance of Payments	
	Improve (+)	Worsen (−)	Unchanged (0)	Improve (+)	Worsen (−)
Less Developed (78)	38	39	1	55	23
Developed (23)	8	15	0	20	3
Total (101)	46	54	1	75	26

Source: Michael Salant, "Devaluations Improve the Balance of Payments Even If Not the Trade Balance."

veloped countries. In over 85 percent of the devaluations by developed countries, and over two-thirds of those by less developed countries, the three-year average of the balance of payments improves. Combining the two samples yields 101 observations. In about three-quarters of the cases the balance of payments improves. Therefore, according to these data, devaluation appears to produce on average a net improvement in the balance of payments.

Salant also examines the trade balance in these same 101 cases. As Laffer did, he defines the trade balance as the difference between f.o.b. exports and c.i.f. imports. However, his data are measured in foreign currency (dollars) rather than in domestic currency. In only about one-half of the less developed country cases and about one-third of the developed country cases does the three year average trade balance improve. For the combined sample, the average trade balance improves in less than one-half of the cases. Thus Salant's results are consistent with Laffer's results, but are at odds with Cooper's conclusions.

The implication of these studies is that there is considerably more evidence of the balance of payments improving following devaluation than of the trade balance. Cooper has evidence of a positive impact effect on the trade balance. Laffer's study also provides evidence of an improvement in the year following devaluation. But the improvement usually follows a worsening of the trade balance in the year of devaluation and tends to be more than offset in subsequent years. In contrast, while the evidence of an improvement in the trade balance is weak, the studies by Connolly and Taylor and by Salant both find evidence that the balance of payments improves in the three years following devaluation. Again, however, it should be cautioned that these studies do not account for other exogenous variables.

INCLUDING THE EFFECTS OF OTHER FACTORS

As repeatedly emphasized, devaluation is often only one part of the government policy package instituted at that time. Using the theory developed in earlier chapters, a method of accounting for these other factors is now described. Following the description, results of a test on the effects of devaluation that employs these methods are presented and analyzed.

From Chapters 12 and 14 it is clear that one potential factor affecting both the trade balance and balance of payments is growth. More precisely, from equation (14–22) changes in the ratio of the trade balance to income should be negatively related to changes in the growth rate of the country relative to the growth rate abroad. From equation (12–16) the change in the ratio of the balance of payments to income should be positively related to changes in the same relative growth rate variable. Any measure of the effects of devaluation must therefore first account for these effects of growth.

Similarly, as shown in Chapter 12, changes in the balance of payments should depend on changes in the domestic money supply relative to changes in the money supplies elsewhere. This same type of argument could be made for the trade balance. If there were a real balance effect, an increase in the domestic money supply would increase the level of real balances, increase the level of expenditure, and worsen the trade balance. If all countries have increasing money supplies, not all trade balances can worsen. Rather, the theory would dictate that the trade balances of the countries with the largest relative money increases, and therefore the largest increases in demand, should be deteriorating. This implication is consistent with the basic concept that goods tend to flow from areas of excess supply to areas of excess demand. Hence, another possible factor to take into account is relative changes in the money supply.

A third possible factor is government expenditure policy. Government consumption represents a possible source of direct expenditure in the economy. Thus, if the government increases the level of its consumption by a dollar, as long as individuals do not immediately view government expenditures as merely replacing their private consumption, total expenditure will rise. Given the level of output, a rise in total expenditure causes the trade balance to deteriorate. So this variable affects primarily the trade balance. As with the growth rate and monetary variables, changes in domestic government consumption relative to government consumption elsewhere should be related (negatively) to changes in the trade balance.

Combining these arguments, in the absence of devaluation the trade balance and balance of payments can be expressed as:

$$\Delta\left(\frac{TB}{Y}\right)_i = a_0 - a_1\Delta(g_i - g_w)$$

$$- a_2\Delta\left[\left(\frac{M}{Y}\right)_i - \left(\frac{M}{Y}\right)_w\right]$$

$$- a_3\Delta\left[\left(\frac{G}{Y}\right)_i - \left(\frac{G}{Y}\right)_w\right] \tag{17-20}$$

$$\Delta\left(\frac{BOP}{Y}\right)_i = b_0 + b_1\Delta(g_i - g_w)$$

$$- b_2\Delta\left[\left(\frac{M}{Y}\right)_i - \left(\frac{M}{Y}\right)_w\right] \tag{17-21}$$

where

TB_i = level of the trade balance in country i

BOP_i = level of the balance of payments in country i

Y_i = level of income in country i

g_i, g_w = growth rates of income in country i and rest-of-world

M_i, M_w = money supply of country i and rest-of-world w

G_i, G_w = government consumption of country i and rest-of-world w.

One possible way of measuring the effects of devaluation alone is to use (17-20) and (17-21) to estimate what the changes in the ratio of the trade balance or balance of payments to income would have been in the absence of devaluation, and then to compare these values to the actual changes. If the actual value is more positive or less negative, devaluation has improved the account more than would have been expected from the other variables.

Such a test was performed by Marc Miles[9] for sixteen devaluations of fourteen countries. Using equation (17-20) and (17-21), values of the various coefficients were estimated using seemingly unrelated regressions. The values of the coefficients, along with the actual data for the variables, provide estimates of how the accounts would have changed in the absence of devaluation. These estimates were then subtracted from the actual changes. The resulting residuals indicate the effect of devaluation. A positive residual indicates that the account improved more than could be expected in the absence of devaluation. A negative residual implies just the opposite effect.

The residuals in turn are divided by the standard error of the equation that was used in computing them. A standard error indicates how much change in the account might be expected for purely statistical reasons. The ratio of the residual to the standard error therefore indicates whether the residual is larger than should be expected for purely statistical reasons.

The average value of the ratio for all sixteen devaluations, from three years before devaluation $(t-3)$ until three years after $(t+3)$ is shown in Table 17-3.[10]

Examine first the values for the trade balance. The average values are small, but positive in the two years prior to devaluation. This result suggests that any deterioration of the trade balance in those years appears on average to be caused by government policies and growth. In the year of devaluation, however, there is a very large negative value. The value is larger in absolute size than the value in any of the other six years. In the following three years there is a positive value only in year $t+1$. But this positive value is only about three-fifths the absolute size of the negative value in the year of devaluation. In other words, there is no evidence of

Table 17-3 Average of Residuals as a Fraction of Their Standard Error—Sixteen Devaluations

Time Period	$t-3$	$t-2$	$t-1$	t	$t+1$	$t+2$	$t+3$
Trade Balance	−0.367	0.050	0.080	−0.376	0.222	−0.305	−0.149
Balance of Payments	−0.073	−0.360	−0.500	0.237	0.384	−0.365	−0.036

devaluation causing even a temporary net improvement in the trade balance. Devaluation has a large negative effect in year t and continues to have a net negative effect in the following three years. In fact, the trade balance deteriorates even more following year t+1.

The pattern of the values for the trade balance contrasts with the pattern for the balance of payments. The average balance-of-payments values are negative for the three years prior to devaluation, peaking in year t−1, the year before devaluation. However, in the year of devaluation the average value suddenly becomes positive. In year t+1 the value is again positive and even larger in value. In year t+2 the value again becomes negative, but since none of the improvement in the balance of payments is offset for at least two years, devaluation has clearly improved the balance of payments.

Furthermore, the improvements in the balance of payments in years t and t+1, followed by a deterioration in year t+2, is consistent with the pattern of behavior associated with a *stock* adjustment of the money supply following devaluation. While the negative value in t+2 does not completely offset the combined improvements of t and t+1, a sizable portion is offset. The remaining improvement may represent the continued return of long-term capital that fled in the years prior to devaluation. In any case, the failure of the trade balance to display a similar behavior indicates that it probably does not play a significant role in such an adjustment.

These results have at least two implications. First, they generally support the positions of Laffer and Salant that devaluation does not improve the trade balance, but improves the balance of payments. There is evidence of Cooper's impact effect, but it shows why Cooper's results can be misleading. The average values for the trade balance are positive in the year following devaluation. In isolation this result implies that the trade balance "improves." But the positive values in that year are smaller in magnitude than the negative values of the year of devaluation. In other words, the improvement is not sufficient to offset the initial worsening and there is no short-run net improvement. Since the values in the next two years are also negative on average, there is no long-run improvement either.

The second implication is the essentially monetary nature of the adjustment to devaluation. While many have suggested that devaluation will be accompanied by changes in real variables such as the trade balance, this test fails to find such evidence. In particular, the behavior of the trade balance provides little evidence of a real balance effect affecting trade. This result can be explained either by the assumption that fiat money is not perceived as net wealth, or that there are only small reactions to changes in the value of monetary wealth. In any case, since devaluation does not improve the trade balance, but improves the balance of payments, by definition the capital account must be improving. Devaluation therefore seems to cause only a simple portfolio adjustment. Rather than affecting the size of the portfolio, and thus net wealth, devaluation causes a simple excess demand for money and excess supply of bonds. The ratio of money to bond holdings is then returned to its desired level through a capital account balance of payments surplus.

Hence, any theoretical model which derives its implications from the assumption that the trade balance improves following devaluation appears to have little empirical relevance. The money-goods model showed both the trade balance and balance of payments improving following devaluation. While that model may be a useful pedagogical device for illustrating the adjustment of the balance of payments, its implications for the trade balance can be misleading. Similarly, the Keynesian IS-LM-FF model of Chapter 16 derives some of its policy implications from the assumption that a depreciation of the domestic currency increases aggregate demand through an improvement in the trade balance. Again, this assumption does not appear to be supported by the empirical evidence. Hence, policies formulated on this assumption lead to other than the expected changes in the economy.

One final note, while the behavior of the balance of payments differs markedly from the behavior of the trade balance, the actual magnitudes of the value for the balance of payments in Table 17–3 are less than might have been expected. The average values are all less than one standard error in size. A possible explanation for this observed behavior will be discussed in Chapter 19 on currency substitution.

SUMMARY

In an integrated world, *devaluation* affects only nominal variables such as prices and the nominal money supply, not real variables such as the trade balance. Prices tend to rise in the devaluing country and fall in the revaluing country in inverse proportion to their size. Adjustment occurs only through financial markets, and the balance of payments and capital account of the devaluing country temporarily improve. *The trade balance is unaffected.*

The early Keynesian models of devaluation were barter models which analyzed the effects of changes in the terms of trade, not the exchange rate. In addition, they tended to focus only on the changes in the demand and supply of imports, neglecting corresponding changes in the demand and supply of exports. When all effects are taken into account, not even a deterioration of the terms of trade tends to generate an improvement in the trade balance.

The analysis of devaluation requires an explicit money market, which in turn requires an explicit demand and supply of money. Inclusion of just a money market with the goods market is useful for explaining some basic concepts. However, a realistic model can only be constructed when a bonds market is included. In a complete model, devaluation reduces money supply relative to money demand, and increases bond supply relative to demand. The excess demand for money and excess supply of bonds are relieved through a temporary improvement in the balance of payments and capital account. The trade balance is unaffected.

Initial empirical investigations of the foreign accounts following devaluation revealed significant improvements in the balance of payments, but not in the trade balance. Subsequent investigation, accounting for the effects of government policies and growth, reinforced this conclusion. Monetary policy and devaluation were both found to influence the balance of payments, but not the trade balance. Devaluation seems to cause only a simple *portfolio adjustment*.

REFERENCES

ALEXANDER, SIDNEY, "Effects of a Devaluation on a Trade Balance," *IMF Staff Papers* (April 1952):263–78; reprinted in R. Caves and H. G. Johnson, eds., *Readings in International Economics*, Homewood, Ill.: Irwin, 1968.

COOPER, RICHARD N., "Currency Devaluation in Developing Countries." *Essays in International Finance*, No. 86, Princeton, N.J.: Princeton University Press, 1971.

FRENKEL, JACOB and CARLOS RODRIGUEZ, "Portfolio Equilibrium and the Balance of Payments: A Monetary Approach," *American Economic Review* 65 (September 1975): 674–88.

LAFFER, ARTHUR B., "Exchange Rates, the Terms of Trade, and the Trade Balance," *Effects of Exchange Rate Adjustments*, Washington, D.C.: Treasury Department, OASIA Research, 1976.

METZLER, LLOYD, "The Theory of International Trade," *A Survey of Contemporary Economics*, H. S. Ellis, ed., Philadelphia, 1948.

MILES, MARC A., *Devaluation, The Trade Balance, and The Balance of Payments*, New York: Marcel Dekker, 1978.

—— "The Effects of Devaluation on the Trade Balance and Balance of Payments: Some New Results," *Journal of Political Economy* 87, No. 3 (June 1979): 600–20.

ROBINSON, JOAN, "The Foreign Exchanges," *Essays on the Theory of Employment*, Oxford: Blackwell, 1947, reprinted in *Readings in the Theory of International Trade*, H. S. Ellis and L. Metzler, eds., Philadelphia: Blakiston, 1948.

SALANT, MICHAEL, "Devaluations Improve the Balance of Payments Even If Not the Trade Balance," *Effects of Exchange Rate Adjustments*, Washington, D.C.: Treasury Department, OASIA Research, 1976.

NOTES

1. See R. Mundell, "The Burden of Adjustment," in his *International Economics*, Chapter 13.

2. See for example, Joan Robinson, "The Foreign Exchanges," in *Essays on the Theory of Employment*, Oxford: Blackwell, 1947 (American Economic Association, *Readings in the Theory of International Trade*); or A. P. Lerner, *The Economics of Control*, New York, Macmillan, 1944; or Lloyd Meltzer, "The Theory of International Trade," in American Economics Association, *A Survey of Contemporary Economics*, Philadelphia, Blakiston, 1948.

3. This criticism of the traditional analysis of devaluation is similar to the critique of the elasticities approach by Sidney Alexander in "Effects of a Devaluation on a Trade Balance," *IMF Staff Papers* (April 1952): 263–78, reprinted in R. Caves and H. G. Johnson, eds., *Readings in International Economics*, Homewood, Ill., Irwin, 1968.

4. For a further discussion of whether government bonds are net wealth, see for example, Martin Bailey, *National Income and the Price Level* (New York: McGraw-Hill, 1971; R. J. Barro, "Are Government Bonds Net Wealth," *Journal of Political Economy* Vol. 82, No. 6 (Nov./Dec. 1974): pp. 1095–1117, or Neil Bruce, "The IS-LM Model of Macroeconomic Equilibrium and the Monetarist Controversy," *Journal of Political Economy* Vol. 85, No. 5 (October 1977): pp. 1049–62. The degree of net wealth is found to depend on, among other things, the private sector's ability to anticipate future tax liabilities, the rate at which these liabilities are discounted as compared with the market interest rate, and intergenerational transfers.

5. Richard Cooper, "An Assessment of Currency Devaluation in Developing Countries," in *Government and Economic Development*, edited by G. Ranis, New Haven: Yale University Press, 1971; and "Currency Devaluation in Developing Countries," *Essays in International Finance*, No. 86, Princeton: Princeton University Press, 1971.

6. Michael Connolly and Dean Taylor, "Devaluation in Less Developed Countries," prepared for conference on devaluation sponsored by the Board of Governors, Federal Reserve System, Washington, D.C., December 14–15, 1972.

7. Arthur Laffer, "Exchange Rates, the Terms of Trade, and the Trade Balance," in *Effects of Exchange Rate Adjustments*, Washington, D.C., Treasury Department, OASIA Research, 1976.

8. Michael Salant, "Devaluations Improve the Balance of Payments Even If Not the Trade Balance," in *Effects of Exchange Rate Adjustments*, Washington, D.C., Treasury Department, OASIA Research, 1976.

9. Marc A. Miles, *Devaluation, the Trade Balance and the Balance of Payments*, New York: Marcel Dekker & Co., 1978; and "The Effects of Devaluation on the Trade Balance and Balance of Payments: Some New Results," *Journal of Political Economy* Vol. 87, No. 3 (June, 1979): pp. 600–620.

10. From Miles, "The Effects of Devaluation on the Trade Balance and Balance of Payments," *op. cit.*, p. 609 and 610.

APPENDIX 17
THE PORTFOLIO EQUILIBRIUM MODEL

The concept presented in Chapter 17 of fiat money representing simultaneously both an asset and a liability is by no means universally accepted. In fact, it is currently a much more common assumption to view money as net wealth. The assumption of the net wealth of money is an important underlying assumption of the *portfolio equilibrium* model of the foreign accounts. The portfolio equilibrium model is now described.[1]

The portfolio equilibrium model explicitly includes all three commodity markets. It is assumed that the wealth represented in an individual's portfolio can be held in two forms, the nominal asset money, and another asset whose value is denominated in terms of goods. This second asset can be thought of as a share of equity like common stock. A share of stock represents the ownership of a fraction of the capital stock of a business. The capital, in turn, represents a tangible, return-producing quantity, not merely a given amount of money.

Notice that since money is still the only nominally denominated asset, only the real value of money changes when prices rise following devaluation. The reduction in real balances is therefore still the motivating force behind any adjustment. And since these real balances are assumed to be viewed as net wealth by the public, an improvement in the trade balance as well as the balance of payments can be expected, just as in the model in the text that considered only the money and goods markets.

The portfolio equilibrium model is summarized in Figure 17A–1. The two axes measure real quantities of the two assets, money (m) and bonds (b). Given the quantity of wealth indicated by the line W_0W_0, the individual has the choice of holding any combination of real balances and bonds that lies along the line. In fact, the precise combination he chooses depends on his tastes and preferences for risk and return, as well as the prevailing rate of interest. This choice process is summarized in the l(r) line. The line shows, given the rate of interest r, into what proportions any given wealth portfolio is divided. In the example shown in Figure 17A–1, given the interest rate r, the individual divides his portfolio into m_0 real balances and b_0 bonds. Were the interest rate to be higher, the l(r) line would rotate clockwise downward, reflecting fewer real balances and more bonds held.

Notice that such a rise in the interest rate produces only a temporary change in the capital account, not the apparent permanent change suggested by the Keynesian IS-LM-FF model in Chapter 16. As the l(r) line rotates downward in response to the higher interest rate, individuals substitute down along the existing wealth line W_0W_0 towards their new desired portfolio combination at the new intersection. The movement along the W_0W_0 line represents exchanging money for bonds, and hence a

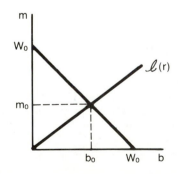

Figure 17A–1   The Portfolio Equilibrium Model

change in the capital account balance. However, once individuals obtain their new desired quantities of bonds, the capital account will again return to the initial equilibrium. Thus once the demand for capital is analyzed within a portfolio framework, changes in the interest rate are shown to cause only temporary capital account adjustments. The assumption that changing interest rates produce permanent capital flow adjustments is now widely recognized to be a specification which limits the Keynesian IS-LM-FF model to, at most, short-run analysis. Policy implications derived from this assumption are therefore often misleading, and if actually put into practice could lead to aggregate economic effects very different from those desired.

For the purposes of analyzing the effects of devaluation, however, the portfolio of the entire country, not just one individual, must be considered. For that reason we must now consider Figure 17A–1 to represent either the portfolio of an entire small country, or the portfolio of a "typical" individual. With that assumption, the effects of devaluation can be determined.

From the previous discussions of devaluation, we know that the impact effect for a small country is to raise the price of all traded goods by the percentage of devaluation. The price rise in turn reduces the real purchasing power or value of the existing stock of cash balances. In terms of Figure 17A–1 this reduction is equivalent to a fall in the value of the m held. This reduction is shown in Figure 17A–2. Devaluation reduces the value of m from m_0 to m_1. The value of bonds which are not nominally denominated remains unchanged. The asset holdings of the country therefore move from point A to point B. Since the small country is a price taker, the desired ratio of money to bonds has not changed. Yet the actual ratio has fallen due to devaluation.

In these portfolio models there is assumed to be two types of adjustment. The first adjustment is the exchanging of money and bonds in order to bring the portfolio back into equilibrium. This adjustment is assumed to occur instantaneously. In Figure 17A–2 this adjustment is indicated by the movement from point B to point C along the new wealth

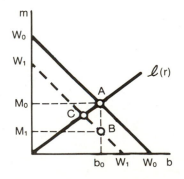

Figure 17A–2   The Effects of Devaluation in The Portfolio Equilibrium Model

line W_1W_1. The new wealth line is closer to the origin than W_0W_0 because devaluation has reduced the real value of one component of wealth, real balances. The movement from B to C represents the exchange of bonds for money in order that the portfolio can return to the desired ratio of the two assets along l(r). The second adjustment is one which occurs over time. This is the adjustment of the total stock of wealth or the size of the portfolio back to its original level. In order to understand this adjustment, it is necessary to understand one more concept, the current account.

Until now the net flow of goods and services has been described by the trade balance. But in this portfolio model the net flow is slightly different. The difference occurs because of the net income from the ownership of foreign bonds. If the domestic country is a net owner of b worth of foreign bonds, then every year it receives an income of rb from these bonds. If, however, the country is a net borrower on the international capital market, then it makes an annual payment of rb. This argument can be summarized by stating that the country's income exceeds its production by the amount rb, where b is the net ownership of bonds. Before the trade balance was defined both as domestic income minus expenditure and the net change in wealth. Now income equals domestic income plus the net income from the ownership of bonds, and the change in net wealth is the difference between this new income concept and expenditure. This difference is called the current account* balance, and its relationship to the trade balance is

$$CA = TB + rb. \qquad (17A-1)$$

If the country is initially in stock equilibrium before devaluation, the current account balance is zero. In other words there is no net addition to or subtraction from the country's stock of wealth. But devaluation causes two effects. First, the portfolio adjustment from point B to point C in Figure 17A–2 means that the country reduces its supply of bonds, worsening the current account. Second, since money is viewed as net wealth and the level of expenditure is positively related to the level of wealth, the reduction in real balances causes the level of expenditure to fall, improving the trade balance and the current account. It can be shown that the second effect is larger than the first so that the net effect is to improve the current account.[2]

The improvement in the current account means that the wealth of the country is increasing. Over time the country is reducing its level of expenditure on goods and increasing its holdings of money and bonds. In terms of Figure 17A–2, starting at point C the wealth line W_1W_1 shifts away from the origin as the level of wealth increases. At every moment the country's portfolio is assumed to remain in equilibrium, so the country is always on the l(r) line. This fact in turn means that any addition to

*In actual practice the current account also includes net foreign remittances and transfers. However, these additional items are assumed to be zero in this simplified example. The current account in this example is therefore equivalent to the balance of goods and services.

the country's wealth must be divided between a balance-of-payments surplus and a capital account deficit in the proportion l(r).

As long as the country continues to run a current account surplus, the wealth of the country increases. At what point will the current account return to equilibrium? The answer is when the level of wealth returns to its predevaluation level. As the level of wealth increases, expenditure also increases, reducing the excess demand. The necessity of a current account surplus declines. For the current account to return to equilibrium, three conditions must be met. Expenditure must have risen sufficiently to eliminate the current account surplus, the supply of money must have risen sufficiently to eliminate the excess demand, and the ratio of money to bonds held must still be l(r). The only level of wealth which can satisfy all these conditions is the initial level of W_0W_0.

So in the portfolio equilibrium model, devaluation is neutral in the long run. Devaluation does not change the final equilibrium level of any asset or of wealth. The final equilibrium levels of the current account, balance of payments, and capital account therefore return to their predevaluation levels. However, in the short run there are changes in all these variables. The reduction in the level of real balances caused by devaluation creates both an excess demand for money that improves the balance of payments and a reduction in expenditure that improves the trade balance and the current account. But as the levels of wealth and money balances return to their initial levels, these effects disappear, and all variables return to their predevaluation levels.

The implications of the portfolio equilibrium model are therefore not very different from those of the model with just money and goods. In both models the trade balance and balance of payments improve temporarily. The source of the improvement in the trade balance in both models is the real balance effect. The improvement in the trade balance contrasts quite sharply with the behavior of the trade balance following devaluation when money is not viewed as net wealth. The contrast emphasizes that in order for devaluation to have real effects, something in the model must not be adjusting properly, in this case individuals' assessments of their future tax liabilities.

APPENDIX NOTES

1. The particular portfolio equilibrium model used in this appendix is adapted from J. Frenkel and C. Rodriguez, "Portfolio Equilibrium and the Balance of Payments: A Monetary Approach," *American Economic Review* 50, (September, 1975): 674–88.

2. For a proof of why the stability conditions require this to be true, see Frenkel and Rodriguez, *op. cit.*, pp. 680–81.

CHAPTER 18

The Reserve Currency Country Model

The discussion in the preceding chapters on how the balance of payments of countries adjust implicitly assumes that all currencies are alike. The world money supply, therefore, is assumed to be a function of the money creation in each country. If any country increases its domestic money supply it has an impact on the entire world, increasing the total world money supply and price level, and causing the increase to be dissipated throughout the world.

But the discussion of the Bretton Woods Agreements showed that not all countries were alike. Specifically, under this system there were two classes of countries—the country which printed the *reserve currency* and all other countries. In the case of the Bretton Woods System, the U.S. dollar was the reserve currency. Under the original agreements the U.S. government was to fix the value of the dollar to gold at the rate of $35 per ounce of gold. Other countries in turn were to fix the dollar value of their currencies. In order to assure the maintenance of the dollar value of their currencies, these other countries held dollar reserves.* So only n−1 of the countries of the world were required to actually fix the value of their currencies. The nth country was not. The reduced responsibility for fixing the value of the currency must have given the reserve currency country some additional degree of latitude over other countries in conducting its monetary policy. The precise degree of latitude is now discussed.

A SIMPLE RESERVE CURRENCY MODEL

Consider a two-country world. Country R is the *reserve currency country* and Country N is the *nonreserve currency country*. Country N is required to fix the value of its currency n in terms of currency r. This

---

*These countries also held some gold as reserves. In the simplified model of this chapter, however, only reserves in the form of obligations of the reserve country are considered.

means that N's central bank intervenes to fix the value of currency in the money market. But with only two currencies, and Country N fixing the value between them, Country R's central bank is not required to perform any intervention.

The discussion can proceed more easily with the aid of a diagram. In Figure 18–1 both countries are divided into two sectors, the public and the central bank. The public in each country is assumed to hold domestic currency and bonds. The bonds in this model are assumed to be fixed in real value and simultaneously denominated in both currencies. Thus individuals in both countries are assumed to hold the same bonds. The public in Country R therefore holds domestic currency r and bonds b, while the public of N holds n and b.

The central bank of each country does not hold domestic currency balances. Instead, it has a printing press and a furnace. If more domestic currency must be supplied to the public, the printing press is used. If the money supply is reduced, the collected currency is burned in the furnace. The central bank of N, however, must hold foreign reserves. Since the central bank of N is the one fixing the value of n in terms of r, if individuals in either country want to exchange units of n in return for units of r, N's central bank must have sufficient r to accommodate the transaction. Conversely, if individuals want to give up r for more n, N's central bank must be willing to print more n and accumulate more r.

Notice that the role of N's central bank as the maintainer of the fixed exchange rate means that it has contact with the public of both N and R. If individuals in either country want to exchange currencies, N's central bank must facilitate the transaction. This is not true for the central bank of R. While R's central bank attempts to increase or decrease the money

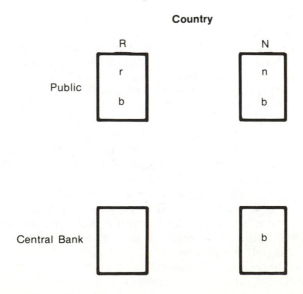

Figure 18–1   The Reserve Currency Model

supply in R (thus having contact with the public of R), since it does not attempt to maintain the exchange rate, it has no contact with the public of N. For this reason, also, R's central bank does not hold any foreign reserves.

The central bank of N has two choices of the form in which it holds its necessary foreign reserves. One possibility, of course, is to just hold units of currency r which pay no explicit interest. A second possibility, however, is to hold interest bearing bonds b. If the bonds are held, then instead of holding idle money balances, the international reserves bring in additional revenue. Furthermore, if units of r are needed, the bonds can be simply sold on the bond market in Country R, and the proceeds can be used to support the exchange rate. Conversely, if units of r are received from the support operation, these can be sold on R's bond market in exchange for b bonds. The incentives for holding b instead of r are therefore strong, and it is assumed that N's central bank acts in this rational manner.

AN OPEN MARKET OPERATION BY THE NONRESERVE COUNTRY

The implications of this model for the policies of each country are now examined. First, the effect on the nonreserve country's ability to carry out an open market operation is shown. Suppose that the central bank of Country N decides to try to increase the domestic money supply through an open market purchase of bonds. The central bank purchases bonds b from the public and gives currency n in exchange. This transaction is shown in Figure 18–2 as transaction (a).

At the prevailing world rate of interest i, the public of N had been happy to hold the initial relative quantities of money and bonds. In order to convince the public to hold more money and fewer bonds, the actions of the central bank must cause an incipient rise in bond prices and an incipient fall in the interest rate. The change in prices is only incipient because markets are assumed to be well arbitraged. Thus, any tendency for bond prices to rise and interest rates to fall in N makes individuals in R want to supply more bonds to N, causing the interest rate to rise again. So the adjustment to the open market purchase in N is most easily analyzed if it is thought to produce an excess demand for bonds and excess supply of money in Country N, and an excess supply of bonds and excess demand for money in Country R.

In order to satisfy these excess demands, bonds b must travel from R to N in exchange for currency r. But the public of N is assumed not to hold balances of r. The units of r therefore must first be obtained from N's central bank. But the central bank is also not holding balances of currency r. It is only holding reserves in the form of bonds. So the next step in this scenario is for N's central bank to sell some of its bonds to R's public in exchange for r. This is shown as transaction (b) in Figure 18–2.

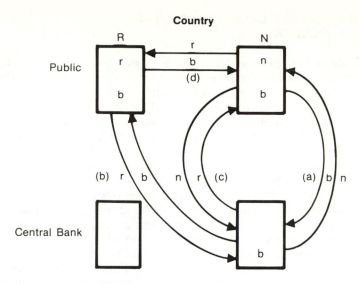

Figure 18–2   An Open Market Operation by the Nonreserve Country

The proceeds of this sale are now given to the public of N in exchange for n. This transaction represents the support operation by the central bank. The central bank is exchanging, as promised, r for n at the fixed price in order that the public of N can make an international purchase. This support operation is shown as transaction (c) in Figure 18–2.

The public of N now has the units of r it needs in order to purchase the bonds it desires. In (d) bonds flow from R to N, and units of r flow in the reverse direction. The effects of the open market purchase are now completed. But what has been the net effects? These can be derived directly from Figure 18–2. First examine what has happened to the original bonds purchased from N's public. In (a) these bonds went to N's central bank. In (b) they went to A's public. In (d) they were then returned to N's public. So the bonds have returned to where they started from. Similarly, the r currency that was purchased by the central bank in (b) was sold to N's public in (c) and returned to R's public in (d). Perhaps most importantly, the units of n that were issued during the open market purchase in (a) were returned directly to the central bank in the support operation (c).

The conclusion is that the open market purchase by the central bank of the nonreserve currency country has been completely offset. After all the effects have been worked through, all sectors hold exactly the same assets as before the open market purchase. The world money supply is unaffected. By fixing the value of its currency, Country N's central bank has become powerless to perform an effective open market operation. As long as the central bank attempts to perform its monetary policy in this way, its monetary policy is impotent.

AN OPEN MARKET OPERATION BY THE RESERVE COUNTRY

The result of the efforts of the reserve currency country to perform an open market purchase is now contrasted with the result of the non-reserve country attempting the same policy. This case is shown in Figure 18–3. In transaction (a) the central bank of R attempts to increase the country's money supply by purchasing bonds in exchange for units of r. The public of R now has more money and fewer bonds than initially. Just as in the previous case where the nonreserve country's central bank performed the open market purchase, there is an incipient rise in bond prices and an incipient fall in interest rates. With a slight fall in i, there is still an excess supply of money and excess demand for bonds by the public of R, and now an excess demand for money and excess supply of bonds by N's public. In fact, the interest rate initially adjusts until the excess demands in the two countries just cancel.

The important question, however, is what the final level of the interest rate will be. Where the nonreserve country performed the open market operation, the adjustment process offset the change in the world quantity of money and bonds, and the interest rate returned to its initial level. So the implications of the reactions by the public to the government's policy must again be analyzed.

With an excess demand for bonds in R and an excess supply in N, the public of R attempts to purchase bonds from the public of N in exchange for money. But in order to complete this transaction, R's public needs units of currency n. These units of n are obtained by requiring N's central bank to perform a support operation. This operation is shown in (b)

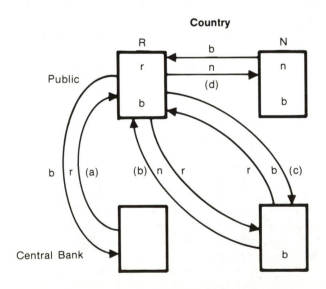

Figure 18–3   An Open Market Operation by the Reserve Country

where units of r are exchanged for newly printed units of n. Since the central bank of N wants to hold bonds, not units of r, as reserves, as shown in (c) the units of r are then sold to R's public in exchange for bonds. Country R's public then takes the units of n it has obtained and gives it to N's public in exchange for b bonds.

As in the previous case, examine what has ultimately happened to the quantities of the various assets. Examine first the quantity of r in circulation. When the central bank of R performed the open market purchase, the quantity of r was increased. The quantity was temporarily decreased in (b) when N's central bank performed the support operation. But the units of r were quickly returned to the public of R in (c) when N's central bank purchased bonds. Thus the quantity of r is unchanged after the net support operation.

Next examine the quantity of n in circulation. When the central bank of N performed the support operation, it printed more units of n to give R's public in exchange for r. These units of n then found their way in (d) to N's public in exchange for bonds. Thus the quantity of n is also increased.

Finally, the quantity of bonds in the possession of the two publics is examined. The movement of bonds from N to R in (d) leaves that quantity unchanged. However, the purchase in (c) of bonds from R's public by the central bank of N reduces the quantity of bonds in the hands of the public. This reduction is in addition to the initial reduction caused by the open market purchase of R's central bank. The quantity of bonds is clearly decreased.

The results of an open market purchase by the reserve currency country's central bank is therefore quite different than the results of a similar operation by any other country. The reserve currency country is clearly able to increase the quantity of its money in circulation relative to the quantity of bonds. Not only that, but the reactions of the public to this increase forces the nonreserve country's central bank to reinforce this operation. The net support operations illustrated in (b) and (c) are equivalent to N's central bank performing an open market purchase. The central bank prints more n, which makes its way to N's public in (d), and reduces the supply of bonds. Thus, not only does the reserve country's open market operation increase the ratio of domestic money to bonds in R, but it increases the ratio in N as well. The central bank of R has forced the hand of the central bank of N.[1]

Notice also that since the ratio of money to bonds has been raised in both countries, the world interest rate should be affected as well. Given the demand functions for money and bonds, a higher ratio of money to bonds requires a lower equilibrium interest rate. Only with a lower opportunity cost of holding money are individuals willing to hold relatively more cash balances. Thus, not only does the central bank of the reserve country control the world money supply, it also controls the world interest rate.

Why should this case differ from the open market operation of the nonreserve country? The answer lies in the nonreserve country's commitment to maintain the relative values of the currencies. This commitment means that the central bank of N must respond to the demands for money by either public, which means that the monetary policy cannot be independent of the exchange rate policy. But the reserve country is not under such a restraint. Since it is not committed to fixing the value of its currency, it has no involuntary contact with the public. The only contact is when it decides to perform an open market operation. Thus any attempts of the public to rid itself of excess units of r are frustrated. Similarly, any attempts by the public to recover the bonds lost to the central bank of R also fail.

Of course, as the Bretton Woods System was arranged, the reserve currency country was not to have this much freedom. While other countries were to fix the relative values of currencies, the reserve country was to fix the value of r in terms of some commodity. The implications of this added constraint are now analyzed.

AN OPEN MARKET OPERATION BY A RESERVE CURRENCY COUNTRY FIXING THE VALUE OF ITS CURRENCY TO A COMMODITY

Assume now that the nonreserve currency countries continue to behave as in the previous two sections. The behavior of the reserve currency country, however, is altered to conform to an additional constraint. The value of the reserve currency must now be maintained constant in terms of a given commodity G (possibly gold).

In order to analyze this case, it is necessary to expand the portfolios of individuals in the public to three assets. Not only money and bonds, but also gold are assumed held by the public. The asset gold in this example has a characteristic that is very similar to the asset money. Both are assumed to pay no explicit interest. In the absence of inflation, the opportunity cost of holding each is therefore i, the interest rate on bonds. With inflation, the opportunity cost of money remains at i, while the opportunity cost of gold is only the real interest rate, since the money price of gold should appreciate at the rate of inflation. So individuals must now decide not only their desired ratio of money to bonds, but also their desired ratio of money to gold.

Suppose the reserve currency country decides to perform an open market purchase of bonds. Again the quantity of r held by R's public increases and the quantity of bonds decreases. This operation, therefore, has the effect of increasing both the ratio of money to bonds and money to gold above their initial equilibrium level. The country can therefore be characterized as having an excess supply of money and excess demands for both gold and bonds. Part of the excess supply of money can be relieved by forcing the central bank of R to undertake a price support operation and exchange gold for units of r. This support operation also has the effect of helping to alleviate the excess demand for gold. The remainder of the excess supply of money can be exchanged for bonds from the public of N. The public of N can then exchange part of the units of r it received for the bonds at R's central bank for gold, and part at N's central bank for units of n.

The final equilibrium is therefore characterized by higher ratios of money to bonds and gold to bonds than initially. While the commitment of R's central bank to fixing the value of r in terms of gold does allow the public to offset some of the initial increase in r, it does not provide a mechanism to immediately recover the bonds lost in the open market operation. While its influence is reduced, as long as the central bank of R is not forced to give up these bonds, it is still able to influence the supply of bonds relative to other assets, and thus the world interest rate.

Does this mean that fixing the reserve currency in terms of gold has no impact? The answer is no. The example analyzed here is of a *marginal* increase in r. While one such marginal operation may be successful, obviously many such operations cannot be. After the open market purchase above, the central bank of R was forced to give up gold. Every time the central bank performs such an open market operation it is forced to give up gold. Since the gold holdings of the central bank are finite, obviously it cannot continue to perform open market bond purchases forever. Of course, the central bank could purchase more gold reserves from the public, say in exchange for bonds. But if the central bank exchanges bonds for gold, it is giving back the asset whose supply it was controlling in order to influence the world interest rate. In other words, the open market operation is successful only to the extent that the reserve currency country has gold reserves. Once these reserves are depleted, the monetary policy becomes powerless, just as in the nonreserve currency country case.

Notice, too, that if the open market actions of the reserve country central bank cause inflation, the point at which open market purchases become useless is arrived at more quickly. While gold pays no explicit interest, since it is an asset fixed in real terms, during periods of inflation its nominal value is expected to appreciate at the rate of inflation. As inflation occurs, individuals want to hold fewer nominally denominated assets such as currency and more real commodities such as gold. Individuals, therefore, desire to reduce their ratios of money to gold by exchanging r for gold at R's central bank, and thus depleting the reserves of gold more quickly. Unless the central bank of R reverses its policy and halts inflation, it loses its ability to determine the market price of gold, and the nominal value of gold appreciates at the rate of inflation relative to r.

A ONCE-FOR-ALL INCREASE IN THE MONEY SUPPLY BY THE NONRESERVE COUNTRY

The above analysis should not be construed as implying that the nonreserve currency countries were completely powerless in affecting their money supplies. One particular monetary policy was still open to them.

Assume, as in Chapters 9 and 12, that the central bank of N decides to increase the supply of n once-for-all by flying a helicopter over the country and dropping out units of n. This monetary policy differs from the open market purchase because the supply of bonds remains unchanged. But the increase in n still has the effect of increasing the public's ratio of n to bonds. At the prevailing world interest rate, there is an excess demand for bonds and an excess supply of money in Country N. The remaining question is whether the attempts by the public to alleviate these excess demands offset the central bank's monetary policy actions.

The effects of the policy are shown in Figure 18–4. In (a) the central bank has increased the quantity of n in the hands of the public. Given the excess demand for bonds and excess supply of money that now exists, the public wants to purchase bonds from Country R's public. To do that, however, units of r must be obtained from the central bank. Thus in (b) the central bank obtains r in exchange for bonds, and in (c) the public exchanges n for the r. Then in (d) the r is exchanged for bonds.

The net effects are similar to the open market case. There is a net increase in the quantity of bonds in circulation and a net decrease in the quantity of n. The difference, however, is that since only n increased initially, to return to the initial equilibrium only n should decrease, that is, b should not increase. Thus the new final equilibrium must differ from the initial one. Specifically, the new equilibrium consists of a higher quantity of both n and b in circulation than initially. One possibility is that the ratio of money to bonds returns to the level consistent with the initial world interest rate, with just a larger numerator and denominator. Only a fraction of the newly printed n is returned to the central bank, and from Figure 18–4 it is clear that the increase in bonds is equal to this

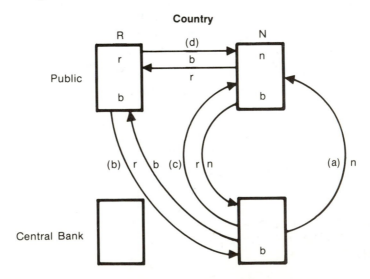

Figure 18–4   A Once-for-All Increase in the Money Supply by the Nonreserve Country

amount. If the initial ratio of money to bonds is defined as $V = n_0/b_0$, then for an increase Δn, this increase is reduced by the public until $\Delta n' = V\Delta b'$, where $\Delta n' + \Delta b' = \Delta n$. The ratio of money to bonds is then consistent with the prevailing world interest rate.

However, the world levels of money balances and bonds are now greater than before. This increase in wealth increases goods demand and thus causes prices to rise. Since, by assumption, bonds are fixed in real value, as prices rise real balances are reduced relative to real bonds, thus affecting the interest rate. So by increasing only the supply of money, the nonreserve country is able to influence the world interest rate.

But as with the reserve country fixing r to gold, the power of the non-reserve country to influence the world interest rate is not unlimited. The influence is limited by the country's supply of reserves. Every time the helicopter drops money, the public of N demands units of r, which in turn depletes the central bank's reserves. Obviously, when the reserves begin to run out, the flights of the helicopter must stop. So even if a country can influence world monetary variables, as long as it is required to fix the value of its currency, this power is constrained.

DEVALUATION BY A NONRESERVE CURRENCY COUNTRY

There is one situation in which it is possible for a nonreserve country to successfully perform an open market purchase. This situation arises when the open market purchase is accompanied by a devaluation of the domestic currency.

Notice that a devaluation of one currency vis-à-vis the other can be performed only by the nonreserve country. Since it is fixing the value of its currency in terms of the reserve currency, by simply changing the relative value that it is supporting, the value can be changed. The reserve country does not have this option. The reserve country can devalue its currency relative to the commodity, but any devaluation relative to other currencies requires the cooperation of other central banks. So devaluation is a policy only at the disposal of the nonreserve countries.*

The effects of devaluation in this model are shown in Figure 18–5. The devaluation reduces the value of real balances in N, causing the ratio of real balances to bonds to decline, and therefore an excess supply of bonds and an excess demand for money. In (a) the public in N sells bonds to R's public in exchange for currency r. The units of r are then exchanged at the central bank for units of newly printed n, as shown in (b). Finally, in (c) the central bank of N sells the units of r it has received

*An example of this fact is the events of August 15, 1971. The U.S. government desired to have the dollar devalued relative to other currencies, but could not devalue unilaterally. The U.S. therefore sought to convince other countries to appreciate by imposing a 10 percent surcharge on all imports, which was removed only after the largest industrial nations agreed to increase the value of their currencies in terms of the dollar.

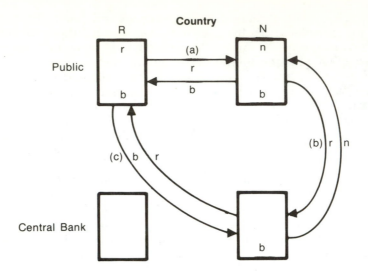

Figure 18–5   Devaluation by a Nonreserve Country

for bonds on R's bond market. Thus there has been no change in the quantity of r held by R's public. But the quantity of n and bonds held by N's public has changed. Bonds that initially were held by N's public are now held by N's central bank. In exchange N's public now holds more units of n. In other words, the equivalent of a central bank open market purchase has occurred. The exchange occurs because the public desires to return to the initial ratio of real balances to bonds.

Where fiat money is not wealth, this open market adjustment is sufficient to achieve a new long run equilibrium. As shown in Chapter 17, when money is not wealth, devaluation produces the equivalent of an open market sale of bonds, increasing the quantity of bonds and reducing the quantity of money. Obviously what is needed to completely offset the excess demands that result from the equivalent of an open market sale is the equivalent of an open market purchase. Thus the adjustment described in Figure 18–5 should completely offset the effect of devaluation.

SOME EMPIRICAL EVIDENCE OF THE RESERVE CURRENCY COUNTRY MODEL

The reserve currency country model corresponds closely to the Bretton Woods System which existed from the late 1940s to the early 1970s. An interesting question is to what extent the monetary variables during this period behaved as the reserve currency model suggests. Such behavior could be observed in at least two ways. First, if the Bretton Woods System operated as described, then the total quantity of money in the world would have been dictated by the reserve currency country's monetary policy. Since the United States was the reserve currency country under the Bretton Woods System, for the empirical evidence to be consistent with the model, the United States' monetary policy would have to dominate the world money supply. Second, different empirical relationships between money and prices would be observed in the United States versus other countries. It is possible for the increase in United States money to increase the world money supply, the world price level, and therefore prices and nominal income in the United States. However, actions to increase the money supply in other countries are successful only to the extent they are in reaction to increases in world money and prices by the United States.

Such asymmetric effects of the monetary policies in the United States and the rest of the world has been observed by researchers. Genberg and Swoboda[2] find that monetary policies in the United States had much larger effects on the world money supply than did the monetary policies of thirteen other countries. They find that whether they define monetary policy as the percentage change in the total monetary base (B) or the proportion of the monetary base due to the domestic monetary authorities (A), the monetary policies of the United States have significantly more effect on the world money supply. For example, the sum of the coefficients reflecting the concurrent and lagged effects of domestic credit expansion (Variable A) in the United States is four times larger than the similar sum for the thirteen other countries. Even more important, the sum of these coefficients for the United States is very close to one for both M1 world money supply (1.33) and the M2 world money supply (0.85). When the United States monetary authorities increased the quantity of domestic credit A by 1 percent, the world money supply increased by about 1 percent. In other words, percentage changes in the world money supply coincide with United States monetary policy.

Putnam and Wilford[3] point out the asymmetry in the relationship between money and prices in the United States and the United Kingdom. Citing conflicting results by Sims and Williams, Goodhart and Gowland,[4] they use the reserve currency model to reconcile the differences. Sims has pioneered a statistical technique to show the direction of causality between variables. Applying this methodology to money and nominal income in the United States he concludes: "The main empirical finding is that the hypothesis that causality is unidirectional from income to money is rejected."[5] In the United States, money appears to "cause" nominal income. However, applying this same statistical technique to the United Kingdom, Williams, Goodhart and Gowland conclude: "We found for the United Kingdom some evidence of unidirectional causality running from nominal incomes to money but also some evidence of unidirectional causality running from money to prices. Taken together, this evidence suggests, perhaps, a more complicated causal relationship between money and incomes in which both are determined simultaneously."[6] Putnam and Wilford argue that the simultaneity of changes in money and prices is what one would expect in a nonreserve currency country. A rise in the reserve currency country's money supply simultaneously raises the nonreserve country's nominal income and nominal demand for money balances, causing the balance of payments inflow into the reserve country that forces that country's monetary authority to increase the money supply.

SOME ADDITIONAL IMPLICATIONS OF THE RESERVE CURRENCY MODEL

The model outlined above has two additional, important implications. First, the fact that the nonreserve country holds its reserves in the form of interest-bearing bonds rather than currency balances implies that there is an additional source of revenue that must be taken into account. With additional revenue, the government does not have to tax as much in order to finance a given level of expenditures. Reduced taxation each year means the present value of the public's tax liabilities is reduced, which in turn means the wealth of the public is increased and the "wedges" in the economy are reduced. So the existence of bonds provides an additional source of wealth and substitution effects for the country that must be kept track of.

Second, the existence of these bonds changes the interpretation of surpluses on the various accounts. For example, in previous chapters a capital account-balance of payments surplus was assumed to represent for the country a net inflow of reserves and a net outflow of bonds. However, for the nonreserve country such a surplus now represents only an increase in the supply of domestic currency. Suppose, for example, that France has such a surplus with the U.S. that French citizens have exchanged some of their bond holdings for dollars. But in this model it is assumed that the French want to hold francs, not dollars. They therefore exchange the dollars for francs at the Bank of France. The Bank of France then converts these dollars into dollar-denominated, interest-bearing assets. In this process there have been equivalent inflows and outflows of dollars, leaving the quantity of dollars in France unchanged. There have also been equivalent inflows and outflows of bonds, leaving the total quantity of bonds held (by the combined public and the central bank) unchanged. The only asset whose quantity has changed is francs. Thus the only net effect of the capital account-balance of payments surplus is an increase in the supply of francs.

Similar implications also hold for a trade balance surplus. There are at least two possibilities. One possibility is for the trade balance surplus to be accompanied by an equivalent capital account deficit, with a zero balance-of-payments surplus. In this case goods are exchanged directly for foreign bonds. These foreign bonds represent a net addition to the country's assets and the level of wealth rises by this amount. A second possibility is for the trade balance surplus to be accompanied by an equivalent balance-of-payments surplus. In this case goods are exchanged for foreign currency. The foreign currency is then exchanged at the central bank for newly printed domestic currency. The central bank then exchanges the foreign currency for bonds. So in this case there is not only an increase in the quantity of foreign bonds held, but also an equal increase in the quantity of domestic money held.

These two cases illustrate another paradox of assuming domestic currency to represent net wealth. In both cases the quantity of bonds rises by the amount of the trade surplus. But in the second case domestic currency also rises by that amount. Thus if money is net wealth, in the second case wealth rises twice as much as in the first case. But why should the change in wealth depend upon the way in which a trade surplus is financed? As discussed previously, a trade surplus represents a given amount of aggregate saving, and that quantity of saving should be the same regardless of how the surplus is financed. The case of a trade surplus of a nonreserve currency country is, therefore, another example of why the assumption that domestic currency is net wealth is not very theoretically satisfying.

SUMMARY

A world monetary system where $n-1$ countries fix the value of their currencies in terms of a reserve currency gives the *reserve currency country* an additional degree of latitude in conducting its monetary policy. The *nonreserve currency country* is incapable of sustaining the effects of a domestic open market operation without first devaluing. An open market purchase of bonds by the reserve currency country, on the other hand, increases the money supply not only in that country, but in the rest of the world as well. Fixing the reserve currency in terms of a commodity such as gold, however, does reduce the freedom of that country's monetary authority. The asymmetric effects of reserve and nonreserve currency countries on money supplies has been observed in empirical studies of the Bretton Woods System.

REFERENCES

GENBERG, HANS and ALEXANDER SWOBODA, "Worldwide Inflation under the Dollar Standard," GIIS-Ford discussion paper No. 12, Graduate Institute of International Studies, Geneva, Switzerland, January 1977.

KEMP, DONALD S., "A Monetary View of the Balance of Payments," St. Louis Federal Reserve Bank *Review.* (April 1975): 14–22; reprinted in *The Monetary Approach to International Adjustment*, B. Putnam and D. S. Wilford, eds., New York: Praeger, 1978.

PUTNAM, BLUFORD and D. SYKES WILFORD, "Money, Income, and Causality in the United States and the United Kingdom," *American Economic Review* 68, No. 3 (June 1978): 423–27; reprinted in *A Monetary Approach to International Adjustment*, B. Putnam and D. S. Wilford, eds., New York: Praeger, 1978.

SWOBODA, ALEXANDER, "Gold, Dollars, Euro-Dollars, and the World Money Stock under Fixed Exchange Rates," *American Economic Review* 68, No. 4 (September 1978): 625–42.

NOTES

1. For an illustration in terms of central bank balance sheets of how the reserve currency country forces an increase in the monetary base of all other countries, see Donald S. Kemp, "A Monetary View of the Balance of Payments," in B. Putnam and D. S. Wilford, *The Monetary Approach to International Adjustment*, op. cit.

2. Hans Genberg and Alexander K. Swoboda, "Worldwide Inflation Under the Dollar Standard," GIIS-Ford discussion paper No. 12, Graduate Institute of International Studies, Geneva, Switzerland, January 1977.

3. Bluford H. Putnam and D. Sykes Wilford, "Money, Income and Causality in the United States and the United Kingdom: A Theoretical Explanation of Different Findings," *American Economic Review* Vol. 68, No. 3 (June 1978): pp. 423–27.

4. Christopher A. Sims, "Money Income and Causality," *American Economic Review* Vol. 62 (September 1972): pp. 540–52; David Williams, C.A.E. Goodhart, and D. H. Gowland, "Money, Income and Causality: The U.K. Experience," *American Economic Review* Vol. 66 (June 1976): pp. 417–23.

5. Sims, "Money Income and Causality," p. 540.

6. Williams, Goodhart, and Gowland, "Money, Income, and Causality," p. 423.

CHAPTER 19

Currency Substitution

INTRODUCTION

Until this point in the book we have followed the standard (domestic and international) monetary assumption that foreign currency is not a substitute in demand for domestic currency, that is, that Americans hold only dollars, French only hold francs, and Germans only hold Deutsche marks. It has been assumed that no foreign currency is held by domestic transactors for transactions or for speculative or precautionary purposes. However, this standard assumption about the international money market differs quite markedly from the standard assumptions about international bond and equity markets. The widely held view of the demand for bonds and equities is that investors are free to diversify their holdings of these assets in order to reduce the overall risk of their portfolios. One source of risk in each of these markets is the uncertainty of exchange rate depreciation, which potentially can inflict capital losses on assets denominated in a given currency. Faced with exchange rate uncertainty, the rational investor will diversify the currency denomination of his asset holdings, thereby reducing the risk of a capital loss.

However, the holder of money balances is not expected to act in such a rational fashion. Regardless of the cost or risk of holding the domestic currency, individuals or firms in a particular country are assumed to demand only the money of that country. In other words, regardless of the recklessness of Federal Reserve policy, Americans are assumed to hold only dollars. The same behavior is assumed to exist among the Germans, the Japanese, and even the Italians. Such behavior can be characterized as a completely inelastic or zero demand for foreign monies.

But such asymmetry of responses in the bonds and equities markets on the one hand, and the money market on the other, is illogical both from theoretical and empirical viewpoints. Theoretically, there is no reason that individuals and firms should not diversify their money portfolios as well as their bond and equity portfolios. Depreciation also inflicts a capital loss on domestic money balances by reducing purchasing power in world markets. By holding money in several different currency denominations, the capital loss on some balances can be offset by the gain in other denominations.*

Empirically, the tremendous increase in the fluctuations of currencies in the last decade has provided an incentive for such diversification of money balances. Furthermore, the expansion of trade between countries, the growth of the Eurocurrency markets, and the increased incidence of corporations with offices in several countries all present abundant opportunities for discretionary choice of the currency of transaction. For example, multinational corporations have strong incentives to diversify the currency composition of their cash balances in order to facilitate their endeavors in various countries. Even individuals and businesses that are clearly domiciled in a particular country often have transactions or precautionary or even speculative motives for diversifying the currency composition of their money holdings. Anyone who consistently makes purchases from foreign countries has at least the same transactions motives for demanding foreign currency balances as for demanding domestic currency balances. Importers and exporters, businesspeople who travel abroad, tourists, and residents of border areas all have incentives to diversify their currency balances. By holding foreign money, the transactions cost of their foreign purchases and the risk of capital losses are reduced.

These theoretical and empirical observations together imply that rather than a completely inelastic or zero demand for foreign monies, we should observe diversification among monies of different denominations, or *currency substitution*.[1] With diversification, a country's money becomes *internationalized* as it finds its way into the money balances of foreigners as well as domestic residents. Money demand within a country now includes foreign as well as domestic money, and the results and conclusions of the traditional monetary models may no longer hold.

In this chapter the implications of currency substitution are examined. First, a simple model of currency substitution is developed. The implications of this model for traditional analysis of monetary policy, flexible exchange rates and the behavior of the balance of payments is then developed. Next, empirical evidence of currency substitution is reported. Finally, the analysis of currency substitution is used to modify the conclusion of traditional models of devaluation. The chapter concludes with a summary of a classic case of the importance of currency substitution— the Mexican devaluation of 1976.

A SIMPLE MODEL OF CURRENCY SUBSTITUTION[2]

The mere ownership of foreign currency-denominated balances by domestic residents is not a sufficient condition for currency substitution to occur. A given amount of foreign currency balances may exist within a

---

*This incentive to diversify money portfolios applies not only to noninterest-bearing money, but also to interest-bearing deposits and near monies.

country for institutional or historical reasons. For currency substitution to exist, not only must there be foreign currency balances, but the level of these balances must change in response to changes in other economic variables. Furthermore, it is not a necessary condition for currency substitution that each individual within a country hold foreign currency balances. Currency substitution involves *marginal*, rather than average, money holdings. It requires only that there exist a group of individuals who, given the current value of economic variables, hold both domestic and foreign currency balances and are indifferent at the margin between holding more domestic or more foreign balances.

In order to discuss the mechanism of currency substitution, assume that such a group of individuals exist. These individuals may be foreign traders, border residents, or even multinational corporations. The important characteristic of each, however, is that they hold a *diversified portfolio* of real money balances. The real balance portfolio is only a fraction of the individual's overall portfolio. In terms of Figure 17A–1 in the appendix of Chapter 17, at initial equilibrium the real balance portfolio is of size m_0. The overall size of this real balance portfolio depends both on the level of real wealth or income and the return r on the alternative assets. The composition of this portfolio, however, varies with the relative opportunity costs of holding real balances of the various types of currencies. For example, if the opportunity cost of holding real balances denominated in currency A rises while the opportunity cost of holding those denominated in other currencies remain constant, all individuals holding diversified portfolios are assumed to reduce their real balances denominated in currency A and to increase their holdings denominated in other currencies.* The overall size of the portfolio, however, remains at m_0.**

Within this portfolio framework a two country model of currency substitution can be analyzed. The two countries A and B are each assumed to supply their own domestic currency-denominated money asset, C_A and C_B respectively. Both countries are also assumed to have a group of individuals who hold real balances denominated in both C_A and C_B in their cash balance portfolios. If we examine the "typical" individual in either country (just as was done for the portfolio model in the appendix to Chapter 17) the ratio in which he holds real balances of the two currencies can be described by

---

*Empirically the change in relative opportunity costs would be reflected in a changed interest differential between countries, or, equivalently, in a change in the forward premium or discount on the exchange rate. Either measure reflects expectations by the private sector that the relative cost of holding the two currencies is changing. In fact, in an integrated world, arbitrage assures that there is a close relationship between the interest rate differential and the forward premium or discount, so that they reflect the same expectations.

**The real balance portfolio may actually shrink below m_0 in size. The rise in the cost of holding currency A increases the weighted average of holding real balances in general. This rise, *ceteris paribus*, is equivalent to increasing r, thus causing a shift in the composition of the overall portfolio away from real balances and towards other assets. Inclusion of this possibility would not substantially alter the present analysis.

$$m(z) = \frac{c_A}{c_B}, \tag{19-1}$$

where $c_A = C_A/P_A$ is the level of real balances denominated in currency A, $C_B = C_B/P_B$ is the level of real balances denominated in currency B, and $z = i_B/i_A$ is the ratio of the opportunity costs of holding real balances in C_B and C_A. A rise in z is assumed to cause a rise in m as well. A rise in z means that the opportunity cost of holding real balances c_B has risen relative to the cost of holding real balances c_A. As z rises, each individual wants to substitute c_A for the now relatively more expensive c_B, raising the value of m. This substitution continues until each individual has adjusted his cash balance portfolio so that he is just indifferent between holding a little more c_A or a little more c_B.

CURRENCY SUBSTITUTION AND MONETARY POLICY

This simple model of currency substitution has an important implication for the effectiveness of monetary policy. An important determinant of the impact of monetary policy is the extent to which any increase (or decrease) in the money supply remains within the domestic country. As we shall see, the existence of currency substitution reduces the ability of the monetary authorities to control the domestic nominal money supply and thus the effectiveness of monetary policy.

Assume now that the central bank is not performing its previous role of fixing the value of domestic currency in terms of foreign currency. Instead, the central bank now refuses to exchange one currency for another. As we saw in Chapter 18, when the central bank fixes the value of domestic currency, monetary policy becomes ineffective. The actions of the central bank in the foreign exchange market makes domestic currency a perfect substitute for foreign currency on the supply side of the market. Thus, if domestic residents find themselves holding too much domestic currency, they simply avail themselves of the central bank's promise to exchange one currency for another, causing an outflow of reserves and a reduction in the domestic money supply. In the present analysis, however, this avenue of monetary escape is eliminated in order to concentrate on the adjustment of the demand side of the market.

Following the examples used in Chapters 9 and 12, the money supply is assumed to increase when the monetary authorities dump units of domestic currency out of a helicopter. There are two possibilities for this increase, a once-for-all increase, or a change in the rate of increase from zero to a positive number. These two possibilities represent the cases in which the opportunity cost of holding c_A falls and rises following the money supply increase. The two possibilities are considered in turn. In both cases it is initially assumed that the entire adjustment to the change in the money supply occurs through a change in the domestic price level. This assumption will be subsequently relaxed.

A Once-for-All Increase in C_A

First suppose that the monetary authorities of Country A unexpectedly decide to perform a once-for-all increase in the quantity of C_A by dumping from a helicopter additional units of C_A. For ease of exposition it is assumed that each individual's cash balances increase in proportion to his initial holdings. If the economy were initially at equilibrium, this monetary shock would require adjustments in order to return the economy to equilibrium. In terms of the present model the adjustments of four variables are of interest. First, how does the monetary shock affect the rate of interest i_A? Second, how does the change in i_A affect desired ratios of real balances m? Third, what change in P_A is required to achieve equilibrium? Finally, do changes in the preceding three variables cause a redistribution of C_A between the two countries? Each of these questions is answered in turn.

If there is a once-for-all increase in C_A, the real quantity of money assets denominated in C_A increases relative to the real value of other assets denominated in C_A. In order for the additional relative amounts of C_A to be absorbed, the cost of borrowing c_A balances must fall. Thus the increase in C_A causes i_A to fall. However, since it is assumed that the real value of C_B and all other assets denominated in C_B remain constant, the cost of borrowing c_B balances remains unchanged. The value of z is observed to rise.

The rise in z makes holding relatively more c_A suddenly more attractive. Thus m also rises. But m does not rise only in Country A. Since individuals anywhere in the world are assumed to face the same opportunity cost of holding real balances denominated in a particular currency, z rises in both countries. Thus the new equilibrium must be characterized by a higher value of m in both countries as compared with the initial equilibrium.

Two other conditions must also hold in the new stock equilibrium. First, in each country the supply of C_A must equal the demand for C_A. This condition is satisified when supply of c_A equals the demand for c_A in each country. Second, if money demand equals money supply in each country, then total world demand must equal total world supply. These two conditions determine the final rise in P_A and the distribution of C_A among countries.

For example, for total world money demand to equal money supply, the excess world supply of real balances denominated in C_A must be eliminated. One possibility is for P_A to rise sufficiently to completely eliminate the excess supply in Country A. This possibility arises because all the increase in the supply of C_A occurs in Country A. But while all the increase in supply occurs in A, all the increase in demand does not. The desired value of m rises in both countries, implying that at even a constant P_A there is excess demand for C_A in Country B. Thus while such a rise in P_A eliminates the excess supply in A, it only increases the excess demand in B. Since such a price rise does not completely eliminate the world excess demand for C_A, it cannot be the equilibrium price rise. Obviously world equilibrium requires a smaller rise in P_A. But with a smaller price rise, there is an excess supply of C_A in country A. The final equilibrium rise in P_A can therefore be determined by where the excess supply of C_A in A is precisely equal to the excess demand for C_A in B.

While the rise in P_A is sufficient to determine world equilibrium in the C_A market, it has not equated the markets within the two countries. The inability for changes in P_A to equate both world and domestic markets is caused by the distribution effect that demand has risen in both countries while supply has risen in only one. The only way for domestic markets to clear, given the P_A that creates world equilibrium, is for units of C_A to flow from Country A where there is excess supply to Country B where there is excess demand. Thus a once-for-all increase in C_A in Country A causes units of C_A to flow between countries.

An Increase in the Rate of C_A Growth from Zero to a Positive Number

Now assume that the monetary authorities of Country A decide to send the helicopter over the country at regular intervals. The monetary authorities inform the public of this decision and that each trip of the helicopter will increase the amount of C_A by a constant percentage. Again, the changes in z, m, P_A and the distribution of C_A between countries is of interest.

In contrast to the once-for-all increase, the decision to increase the supply of C_A at a constant rate creates expectations of inflation which causes i_A to rise. The rise in i_A causes z to fall. The fall in z causes the desired m to fall in both countries as individuals try to reduce the share of real balances denominated in C_A.*

The ensuing rise in P_A in each period can be divided into two parts, the rise in P_A necessary to maintain the initial level of relative real balances in each country, and the rise in P_A that reduces m from its initial level. The second source of a rise in P_A has a positive value in the first period, and a zero value in subsequent periods. For example, consider the first period. The supply of C_A has been increased in Country A. Ignoring for a moment any change in desired m, the analysis is very similar to the once-for-all increase case. The level of P_A must rise in order to equilibriate the world supply and demand for C_A. But in order for the supply of C_A to equal demand in both countries, units of C_A must flow from A to B. Again the increase in C_A causes a flow of currency between countries.

But the expectation of inflation causes i_A to rise, and m does not remain constant. The value of m must fall in both countries. Assuming

*As in the once-for-all case, additional money balances are distributed in proportion to initial rather current money balances. The intention is to prevent individuals from raising their "interest" payments by holding more money, and thus creating an additional effect on the demand for money.

symmetrical responses, the desired level of m will fall by the same percentage in the two countries. This adjustment can be accomplished by a once-for-all rise in P_A equal to the percentage fall in m. Such a rise reduces c_A in both countries by the desired amount and does not require further flows of C_A between the countries.

So only one of the two rises in P_A causes a net flow of C_A in the first period, and the flow is again from Country A to Country B. Furthermore, once the level of m adjusts to the level consistent with the expected inflation, there is no longer any force creating the second source of a rise in P_A. In subsequent periods P_A adjusts only to maintain real balances at the initial level of m, and as has been shown, this adjustment requires a movement of C_A in each period.

Allowing P_B Also to Adjust

Until now it has been assumed that when C_A increases, all the adjustment in the level of real balances occurs through a rise in P_A. However, if currencies are substitutes in demand, it is quite possible that at least some of the adjustment can occur through a rise in P_B. When C_A is increased by the monetary authorities in A, the overall level of real balances in the world is increased above the level of world demand. To this point it has been assumed that the overall level is reduced back to an equilibrium level by lowering only c_A. But lowering c_B can also have the desired effect on m. For example, in the case of the once-for-all rise in C_A, a rise in P_B helps to cause m to rise to the desired level, and P_A does not have to rise as much as in the previous case.

SOME IMPLICATIONS OF THIS ANALYSIS

The previous section shows that even if the central bank is not intervening in the foreign exchange market there can be flows of currency between countries. Thus another avenue for the adjustment of the money supply exists. Hence, the assumptions in this book of correlated movements of national price levels and the movements of money from areas of excess supply to areas of excess demand are not necessarily dependent on the assumption of the central bank maintaing a fixed exchange rate. While the fixed exchange rate allows these adjustments to occur by exchanging supplies of currencies through the central bank, the adjustments could just as easily occur through changing demands for currencies in the private foreign exchange markets. Private individuals in Country A can simply sell units of either C_A or C_B directly to individuals in Country B in exchange for goods or bonds without requiring any services of the central bank.

This conclusion has an important implication for the theory of flexible exchange rates. One of the traditional arguments for flexible rates is that they allow a country to insulate its monetary policy from the monetary policies of other countries. Such insulation is assumed to occur, because, under perfectly flexible rates, the central banks agree not to intervene at all in the foreign exchange market, thus eliminating the substitution of currencies on the supply side. Combining this nonintervention with the usual assumption that individuals hold only their domestic currency implies that there is no avenue for money to move from one country to another. However, as the possibility of substitution among currencies in private portfolios increases, a new avenue of money flows begins to open up. When the monetary authorities of A increase the supply of C_A, rather than the entire increase remaining with Country A, and P_A adjusting to eliminate the domestic excess supply of real balances, some units of C_A are redistributed through private markets to Country B. The effects of monetary policy are no longer internalized within A. P_A rises by less than the percentage increase in C_A. Without any intervention by the governments of either Country A or Country B, the nominal money supply ($C_A + C_B$) rises in B.

Once possible changes in P_B are introduced, the implications become even more obvious. As long as c_A and c_B are substitutes in demand, a rise in C_A can cause not only P_A to rise, but also P_B. Thus inflation is transmitted between countries without having to assume any government intervention in the foreign exchange market. Yet transmission of inflation is precisely the type of phenomenon from which flexible rates, and the accompanying monetary independence, are assumed to insulate a country.

The degree to which changes in the money supply and inflation are transmitted between the countries is of course proportional to the degree of substitution between currencies. The limiting case is where c_A and c_B are perfect substitutes. In that case there is the equivalent of one world currency, just as when central banks make currencies perfect substitutes on the supply side by fixing exchange rates. In that case no distinction can be drawn between either c_A or c_B, or between P_A or P_B, just as in the one world currency model that has been used throughout the book. An increase in the nominal money supply in either country increases the real balances used in both countries and causes the price level in both countries to rise by precisely the same amount.

The existence of currency substitution therefore implies that the traditional concepts of the sources of supply and demand in domestic money markets must be reexamined. Furthermore, it can explain part of the disenchantment with the current system of floating rates. For example, conventional monetarists who recognized under the fixed rate system that, say, the U.S. money market was highly integrated into the world money market, welcomed the current floating rate regime as an opportunity to separate the U.S. and world markets. The separation of money markets in turn was to provide U.S. policy makers additional powers to influence the economy. The basis of this belief, however, was that Americans hold only their domestic money. Hence, if the Federal Reserve increases the supply of dollars, these dollars must ultimately be returned to the U.S. since no one elsewhere in the world will hold them. All effects of U.S. monetary policy are therefore felt within the U.S.

However, if under floating rates individuals and firms hold diversified money portfolios, then dollars are held abroad as well as in the U.S. Increases in the dollar money supply by the Federal Reserve may therefore not all remain in the U.S., but instead may become dispersed throughout the world as private market money portfolios respond to changing market forces. Despite the increased flexibility of exchange rates, governments still find money supplies among countries interrelated and the promised absolute control over the domestic money supply elusive. The lack of control can be traced in part to the diversification of money portfolios.

But even if some monetary authorities could control the quantity of domestic money within their borders, such an ability to regulate is no longer a sufficient condition to produce an independent monetary policy. With the private sector holding diversified money portfolios, domestic money is only part of the relevant "money supply." The remaining portion, foreign currency-denominated money, is beyond the control of the domestic monetary authorities. Flows of money now occur between countries through the private market, and the usefulness of monetary policy for "tuning" the economy is again reduced.

Hence, with substitution among monies, the relevant concepts of money demand are the demand for dollars worldwide and the demand for money in the U.S. The *demand for dollars* is now the sum of dollar demands in every country, or the total world dollar demand. The *demand for money in the U.S.* is the U.S. demand for dollars and any other monies held in domestic portfolios. Notice that the conventional concept, the demand for dollars in the U.S., is only part of each of these two demands, and its usefulness as an economic indicator is therefore very limited.[3]

The issue of currency substitution also has an important implication for the behavior of the observed balance of payments. Until this point the balance of payments have been assumed to represent the net inflow of money. When foreign currency flows in, domestic residents present the foreign currency at the central bank and exchange it for domestic currency. The domestic money supply increases, as do the reserves held by the central bank. Thus the net flow of official reserves (the balance of payments) is directly related to changes in the domestic money supply. However, with currency substitution it is no longer certain that an inflow of foreign reserves will be presented at the central bank by the public, even where the central bank is fixing the exchange rate. Instead, the public may choose to simply add the foreign currency to their diversified cash balance portfolio. In this case the reserves held by the central bank, and thus the balance of payments, are unaffected. The country's money supply, however, has still risen by the amount of the foreign currency inflow. Thus, where currencies are substitutes on the demand side, the balance of payments may no longer be an accurate measure of the net change in money.

The issue of currency substitution therefore has important implications for some fundamental conclusions of the traditional monetary approach to the balance of payments. The greater the degree of currency substitution, the less the traditional conclusions hold. The degree of substitution in demand between currencies therefore becomes an important empirical question.

EMPIRICAL MODELS OF CURRENCY SUBSTITUTION

There are at least two different methods for testing the presence of currency substitution. One method is to directly search for evidence of the type of money portfolio behavior that currency substitution implies. With diversified money portfolios, money demand within a country should include foreign as well as domestic money, and the relative composition between the two should depend on the usual portfolio composition determining variables, the expected return and risk of return of the various monies. Changes in the composition of money portfolios in response to changes in expected return or risk of return would therefore represent direct evidence of the currency substitution phenomenon.

A second method is to examine more aggregative data for consistency with the currency substitution phenomenon. Conventional monetary theory suggests that a certain relationship should exist between money supplies, national incomes and exchange rates. The currency substitution hypothesis suggests an alternative relationship. Aggregate data for several countries can be examined to distinguish between the two hypotheses.

This section describes both the direct and indirect tests of currency substitution. The section shows how such tests can be formulated, and reviews the empirical results.

Direct Measurements of Portfolio Behavior

Economists have begun to uncover evidence that not only do the incentives for diversification now exist, but that money portfolios respond to these incentives. For example Haim Levy and Marshall Sarnat[4] have calculated how the mean rates of return and standard deviations (risks) of return of foreign currencies differed during the fixed rate period as compared with after the advent of floating rates. They conclude that during the fixed rate period the changes in the exchange rates were not sufficiently large to create an incentive for money portfolio diversification. But with the breakdown of the Bretton Woods System, the mean rates of return and standard deviations rose dramatically, providing a strong incentive for money diversification.

In other words, during fixed rate periods the central banks of various countries make all currencies perfect substitutes on the supply or central bank intervention side. By holding a dollar or a Deutsche mark, an equivalent amount of all other currencies is simultaneously held. There is little, if any, difference between the expected returns or risks of return of individual currencies. Individuals and firms therefore tend to hold only the currency with the greatest convenience factor to them, in most cases the domestic currency. But when central banks eliminate this value guarantee among the currencies during floating rate periods, the private market has the incentive to deal with the new uncertainties by diversifying or substituting among monies through money demand.

Tests by Miles[5] on United States, Canadian, and German money data have shown that not only does the advent of floating rates create an incentive for money diversification, but that the private sector responds to these incentives. In each of these three countries the degree of responsiveness of relative holdings of foreign and domestic money to relative changes in the opportunity costs or interest rates associated with the two monies is measured. These relative changes in interest rates algebraically correspond closely to changes in relative expected returns on the two types of money. These tests therefore measure the portfolio substitution between currencies in response to changes in expected return. The degree of substitution is summarized in a variable called the *elasticity of substitution*.

The model for testing the degree of substitution between domestic and foreign currency is developed using a procedure similar to one employed by Chetty.[6] Real balances, denominated in terms of both domestic and foreign currencies, from an individual's cash balance portfolio are combined in a production function for money services. Given the relative efficiencies of domestic and foreign currencies in producing money services (defined by the production function) and the relative opportunity costs of holding different currencies (reflected in the asset constraint), the individual tries to maximize the production of money services.

The equation which is finally estimated is

$$\log \frac{M_d}{eM_f} = \sigma\log\left(\frac{\alpha_1}{\alpha_2}\right) + \sigma\log\left(\frac{1 + i_f}{1 + i_d}\right) + \mu^* \qquad (19\text{-}2)$$

where

M_d, M_f = the domestic currency-denominated and foreign currency-denominated cash balances held, respectively

e = the exchange rate (units of domestic currency per unit of foreign currency)

α_1, α_2 = weights reflecting the efficiency of domestic and foreign balances in producing money services

i_d, i_f = interest rates on domestic currency-denominated and foreign currency-denominated cash balances respectively

σ = the elasticity of substitution between domestic and foreign currency-denominated cash balances respectively

μ = statistical error term

Thus, the elasticity is directly estimated in the equation. The elasticity measures the percentage change in the holdings of domestic relative to

---

*This equation is derived in the Appendix to this chapter.

foreign money balances when there is a one percent rise in the cost of holding foreign relative to domestic money. A high elasticity of substitution implies that the two currencies are regarded as close substitutes, so that a small change in the relative opportunity costs of holding them causes a large change in the relative proportions in which they are held. Alternatively, if currencies are nonsubstitutes, the relative holdings of currencies should be unresponsive to changes in relative costs, and the estimated elasticity of substitution should be zero.

In the U.S. and German tests, the elasticity of substitution between domestic money and major foreign currencies is estimated. Holdings of major foreign currencies are measured by the foreign currency-denominated short-term assets of the nonbank private sector. Domestic money holdings are measured by the conventional domestic money supply, and Euromarket rates are used as the opportunity costs. In the Canadian test, the elasticity of substitution between Canadian and U.S. money is estimated. Foreign currency is measured by the short-term U.S. dollar assets of nonbank nonofficial Canadians, and the opportunity costs are measured by the yields on U.S. and Canadian treasury bills.

The conventional monetary model assumption is that the demand for these foreign monies relative to domestic money will always be unresponsive to changes in the expected returns or costs. In contrast, the portfolio diversification assumption is that relative holdings will be unresponsive where no incentive for diversification exists (fixed rate periods), but that a significant degree of responsiveness will appear when incentives arise (floating rate periods).

The results for the three countries during fixed and floating rate periods are presented in Table 19-1. In all three countries during fixed rate periods, the measured degree of responsiveness of relative money holdings to changes in relative expected returns is statistically insignificantly different from zero. However, during the floating rate periods, the elasticities of substitution become larger and statistically significant. Relative money holdings become responsive to expected returns in all three countries, and the conventional monetary assumptions are rejected. Money appears to flow between countries without the help of the central bank, domestic money has become *internationalized*, and an isolated or independent domestic monetary policy cannot exist.

Some evidence of the money substitution phenomenon in response to changes in relative risk exists as well. For instance, one might expect the currency in which a Eurocurrency market loan or deposit is denominated, or international trade is consummated, to depend on the risk of contracting in the different currencies. For example, a German company and its customers in South America may initially denominate their transactions in dollars. The dollar in its role as an international reserve currency is readily accepted in most countries, and it is the most convenient form in which the German company can denominate these international transactions. However, if the risk or uncertainty of holding dollars increases, the company and its customers may decide to denominate their transactions in more stable currencies. Even if the expected return on the

**Table 19–1   Estimates of the Elasticity of Substitution During Subperiods of
Fixed and Floating Exchange Rates**

	Subperiod	Exchange Rate Regime	Type of Equation	Elasticity of Substitution	$\bar{R}^2$	D.W.	Rho
	Q4/60–Q2/62	Floating	OLSQ	12.8 (2.54)	0.48	1.66	
Canada	Q3/62–Q2/70	Fixed	CORC	2.66 (0.79)	0.78	1.41	0.90
	Q3/70–Q4/75	Floating	CORC	5.78 (1.83)	0.79	1.27	0.81
	Q1/67–Q2/71	Fixed	CORC	0.85 (0.35)	0.44	2.04	0.64
United States	Q3/71–Q3/78	Floating	CORC	3.94 (2.77)	0.69	1.81	0.83
	Q1/65–Q2/71	Fixed	CORC	1.51 (0.51)	0.69	2.00	0.81
Germany	Q3/71–Q3/78	Floating	CORC	2.78 (2.23)	0.89	2.28	0.97

Note: t-statistics are in parentheses below the estimated coefficients.
OLSQ is an ordinary least squares regression.
CORC is a regression employing the Cochrane-Orcutt procedure for eliminating first-order autocorrelation in the residuals.
D.W. is the Durban-Watson statistic.
Rho is the first-order autocorrelation estimated by the Cochrane-Orcutt technique.

Source: Marc A. Miles, "Currency Substitution, Flexible Exchange Rates, and Monetary Independence," and "Currency Substitution: Some Further Results and Conclusions."

dollar does not change, an increase in the uncertainty or variance of return increases chances that either the seller or purchaser will experience a capital loss.

Similarly, when dollar risk increases, both borrowers and lenders in the Eurocurrency markets now find contracting in dollars more risky. Hence, both groups should now be expected to desire more of their agreements to be denominated in other, relatively more stable currencies. In other words, the risk of a currency should affect decisions on both the asset and liability sides. The proportion of both Eurocurrency assets and liabilities denominated in currencies other than dollars is expected to rise.

Evidence of precisely this type of composition substitution in the Eurocurrency market has been found by Putnam and Wilford.[7] They find that increased risk (standard deviation) in the dollar/mark exchange rate is positively and significantly correlated to the nondollar/dollar currency composition ratio of European banks' external portfolios. In fact the exchange risk explained about 42 percent of the variation of this ratio on the banks' asset side, and about 29 percent of the variation on the liability side.

Similarly, Miles and Stewart[8] find that money portfolios in both the U.S. and Germany respond to uncertainty as well as expected return. Extending the tests by Miles for the degree of currency substitution, an additional risk variable is included in equation (19–2). The additional risk variable measures the risk or uncertainty of the dollar relative to the Deutsche mark. More specifically, the standard deviation of the weekly dollar/Swiss franc exchange rate is compared to the standard deviation of the DM/Swiss franc rate. When this variable is included during the floating rate period, not only does the degree of substitution in response to changes in expected returns remain significant, but evidence is provided that portfolios diversify out of domestic money when its risk or uncertainty rises relative to that of foreign money.

The response of relative money holdings to changes in expected return together with the evidence of substitution due to changes in relative risk, imply that the portfolio diversification model probably summarizes well the forces within the international money market.

An Alternative Test for the Presence of Currency Substitution

A less direct but still plausible test of currency substitution is to measure whether the more aggregate empirical data are consistent with the hypothesis. Such a test has been performed by Evans and Laffer.[9] Evans and Laffer focus in their tests on the relationship between excess demand for money in the domestic country, excess demand for money in the foreign country, and the exchange rate. If currencies are perfect nonsubstitutes, then during periods where the exchange rate is not fixed, adjustments must occur through price rather than quantity changes. Changes in the exchange rate are determined by changes in the excess demand for money in one country relative to another. If Country A increases its money supply, *ceteris paribus*, then the supply of money increases relative to demand in A, creating excess supply, a rise in A's price level, and a depreciation of A's currency. However, if currencies are perfect substitutes in demand, such price adjustments can be alleviated by C_A flowing to B, and the price level rising by the same percentage in both countries. The exchange rate is unaffected.

The test used by Evans and Laffer is to differentiate between these two cases by observing whether the exchange rate responds to changes in relative excess supplies of money. The model tested is derived from three equations: (a) the purchasing power parity relationship

$$ER_{i/j} = \frac{P_i}{P_j} \tag{19–3}$$

where $ER_{i/j}$ is the number of units of Country i's currency per unit of Country j's currency, and P_i, P_j are the price levels in the two countries; (b) a quantity theory equation for Country i

$$M_i V_i = P_i y_i \tag{19-4}$$

where V_i is the income velocity of money and y_i is real income; (c) a quantity theory equation for Country j

$$M_j V_j = P_j y_j. \tag{19-5}$$

Solving equations (19-4) and (19-5) for the price levels and substituting into (19-3) yields

$$ER_{i/j} = \frac{V_i}{V_j} \cdot \frac{M_i}{M_j} \cdot \frac{y_j}{y_i}. \tag{19-6}$$

Taking the logarithm of (19-6) and computing the period-to-period change yields the percentage change form

$$\% \Delta ER_{i/j} = b_0 \% \Delta\left(\frac{V_i}{V_j}\right) + b_1 \% \Delta M_i$$
$$- b_2 \% \Delta M_j - b_3 \% \Delta y_i + b_4 \% \Delta y_j. \tag{19-7}$$

Equation (19-7) becomes the testable model. If currencies are perfect nonsubstitutes, then the exchange rate should be proportionately affected by a change in any of the right hand variables. In other words, the estimated coefficients of b_0 to b_4 on each of the right hand variables should be one in value. Conversely, if currencies are perfect substitutes, there should be no systematic relationship between the exchange rate and the right hand variables. In other words, the estimated coefficients b_0 to b_4 should all be zero in value. So estimated values close to one are consistent with nonsubstitutability, and estimated values near zero are consistent with currency diversification.

Equation (19-7) is tested on monthly data from the period January 1968 through September 1975 for France, Germany, Italy, the United Kingdom, Canada, and Japan. The results are summarized in Table 19-2. Notice that the largest of the coefficients is only 0.38, which is far below one in value. All other coefficients are below 0.19 in value, some are even negative, and most are not significantly different from zero. The empirical results are again clearly more consistent with a world with a significant degree of currency substitution than a world where currencies are nonsubstitutes. So whether a direct or indirect test is used, currency substitution appears to be a significant phenomenon for explaining the behavior of the international money markets.

THE IMPLICATIONS OF CURRENCY SUBSTITUTION FOR DEVALUATION[10]

The standard monetary approach analysis of devaluation was described in Chapter 17. According to this approach, devaluation causes the domestic price level to rise, which in turn reduces the real value of the given stock of money balances. The reduction in the value of real balances

Table 19–2　Testing the Exchange Rate Market for the Presence of Currency Substitution

Country	b_0	b_1	b_2	b_3	b_4	R^2	F	D.W.
Canada	.001	−.002	.117	−.000	.011	.01	.1	1.61
	(.89)	(−.04)	(.59)	(−.01)	(.27)			
France	.001	.132	.149	.020	.082	.04	1.0	1.78
	(.46)	(1.10)	(1.22)	(1.38)	(.82)			
Germany	.005	.149	.059	.076	.032	.04	1.0	1.56
	(1.75)	(1.27)	(.56)	(1.55)	(.25)			
Italy	−.001	.120	.190	−.008	.074	.09	2.2	1.97
	(−.21)	(1.73)	(2.67)	(−.87)	(−1.14)			
Japan	.001	−.027	−.001	−.002	.158	.06	1.4	1.86
	(.58)	(−.42)	(−.02)	(−.08)	(2.23)			
U.K.	−.001	.383	.107	.007	.135	.11	1.3	1.56
	(−.26)	(2.12)	(.96)	(.15)	(1.19)			

Note: The t statistic for each coefficient appears below it in parentheses.
Source: Evans and Laffer.

reduces the real value of money assets relative to other real assets, and causes an excess demand for money and a portfolio disequilibrium. The excess demand for money must then be satisfied, in the absence of domestic credit creation, by an inflow of money from abroad. The balance of payments therefore improves temporarily until a new stock equilibrium is achieved.

This monetary approach argument, however, is making the implicit argument that different national currencies are perfect nonsubstitutes in demand. Thus when real money balances are reduced, only domestic money balances can help to bring the supply of balances up to the desired level. This assumption of perfect nonsubstitutability has two implications for the adjustment process of the money supply. First, a central bank is needed in order to convert foreign currency into domestic currency. Second, any inflow of foreign currency always ends up at the central bank, which results in an increase in the foreign reserve holdings of the central bank, and thus permits any foreign currency inflow to be measured as an improvement in the balance of payments.

However, if currency substitution is assumed to exist, the adjustment process of the money supply following devaluation is possibly quite different. Since individuals now hold both domestic and foreign currency balances to provide money services, either can now be used to satisfy the excess demand for money that occurs following devaluation. When foreign currency flows into the country, it may now simply remain in private portfolios in its present form. Currency substitution therefore has two important implications for the adjustment process:

1. There is no longer a need for a central bank in order to increase the real supply of money following devaluation. Since individuals now

hold foreign currency balances, there is no compelling reason to first convert foreign currency balances into domestic currency. Thus the money supply can increase without any intervention by a central bank.* Notice, however, that to the degree foreign and domestic currencies are not perfect substitutes, the domestic currency equivalent of the increase in the money supply is larger if foreign currency rather than domestic currency is used to satisfy the excess demand.

2. As already discussed, the inflow of foreign currency appears as an inflow of reserves only to the extent that foreign currency is presented at the central bank to be converted into domestic currency. This fact in turn has an important implication for the behavior of the balance of payments. To the extent that the foreign currency is retained in private portfolios, there is no record of foreign inflows on the balance sheet of the central bank, and the balance of payments does not improve. Thus, in the presence of currency substitution, the balance of payments does not improve as much following devaluation as one would expect from a strict monetary approach model.

This last point may provide at least a partial explanation for the behavior of the balance-of-payments residuals in Table 17–3. Recall that those residuals indicated on average an improvement in the balance of payments for about two years following devaluation. This contrasts with a similar measure for the trade balance which indicated no net improvement in that account following devaluation. Yet the magnitude of the average value for the balance of payments is less than expected. The improvements average only one-quarter to one-third of the standard error. Such a value does not indicate the significant improvement predicted by the monetary approach.

However, these results are consistent with the theory of currency substitution. The positive residuals indicate that on average more reserves flowed into the central banks of the countries following devaluation than normally could be expected. Yet the small magnitude may indicate that some of the foreign currency imported may simply have remained in the portfolios of the private sector and is not recorded as an inflow of reserves.

Currency substitution also has implications for the adjustment of money demand. As pointed out above, the traditional monetary approach argument for devaluation is that it relieves an excess supply of money. Following devaluation, the demand for real balances is unchanged, or falls less than money supply, thereby improving the balance of payments. However, once the concept of currency substitution is introduced, larger changes in money demand become possible, and it is no longer obvious that devaluation should improve the balance of payments.

*This analysis concentrates on foreign sources of additional money. It is recognized that the domestic money supply can also increase without any intervention by the domestic central bank to the extent the public lowers its desired ratio of currency to bank deposits, banks lower their desired level of excess reserves, or the private sector makes greater use of money substitutes.

Essentially devaluation implies a reneging on a promise by the central bank of a country to exchange domestic and foreign currency at a fixed price. The memory of the reneged promise adds a risk factor to future holdings of that currency and thus increases the perceived cost of holding the currency. The higher opportunity cost affects the relative demand for domestic currency not only in the domestic country, but also in any other country where these currency balances are actually or potentially held. In all these countries individuals want to reduce the ratio of real balances held in the devalued currency relative to real balances held in other currencies. Given the demand for other currencies, the reduced desired ratio implies an absolute fall in the demand for real balances of the devalued currency.

From Equation (19–2) it is clear that the change in the desired ratio of real balances depends upon two factors: (a) the degree to which devaluation changes perceived risk, and (b) the degree to which currencies are substitutes. The more the perceived risk is raised and the greater the degree of substitution between currencies, the more the demand for real balances of the devalued currency falls. In fact, if these two variables are sufficiently large, the world demand for real balances of the devalued currency may fall more than does the world supply, exacerbating the excess supply of money rather than relieving it.

Devaluation of the Mexican Peso

A classic case where the change in the demand for real balances probably dominated the change in supply was the devaluation of the Mexican peso in August 1976. The devaluation represented the first break in the fixed parity between the dollar and the peso in twenty-two years. Thus while the devaluation was to some extent anticipated, it did not occur within an environment in which devaluation was a common occurrence. With the actual devaluation, therefore, the perceived risk of holding pesos probably rose dramatically.

Furthermore, the peso and the dollar were quite close substitutes, particularly in the border areas and tourist towns.[11] For example, prior to devaluation, prices in the tourist industry were traditionally denominated in both dollars and pesos. In order to facilitate transactions in either currency, firms and individuals engaged in the tourist industry certainly had to hold both currencies in some desired ratio. Similarly, in border towns such as Laredo, Texas where Mexicans did much purchasing, prices were also simultaneously denominated in both currencies prior to devaluation. Again, merchants in this town held a desired ratio of both currencies in order to be prepared to complete a transaction in either currency.

However, following devaluation and the related uncertainty, these transactions patterns changed. The tourist industry moved from a dual price system to prices denominated almost exclusively in dollars. In the border towns, too, prices were now denominated in the more stable dollar. And accompanying this shift to dollar prices was a reduction in the proportion of peso balances held.

Not surprisingly, the Mexican devaluation did not produce the move-ment towards stability that traditional monetary approach economists ar-gued would occur. Mexican officials were perplexed by the large runs on the peso *following* devaluation. Stories of Mexicans landing in Texas with suitcases of dollars were very common. The Mexican central bank found that it could not maintain even the new, lower value of the peso, and they were forced to allow the peso to float even lower.

To some economists the Mexican experience seemed inconsistent with economic theory. However, when viewed in terms of a large increase in the perceived cost of holding a currency for which a close substitute ex-ists, the Mexican experience is not at all unexpected. While devaluation may have reduced the real supply of pesos, it simultaneously reduced real demand. And given the ability of individuals to shift from using pesos to dollars, the real demand for pesos simply fell by more than the real supply. Devaluation simply served to exacerbate the existing excess supply of pesos, and the additional outflows of capital were a symptom of this increased excess supply.

SUMMARY

The demand for money, like the demand for bonds and equities, is diver-sified across currencies. This diversification and internationalization of monies is called *currency substitution*. Where such a phenomenon exists, it is impossible for a country to run a monetary policy which is indepen-dent of monetary policies in other countries. Currency substitution there-fore alters some of the basic conclusions of the traditional monetarist and the monetary approach to the balance of payments theories. The conclu-sions changed include an alleged benefit of floating exchange rates and the effect of devaluation on the measured balance of payments.

Currency substitution requires only that there exist a group of indi-viduals who are indifferent on the *margin* between domestic and foreign monies, and who change the composition of their money portfolios in response to changing incentives. Empirical evidence suggests that such behavior exists in several major countries.

REFERENCES

BOYER, RUSSELL S., "Currency Mobility and Balance of Payments Adjustment," *The Monetary Approach to International Adjustment*, B. Putnam and D. S. Wilford, eds., New York: Praeger, 1978.

KING, DAVID T., BLUFORD H. PUTNAM, and D. SYKES WILFORD, "A Currency Port-folio Approach to Exchange Rate Determination: Exchange Rate Stability and the Independence of Monetary Policy," *The Monetary Approach to Interna-tional Adjustment*, B. Putnam and D. S. Wilford, eds., New York: Praeger, 1978.

LEVY, HAIM and MARSHALL SARNAT, "Exchange Rate Risk and the Optimal Diver-sification of Foreign Currency Holdings," *Journal of Money, Credit and Bank-ing* 10, No. 4 (November 1978): 453–63.

MILES, MARC A. "Currency Substitution, Flexible Exchange Rates, and Monetary Independence." *American Economic Review* 68, No. 3 (June 1978): 428–36.

—— "Currency Substitution: Perspective, Implications, and Empirical Evidence," *The Monetary Approach to International Adjustment*, B. Putnam and D. S. Wilford, eds., New York: Praeger, 1978.

PUTNAM, BLUFORD H. and D. SYKES WILFORD, "How Diversification Makes the Dollar Weaker." *Euromoney* (October 1978): 201–04.

NOTES

1. See for example, Russell S. Boyer, "Currency Mobility and Balance of Payments Adjustment, Chapter 13 in Putnam and Wilford, eds., *The Monetary Approach to International Adjustment*, op. cit.; Lance Girton and Don Roper, "Theory and Implications of Currency Substitution," Federal Reserve Bank, *International Finance Discussion Papers* No. 86, August 1976; David King, Bluford Putnam and D. Sykes Wilford, "A Currency Portfolio Approach to Exchange Rate Determination: Exchange Rate Stability and Independence of Monetary Policy," Chapter 14 of Putnam and Wilford, eds., *The Monetary Approach*, op. cit.; Marc A. Miles, "Currency Substitution: Perspective, Implications, and Empirical Evidence," Chapter 12 of Putnam and Wilford, op. cit.; and Marc A. Miles, "Currency Substitution, Flexible Exchange Rates, and Monetary Independence," *American Economic Review* 68, No. 3 (June 1978): 428–436.

2. Adapted from Marc A. Miles, "Currency Substitution, Flexible Exchange Rates, and Monetary Independence," *American Economic Review* 68, No. 3 (June 1978): 428–436.

3. Currency substitution, then, represents one way in which the relevant money supply of a country becomes endogenous, that is, determined by the demand of the private sector, not the policy of the central bank. Other phenomena such as the existence of domestic money substitutes (money market funds, Eurodollars, repurchase agreements, etc.) also make the money supply endogenous. The usefulness of monetary policy for "tuning" the economy is therefore compromised for reasons besides just currency substitution.

4. Haim Levy and Marshall Sarnat, "Exchange Rate Risk and the Optimal Diversification of Foreign Currency Holdings," *Journal of Money, Credit, and Banking* Vol. 10, No. 4 (November 1978): pp. 453–463.

5. Marc A. Miles, "Currency Substitution, Flexible Exchange Rates, and Monetary Independence," op. cit.; and "Currency Substitution: Some Further Results and Conclusions," Rutgers College, May 1979.

6. V. K. Chetty, "On Measuring the Nearness of Near-Money," *American Economic Review* Vol. 59. (June 1969): pp. 270–281.

7. Bluford H. Putnam and D. Sykes Wilford, "How Diversification Makes the Dollar Weaker," *Euromoney* (October 1978): pp. 201–204.

8. Marc A. Miles and Marion B. Stewart, "The Effects of Risk and Return on the Currency Composition of Money Demand," *Weltwirtschaftliches Archiv*.

9. Paul Evans and Arthur Laffer, "Demand Substitutability Across Countries," University of Southern California, 1977.

10. Adapted from Marc A. Miles, "Devaluation, Currency Substitution, and Bal-

ance of Payments," paper presented at the Southern Economic Association Meetings, November 1977, New Orleans, Louisiana.

11. See for example D. King, B. Putnam and D. S. Wilford, "A Currency Portfolio Approach to Exchange Rate Determination: Exchange Rate Stability and the Independence of Monetary Policy," op. cit.

APPENDIX 19
DERIVATION OF THE EQUATION FOR DIRECTLY ESTIMATING THE ELASTICITY OF SUBSTITUTION BETWEEN CURRENCIES

Chapter 19 presents empirical evidence of the degree of substitution between money balances of different currency denominations, estimated from equation (19-2). Equation (19-2), however, is derived from maximizing the production of money services subject to an asset constraint.

More specifically, if a constant elasticity of substitution (CES) production function is assumed, the level of money services produced by M_d/P_d domestic currency real balances and M_f/P_f foreign currency real balance is

$$\frac{MS}{P_d} = \left[\alpha_1\left(\frac{M_d}{P_d}\right)^{-\rho} + \alpha_2\left(\frac{M_f}{P_f}\right)^{-\rho}\right]^{-(1/\rho)} \qquad (19A-1)$$

where

$\quad MS$ = level of money services

M_d, M_f = the domestic currency- and foreign currency-denominated cash balances held, respectively

$\quad P_d, P_f$ = domestic and foreign currency price indices, respectively

$\quad \alpha_1, \alpha_2$ = weights reflecting the efficiency of domestic and foreign real balances in producing money services.

This production function directly relates the level of real balances to the level of money services. Notice that since real balances in both currencies are denominated in units of goods, there is no need for an exchange rate. However, for empirically estimating this relationship, it is desirable to express the production function in terms of nominal cash balances and exchange rates. Defining the exchange rate as $e = P_d/P_f$ from purchasing power parity, and since P_d and P_f are indices defining $P_d = 1$, equation (19A-1) becomes

$$MS = (\alpha_1 M_d^{-\rho} + \alpha_2 e M_f^{-\rho})^{-(1/\rho)}. \qquad (19A-2)$$

The asset constraint for money balances is constructed to reflect two factors: (a) that there is an opportunity cost to holding real balances, and (b) this opportunity cost may differ between the two types of real balances. The overall portfolio of the nonbank private sector of the country is assumed to consist of holdings of all types of real assets, only one of which is money. Given the overall portfolio size and the relative returns on each type of asset, the demand for each type of asset, and thus the corresponding asset constraint, could be constructed. The asset constraint for real money balances is one such constraint. It is assumed that in determining the composition of the overall portfolio, the private sector decides to hold M_0/P_d real cash balances. These cash balances are then divided between M_d/P_d domestic currency-denominated real balances and M_f/P_f foreign currency-denominated real balances on the basis of the relative cost of holding these different types of balances (reflected in the asset constraint) and their relative efficiencies in providing money services (reflected in the production function).

The asset constraint is therefore of the form

$$\frac{M_0}{P_d} = \frac{M_d}{P_d}(1 + i_d) + \frac{M_f}{P_f}(1 + i_f) \qquad (19A\text{--}3)$$

where i_d and i_f are the interest rates on domestic and foreign currencies balances respectively. In terms of nominal balances and exchange rates equation (19A–3) becomes

$$M_0 = M_d(1 + i_d) + eM_f(1 + i_f) \qquad (19A\text{--}4)$$

The asset constraint reflects the fact that M_0 is the total money assets that must be held to provide the money services of M_d and eM_f money assets. If, for example, the money balances are borrowed each period, since it costs $M_d \cdot i_d$ and $eM_f \cdot i_f$ to borrow M_d and eM_f balances respectively, a total of $M_d(1+i_d)$ and $eM_f(1+i_f)$ money balances must be held in order to pay off the loans at the end of the period.

Maximizing the production function subject to the asset constraint provides the following marginal conditions:

$$\frac{\partial MS}{\partial M_d} = -\rho\alpha_1 M_d^{-\rho-1}MS^{-1} = \lambda(1 + i_d) \qquad (19A\text{--}5)$$

$$\frac{\partial MS}{\partial M_f} = -\rho\alpha_2 M_f^{-\rho-1}MS^{-1} = \lambda(1 + i_f) \qquad (19A\text{--}6)$$

$$M_0 = M_d(1 + i_d) + eM_f(1 + i_f) \qquad (19A\text{--}7)$$

where λ is the LaGrangean multiplier. Dividing (19A–5) by (19A–6) relates the relative marginal productivities of the two types of balances to their relative prices,

$$\frac{\alpha_1}{\alpha_2}\left(\frac{M_d}{eM_f}\right)^{-(1+\rho)} = \frac{1 + i_d}{1 + i_f}. \qquad (19A\text{--}8)$$

Taking the logarithm of both sides, rearranging some terms and adding a disturbance term provides the functional form for the estimation,

$$\log\frac{M_d}{eM_f} = \frac{1}{1 + \rho}\log\left(\frac{\alpha_1}{\alpha_2}\right) + \frac{1}{1 + \rho}\log\left(\frac{1 + i_f}{1 + i_d}\right) + \mu. \quad (19A\text{--}9)$$

In this equation to be estimated the elasticity of substitution σ is equal to $1/1+\rho$.

CHAPTER 20

Fixed vs. Flexible Exchange Rates

How important is the exchange rate system? The discussion in Chapter 13 of the rise in world inflation following the breakdown of the Bretton Woods Agreements found that one system may have a much different effect on the world economy than another system. The question then is what type of criteria one should use in determining the optimal type of exchange rate system. A number of criteria have been put forth as the basis for choosing one system over another. In this chapter some of these traditional arguments are analyzed within the international framework that has been developed in this book.

While there are an infinite number of conceivable exchange rate systems, four basic types can be distinguished. One type is a system of *perfectly flexible exchange rates* where governments in no way interfere in foreign markets in order to affect the rates. Since governments do not intervene, there are no official settlements flows between countries, implying that the balance of payments between countries is always zero. The opposite extreme is where all governments agree in perpetuity to buy and sell currencies at fixed prices. This is the system of *truly fixed rates* that has been assumed to exist in most of the book. A third system is the *adjustable peg*. Under this system governments support exchange rates until reserve changes exceed some normatively determined limits, at which time the rates are reset. A final possibility is that nations can literally not transact with each other so that there is no exchange rate system at all.

While it is clear that none of these systems ever existed in its pure form, actual systems can be more or less characterized as different combinations of these four. A discussion of these extreme cases can orient the reader to the issues at hand and help him to determine the direction he would prefer to see the system move. The discussion that follows focuses most heavily on the differences between truly fixed and purely flexible rates.

THE NATURAL EQUILIBRATION ARGUMENT

One criterion for choosing an exchange rate system that has been repeatedly put forward by advocates of flexible rates is whether one system brings a country to balance-of-payments equilibrium more automatically than another system. The assertion is usually then made that flexible rates fulfill this criterion better. The argument is developed in terms of the trade balance. If a country is importing too much relative to its exports, the exchange rate will depreciate in value, making its exports more attractive and its imports more expensive, thus eventually eliminating the imbalance. This automatic adjustment process is described in Milton Friedman's classic article, "The Case for Flexible Exchange Rates."[1]

> A rise in the exchange rate produced by a tendency toward a surplus makes foreign goods cheaper in terms of domestic currency, even though their prices are unchanged in terms of their own currency, and domestic goods more expensive in terms of foreign currency, even though their prices are unchanged in terms of domestic currency. This tends to increase imports, reduce exports, and so offset the incipient surplus. Conversely, a decline in the exchange rate produced by a tendency toward a deficit makes imports more expensive to home consumers, and exports less expensive to foreigners, and so tends to offset the incipient deficit.

Two obvious comments can be made about this argument from previous discussions. First, this argument is again equating the trade balance and the balance of payments by ignoring the capital account. As has been repeatedly pointed out, in the modern world the capital account is not insignificant. In fact there is evidence that it responds to economic changes more quickly and by larger absolute amounts than does the trade balance. Since the balance of payments is the sum of the trade balance and capital account balance, the relevance of any argument about balance-of-payments adjustment that ignores the capital account must be questioned.

Second, as discussed in Chapter 17, the arguments about how reductions in the value of currency improve the trade balance are not theoretically complete, reflecting a partial equilibrium rather than a general equilibrium approach. Furthermore, the empirical study by Lee cited in Chapter 11 failed to find evidence of exchange rate changes producing sustained changes in countries' relative price levels (terms of trade), and the empirical study by Miles failed to find any evidence that depreciations of the exchange rate improve the trade balance. Thus, this argument for flexible rates can be dismissed on either its theoretical incompleteness or the lack of empirical verification.

INDEPENDENT MONETARY POLICY

A second criteria on which support for particular exchange rate policies are often decided is the degree to which one regime increases the ability of the government to implement its policies. This criteria is usually also used as an argument in favor of flexible rates because flexible rates traditionally are thought to provide monetary independence for a country. For example, Professor Friedman states:[2]

> In effect, flexible exchange rates are a means of combining interdependence among countries through trade with a maximum of internal monetary independence; they are a means of permitting each country to seek for monetary stability according to its own lights, without either imposing its mistakes on its neighbors or having their mistakes imposed on it.

Since the central bank does not intervene at all in the foreign exchange market, one avenue of monetary escape for the public is closed off. Individuals can no longer convert foreign currency into domestic currency at the central bank, so there will be no net flows of currency between countries. Currency will remain in or return to the country of origin, the balance of payments will always be zero, and all the effects of monetary policy will be felt within the domestic country.

There are two different sets of arguments that can be used to evaluate this assertion. First, it can be questioned whether the assertion that perfectly flexible exchange rates provide an independent monetary policy is even correct. As pointed out in Chapter 19, the argument that the actions of the monetary authorities will be felt only within the domestic country is dependent on one very important assumption—that the domestic currency is used as a transactions medium only in the country of origin. When domestic currency leaks out of a country in exchange for goods or bonds, foreigners do not hold onto any of it. Instead foreigners try to get their own currency in exchange, which leads to the domestic currency being sent back to the original country. In other words, a very important assumption of the independent monetary policy argument is that there is no currency substitution in money demand, that is, French hold only francs and Germans only Deutsche marks. But as was also discussed in that chapter, currency substitution is probably an important, observable phenomenon. The stronger the degree of currency substitution, the less valid the independent monetary policy argument.

Second, suppose that the assertion that flexible rates provide monetary independence is true. Suppose all dollars remain in the U.S. and all pounds in the United Kingdom. Essentially, what this situation implies is that there is no net trade in currency. If the Federal Reserve increases the U.S. money supply, by definition those dollars remain in or return to the U.S. Any dollars leaving the U.S. in exchange for, say, goods cannot remain abroad, because foreigners by assumption have no use for dollars and no central bank stands ready to convert dollars into foreign currency. There is no way to share some of the additional money with foreigners. Flexible rates provide a complete barrier to trading in money between countries, preventing money from moving from areas of excess supply to areas of excess demand.

The pure trade theory section of this book described what barriers to trade in the goods market can do. Recall that when a country in a barter model goes from an autarkic state to a trading state it experiences gains from trade which make it better off. By returning the country to autarky the gains from trade would again be lost. Thus there is a cost equal to the gains from trade by imposing barriers to the trading of goods. The same type of analysis that was applied to the commodity goods can be applied to the trading of the commodity money. Again there are gains from trade by allowing money to flow from areas of excess supply to areas of excess demand. And again, by imposing barriers to the flow of this commodity, these gains will be lost. So from this point of view, even if perfectly flexible rates did prevent the outflow of domestic currency, it is questionable whether barriers to the movement of money are any more desirable than barriers to the movement of goods.

Another way of describing the barrier to trade arguments is in terms of the arbitrage of markets and the ability of the world to achieve overall efficiency. In an efficient market with free trade in goods and bonds, equilibration of real rates of interest must occur. From a resource allocation standpoint, arbitrage of real interest rates improves overall world efficiency. In an integrated world, fixed exchange rates should bring about an equilibration of real rates of interest. If exchange rates truly will not change, then spot as well as forward rate contracts will be literally the same. Therefore, if commodity prices are arbitraged, the change in commodity prices in a given time period within all the fixed rate countries must be expected to be the same. This fact in turn implies that not only will real interest rates be arbitraged in such a market, but the nominal interest rates will be as well.

This theoretical result contrasts with two implications of a flexible exchange rate system. In an integrated world flexible rates will also lead to the equilibration of real rates of interest internationally. But with independent monetary policies and divergent rates of inflation, nominal rates of interest should reflect each country's specific rate of inflation. With the arbitrage of goods' prices, spot exchange rates should reflect current commodity price arbitrage and forward exchange rates should reflect the market's best guess of future commodity price arbitrage. Thus the difference between spot exchange rates and forward exchanges rates should reflect the market's best guess as to the difference in price changes between any two countries. This difference is precisely the difference between the two countries' nominal rates of interest.

Both systems arbitrage the real rate of interest among countries. But while the equilibration of real interest rates is a necessary condition for maximizing the efficiency of resource allocation, it is not a sufficient condition to guarantee the most efficient allocation of resources. The most efficient allocation of resources requires the equilibration of the costs of all factors of production. In particular, a system of flexible rates does not guarantee equilibration of the cost of holding real money balances. Fixed exchange rate systems do. The cost of holding real balances is of course equal to the nominal interest rate. Since flexible rates are being assumed here to permit divergent rates of inflation, they also permit divergent nominal rates of interest. The real costs of holding money can therefore differ.

The inefficiencies in resource allocation that the differing prices create can then be seen if money is considered a factor of production. The classic example is the errand boy of the local merchant. The local merchant has a choice of the production technique to use for making change for the customer in his store. One possibility is to hire an errand boy to run to the bank to get change every time a sale is made. This technique requires two real resources, the time of the errand boy and the shoe leather he wears out running to and from the bank. The alternative possibility is to hold real cash balances in the cash register. This technique requires only a resource which is almost costless for society to produce. Obviously the more efficient production technique from society's point of view is to use real balances since these require less real resources. The time and shoe leather of the errand boy are then released for other, more productive uses. But the local merchant makes his decision by weighing the cost to him of hiring the errand boy relative to the cost to him of holding real balances. As the domestic inflation and nominal interest rate rise, the cost of holding real balances rises relative to the cost of hiring errand boys. The merchant hires more boys and holds fewer balances, thus substituting real resources for cash balances and producing an inefficiency.

This inefficiency is compounded on the world level if the domestic inflation and nominal interest rates differ among countries. Those countries with high inflation rates conserve on the use of real balances and use more of the valuable resources instead. Countries with low inflation rates do just the opposite. It is easy to see that the world would operate more efficiently if money were instead allowed to move freely between these two sets of countries. In that case money would flow so as to even its cost among countries. Countries where the cost had been high would now use more real balances and less real resources, freeing these real resources for other, more productive uses.*

So inequality of real money balance costs tends to distort production decisions. A more efficient solution would be for each country to have the same percentage rate of inflation and thus allow money balances to be arbitraged efficiently between countries. Efficient arbitrage is the natural result if countries have a common currency or rigidly fixed exchange rates. Nominal rates of interest in all countries would be identical. Any deviation in interest rates would be immediately offset by arbitrage. Thus, with truly fixed rates not only are real rates of interest arbitraged between countries, but the real costs of holding money balances are also equilibrated. On the grounds of overall efficiency, therefore, fixed rates are to be preferred to flexible rates.

Notice, however, that if a competitive rate of interest were paid on all money including the reserves held by banks, this efficiency distortion between fixed and flexible rates would disappear.** In this case the rate of

---

*This argument is made, of course, given the average rate of world inflation. Inefficiencies are also reduced by lowering average world inflation. As we will argue, fixed rates can also have this desirable effect.

**With the introduction of money market funds and NOW accounts, it is easy to imagine competitive interest paid on deposits. It is also conceivable that the Federal Reserve could pay interest on bank reserves held at the Fed. However, there is still a problem of how to pay interest on currency. To the extent that money in wallets, cash registers, bank vaults, etc. do not receive interest, the inefficiencies remain.

interest paid on money would rise as the nominal interest rate rose, off-setting the higher cost of holding real balances. Thus inefficiencies in the use of real resources would occur neither within a country due to inflation nor between countries due to differing rates of inflation.

FREEDOM FOR ALL PRICES TO ADJUST

Another argument used to promote flexible rates is that under a flexible rate system all prices are allowed to adjust. This argument is often put forward by advocates of free markets. They argue that fixing the value of a currency resembles price controls by artificially holding a price constant. Such controls keep markets from adjusting completely, and only by permitting exchange rates to freely adjust does proper adjustment occur.

On one level this argument is just another version of the assertion that freely fluctuating exchange rates always cause the trade balance to equilibrate. The merits of this assertion have already been discussed at length and do not need further elaboration. On another level, it has been shown that complete elimination of excess demand and supply in the money market does not occur through price changes, and thus flexible rates do not increase the ability of the money market to adjust. Rather, price changes only permit the equilibration in the world money market or at most n-1 countries. The remaining adjustment must occur through quantity changes. This point can be illustrated within a two-country model. Suppose there is an excess supply of money in both Countries A and B. Under fixed rates the world price level rises until the excess demand in one country equals the excess supply in the other. Money then flows from the country with excess supply to the country with excess demand. Under flexible rates, one country devalues, raising its domestic price level and reducing the excess supply of money. Perhaps the devaluation completely eliminates this excess supply. But nothing has been done to alleviate the excess supply of money in the other country. While the flexible rate can eliminate the excess supply in one country, it cannot alleviate the excess supply in both. Prices alone cannot equilibrate markets. Again the optimal price (exchange rate) change would be one that causes the remaining excess supply of money in one country to equal a newly created excess demand in the other. Complete equilibrium would then be achieved by a flow of money from the area of excess supply to the area of excess demand. But flexible rates are assumed not to permit such flows of money, so complete equilibrium is not even possible under flexible rates. This results in differences in nominal interest rates, which previously have been shown to be a symptom that money markets are not completely adjusting.

SURVEILLANCE

Whether countries choose a system of permanently fixed or perfectly flexible rates, a set of rules must be followed by all central banks. In order to assure that these rules will be adhered to, either system must have surveillance mechanisms, judicial procedures and enforceable penalties. With regard to the judicial procedures or the enforcement of penalties, there is little reason to expect differences of one system over another. However, with regard to both rules and surveillance, it appears that flexible rates may require the more difficult task, providing numerous circuitous routes for government to influence exchange rates.

Under perfectly flexible exchange rates the government is supposed to refrain from any intervention in the currency market. But how do you assure that the government does not enter to influence the value of its currency? In other words, how will the surveillance be performed under flexible rates? It is not a small job. Surveillance is particularly difficult under flexible rates primarily because there are so many relatively obscure methods that governments can use to influence exchange rates. Even if it were possible to accurately monitor the direct actions of all central banks in the foreign currency market, there still would be no guarantee that the central banks were not covertly entering the market. It is not uncommon for central banks to have commercial or merchant banks do the intervention for them. And which markets are going to be monitored? Will central banks be barred from entering only the spot exchange market, or should they also be excluded from all forward markets as well? The forward markets can be instrumental in influencing the attractiveness of investing money temporarily in a country. But the greater the number of markets that central banks must be kept out of, the more surveillance that is necessary. Furthermore, the surveillance becomes more difficult because information on the sale and purchase of forward exchange contracts are not included in reserve data. Also, it is often difficult to ascertain whether the purchase of spot or forward currency can be justified because the government needs foreign commodities.

Governments can also directly and indirectly subsidize private parties to hold more or less in the way of foreign assets. This can be done with exchange guarantees or even with moral-suasion. Subsidies on exportable products and taxes on importable products, all forms of indirect taxes, can also have major effects on exchange markets. Thus under flexible rates, the rules of behavior and surveillance techniques must be complex and elaborate.

The complexity of the rules under flexible rates contrasts with the simplicity of the comparable rules under fixed rates. With fixed rates, each country has only one price rule which is simple to observe. All buyers of foreign exchange (or the intervention commodity) who wish to purchase from a given government must be allowed to purchase unlimited quantities at the floor price. Any failure to meet this obligation is literally a violation of the agreement. Beyond this, no additional rules or surveillance are required.

WELFARE

Another issue that has been raised in the fixed versus flexible exchange rate controversy is welfare, that is, do fixed or flexible rates make a country better off? More specifically, does a country reap large benefits from being able to run its own monetary policy? The argument postulates that under a regime of fixed exchange rates the rest of the world runs the domestic country's money supply. Under flexible exchange rates, however, each country retains autonomy over its monetary policy. Does the economy benefit from this autonomy?

If the rest of the world is expanding its money supply too rapidly and there are fixed exchange rates, then the domestic economy will have excessive inflation. However, under the flexible exchange rates, the excessive monetary policy abroad would not lead to domestic inflation. Instead it would cause only an appreciation of the domestic currency relative to foreign currencies. Thus, would not it be better if there were flexible exchange rates where, instead of having to import inflation, the appreciating exchange rate allows the domestic price level to remain stable?

The analogy holds also when foreigners have excessively contractionary monetary policy. Abroad, the contracting money supplies lead to deflation. Under fixed rates, the domestic country would share this deflation and any accompanying unemployment. However, with flexible rates the contracting money supply and falling price level would simply lead to a depreciating domestic currency and a stable price level.

While these arguments may be valid, there is still a problem. An implicit assumption in these arguments is that the domestic monetary authorities are following an optimal monetary policy. Certainly if the domestic authorities are so well behaved, the country does not want their behavior affected by less prudent foreign monetary authorities. But not every country will be facing excessive monetary policies from abroad. Obviously at least one country must be the country with the monetary authority that tends to be excessive at times. From that country's point of view, there is a preference to export money balances and thereby inflation to the rest of the world. This country clearly would prefer not to have monetary independence. It would rather have less inflation. Similarly, if a country's monetary authority tends to increase the money supply too slowly, the inhabitants of that country would also prefer not to have monetary independence. They would prefer to import money from abroad and reduce their rate of deflation. Thus, from a purely nationalistic standpoint, the decision between fixed and flexible rates depends upon whether the specific country is the one that perpetrates the nonoptimal monetary polcy or whether it is the one upon whom it is perpetrated. The independence issue is therefore a two-bladed sword. Whenever there is at least one country which feels its welfare will be increased by flexible rates, there is probably at least one country that feels its welfare will be increased by fixed rates. The welfare issue therefore cannot be used exclusively as an argument for flexible exchange rates.

MONETARY CONSTRAINTS

The question of fixed versus flexible rates also raises the issue of constraints on the monetary authorities. As pointed out in the discussion of the Bretton Woods Agreements, requiring all governments to maintain the value of their currency in terms of other currencies or some commodity puts a definite constraint on the quantity of money that they can print. If all countries are fixing their currencies to the dollar as under the Bretton Woods System, then they can increase the quantity of their domestic currency only at about the same rate that dollars are increasing. As was shown in Chapter 18, the system of constraints prevented the countries from increasing their money supplies by open market operations at a faster rate. And if a country repeatedly tried to maintain a faster rate of money creation, it would find its reserves diminishing and its ability to maintain the exchange rate declining. Similarly, as long as the U.S. adhered to the rules of the system, the rate at which dollars would increase was affected by the quantity of gold reserves, the demand for world liquidity, and how fast they were increasing. So the rate at which one country could increase its money supply was interrelated to the rate at which all other countries could increase theirs. And the rate at which they could all increase their money supplies was essentially linked to the rate of gold production. Such a system obviously provided a tremendous constraint over the inclinations of governments to print money.

But, as described in Chapter 13, once the various links of the system were broken, these constraints disappeared. The breaking of the price relationship between the reserve currency and gold meant that the reserve currency, and thus all countries, were free to increase the rate of money creation. Similarly, countries that decided to no longer fix the value of the domestic currency to the dollar were now free to increase their money supplies even faster than this new, higher average rate. A faster than average increase in the money supply would be simply reflected in a depreciating exchange rate.

Of course the removing of constraints also permitted countries to move their monetary policies in the opposite direction, that is, reduce the rate of money creation. Yet, given the explosion in the world money supply, apparently not enough countries chose this alternative. Why should governments be biased towards increasing the money supply at a faster rate? There are essentially two incentives—a political incentive and a financial one. The political incentive is political survival. Many politicians, especially those up for reelection, are familiar with the theory that increases in the money supply promote expenditure, increase GNP, and reduce unemployment. These changes in turn are assumed to make the citizen of the country look more kindly upon the incumbent government. While there may be some validity in this theory, unfortunately it is often implemented under the notion that if a little money creation is good, a lot must be even better.

The financial motive for printing money is the fact that while money is practically costless to produce, it can be used for purchasing goods and services. The resulting seigniorage represents revenue to the government. Revenue gathered in this way means less revenue must be gathered in another way, say, through direct taxation.

Given these incentives to print money, it can be seen why removal of the monetary constraints on governments tends to create inflation rather than deflation.

Even if countries recognize that increasing their money supplies exacerbates world inflation, there is still a distributional problem which creates an incentive to print more money. While increased supplies create more inflation, they also realize that they gain all the benefits from printing the money, while suffering only a fraction of the inflationary consequences. The rest of the world absorbs the remaining costs. As long as these marginal benefits outweigh the marginal costs, the money creation will continue.

But while this reasoning may be true for one country, it certainly cannot be true for all countries as a whole. One country assumes it can gain because it causes only a slight increase in world inflation. But if all countries try to implement such policies, the increase in world inflation must be large, and at best some countries must be frustrated in their attempt to gain. The effect of countries following their individual incentives is increased worldwide inflation.

ENDING WORLD INFLATION—THE CASE FOR A NEW PRICE RULE[3]

The most pressing argument for a return to fixed rates, then, is to reestablish a constraint on the quantity of money that governments create, and return the world to price stability. An alternative suggestion for slowing the rate of world money growth has been to encourage individual countries to reduce their rate of money creation. However, given the difficulty or even impossibility of effective worldwide curbs on money and credit, the most practical mechanism for achieving this goal is the establishment of a new international system of fixed exchange rates, that is, an international *"price rule."* By stabilizing the value of money in terms of goods, a price rule is also the most direct approach for pegging inflation to a rate near zero.

Such a "price rule" could take several possible forms. For example, the world could return to a Bretton Woods-like agreement where n-1 countries peg their currencies to the nth currency. The nth country could then maintain a stable price level by pegging its currency to a commodity like gold, or to a basket of commodities via a price index. Since, if the system is successful the n-1 countries experience the same inflation as the nth country, confidence in the system would, of course, be maximized if the nth country has a demonstrably favorable inflation record. Tying the other European currencies, for instance, to the German post-War penchant for lower inflation seems to have been one of the original motivating forces behind the creation of the European Monetary System in 1979.

Given the history of the Bretton Woods System, countries may be reluctant to return to another two-tier system. The same effects, however, could be achieved by tying all n currencies of the world directly to an outside commodity. Such a system simply involves each country agreeing to adopt a "price rule." Each country is responsible for stabilizing the price of a commodity such as gold, or a basket of internationally traded goods, in terms of its currency.

The return to an international system of price rules does have its opponents. There are those, for example, who are afraid that a gold-based system would benefit such large holders of gold as the French, Russians and South Africans. One can argue, however, that just the opposite effect is likely to occur. A system which returned stability to paper money would diminish the demand for (and the price of) gold relative to currency. Such a system would therefore benefit large holders of paper money at the expense of large holders of gold.

Given the current prejudices against a commodity-based system, such an international agreement may prove difficult to conclude. Yet, even in the absence of an international agreement, individual countries can establish their own "price rules" to eradicate inflation in their own domestic currency. The United States, for example, is capable of taking sufficient unilateral steps to eradicate dollar inflation. Regardless of the policies of other governments, the Federal Reserve could simply adopt a dollar "price rule." The Fed would simply take actions necessary to stabilize the value of the dollar in terms of one or more commodities.

For instance, dollar prices of both gold and oil increased about tenfold between 1965 and the Soviet-Afghan crisis of December 1979. In other words, while the dollar has purchased progressively less of either commodity, over this period an ounce of gold has maintained its power to purchase about twenty barrels of Saudi light crude oil. As Figure 20-1 shows, the rises in the dollar price of oil are closely related to the rises in the dollar price of gold. If the Fed had retained the dollar/gold "price rule" throughout this period, there would have been no need for dollar oil prices to rise.

As with the international "price rule," the Fed would institute its dollar "price rule" by stabilizing the value of the dollar in terms of an external standard. This standard could be a single commodity or a basket of commodities (a price index). As was observed in gold markets in 1979, following the disturbances in the Middle East, the price of a single commodity can deviate significantly from other commodities. On theoretical grounds, then, use of an index may be preferable since it governs dollar prices across a broader spectrum of goods. A potential drawback to the use of an index, however, is the fact that it is a human construct. There is a possibility of pressure to manipulate such an index for political purposes by changing its construction. Consider, for example, the recent political controversies in the U.S. surrounding the consumer price index to which government spending programs are indexed.

Regardless of precisely which external standard is chosen, there are two basic rules of Fed behavior under the price rule. First, if the dollar price of the standard starts to rise (the dollar falls in value), the Fed must reduce the quantity of dollars through open market sales of bonds, foreign exchange, gold, or other commodities. Second, if the dollar price

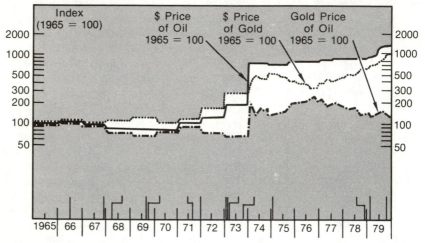

Figure 20–1   Gold, Oil, and the Dollar

starts to fall (the dollar rises in value), the Fed must increase the quantity of dollars through open market purchases of bonds, foreign exchange, gold, or other commodities. The Fed is charged with keeping the value or price of the dollar stable in terms of the external standard. The body politic knows that the Fed is maintaining its commitment as long as the dollar price of the external standard, or the price index, remains stable.

Given the decision to adopt a "price rule," the precise choice of the intervention asset (the item for which dollars are exchanged) can also be important. An open market sale of bonds or gold not only reduces the quantity of dollars, but also the total world quantity of paper money. Not only dollar inflation, but world inflation, falls. On the other hand, a foreign exchange intervention merely exchanges foreign currency for dollars. Only the composition of the world's money changes. While dollar inflation falls, foreign currency inflation rises, leaving average world inflation unaltered.

HOW A "PRICE RULE" DIFFERS FROM A "QUANTITY RULE"

While the "price rule" described in the previous section should be expected to slow a country's inflation, it is not the only kind of rule advanced by economists to deal with rising prices. An alternative policy is a "money supply" or *"quantity"* rule. This policy is often associated with monetarist economists such as Milton Friedman, and in October 1979 it became part (at least in rhetoric) of the Federal Reserve's working policy. The basis of the "quantity rule" is for the monetary authorities to stabilize the growth rate of the domestic money supply. So, for example, in the United States, a "quantity rule" would be for the Fed to keep an appropriately chosen definition of the money supply growing at an even, say, five percent rate. The Fed would forgo any possibilities of expanding the money supply at faster or slower rates as the level of economic activity in the U.S. fluctuates. The Fed's only target is a stable growth of money aggregates. The presumption, then, is that if the Fed can keep the growth of the money supply at a sufficiently slow rate, inflation will also be low.

If all countries of the world, or the U.S. by itself, were to adopt such "quantity rules," this action would certainly be a step in the direction of reducing the growth of the world money supply and world inflation. But while adoption of a quantity rule in, say, the United States is a step towards restraining the supply of dollars, it is still inferior to a "price rule" for several reasons.

First, with the growth of Eurodollars, money market funds, and other dollar substitutes, conventional money supply measures represent only a fraction of dollar money holdings, and fail to describe the behavior of the total quantity of dollars. Even the Fed admitted the shortcomings of traditional money measures when it unveiled, in February 1980, new aggregates which include some of the substitutes for conventionally defined money.

Second, even if traditional M1 or M2, or one of the newer measures just introduced by the Fed, could be used as a guide to the total money supply, estimating these figures is problematical. Figures must be collected from many banks, and pass through several hands. The data must be corrected for seasonality and trading day variations. The possibility for substantial measurement errors is great, as money markets found in the fall of 1979 when a mistake by one New York bank caused the weekly money supply figures to be misquoted by $3.5 billion.

Third, and most importantly, the supply of dollars, *per se*, is not the critical factor. A successful quantity rule must be continually adapted to fluctuations in the *demand* for dollars. And, in practice, to the extent these fluctuations can be measured at all, they are rarely recognizable in advance. For example, the explosive increase in the supply of Swiss francs in 1978 was accompanied by low Swiss inflation, because the total world demand for Swiss francs was growing proportionately. Like Swiss franc inflation, dollar inflation is determined by the difference in the world supply relative to the world demand for dollars. Deceleration of inflation requires, then, an ability to cause world dollar demand to keep pace more closely than it has with world dollar supply.

In an unchanging world where all information is freely available, there of course would be a "quantity rule" which would correspond to a given "price rule." With complete information, the Fed would know precisely which path of money growth would lead, say, to stable prices. But as the world begins to change over time, as the proper definition of money becomes less clear, and as money demand becomes more difficult to estimate, finding the "quantity rule" which corresponds to stable prices becomes more and more complicated.

In contrast, a "price rule" is straightforward and uncomplicated. All relevant information concerning the Fed's policy actions is available directly and continuously from the marketplace. The Fed knows precisely what actions are necessary to stabilize prices. The Fed simply continues to intervene in private markets until any deviations from the fixed dollar price of the external standard is eliminated. The private sector knows if the Fed is maintaining its commitment. The private sector simply watches the dollar price of the external standard on the ticker. The probability of error is greatly reduced.

SUMMARY

This chapter critically examines some of the most popular arguments for floating rates. Some of these arguments are that floating rates cause the trade balance to naturally equilibrate, that monetary independence is assured and desirable, and that flexible rates allow all prices to adjust and all markets to clear. Flexible rates are also contrasted with fixed rates in terms of ease of surveillance, increasing country welfare, and constraining the world's monetary authorities to hold down inflation. The chapter concludes with a description of why a new international *"price rule"* is needed to reduce or eliminate world inflation.

REFERENCES

FRIEDMAN, MILTON, "The Case for Flexible Exchange Rates," *Essays in Positive Economics.* Chicago: University of Chicago Press, 1953; reprinted in *Readings in International Economics,* R. Caves and H. G. Johnson, eds. Homewood, Ill.: Irwin, 1968.

JOHNSON, HARRY G., "The Case for Flexible Exchange Rates, 1969," *International Trade and Finance: Readings,* R. E. Baldwin and J. D. Richardson, eds., Boston: Little, Brown, 1974.

LAFFER, ARTHUR B., "Balance of Payments and Exchange Rate Systems," *Financial Analysts Journal* (July–August 1974): 26–32, 76–79.

—— "Two Arguments for Fixed Rates," *The Economics of Common Currencies,* H. G. Johnson and A. Swoboda, eds. London: George Allen and Unwin, 1973.

MILES, MARC A., "Currency Substitution, Flexible Exchange Rates, and Monetary Independence," 68 *American Economic Review,* No. 3 (June 1978): 428–36.

MUNDELL, ROBERT A., "Uncommon Arguments for a Common Currency," *The Economics of Common Currencies,* H. G. Johnson and A. Swoboda, eds. London: George Allen and Unwin, 1973.

SOHMEN, EGON, *Flexible Exchange Rates: Theory and Controversy,* Chicago: University of Chicago Press, 1969.

NOTES

1. Milton Friedman, "The Case for Flexible Exchange Rates," in his *Essays in Positive Economics*, Chicago: University of Chicago Press 1953; reprinted in R. Caves and H. G. Johnson, *Readings in International Economics*, Homewood, Ill.: Irwin 1968.

2. Milton Friedman, "The Case for Flexible Exchange Rates," *op. cit.*, p. 430.

3. Adapted from Marc A. Miles, "One Way to Halt Inflation: A 'Price Rule' For Monetary Policy," H. C. Wainwright & Co., *Economic and Investment Observations*, May 5, 1980.

CHAPTER 21

Some Recent Developments in the International Economy

The true measure of any theory is how well it allows us to understand and anticipate what is occurring in the world. A coherent new theory may provide us with generous amounts of mental satisfaction, but unless it also provides new insights into how the world "works," its value in the long run is not very great. The purpose of reading a book like this in a course in economics is to create a useful framework for dealing with the real problems of the world. Some real world problems occur over and over, and most new theories are carefully tailored to include explanations of the pressing problems of the past. However, other real world problems cannot be so easily anticipated because they do not arise frequently, or perhaps have not even yet occurred. When these events happen, theorists scramble to show that although their models may not have correctly anticipated the actual events, what has occurred is consistent with their basic theory. Sometimes the theorists are successful, and sometimes they are simply forced to face the limitations of their theory. Recent examples of events which have caused such theoretic scrambling include the sudden burst of inflation in the spring of 1973, and the so-called stagflation of the mid-1970s.

A useful theory must therefore be sufficiently general not only to explain the past, but also to anticipate and understand the future. Perhaps the theory does not explain one hundred percent of future events, but it should certainly provide a first approximation to the mechanics of the world economy, providing correct estimates of both the direction and general magnitude of the changes in economic variables.

This criterion is especially important for the theory of integrated world markets presented in this book. Much of the theory was developed in terms of a fixed exchange rate framework at a time when the world's economy was very tranquil. Yet the world has not been on a true fixed exchange rate system since at least 1971, and the world's economy in the 1970s has been far from tranquil. How useful has the theory of the integrated world been over this period?

Obviously no theory has a perfect record. Yet our theory has continued to be extremely useful for understanding and anticipating the effects of government actions. To illustrate how one would use the model of the integrated world to interpret the effects of government policies, let us assume that by June 30, 1977 you have read the previous chapters of the book. You now prepare to tackle world problems as an investor, corporate executive, or government official. Over the next two years you encounter government reversals on exchange rate policy, tremendous depreciations of the dollar, a dramatic attempt by the U.S. President to stop the dollar's slide, and the establishment of a European currency area. What information can you glean from these events? How would you apply the theory you have just read? What are the expected effects of these actions? What will these events do to inflation and GNP in the U.S. and the rest of the world? What would be your general estimates at each step? Would these estimates be in the correct direction and of the proper magnitude? Attempting to answer these questions, we now examine some the these major events within the integrated world framework. ·

THE DOLLAR'S DOWNWARD SLIDE[1]

We begin in the summer of 1977. The United States is faced with sudden massive trade deficits (a record $24 billion at an annual rate in the first half of 1977), and high unemployment (7.1 percent in June 1977). Inflation, however, is low by recent standards, averaging only 5 percent (annual rate) in the second quarter of 1977. Congress, particularly the chairman of the House Banking Committee, is busy criticizing the Treasury Department's apparent "complacent" position on the trade deficit matter. The Commerce Department, too, expresses its concern over the trade deficit. Pressure mounts for the Carter Administration to do something about the deficit. In this atmosphere, Treasury Secretary Blumenthal unveils his plan to "talk down" the dollar.

The Treasury Secretary's plan is quite simple. The dollar will be managed downward as a sure way to stimulate the economy. After all, does not a falling exchange rate increase American competitiveness by making American exports cheaper to foreigners and American imports more expensive? Would not the increased net demand for American goods simultaneously increase domestic output and employment? What alternative policy prescription could deal better with America's ills?

Some officials, such as Federal Reserve Chairman Arthur Burns, worry publicly that the downward movement of the dollar will add to U.S. inflation. However, he and others view the weakening currency as causing higher inflation simply by virtue of raising import and export prices. With external trade only about 10 percent of U.S. economic activity, each percentage of depreciation is expected, at most, to lead to only one-tenth of 1 percent of inflation.

So in the summer of 1977 the dollar was allowed to begin a depreciation that accelerated in the fall of 1977 and continued into 1979. The primary aim of the decline was to eliminate the trade deficit. Yet what information would the theory of integrated markets have provided about the effects on the economy of the Treasury Secretary's program?

First of all, the theory of the trade balance presented in Chapter 14 would have provided insight into why the deficit was suddenly so large. Recall from that chapter that changes in the ratio of the trade balance to income are related negatively to changes in the income growth differential between the domestic country and the rest of the world. Real income growth in the U.S. had increased sharply in the first half of 1977. Whereas output had grown at only a 2.5 percent annual rate in the last six months of 1976, output increased at a 6.4 percent rate in the first six months of 1977. In contrast, income growth abroad was relatively unchanged between the two periods. Hence, the relative increase in U.S. growth should have been expected to widen the trade deficit. Alternatively we could have said that the trade deficit was a sign of a relatively healthy economy, not a cause for alarm.

Second, the theory of currency depreciation in an integrated world presented in Chapter 17 would have warned that the depreciating dollar would not produce the results for which the Treasury Secretary had hoped. The trade balance would not be expected to improve substantially. The decline in the dollar, through added dollar inflation, would not change the "competitiveness" of the U.S., and hence would not improve the net demand for U.S. goods. Instead, the primary effect of the dollar depreciation would simply be the added inflation over and above that of the rest of the world. And the added inflation would not be one-tenth of the decline in the dollar. Rather the added inflation should match the depreciation percentage point for percentage point.

So analyzing the U.S. economy in the summer of 1977 from the integrated markets perspective, one would have been primarily warning one's clients or rearranging one's portfolio in anticipation of higher U.S. inflation. With hindsight we can say that such a strategy would have paid off. Since the dollar began to depreciate in 1977, U.S. inflation has exceeded inflation elsewhere in the world. Comparing the behavior of prices (WPI) in the U.S. to those in Germany (Figure 21–1), Japan (Figure 21–2), and Switzerland (Figure 21–3) shows a sudden divergence of inflation rates after the commencement of dollar depreciation. Prior to August 1977, inflation rates in the four countries were very similar. Wholesale prices in the U.S. actually declined between July and August. But after August, U.S. prices began to climb faster and faster, while foreign prices continued to fall. In the five remaining months of 1977, prices fell by 0.1 percent in Germany, 1.2 percent in Japan, and 1.1 percent in Switzerland, while prices rose by 1.8 percent in the U.S. As the dollar continued to fall sharply relative to these foreign currencies, the rate of U.S. inflation continued to increase sharply relative to foreign inflation. By April 1979 the dollar had depreciated by 20 percent against the Deutsche mark, 18.7 percent against the Japanese yen, and 33 percent against the Swiss franc. Over the same period the U.S. experienced about 12 percent more inflation than Germany, 16 percent more than Japan, and about 17 per-

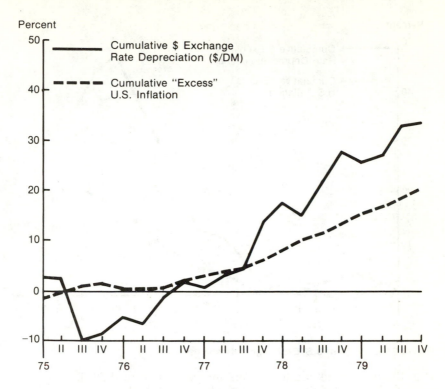

Figure 21–1   Germany–U.S. Exchange Rate and Inflation

cent more than Switzerland. And over the first four months of 1979, inflation continued at a higher annualized rate in the U.S. (16.4 percent) than
in Germany (8.4 percent), Japan (12 percent), or Switzerland (9.9 percent).
     While the additional U.S. inflation had not completely matched the
dollar depreciation percentage point for percentage point, the additional
inflation was significantly above the approximately ten-to-one relationship suggested by those employing a more conventional framework. The
relationship between dollar depreciation and additional U.S. inflation
ranges from about one-half the dollar-Swiss franc depreciation to over 85
percent of the dollar-yen depreciation. Furthermore, within the integrated markets framework, the fact that the cumulative difference in inflation rates did not yet reach the level of cumulative depreciation of the
dollar for these countries, indicated the likelihood of even more months
of relatively high inflation in the U.S.
     Not surprisingly, the trade balance has also behaved as the integrated
markets theory would predict. The substantial depreciation of the dollar
over this period failed to produce either a substantial or sustained improvement in the net exports of U.S. goods. The trade deficit in the third
quarter of 1977, when the dollar began its long decline, was about $25.8
billion at an annual rate. The deficit continued to expand, not improve,

Percent

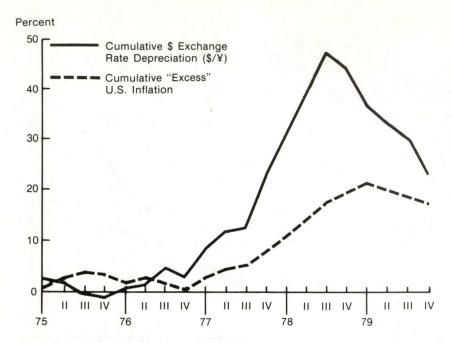

Figure 21-2 Japan–U.S. Exchange Rate and Inflation

over the next three quarters. Even one year later, in the third quarter of 1978, the trade deficit was a practically unchanged annual rate of $25.1 billion. The enormous trade deficit of $26 billion in 1977 actually deteriorated to $28 billion in 1978. And even two years later, despite the interruption of Iranian oil flows, the deficit in 1979 was still close to $25 billion ($24.7).

Currency depreciation, then, does not seem to stimulate the net demand for a country's goods. Certainly in the case of the U.S., net demand was not stimulated. Real GNP growth dropped to 4.4 percent in 1978 from 5.3 percent in 1977, and in 1979 growth declined further to only 2.3 percent. The decline in real GNP growth can in part be attributed to the additional inflation accompanying depreciation. On the one hand, inflation raises the cost of doing business. The costs of borrowing money, of holding inventories, of covering transactions in foreign exchange, of hiring labor, and of investing in capital all rise as the rate of inflation rises. On the other hand, inflation tends to reduce the net rewards from doing business. Even if the dollar rewards to firms and individuals rise sufficiently to maintain the real purchasing power of their gross incomes, net rewards fall. Higher dollar incomes push more firms' and individuals' incomes into higher progressive marginal tax brackets. After-tax real incomes fall.

The reduction in after-tax real incomes in turn creates forces which reduce the level of economic activity. On the demand side, smaller real net incomes mean smaller net demands. On the supply side, higher mar-

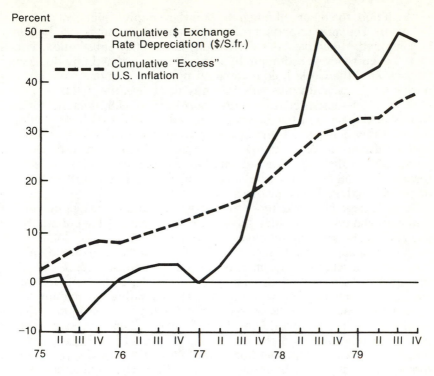

Figure 21–3 Switzerland–U.S. Exchange Rate and Inflation

ginal tax rates, or lower net returns, reduce the incentives for factors of production to supply their services to the productive market. Hence, combining the contractionary effects of reduced net returns with the retarding effects of higher business costs leads to a very important conclusion: investors would be wise to move their investments out of companies whose business or assets are primarily in countries with depreciating currencies, and into businesses centered primarily in stable or appreciating currency countries.

DETERMINING THE DOLLAR'S VALUE[2]

Over this period in which value of the dollar was declining, considerable effort was exerted in both the private and government sectors to ascertain precisely the important factors for determining the behavior of the dollar's market price. Businesses are interested in anticipating changes in the dollar's value in order to protect their foreign currency investments against capital losses. Governments are interested in the determinants of the exchange rate in order to influence their currency's value. Hence a theory which can provide accurate information about the direction and magnitude of exchange rate changes is very valuable.

What does the theory of integrated markets imply about exchange rate behavior? The most important information about exchange rate behavior is contained in Chapter 19's discussion of currency substitution. Recall that the currency substitution hypothesis asserts that individuals and firms around the world hold diversified portfolios of money, not just domestic currency. With diversified money portfolios, the dollar/mark exchange rate is determined by more than just the U.S. demand for and supply of dollars, and the German demand for and supply of Deutsche marks. Individuals and firms in many countries now hold both dollars and Deutsche marks. A change in the cost or risk of holding dollars, which affects the U.S. demand for dollars, should therefore affect the foreign demand as well. Portfolios around the world readjust as the cost or risk of holding dollars changes.

In an integrated world, those interested in dollar exchange rate determination should be watching the total world demand for dollars. More specifically, in order to anticipate the behavior of, say, the dollar/mark exchange rate, one should be estimating the *total world demand* for dollars and Deutsche marks compared to the *total world supplies* of these currencies. As described in Chapter 19, the world demand for either money is affected by the cost and/or risk of holding that money. Anything which raises the cost or risk of holding a particular money causes portfolios around the world to diversify away from it, and into other monies or other assets. A rise in the cost or risk of holding a particular money, *certeris paribus*, therefore causes a world excess supply of that money and a depreciation of the currency. Similarly, any increase in the world supply of a money (including, say, Eurocurrency holdings) relative to demand, should be associated with a depreciation of that money.

An important implication of this analysis, then, is that the proper framework for analyzing exchange rate behavior is the entire world. In contrast, the currently popular method among international theorists for analyzing the behavior of, say, the dollar/mark exchange rate, is simply to compare changes in the conventional demand and supply of dollars in the U.S., to changes in the conventional demand and supply of Deutsche marks in Germany. But the demand for dollars in the U.S. is only part of the total world demand for dollars. While the demand for dollars is falling in the U.S., an offsetting increase in demand could be occurring elsewhere in the world as foreign money portfolios expand. Similarly, changes in the German Deutsche mark demand may not accurately reflect changes in the total world demand for Deutsche marks. Reliance on simple monetary models for anticipating exchange rate behavior may therefore lead to substantial forecast errors due to a misspecified framework.

One type of error these conventional monetary models are likely to produce is an underestimation of exchange rate changes. By concentrating primarily on the percentage change in the (domestic) money demands and supplies, the conventional models probably provide less sensitive estimates of change than the global portfolio demand approach. The percentage change is equivalent to an average rate of change, and corresponds roughly to measuring the average expected return or cost of holding a currency. In an efficient market, a 10 percent average increase in the supply of dollars, *ceteris paribus,* leads to anticipations of roughly 10 percent dollar inflation and fewer dollars being held. The dollar depreciates. On the other hand, a 10 percent rise in dollar demand lowers expectations of inflation, reducing the expected cost of holding dollars. More dollars are demanded, and the dollar appreciates.

But, as pointed out in Chapter 19, a portfolio is affected not only by expected returns, but also by risk or uncertainty. For example, an average rate of increase of 10 percent in the world supply of dollars can be perceived by the market and reflected in interest rate differentials and forward exchange rate premiums. However, if the 10 percent increase is the average of large and erratic fluctuations in the amplitude of the rate of dollar increase, an increased risk cost has been created which is harder to incorporate into market compensation. Over time the increase averages 10 percent, but at any time, uncertainty exists as to whether the dollar increase will be 1 percent, 5 percent, or 20 percent. The actions of the Fed are unpredictable! Hence, an increased frequency or magnitude of fluctuations in the quantity of dollars, by raising dollar risk, should reduce the relative demand for dollars everywhere. Money portfolios throughout the world now will diversify towards fewer dollars and greater quantities of more stable currencies.

Thus, any action of the U.S. monetary authorities which increases the uncertainty about the future value of the dollar will reduce the demand for dollars not only in the U.S., but in other countries as well. The fall in total dollar demand, and hence the depreciation of the dollar, should be larger than anticipated from considering only the average change in money supplies and demands. Reliance on the simple monetary model may lead to substantial errors.

Evidence of precisely this type of steeper than expected decline in the dollar is presented in Figures 21–4 and 21–5. For example, Figure 21–4 presents the difference between the actual seasonally adjusted percentage change in the dollar/mark exchange rate, and the change predicted by a simple monetary model. The simple monetary model compares the difference between the quarterly seasonally adjusted rates of growth of money and income in Germany and the United States. This approach predicts that if money is growing faster relative to income in the U.S. than in Germany, the dollar exchange rate (DM/$) will depreciate, and vice versa. Similar reasoning holds in Figure 21–5 for the dollar/Swiss franc exchange rate, and the rates of growth of money and income in the U.S. and Switzerland.

The shaded areas of the figures represent estimated periods of monetary uncertainty. These periods are defined as the quarters with the largest (upper quartile) fluctuations (standard deviations) of the weekly percentage change in the seasonally adjusted U.S. monetary base. Notice that for Germany (Figure 21–4), in six of the eight shaded quarters the actual depreciation (appreciation) of the dollar is greater (less) than anticipated. In four of the six cases, the discrepancy between the actual and

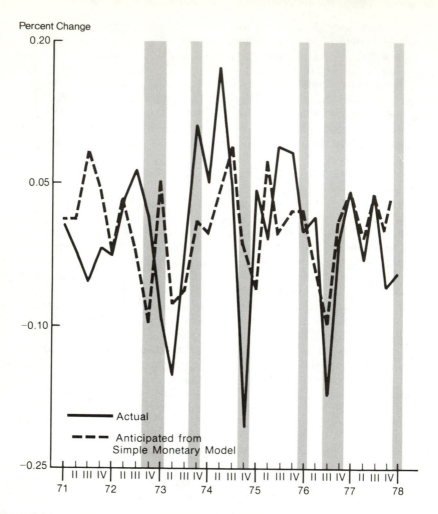

Figure 21–4   Actual and Anticipated Changes in DM/$

anticipated change is quite large. Similarly for Switzerland (Figure 21–5), in five of the eight shaded areas the actual depreciation exceeds the anticipated depreciation. In four of the five cases the negative discrepancy is again quite large.

For Germany, the periods corresponding to the four largest underestimates of depreciation after 1971 are all periods of exceptionally erratic growth rates in the dollar monetary base. For Switzerland, two of the three exceptionally large underestimates of dollar depreciation after 1971 are in similar periods of U.S. monetary uncertainty. The only other large negative errors missed in both figures occurred in the third quarter of 1971. The middle of that third quarter was August 15, when President Nixon closed the gold window. That unilateral action increased the risk of holding dollars, and therefore, according to the currency substitution

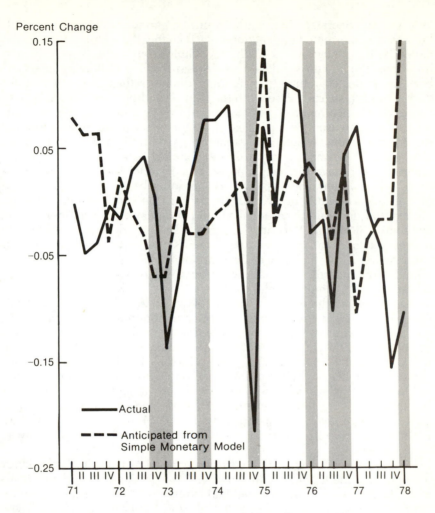

Figure 21–5   Actual and Anticipated Changes in S.fr./$

hypothesis, should be expected to produce the large negative errors in the two figures. That increase in dollar risk, however, would not be expected to be reflected in the fluctuations of the quarter's monetary base, and hence it would not be captured by the measure of monetary policy risk used in this analysis.

In sum, large or erratic changes in the monetary base or new monetary policy initiatives provide an additional signal that a readjustment of currency portfolios may be underway. Actions that increase the risk of a currency are a sign that holders of that currency abroad as well as at home will be substituting away from that currency, and hence that the downward swing of that currency will be greater than anticipated from conventional models.

What implications do these conclusions have for the post-summer

1977 period? Secretary Blumenthal's public announcement that the dollar was to be permitted to float downward changed the cost and risk associated with holding dollars. With the Administration no longer trying to mimimize the downward drift of the dollar through stabilizing intervention, the expected return from holding dollars rather than other major currencies fell sharply. Also, with the diminished presence of the U.S. in foreign exchange markets, the chance of erratic movements in the dollar's value increased. Both of these effects have the same implications for the dollar's behavior. Both imply that money portfolio holders around the world would be shifting towards fewer dollar balances and more balances in other, now relatively more stable, currencies. This portfolio shift in turn has two implications. First, as the dollar becomes a smaller share of portfolios around the world, the fall in the dollar is exacerbated. Hence, the decline in the dollar should be greater than anticipated by conventional models. Second, the smaller share of dollars in worldwide money portfolios means the dollar's role as an international currency of exchange will be diminished. Transactions which previously were denominated primarily in dollars will now be denominated in currencies whose values are more stable.

The history of the dollar is remarkably close to this scenario. The dollar began to fall in the summer of 1977 and continued to fall as long as the U.S. government failed to act to reduce the risk of the dollar. Figures 21–4 and 21–5 show that not only did the dollar decline, but through the first quarter of 1978, the decline was generally much steeper than conventional monetary exchange rate models could explain. Furthermore, on the two occasions the U.S. government did attempt to reduce the dollar uncertainty, April and November 1978 (see the next sections), the foreign exchange market responded with record rallies for the dollar. Portfolios apparently are capable of shifting towards, as well as away from, dollars.

This period of dollar decline was also marked by a diminished role for the once dominant dollar in international transactions. With the reliability of the dollar reduced, international transactors turned increasingly towards more stable currencies, primarily the Deutsche mark and Swiss franc. Rather than one international medium of exchange, there were now two or three. Not surprisingly, the values of these currencies with new international roles rose far in excess of what conventional theory would suggest, as money holders clamored to make these currencies share larger fractions of their money portfolios.

THE BUCK STOPS HERE[3]

The fall of the dollar reached crisis proportions in October 1978. For example, in that month alone the dollar fell 11 percent against the Deutsche mark and over 7 percent against the Japanese yen. Pressure mounted to do something to reverse the steady decline in the dollar for almost a year and a half.

On November 1, President Carter announced his plan for rescuing the dollar. The plan included a one percentage point rise in the Federal Reserve discount rate, a rise in reserve requirements on large CDs from 2 to 4 percent, the arrangement of $15 billion in swap lines with foreign central banks and $3 billion in tranche* at the IMF, the issuing of $10 billion in foreign currency-denominated treasury bills, increasing the monthly auction of gold to $300 million per month, and the sale of $2 billion in Special Drawing Rights (SDRs). What effect, within the integrated market framework, would these actions be expected to have on the dollar money supply, the world money supply, U.S. inflation, world inflation, and the dollar's value?

Two of the points of the plan, the rise in the discount rate and the increased reserve requirements on CDs, would be expected to have very little effect. For example, the one percentage point increase in the discount rate, while dramatic in historical perspective, only increased the cost of a relatively unimportant source of reserves to member banks of the Federal Reserve System. Furthermore, the discount rate in recent years has tended to trail the behavior of other interest rates. So rather than indicating a future rise in other interest rates, the change in the discount rate represented an attempt to adjust this administered rate to market realities.

Similarly, the increased reserve requirement on large CDs would not be expected to greatly affect the total supply of dollars. If the United States were completely isolated from the rest of the world, a rise in the reserve requirement might reduce the potential dollar supply. But in an integrated world, the U.S. money market is not isolated from the money markets elsewhere. In particular, as shown in Chapter 13, the U.S. money market is closely intertwined with the Eurodollar market, providing one route for circumventing such regulations by the Federal Reserve. For instance, doubling the reserve requirement on large CDs from 2 to 4 percent does mean that, for a given amount of CDs booked in the United States, fewer excess reserves are available, and hence fewer loans can be made by U.S. banks. But recall from Chapter 13 that there are no such reserve requirements on CDs booked in the Eurodollar market.

The Eurobanks are then able to attract funds for a lower interest expense (after accounting for the lost interest of required reserves in U.S. banks), even as they pay depositors a higher rate of interest. Hence, when the reserve requirement distortion in the U.S. money market is raised, banks have an incentive to simply shift the booking of CDs from the U.S. to the Eurodollar market. The reserves obtained by the Euro-branches can then be returned to the head office in exchange for dollar deposits in New York. The total quantity of dollar CDs and reserves available for making loans need not change. Only the location of book-

---

*Members of the IMF may borrow foreign currencies or SDRs through credit tranche drawings under specified conditions. Most credit tranche drawings are made under stand-by agreement.

ings changes. Therefore the total world supply of dollars is likely to be comparatively unchanged by this action of the Federal Reserve.

On the other hand, the other points of the plan are likely to have an effect on the total quantity of dollars or other currencies. For example, the decision to issue $10 billion of Treasury securities, denominated in foreign currencies, in foreign markets is equivalent to a massive, reverse U.S. open market operation. Such an action is virtually the equivalent of a $10 billion incremental sale of dollar-denominated Treasury bills in domestic money markets. In the former case, foreign currency is first obtained from one group of participants in the international money markets in exchange for a foreign currency-denominated debt instrument of the U.S. government. The foreign currency is then transferred through foreign exchange intervention to another group of participants in the money markets in exchange for dollars. In the latter case, the Treasury security is sold directly to holders of dollars. Both actions reduce the net supply of dollars.

To the extent that there is a net reduction in the quantity of dollars in circulation, the world money supply is reduced. As discussed in Chapter 13, slower growth in the world money supply should imply slower world inflation. Furthermore, since the quantity of dollars relative to other currencies is reduced, the dollar is likely to strengthen relative to other currencies on the foreign exchange market. Recall from Chapter 17 that an appreciating currency country is expected to have less inflation than other countries. Such an open market sale by the Treasury is therefore likely to mean not only lower levels of world inflation, but an even larger reduction in U.S. inflation. In addition, the decision to denominate Treasury debt in foreign currencies introduces an incentive for the Treasury to maintain or increase the dollar's value. Any depreciation of the dollar would increase the real value of this liability on the Treasury's balance sheet.

The effect of the decision to increase the rate of gold sales is similar in some aspects to the Treasury's sale of debt on the open market. Both actions tend to reduce the net quantity of dollars in circulation. Hence both actions tend to reduce average world inflation, and reduce dollar inflation even more. But, in addition, the gold sales increase the supply of gold in private hands, reducing the value of foreign reserves held by governments. Smaller foreign reserves imply decreased ability for governments to maintain existing money supplies, and thus reinforce the trend towards lower world inflation.

So the sale of bonds and gold by the Treasury has, in the integrated market framework, straightforward implications about the level of world inflation and relative inflation in the U.S. The remaining two parts of the plan, however, cloud the net effect of the program. For example, the sale of $2 billion in Special Drawing Rights (SDRs) by the Treasury does not have the impact of selling gold. Special Drawing Rights can only be held by central banks. And foreign central banks ordinarily would pay for the SDRs with newly created money. Hence, the sale of SDRs by itself actually increases world reserves. Even if the Treasury then used the full proceeds of the sale to extinguish dollars in the world money market, the world money supply and average world inflation rate would be unchanged. Only the composition of the world money supply would change to fewer dollars and more foreign currency. So, to the extent that U.S. inflation is lowered, it is accomplished through higher foreign inflation.

Similarly, the major effect of using the new swap lines or the tranche line at the IMF is probably only to affect the composition of the world money supply in the short run. The swap lines, for example, are short-term lines of credit denominated in foreign currencies with a foreign government. So when the U.S. uses these lines, it is exchanging newly created foreign currency for dollars. Such an action increases the proportion of foreign currency and reduces the proportion of dollars in circulation, but leaves the total world money supply unchanged. Only if the foreign governments were to fund these loans to the U.S. through open market sales in the private market would world money supplies be reduced. In the absence of such actions, however, lower dollar inflation is accomplished only at the expense of higher foreign inflation.

Furthermore, the way in which the Treasury pays off the swap lines determines the permanence of these effects. If the Federal Reserve creates dollars to purchase the foreign currency owed to the foreign central bank, the initial intervention would be offset. There then would be no permanent effect on the composition of the world money supply, the dollar's value, or the rate of dollar price increases. Only if the Treasury finances the purchase with tax revenue or an open market sale of new debt would the effect of swap line intervention be sustained.

It should also be pointed out that even if one knew how these swap lines were to be used and repaid, the behavior of the dollar and inflation could still not be completely anticipated. Foreign exchange operations are performed by the foreign exchange trading desk of the Federal Reserve Bank of New York, under guidelines provided by the Treasury. However, the same New York Federal Reserve building also houses the domestic trading desk of the Federal Reserve System, which in recent years has aimed for federal funds rate targets under guidelines provided by the Federal Reserve Board Open Market Committee. While housed in the same building, these desks belong to separate departments in separate areas, and operate independently. Hence, the $30 billion in swap lines, IMF tranches, gold, SDRs, etc. amassed by the Treasury to defend the dollar could be viewed by the domestic desk as simply a buffer for domestic monetary policy. The Fed's domestic open market desk could then, say, pursue more purchases in an attempt to keep interest rates low. But as discussed in Chapters 12 and 17, such actions of the domestic desk simply offset actions in the foreign exchange market. Just as in the fixed exchange rate world of those chapters, faster money creation prevented the balance of payments from improving, so in the flexible rate world it prevents the dollar from realizing its potential appreciation. The actions of the foreign exchange desk cannot, therefore, be analyzed in isolation.

Instead, one is interested in the net intervention of the two desks. Are the dollars removed by the foreign exchanging trading desk simply put back into circulation by the domestic trading desk?

An additional aspect of the dollar defense program worth noting was the apparent decision by foreign banks to support the dollar's defense by intervening (buying dollars) for their own account. The analysis of the nonreserve currency country in Chapter 19 indicates the likely effect of such actions. The foreign central banks pay for the dollars they buy with newly created foreign currency. This action by itself changes the composition, but not the total quantity of world money. But the foreign central banks do not keep the dollars in currency form. Instead, they convert them to interest-bearing securities by performing an open market purchase from the public. Hence, the net effect of the intervention is to leave the quantity of dollars in circulation unchanged, while increasing the quantity of foreign currency. While dollars are now a smaller proportion of the world money supply, the total world money supply has increased. Average world inflation and foreign inflation increase.

Only one clear conclusion can be drawn from this analysis of the dollar defense program: defending the dollar reduces U.S. relative to foreign inflation. However, an equally important question is how the relative change will be brought about. Will U.S. inflation be reduced to the level of foreign inflation, or will foreign inflation be brought up to the level of the U.S.? Unfortunately, as just shown, such a projection would depend on which intervention mechanism dominates.

The importance of choosing the correct intervention mechanism for stabilizing the dollar should not be underestimated. Different rates of inflation produce different effects on interest rates, investment, output, etc. For example, an intervention plan which raises the total world money supply, creating additional inflation, raises average world interest rates. In contrast, if the plan caused the world money supply to grow more slowly, average rates would fall. Also, the lower the rates of inflation, the lower the levels of illusory profits from undercosting of goods sold and underdepreciation of fixed assets, and hence, the lower the effective tax rates on corporate-held capital. Lower rates of inflation also mean that individuals will be pushed less rapidly into higher marginal tax brackets as their nominal incomes increase enough to keep their real incomes constant. So lower inflation implies an improved outlook for incentives to supply work effort and capital, higher levels of economic activity, and lower interest rates. Thus the U.S. and world economies would be better off under an intervention program which reduced world inflation.

Unfortunately, with hindsight we can say that the less desirable mechanisms dominated after November 1, 1978. Rather than lowering U.S. inflation, the support of the dollar by foreign central banks increased foreign and world money supplies at a faster rate, quickly raising foreign inflation towards the previous U.S. level. In the three months ending in November 1978, inflation (annualized rate) was 1.8 percent in Germany, −1.9 percent in Japan, and 0.4 percent in Switzerland. But by April 1979, these three-month rates had leaped by almost 7 percent in Germany, by over 15 percent in Japan and by over 10 percent in Switzerland. In contrast, the inflation rate in the U.S. during these periods increased less than six percentage points (9.9 percent to 15.8 percent).

THE EUROPEAN MONETARY SYSTEM[4]

The discussion of currency substitution has several implications for flexible exchange rate systems. One is that when the relative cost or risk of holding a given money rises, not only domestic portfolios, but also foreign portfolios, shift towards smaller proportions of that money. The implication then is that where currency substitution exists, the reaction of the international money markets to a given change in expected cost or risk in a certain currency should be larger or faster than in its absence. Exchange rate changes should therefore exhibit larger variance in the presence of currency substitution. The larger variance in turn leads to higher bid-ask spreads or foreign exchange costs, which in turn raises the cost of conducting business under a flexible rate system. These higher costs reduce the attractiveness of a flexible rate system.

Another implication concerns the issue of the proper world monetary system. Should the world system emphasize independent country control for internal stability? Alternatively, should the system emphasize cooperation and coordination at the expense of monetary independence? Currency substitution provides a good criterion for resolving this issue. If the currencies of two countries are close substitutes in demand, then for small changes in the money supply, the monetary policies of these two countries cannot be independent. Only by continually changing the monetary policy by a sufficiently large amount to change the perceived cost or risk of holding the domestic currency, can the central bank achieve any degree of monetary independence. But as just discussed, the large swings in monetary policy will produce larger than expected swings in the exchange rate, raising business costs and lowering output. These large swings in monetary policy are precisely the type of monetary policy that even more traditional monetarists have argued against.[5]

In the presence of currency substitution, a world system which emphasizes independent policies would therefore be less than optimal. Rather, where two currencies are close substitutes and money is freely mobile between countries, countries should be encouraged to coordinate their monetary policies as a *bloc* rather than moving in separate directions. The more currencies which are close substitutes, the larger should be the bloc.

One empirical result reported in Chapter 18 is that Deutsche marks and foreign currencies appear to be close substitutes in Germany. This result appears to strengthen the argument for the European Monetary System (EMS) of fixed exchange rates which began operation in March 1979. The stated purpose of the EMS was to create "closer monetary cooperation leading to a zone of monetary stability in Europe."[6] Certainly a system which reduces exchange rate fluctuations among member currencies would be a step in the direction of the world exchange rate system which is optimal from an integrated market viewpoint. But as was found in the case of President Carter's November 1, 1978 program for defending the dollar, two policies which both appear to stabilize a currency can have very different implications for inflation and success in the long run. Hence some details of the EMS are examined to show the implications of the system in an integrated world. Specifically, how is the system proposed to work? Is it likely to make member currencies resemble more closely the Deutsche mark or the Italian lira? Is the system likely to reduce inflation in the world, in Europe, and in the U.S.?

The EMS consists of two separate constraints on the member currencies (currently Germany, France, Italy, the Netherlands, Belgium, Luxembourg, Denmark, and Ireland). One constraint restricts movements of member currencies relative to a common unit of account. The second constraint restricts movements relative to other member currencies. The common unit of account, called the European Currency Unit (ECU), is simply a weighted average of all the member currencies.

Each member currency must determine a central rate for its currency in terms of the ECU. The currency is then allowed to fluctuate within a band around its central rate. Under the rules of the system, once a currency deviates by approximately 75 percent of its permitted band around the central rate, a "threshold of divergence" has been passed. Beyond this threshold, a country is expected to attempt to correct the movement of the currency through intervention in the foreign exchange markets, that is, by using its foreign exchange reserves to purchase or sell its own currency in world markets. It can also adjust domestic policy by exchanging assets for domestic currency, or it can change the central rate of (devalue or revalue) its currency.

Since the ECU is a weighted average, a given currency can fluctuate against the ECU for two reasons. First, holding all other ECU-related currencies constant against, say, the dollar, an individual currency may fluctuate against the dollar, and therefore against the relatively stable ECU. Second, holding the dollar value of the individual currency constant, the value of all other member currencies can depreciate or appreciate against the dollar. In this case, the ECU changes relative to the dollar, and the ECU fluctuates relative to the currency. The necessity for a country to maintain its currency within the threshold values therefore may not be the result of the country's own actions. As a result, the intervention mechanism presents the likelihood that one country, or a group of countries, could force all other members to conform to its policies. Which country dominates in this way of course depends on which countries bear the burden of adjustment.

The task of determining which country will dominate the EMS is mathematically complex, depending on several factors including (a) which currencies carry the largest weights in calculating the value of the ECU, (b) whether the multilateral (ECU) or the bilateral constraint is more effective, (c) whether weak or strong currencies are presumed to bear the burden of adjustment, and (d) the relative widths of the bands of permissible currency fluctuations. The European solution to the nettlesome issue of domination appears to have been a diplomatic one. No one country clearly dominates the system, and the question of whether weak. or strong currencies in practice will bear the burden of adjustment has been left unanswered. At least on paper, all currencies seem to be on relatively equal footing. A priori Germany seems no more likely to dominate the system than Italy.

Furthermore, there appears to be nothing inherent in the EMS to increase or reduce European inflation. The EMS system, like other fixed rate systems, does restrict the amount of money that a member country can create. The monetary policy of that country must reflect that of its partners. If its money creation exceeds that of other member countries, then its currency tends to depreciate, requiring a support operation for the exchange rate, reducing the monetary base. But if its money supply increases too slowly relative to their member countries, it would be forced to intervene by expanding its monetary base. Thus, if the consensus or average monetary policy emulates Germany's historically restrictive policy, then the EMS will tend to reduce European inflation. Alternatively, if the consensus emulates Italian monetary policy, European inflation would tend to increase.

But what determines the consensus monetary policy? Historically the consensus among countries in a fixed exchange rate system has been predetermined in one of two ways. First, a commodity such as gold could be adopted as the standard for all currencies. In this case there are n exchange rates with respect to the commodity, and the monetary policies of all countries are restricted by the commitment to maintain the fixed price of gold. Second, n-1 countries could fix their currencies to a reserve currency, and the reserve currency in turn pegs its currency to the commodity. The nth (reserve) currency is restricted to creating money in such an amount as to keep the price of gold constant, and the remaining countries increase their monies approximately at the same rate as the reserve country. This second alternative was essentially the Bretton Woods System discussed in Chapters 13 and 19.

The key ingredient in both systems is a commodity to which at least one currency is tied. Unfortunately, such a provision was eliminated before the creation of the EMS. Prior to December 31, 1977, the forerunner to the ECU (the EUA) was defined as .88867088 grams of fine gold. If this definition had been maintained and adhered to, money creation would have been restricted. In its absence, there is no inherent reason for the member countries as a whole to reduce their money creation.

So if Germany dominates, then the remaining countries would tend to emulate Germany's monetary policy. The rate of European money creation likely would fall, as would world inflation. Alternatively, if Italy dominates European money creation, world inflation likely would rise. The Germans indicate that they are determined not to let the EMS force them to print money at a faster rate. If so, the EMS could be tied to the

Germans' historical penchant for stable prices. However, there is no provision in the EMS to guarantee this result.

What does the establishment of the EMS mean for the dollar and U.S. inflation? Successful implementation of the European Monetary System likely could produce a change in global monetary forces capable of testing any U.S. government policy to maintain a stable dollar. Stability among the European currencies would tend to increase each currency's "moneyness" or usefulness. As the theory of currency substitution would predict, companies with trans-European operations, for example, would become less concerned over the European currency in which they hold their money balances. As currency values stabilize, the monies become more equivalent. This gain in moneyness implies that money holders would tend to shift more of their holdings into EMS currencies from third currencies such as the dollar. This reduction in the global demand for dollars alone would, holding U.S. monetary policy constant, lead to a fall in the value of the dollar.

Of course this movement from dollars could be moderated by the covariance factor. Since all EMS currencies would move together, a money holder wishing to reduce the overall variance of the value of his money portfolio in terms of goods would desire to hold larger amounts of non-ECU currencies such as dollars. However, since the covariance factor most likely would not offset the substitution into European currencies due to their increased moneyness, the net decline in the global demand for dollars could hasten the displacement of the dollar as the international numeraire. Without a concerted effort by the Treasury and Federal Reserve to offset this exogenous decline in the demand for dollars, the value of the dollar would tend to fall relative to the ECU, exacerbating U.S. inflation and undermining further the dollar's role as the international currency.

The continued decline in the prominence of the dollar could in turn force the United States to strengthen its efforts to assure future dollar stability both in terms of other currencies and in terms of the price of goods. For example, the Treasury could peg the dollar to the ECU. Such a step might be the precursor to the reestablishment of a worldwide fixed exchange rate system.

On the other hand, the European Monetary System may meet with only limited success. To the extent that governments fail or refuse to take the steps necessary to maintain the agreed relationships among their domestic currencies, the ECU, and other currencies, the EMS would have a reduced impact. In the extreme, if governments ignore the restrictions completely, following whatever policy they desire without regard for the relative value of their domestic currency, the EMS would have no impact at all. There would be no effective constraints on money creation, and world and dollar inflation are likely to be what they would have been in the absence of EMS. Unfortunately, within the first six months of operation, the Danish Krone crisis, and its subsequent devaluation, showed that the constraints within the EMS are substantially less than permanently binding.

SUMMARY

This chapter applies the theory of integrated world markets to international events of the late 1970s. It is shown that Treasury Secretary Blumenthal's attempt to "talk down" the dollar did not stimulate the U.S. economy or improve the trade balance, but rather led primarily to higher rates of U.S. inflation. The Secretary's actions also lowered the expected returns and increased the risk from holding dollars, exacerbating the dollar's decline and reducing the role of the dollar as an international currency. Even President Carter's attempt to stop the dollar's slide in November 1978 was largely misguided. While strengthening the dollar can be very desirable, the intervention plan chosen served only to exacerbate foreign inflation rather than lowering the U.S. rate. The European Monetary System held out the hope at the end of the decade that the European countries might be taking steps to lower world inflation. The constraints in the system, however, have not proven sufficiently binding to provide for this result.

NOTES

1. This section is adapted from Marc A. Miles, "Myth of Currency Depreciation As Panacea Is Being Disproved," *The Money Manager,* August 6, 1979, pp. 10, 16.

2. This section is adapted from Marc A. Miles, "Money Substitution, Dollar Demand, Exchange Rates, and Financial Markets," H. C. Wainwright & Co., *Economic and Investment Observations,* 1979.

3. Based on Charles W. Kadlec, Arthur B. Laffer, and Marc A. Miles, "The Carter Turnaround: A New Policy for the Dollar," H. C. Wainwright & Co., *Economic Study,* December 18, 1978.

4. Based on Marc A. Miles, "The European Monetary System," H. C. Wainwright & Co., *Economic and Investment Observations,* July 3, 1979.

5. See, for example, Milton Friedman, "The Role of Monetary Policy," *American Economic Review* Vol. 58, No. 1 (March 1968): pp. 1–17.

6. "European Community News," December 6, 1978, Section A–1.1 of *The European Council's EMS Resolution.*

INDEX